Emma Hardinge Britten

Ghost Land

Or Researches into the Mysteries of Occultism

Emma Hardinge Britten

Ghost Land
Or Researches into the Mysteries of Occultism

ISBN/EAN: 9783337030773

Printed in Europe, USA, Canada, Australia, Japan

Cover: Foto ©Lupo / pixelio.de

More available books at **www.hansebooks.com**

GHOST LAND;

OR

RESEARCHES INTO THE MYSTERIES.

OF

OCCULTISM.

ILLUSTRATED IN A

SERIES OF AUTOBIOGRAPHICAL SKETCHES.

IN TWO PARTS.

BY THE AUTHOR OF "ART MAGIC"; WITH EXTRACTS FROM THE RECORDS OF
"MAGICAL SÉANCES," ETC. ETC.

TRANSLATED AND EDITED

By EMMA HARDINGE BRITTEN.

"I am He that liveth and was dead,
And behold, I am alive for evermore."

PUBLISHED FOR THE EDITOR:
AT BOSTON, AMERICA.
1876.

Stereotyped and Printed by
ALFRED MUDGE & SON, PRINTERS, BOSTON.

CONTENTS.

AUTHOR'S PREFACE.

BEFORE the subjoined papers are submitted to the critical reader, the author desires most emphatically to protest against their being ranked in the same category of literature as his recently published volume on "ART MAGIC."

The autobiographical sketches now presented to the public were written, or rather collated from private memoranda, some four years since, at the earnest request of Mrs. Emma Hardinge Britten, and that with the simple design of contributing such a series of magazine papers to her admirable periodical, "The Western Star," as would be in harmony with its general tone and design.

When it is remembered that these papers are only off-hand sketches of a fateful life, in which striking illustrations of the spiritual philosophy may be found in a less stately guise than abstract essays, and that at most they are only to be considered as magazine sketches, the author trusts that his work will be held exempt from that severity of critical analysis which he would have courted for "Art Magic" had it been placed before the world under similar circumstances.

The only claim that the author can advance for the present work is that of strict veracity. Although the same reasons that induced him to withhold his name when it was first produced prevail with him to-day, all the incidents narrated have been faithfully set down with the strictest regard to truth as far as the present volume carries the history forward.

To the author himself the details of his life convey in retrospection the most important lessons, but their value to the world is entirely dependent upon their actuality. As a mere tale of fiction far more interesting subjects could doubtless have been found in any sensational novel or newspaper romance; but if the narratives herein detailed faithfully represent the mystic action of mind upon mind, the fearful phenomenon of obsession, the possibility of an actual *life transfer*, and the interposition of beings in human affairs whose existence supplies the missing link which connects the realm of animate and inanimate nature, then is this work, however crude in style or imperfect in philosophical deduction, a most important and noteworthy one.

It is because it ought to be thus regarded, because it narrates step by step and incident by incident, actualities which may one day become the experience of the many rather than the few, that the author is again persuaded to brave the idle sneer and vulgar jeer of those who are only capable of appreciating the facts that may have come within the narrow circle of their own observation. That those persons who call themselves "spiritual teachers" and claim to be "interpreters and exponents" of the spiritual philosophy (?) have not *all* the truth — nay, not even a tithe of the experience necessary to qualify them for the office they have assumed — becomes more and more painfully evident to the earnest student into spiritual *mysteries* the more he compares the immensity of the realms to be traversed with the shallow pretences at *explanation* put forth by the self-elected spiritual teachers of this generation.

By these great authorities occultion is assumed to be a word invented by a few individuals, whose chief aim is to destroy Spiritualism and substitute "black magic" in its place, whilst occultists are renegades, who would "roll back the car of progress" (a favorite expression, by the way, of those who deny the right of any one to progress beyond their own standard of knowledge) and presume to add to the sublime philosophy enunciated through the table-tipping and trance-speaking media for "spirits of the seventh sphere," the antiquated stuff of Oriental cabalists, Chaldean astrologists, Hindoo, Egyptian, and Persian magi, Greek philosophers, Arabian alchemists, and mediæval Rosicrucian mystics. Of course all these are mere *ignoramuses*, who for thousands of years have been blundering through the mysteries of occult science, which the aforesaid table-tipping and seventh-sphere-inspiring spirits instantly sweep away with the knock-down argument of "What I don't know is n't true; and what I can not explain has no existence."

That the author of "Ghost Land" has attempted to explain occultion, or present a concrete scheme of occult philosophy in these pages, must not for one moment be assumed. He has simply introduced such scenes in his own life experience as will show what a vast amount of phenomena remain to be explained, which the spiritual *philosophy* of the present day has not touched, and which many modern Spiritists, following out the rude and illogical example of their own materialistic opponents, find it easier to deny altogether than to elucidate. No one has more faithfully, humbly, and reverently sought for truth wherever it may be found than the author of "Ghost Land"; yet he is fain to confess the table-tipping and trance-inspiring spirits of America and England have not, to his blundering apprehension, covered the whole ground of the experiences which he has ventured to detail in this volume. When he adds that an additional score of years' experiences still more wonderful and occult yet remain to be accounted for, and that during his wide wanderings over the world he has encountered hundreds of individuals who have an array of equally occult testimony to render, the *Illuminée* of the modern spiritual movement may forgive him if he ventures to question whether there may not be some few things, scenes, and persons more in the spiritual universe than their seven spheres of purely human intelligence can account for.

The author could have wished that his esteemed editor had dispensed with the chapters interpolated by their mutual and highly valued friend, "John Cavendish Dudley"; not that any portion of this gentleman's writings are lacking in that strict fidelity to truth which has been the ruling genius of the entire work, whilst in style and interest they far surpass the attempts of a foreigner to express his ideas in an unfamiliar language; but the author has marked with deep regret the many eulogistic allusions to himself with which Mr. Dudley's diary is seasoned; and whilst he knows they are dictated in all sincerity by a too partial friend, he feels their association with autobiographical sketches will subject him to a charge of vanity which is equally repulsive to his habits of thought and action. On this point he has no other excuse to offer than the all-potential will of his editor. Mrs. Hardinge Britten alleges that the diary of Mr. Dudley was given to her in the same unconditional spirit as the "Ghost Land" papers; also, that it was not until she came to examine the MSS. separately that she discovered how intimately they were related and how impossible it would have been to continue the narrative after the eleventh chapter without the assistance of Mr. Dudley's journal.

When Mrs. Hardinge Britten further added I will to I wish, the author of "Art Magic," himself the strongest possible pleader for the omnipotence of will, found all his arguments on the *per contra* of the question silenced.

With a final allegation that though the style of composition is all too faulty, the details are a faithful representation of facts known to and witnessed by many most honorable persons in the present generation, the author gives his work to the winds of public opinion. Blow hot or cold as they will, they only represent the source from whence they come, but can not make or mar the work they ban or bless.

PUENTES GRANDES,
THE HAVANA, ISLE DE CUBA, 1876.

INTRODUCTION.

By the Editor.

The following series of papers was first prepared for the press in 1872, when a few ladies and gentlemen interested in the cause of Spiritualism, and believing its interests would be promoted by the publication of a high-toned periodical, agreed to sustain me in the production of "The Western Star," a magazine issued expressly to meet the above design. As soon as I had decided upon the expediency of this undertaking I applied to several European friends from whom I deemed I might obtain literary assistance of the highest value, and contributions which would be more fresh to my American readers than those of the writers on this side of the Atlantic.

The foremost and perhaps the most urgent applications I made were addressed to two gentlemen from whose friendship for me and their talent as writers I anticipated the most favorable results. I knew that both had enjoyed rare opportunities of research into the realms of spiritual existence.

One, whom I shall henceforth speak of as the Chevalier de B——, was, as I well knew, a member of several Oriental and European societies, where he had enjoyed the privilege of initiation into the ancient mysteries, and opportunities for the study of occultism rarely open to modern investigators. I had myself witnessed many evidences of this gentleman's wonderful powers as a seer and adept in magical rites, no less than what is now called "mediumship," for every conceivable phase of spirit power. Already familiar with many of his remarkable experiences, and believing I could obtain still further information on the subject from his intimate and near connexion, an English nobleman, to whom I give the *nom de plume* of John Cavendish Dudley, I laid my case before both parties, soliciting from them such a series of papers as would embody their joint experiences in Spiritualism without impinging upon any points they might desire to reserve from the public eye. The cordial response which I obtained from these well-tried and valued friends was accompanied, however, with some restrictions, the most important of which was the positive charge to withhold their names, also to arrange their MSS. under such veiled expressions as would effectually conceal their identity. Both gentlemen were aware that their personalities would be recognized by their own immediate circle of acquaintances should the narratives ever fall into such hands; but whilst they were most willing to oblige me, and deemed their remarkable experiences might benefit and instruct many a spiritualistic reader, they protested strongly against subjecting themselves to the rude criticism and cold infidelic sneers of an unsympathetic world.

"I would not wear my heart upon my sleeve for daws to peck at," said my English friend, in the words of the immortal bard of Avon; whilst the Chevalier de B—— urged private and personal reasons still more stringent. To mask the identity of my authors then, and even maintain a strict *incognito* for all those associated with them, became the conditions upon which the terms of my editorship in these papers were founded.

Less, perhaps, with a view of enlightening a generation which is not always prepared to recognize its need of enlightenment, than with a desire to embellish my periodical with a series of papers which I deemed eminently worthy of the place assigned them, I cheerfully accepted the offer of my two friends, subject to the restrictions they laid upon me. On examining the MSS. committed to my charge, I found that I could commence the publication of the Chevalier de B——'s papers in a serial entitled "Ghost Land," and from the mass of records furnished me by Mr. J. C. Dudley I extracted the humorous and racy description of that gentleman's experiences in America, to which he had given the caption of "Amongst the Spirits." The autobiographical sketches of the Chevalier were written originally in German, but as I was not sufficiently familiar with that language to read or translate it, my kind friend, himself an excellent linguist, engaged to furnish me with a literal translation, — that is, to render his writings into "rough English," and leave to me the task of arranging the phraseology and construction of the sentences. In many instances I found this task unnecessary, although in others I have had much labor in re-transcribing, arranging, and compiling fragmentary memoranda, written not unfrequently in French or imperfect English.

As I proceeded with my work, I found that the MSS. would be wholly incomplete without that of Mr. Dudley, and as I had the good fortune to be in possession of the latter's journal, I selected from it such chapters relating to the Chevalier as supplied the hiatus in question, and enabled me to form a consecutive narrative of that gentleman's singular and eventful career.

I encountered some opposition from both my friends in this course of procedure, the Chevalier objecting strongly to the eulogistic tone adopted by his friend in reference to himself, and Mr. Dudley urging me to say more on the same subject than I deemed it prudent to insert. Another and still graver difficulty in my path has been the necessity of transcribing a foreigner's ideas and statements to a considerable extent in my own language, and clothing thoughts, opinions, and even the framework of the dialogues given by the author in my own form of expression. I feel keenly the loss the reader must sustain in many instances by this infusion of my personality into the author's sublime and exalted ideality. I am aware, also, what a handle it affords to those untruthful and uncandid critics who see themselves in others' acts, and who, being naturally deceptive and tricky themselves, cannot recognize truth and honesty even when it stares them in the face.

Although I have been and shall be again, induced from the force of circumstances to mask the noble sentiments of the Chevalier de B—— in my own peculiarities of style, I have in vain labored to persuade him to place his works in other hands or avail himself of a less *prononcée* style of compilation. Had I not devoted myself to this work it would never have been accomplished, and that thought has been my chief recompense for the slander and misrepresentation that has been cast on my share of the publication. Although my friend's courtesy has induced him to treat these misrepresentations lightly, and even to allege that he felt honored in hearing the authorship of his works attributed to me, such a slander upon him, no less than the wrong done to my veracity and the character for straightforward candor which I deemed my life had earned, has been the worst stab my enemies could have inflicted upon me, and calls for this explanation concerning the necessary share which I have had in characterizing the Chevalier de B——'s writings.

In view of the stringent charge I received from each of my authors, not only to preserve their *incognito*, but even to represent an ideal personage as the vehicle of the thoughts rendered, I drew up an introductory sketch of the supposed author of "Ghost Land," which I printed in the first number of "The Western Star."

In becoming more familiar with the later portions of the autobiography, I found that the author had stated the real events of his life so candidly, and alluded to the various dates and epochs that marked it with such fidelity of detail, that my ideal sketch had to be abandoned; the two histories would not cohere together; hence in republishing the first five chapters of "Ghost Land" in their present form I have felt obliged to present the author in his real character from beginning to end ; and although I have observed all the other restrictions laid upon me in respect to the names of persons and places, the incidents of this strange life are so TRUE, so candidly and simply detailed, that I doubt whether the lovers of fiction will be able to recognize that truth, and I shall not be surprised to hear that the whole narrative is a *made-up affair.*

I have some reason to believe this view would not be displeasing to the author himself, who, although compelled to write under the *efflatus* of the same power that obliges the "sibyl to *vaticinate*" even when she is not believed in, still feels sensitively opposed to parading his peculiar and often most painful personal experiences before a hard, unkind, and unsympathetic world. I, on the contrary, have a deep and religious interest in urging the exact truth of these experiences, and as I have been mainly instrumental in inducing my friend to narrate them, I would gladly, most gladly, add the lustre of a far more authoritative name than my own to the solemn assurance that they are all literal transcripts of history, and that they ought to be studied and classified by every philosophic thinker as amongst the rarest and most important psychological facts on record.

It simply remains for me to explain how and why this autobiography appears at this particular time. I need not remind those of my readers who may have been subscribers to "The Western Star," that just after the issue of the sixth number, the occurrence of the disastrous Boston fires and the immense losses sustained by some of my principal supporters, compelled me to suspend that periodical ; but immediately upon the announcement of this suspension and up to the present time I have been literally besieged with requests to issue a reprint and continuance of "Ghost Land," my correspondents assuring me that those delightful and absorbing papers were more to them than all the rest of the magazine. The same request has been repeatedly made in reference to the articles of Mr. Dudley, entitled "Amongst the Spirits." In a word, the high appreciation accorded to those two serials made me often regret that leisure and opportunity were not afforded me for their publication in separate and continuous forms.

It was some three years after the suspension of "The Western Star" that my esteemed friend, the Chevalier de B——, made a second visit to the United States, travelling as was his custom in a private and unostentatious manner under an *incognito*, and employing his time in the observation and study of those spiritualistic facts which it has been the main object of his life to gather up. It was then that I learned from him that two works, the scheme of which he had often laid out in project to me, were nearly completed ; and as he was unable to undertake the fatigue and master the harassing details of their publication, he offered to present me with the MSS., although he wished that their production should be deferred for a stated period.

One of the MSS. thus intrusted to me was "Art Magic." It was written, like "Ghost Land," partly in French and partly rendered into English, for the sake of aiding me in its translation. Much of the language I found capable of representing the author's ideas without any alteration ; but the whole work struck me as so important, sublime, and beautiful that I urged upon my friend its immediate production without waiting for further contingencies.

Tendering all the services I deemed likely to be available on the occasion, I at last succeeded in overcoming the Chevalier's reticence, and provided that I would give it to the world under the conditions which he dictated, he said the work was at my disposal. My friend then laid down those conditions of publication which have called forth the clouds of abuse, scandal, and insult which it has been my privilege to endure in so good a cause, and I dictated the financial terms by which I had hoped to save him from loss. In this respect the results belong to ourselves, not to the world. It is enough that I have been instrumental in launching a noble work upon the ocean of human thought. Many a bitter experience has been added to those which both author and editor have had to endure, many that might have been more gracefully spared by those who inflicted them. The effect of these experiences, however, it may not be amiss to notice a little more in detail, for it is evident they have not fulfilled the exact purpose with which they were freighted. In the first place, they have taught the sensitive author to rise superior to all human opinion, by showing him that which the editor has long since understood, namely, that there is always a certain amount of journalistic criticism which can be *bought* or *sold*, according to the purchaser's disposition or means of payment ; another class from which praise would be dishonor ; still another, who never waste time one way or the other on any subject that is not a marketable commodity and likely to pay well ; and a fourth class, but one alas ! greatly in the minority, who can and will recognize truth and beauty wherever they find it : and to this class "Art Magic" has indeed been "the gem of spiritualistic effort of this and every other generation."

All this the author has had to learn. That he was not entirely ignorant of the crucible through which his work would have had to pass had it been published for "the masses" instead of the few, he himself proved, as I find in a letter addressed to me on this very subject the following *complimentary* expressions of opinion concerning the "great public":—

"The *masses*, to whom you so enthusiastically would have me commend the perusal of 'Art Magic,' ever halt between two horns of a dilemma. If you tell them what they do not already know, they will cry, 'We can not understand this writer!' If you repeat old truths, no matter how new may be your methods of representation, they will scream against you for telling them nothing new; and herein lies the real power of the critic, which is just to tell the world, according to his own personal predilections, what that poor imbecile thing ought to believe or reject, exalt to the skies or trample in the dust."

I have learned something as well as the author in this publication, for despite the infamous slanders of one part of a press calling itself "spiritual," and the significant silence of others, the subscribers to this work have in general been of that class which bravely and boldly takes the task of thinking into its own hands; hence they have not only written to me in the most glowing and enthusiastic praise of this "great and sublime work," but they have insisted upon having something more from the same "facile and fascinating pen."

Now, although this gentleman has submitted to me the rough draft of a still more elaborate exposition of the subjects on which "Art Magic" treats than even that admirable work itself, it may be some time before it can be completed and ready for press. In the interim the continued demand for "another work from the same author" induces me to turn my attention to the long-promised continuation of "Ghost Land," the deeply interesting and instructive character of which is fully equal to "Art Magic"; and besides, I am still more inclined to pursue this course from the very natural and spontaneous desire of many readers to know more about the gifted individual who wrote "Art Magic." That these autobiographical sketches will prove as acceptable as they are instructive I can not doubt, and I once more commend them to the reader with the assurance that, though the truths in these pages are, as truth generally is, stranger than fiction, I respect myself and my friend too highly to apologize further for the fact that some of those truths may be unprecedented, hence difficult of realization.

I now commit the precious MSS. intrusted to me to the tender mercies of a world of which my respectful but candid opinion may be gathered from the aphorism which has been my life's motto, and the one which has urged me forward to the publication of this volume, namely, "The truth *against* the world!"

Boston, 1876.   EMMA HARDINGE BRITTEN.

Ghost Land.

CHAPTER I.

ON THE THRESHOLD

As the sole object of these sketches has been to present to the investigator into spiritual mysteries some experiences of a singular and exceptional character, I would gladly have recorded them as isolated facts, or even communicated their curious details to such Spiritualistic journalists as might have deemed them worthy of a place in their columns; but on attempting to arrange them in such a form as would accord with this design, I found it impossible to separate the phenomenal portions of the history from the person with whom they were most immediately connected.

Had I been a mere spectator of the scenes detailed, I could have easily reduced them to narrative form, but as in most instances I was either the "medium" through whom the phenomena worthy of record transpired, or their interest was derived from their association with a consecutive history, I found I must either relinquish the design of contributing my experiences to the world, or consent to the repulsive task of identifying them with one who has sufficient reason to shrink from publicity, and sighs for nothing so much as the peaceful retirement which should precede the last farewell to earth. As my own desires have been completely overruled by one whose wishes I gladly prefer to my own, I find myself either obliged to identify my Spiritualistic experiences with a fictitious personage, or accept the repulsive alternative of adding to the many characters I have been compelled to act out on the stage of life's tragic drama the unwelcome one of an autobiographer.

For many reasons unnecessary to detail, I have a special dislike to tales of fiction. Life is all too real, too thoroughly momentous, to be travestied by fictional representations. Truth appeals to the consciousness of true natures with much more earnestness than fiction; and Spiritualistic narratives in particular, as pointing the way on a new path of discovery, and one wherein the eternal interests of the race are concerned, are simply degraded by fictional contrivances. Even the too common tendency to exaggerate the marvels of Spiritualistic phenomena should be carefully avoided, for the sake of arriving at the heart of truths so important and unfamiliar as those which relate to the spiritual side of man's nature.

It is with these reverential views of truth that I enter upon the task of narrating my singular and exceptional experiences. The only departure I have permitted myself to make from the line of stern and ungarbled fact is in relation to my own identity and that of the persons associated with me. My reasons for suppressing my real name, and in every possible way veiling the identity of those connected with me, are imperative, and if fully understood would be fully appreciated. In all other respects I am about to enter upon a candid history of myself, so far as I am connected with the incidents I am required to detail.

My father was a Hungarian nobleman, but having deemed himself wronged by the ruling government of his country, he virtually renounced it, and being connected on the mother's side with one of the most powerful native princes of India, from whom he received tempting offers of military and official distinction, he determined to prepare himself for his new career by the requisite course of study in England; hence, the belief very generally prevailed that he was an English officer, an opinion strengthened by the fact that for many years he abandoned his title, and substituted for the rank which he had once held in his native country that which was to him far more honorable, namely, a military distinction won on the battle-fields of India by services of the most extraordinary gallantry. Before his departure for the East my father had married a beautiful Italian lady, and as he resolved to maintain his Hungarian title and estates, barren as they were, for the benefit of his children, he left his eldest son, my only brother, in Austria, for education, in the charge of near relatives. I was born on the soil of Hindostan shortly after my parents arrived there, and as my eldest brother died when I was about ten years of age, I was sent to Europe to take his place, receive a European education, and become formally installed into the empty dignity, title, and heirship of our Hungarian estates. As my poor father tenaciously adhered to these shadowy dignities for his children, even though he despised and rejected them for himself, I was accustomed from early childhood to hear myself addressed as the Chevalier de B——, and taught to believe, when my brother died, I had become the heir of a noble house, the prerogatives of which I have never realized, except in the form of the same wrong, oppression, and political tyranny which made my father an alien and a professed subject of a foreign power.

I was about twelve years of age, as well as I can remember, when, returning one day late in the afternoon from the college I attended at B., just as I was about to enter the gate of the house where I boarded, I felt a hand laid on my shoulder, and looking round, I saw myself confronted with one of my teachers, a man who, during the period of my ten months' study in that place, had exerted a singular and irresistible influence over me. He was a professor of Oriental languages, and though I had not been regularly entered in his class, I had joined it because he one day suddenly asked me to do so, and I as suddenly felt impelled to accept his offer. From the very moment that I entered Professor von Marx's class, I became absorbed in the study of Eastern literature, and the proficiency I made was doubtless owing to my desire to master the subjects to which these Oriental tongues formed the key. On the morning of the day from which I commence my narrative, Professor von Marx had abruptly asked me if I were a dreamer. I replied in the negative, adding that I thought I often dreamed something, but the memory of what it might be only remained with me on awaking sufficiently long to impress me with the opinion that I had been somewhere in my sleep, but had forgotten where. When the professor touched me on the shoulder, as above mentioned, at my own doorstep, he said,—

"Louis, my boy, how would you like to have some dreams that you could remember, and go to places in your sleep from which you should return and give accounts of?"

"O professor!" I exclaimed, in astonishment, "could I do this, and how?"

"Come with me, boy," replied my teacher. "I belong to a philosophical society, the existence or at least the real nature of which is but little known. We want the aid of a good smart lad, like you, especially one who is not a conscious dreamer. I have long had my eye upon you, and I think I can not only trust you with our secrets, but, by making you a partaker of them, instruct you in lore of great wisdom, which few children of your age would be thought worthy to know."

Flattered by this confidence, and more than usually thrilled by the strange shivering which always seemed to follow the touch of the professor's hand, I suffered myself to be led on until I reached with him the fourth story of a large house in a very quiet part of the city, where I was speedily introduced into an apartment of spacious dimensions, parted off by screens and curtains into many subdivisions, and half filled with an assemblage of gentlemen, several of whom, to my surprise, I recognized as belonging to the college, some to neighboring literary institutions, and two others as members of one of the princely families of Germany.

There was an air of mystery and caution attending our entrance into this place and my subsequent introduction to the company, which inclined me to believe that this was a meeting of one of those secret societies that, young as I was, I knew to have been strictly forbidden by the government; hence the idea that I was making one of an illegal gathering impressed me with a sentiment of fear and a restless desire to be·gone. Apparently these unexpressed feelings were understood by my teacher, for he addressed me in a low voice, assuring me that I was in the society of gentlemen of honor and respectability, that my presence there had only been solicited to assist them in certain philosophical experiments they were conducting, and that I should soon find cause to congratulate myself that I had been so highly favored as to be inducted into their association.

Whilst he spoke the professor laid his hand on my head, and continued to hold it there, at first with a seemingly slight and accidental pressure; but ere he had concluded his address, the weight of that hand appeared to me to increase to an almost unendurable extent. Like a mountain bearing down upon my shoulders, columns of fiery, cloud-like matter seemed to stream from the professor's fingers, enter my whole being, and finally crush me beneath their terrific force into a state where resistance, appeal, or even speech was impossible. A vague feeling that death was upon me filled my bewildered brain, and a sensation of an undefinable yearning to escape from a certain thraldom in which I believed myself to be held, oppressed me with agonizing force. At length it seemed as if this intense longing for liberation was gratified. I stood, and seemed to myself to stand, free of the professor's crushing hand, free of my body, free of every clog or chain but an invisible and yet quite tangible cord which connected me with the form I had worn, but which now, like a garment I had put off, lay sleeping in an easy-chair beneath me. As for my real self, I stood balanced in air, as I thought at first, about four feet above and a little on one side of my slumbering mortal envelope; presently, however, I perceived that I was treading on a beautiful crystalline form of matter, pure and transparent, and hard as a diamond, but sparkling, bright, luminous, and ethereal. There was a wonderful atmosphere, too, surrounding me on all sides. Above and about me, it was discernible as a radiant, sparkling mist, enclosing my form, piercing the walls and ceiling, and permitting my vision to take in an almost illimitable

area of space, including the city, fields, plains, mountains, and scenery, together with the firmament above
my head, spangled with stars, and irradiated by the soft
beams of the tranquil moon. All this vast realm of
perception opened up before me in despite of the enclosing walls, ceiling, and other obstacles of matter which
surrounded me. These were obstacles no more. I saw
through them as if they had been thin air; and what is
more I knew I could not only pass through them with
perfect ease, but that any piece of ponderable matter in
the apartment, the very furniture itself, if it were only
brought into the solvent of the radiant fire mist that
surrounded me, would dissolve and become, like me
and like my atmosphere, *so soluble* that it could pass,
just as I could, through everything material. I saw,
or seemed to see, that I was now *all force;* that I
was soul loosed from the body save by the invisible
cord which connected me with it; also, that I was in
the realm of soul, the soul of matter; and that as my
soul, and the soul-realm in which I had now entered,
was the real force which kept matter together, I could
just as easily break the atoms apart and pass through
them as one can put a solid body into the midst of
water or air.

Suddenly it seemed to me that I would try this newly
discovered power, and observing that the college cap
I had worn on my poor lifeless body's head was lying
idly in the hands, I made an effort to reach it. To succeed, however, I found I must come into contact with a
singular kind of blue vapor which for the first time I
noticed to be issuing from my body, and surrounding it
like a second self.

Whilst I was gazing at this curious phenomenon I felt
impressed to look at the other persons in the room, and

I then observed that a similar aura or luminous se cond self issued from every one of them. The color and density of each one varied, and by carefully regarding the nature of these mists, or as I have since learned to call them "photospheres," I could correctly discern the character, motives, and past lives of these individuals.

I became so deeply absorbed in tracing the images, shapes, scenes, and revelations that were depicted on these men's souls that I forgot my design of appropriating the cap I had worn, until I noticed that the emanations of Professor von Marx, assuming the hue of a shining rose tint, seemed to permeate and commingle with the bluish vapor that issued from my form. I noticed then another phenomenon. When the two vapors or photospheres were thoroughly commingled, they too became force, like my soul and like the realm of soul in which I was standing. To *perceive,* in the state into which I was inducted, was to see, hear, taste, smell, and understand all things in one new sense. I knew that as a mortal I could not use more than one or two of the senses at a time; but as a soul, I could realize all sensations through one master sense, perception; also, that this sublime and exalted sixth sense informed me of far more than all which the other senses separately could have done. Suddenly a feeling of triumph possessed me at the idea of knowing and understanding so much more than the grave and learned professors into whose company I had entered as a timid, shrinking lad, but whom I now regarded with contempt, because their knowledge was so inferior to mine, and pity, because they could not conceive of the new functions and consequent enjoyments that I experienced as a liberated soul.

There was another revelation impressed upon me at

that time, and one which subsequent experiences have quickened into stupendous depths of consciousness. It was this: I saw, as I have before stated, upon my companions, in distinct and vivid characters, the events of their past lives and the motives which had prompted them to their acts. Now it became to me clear as sunlight that one set of motives were wrong, and another right; and that one set of actions (those prompted by wrong motives, I mean) produced horrible deformities and loathsome appearances on the photosphere, whilst the other set of actions (prompted by the motives which I at once detected as right) seemed to illuminate the soul aura with indescribable brightness, and cast a halo of such beauty and radiance over the whole being, that one old man in particular, who was of a singularly uncomely and withered appearance as a mortal, shone, as a soul, in the light of his noble life and glorious emanations, like a perfect angel. I could now write a folio volume on the interior disclosures which are revealed to the soul's eye, and which are hidden away or unknown to the bodily senses. I cannot pause upon them now, though I think it would be well if we would write many books on this subject, provided men would read and believe them. In that case, I feel confident, human beings would shrink back aghast and terror-stricken from crime, or even from bad thoughts, so hideous do they show upon the soul, and so full of torment and pain does the photosphere become that is charged with evil. I saw in one very fine gentleman's photosphere the representation of all sorts of the most foul and disgusting reptiles. These images seemed to form, as it were, out of his misty emanations, whilst upon his soul I perceived sores and frightful marks that convinced me he was not only a libertine and a sensualist, but a man imbued with many base and repulsive traits of character.

What I saw that night made me afraid of crime, afraid to cherish bad thoughts or harbor bad motives, and with all my faults and shortcomings in after life, I have never forgotten, or ceased to try and live out, the awful lessons of warning I then learned. I must here state that what may have taken me some fifteen minutes or more to write, flashed upon my perceptions nearly all at once, and its comprehension, in much fuller detail than I have here given, could not have occupied more than a few seconds of time to arrive at.

By this time, that at which I now write, " clairvoyance," as the soul's perceptions are called, has become too common a faculty to interest the world much by its elaborate description. Thirty or forty years ago it was too much of a marvel to obtain general credit; but I question whether those who then watched its powers and properties did not study them with more profound appreciation and understanding than they do now, when it seems to be a gift cultivated for very little use beyond that of affording a means of livelihood, and too frequently opens up opportunities of deception for the quack doctor or pretended fortune-teller. But to resume my narrative.

I had not been long free from the fetters of my sleeping body and the professor's magical hand, when he bent down over my form and said, —

"Louis, I WILL you to remember all that transpires in the mesmeric sleep; also, I desire that you should speak, and relate to us, as far as you can, all that you now see and hear."

In an instant the wish of my childish life, the one incessant yearning that possessed my waking hours, returned to me, namely, the desire to behold my dearly loved mother, from whom I had been separated for the past two years. With the flash of my mother's image across my mind, I seemed to be transported swiftly across an immense waste of waters, to behold a great city, where strange-looking buildings were discernible, and where huge domes, covered with brilliant metals, flashed in a burning, tropical sun. Whirled through space, a thousand new and wondrous sights gleamed a` moment before my eyes, then vanished. Then I found myself standing beneath the shade of a group of tall palm-trees, gazing upon a beautiful lady who lay stretched upon a couch, shaded by the broad verandah of a stately bungalow, whilst half a dozen dusky figures, robed in white, with bands of gold around their bare arms and ankles, waved immense fans over her, and seemed to be busy in ministering to her refreshment. "Mother, mother!" I cried, extending my arms towards the well-known image of the being dearest to me on earth. As I spoke, I could see that my voice caused no vibration in the air that surrounded my mother's couch; still the impression produced by my earnest will affected her. I saw a light play around her head, which, strange to relate, assumed my exact form, shape, and attitude, only that it was a singularly *petite* miniature resemblance. As it flickered over the sensorium, she raised her eyes from her book, and fixing them upon the exact point in space where I stood, murmured, in a voice that seemed indescribably distant, "My Louis! my poor, far-away, deserted child! would I could see thee now."

At this moment the will of my magnetizer seemed to intervene between me and my unexpected vision.

I caught his voice saying in stern tones, "Do not

interfere, Herr Eschenmayer. I do not wish him to see his mother, and the tidings he could bring from her would not interest us."

Some one replied; for I felt that the professor listened, though for some cause unknown to me then, I could not hear any voice but his. Again he spoke and said, "I wish him to visit our society at Hamburgh, and bring us some intelligence of what they are doing there." As the words were uttered, I saw for one brief second of time my mother's form, the couch whereon she lay, the verandah, bungalow, and all the objects that surrounded her, turn upside-down, like forms seen in a reversed mirror, and then the whole scene changed. Cities, villages, roads, mountains, valleys, oceans, flitted before my gaze, crowding up their representation in a single instant of time, and ending their panoramic delineation in a large and splendidly furnished chamber, not unlike the one I had entered with the professor.

I perceived that I was at Hamburgh, in the house of the Baron von S., and that he and a party of gentlemen were seated around a table on which were drinking cups, each filled with some hot, ruby-colored liquid, from which a fragrant, herb-like odor was exhaled. Several crystal globes were on the table, also some plates of dark, shining surfaces, together with a number of open books, some in print, others in MSS., and others again whose pages were covered with characters of an antique form, and highly illuminated.. As I entered, or seemed borne into this apartment, a voice exclaimed, "A messenger from Herr von Marx is here, a 'flying soul,' one who will carry the promised word to our circle in B."

"Question him," responded another voice. "What tidings or message does he bring?"

"He is a new recruit, no adept in the sublime sciences," responded the first speaker, "and cannot be depended on."

"Let me speak with him," broke in a voice of singularly sweet tone and accent; and thereupon I became able to fix my perceptive sense so clearly on this last speaker that I fully realized who and what he was, and how situated. I observed that he stood immediately beneath a large mirror suspended against the wall, and set in a circular frame covered with strange and cabalistic looking characters. A dark velvet curtain was undrawn and parted on either side of the mirror, and in or on, I cannot tell which, its black and highly polished surface, I saw a miniature form of a being robed in starry garments, with a glittering crown on its head, long tresses of golden hair, shining as sunbeams, streaming down its shoulders, and a face of the most unparalleled loveliness my eyes had then or have ever since beheld. I cannot tell whether this creature or image was designed to represent a male or female. I did not then know and may not now say whether it was an animate or inanimate being. It seemed to be living, and its beautiful lips moved as if speaking, and its strangely-gleaming, sad eyes were fixed with an expression of pity upon me.

Several voices, with the tones of little children, though I saw none present, said, in a clear, choral accent, " The crowned angel speaks. Listen! " The lips of the figure in the mirror then seemed to move. A long beam of light extended from them to the fine, noble-looking youth of about eighteen who stood beneath the mirror, and who pronounced, in the voice I had last heard, these words: —

"Tell Felix von Marx he and his companions are searching in vain. They spend their time in idle efforts

to confirm a myth, and will only reap the bitter fruits
of disappointment and mockery. The soul of man is
compounded from the aromal life of elementary spirits,
and, like the founders and authors of its being, only
sustains an individualized life so long as the vehicle
of the soul holds together and remains intact. If the
spirits of the elements, stars, and worlds have been
unable during countless ages to discover the secret of
eternal being, shall such a mere vaporous compound of
their exhaled essence as the soul of man achieve the
aim denied to them? Go to, presumptuous ones! Life
is a transitory condition of combinations, death a final
state of dissolution. Being is an eternal alternation
between these changes, and individuality is the privilege of the soul once only in eternity. Look upon
my earthly companion! look well, and describe him, so
that the employers who have sent you shall know that
the crowned angel has spoken."

I looked as directed, and noticed that the young man
who spoke, or seemed to speak, in rhythmic harmony
with the image in the mirror, wore a fantastic masquer-
ade dress, different from all the other persons present.
He on his part seemed moved with the desire that those
around him should become aware of my presence, as he
was. Then I noticed that his eyes looked intelligently
into mine, as if he saw and recognized me; but the
gaze of all the rest of the company met mine as if they
looked on vacancy. They could not see me.

"Flying soul," said the youth, authoritatively addressing me, "can you not give us the usual signal?" Instantly I remarked that dim, shadowy forms, like half
erased photographic images, were fixed in the air and
about the apartment, and I saw that they were forms
composed of the essence of souls that, like mine, had

visited that chamber, and like mine had left their tracery behind. With the pictures thus presented, however, I understood the nature of the signals they had given, and what was now demanded of me. I willed instinctively a strong breath or life essence to pass from myself to the young man, also I noticed that his photosphere was of the same rosy tint as Professor von Marx's.

I saw the blue vapor from my form exhale like a cloud by my will, commingle with his photosphere, and precipitate itself towards his finger-ends, feet, hair, beard, and eyelashes.

He laid his hand on a small tripod of different kinds of metal which stood near him, and, by the direction of my will, five showers of the life essence were discharged from his fingers, sounding like clear, distinct detonations through the apartment.

All present started, and one voice remarked, "The messenger has been here!"

"And gone!" added the youth, when instantly I sunk into blank unconsciousness.

CHAPTER. II.

"The original of all things is one thing. Creation is one whole. The differences a mortal sees are diverse only to the finite mind."—FESTUS.

As I recall the singular experiences which marked my early boyhood, it seems but yesterday that I, now a man in the meridian of life, was the lad of twelve summers, led to my home by the hand of Professor von Marx, on the memorable night when I first realized the marvel of magnetic influence and somnambulic lucidity, in the experiment detailed in the last chapter. As such experiments were constantly repeated, and spread over a period of full six years, I do not propose to recapitulate them *seriatim*, but will endeavor to occupy my readers' time more profitably by presenting them with a summary of the revealments which those six years of occult practices disclosed to me.

On the night of what I may call my initiation into the society associated with Professor von Marx, that gentleman informed me, on our way to our lodgings, that the unconscious condition into which I had fallen after my spiritual visit to Hamburgh was occasioned by the lack of force necessary to sustain my system to the close of the séance.

He added that as I grew stronger and more accustomed to the magnetic control, I should be privileged to retain a recollection of what had transpired; and where this power failed, as it might do, my memory should be refreshed by a perusal of the memoranda which he kept of every séance, a storehouse of information which he intended to transcribe and correct in my presence.

In fulfilment of this promise, the professor spent· some hours of every week with me; and as I was permitted to propound any questions which arose in my mind, and he seemed to take a singular pleasure in explaining the philosophy connected with the facts he recorded, I soon became possessed of the opinions entertained by the society with whom I was unwittingly associated.

Professor von Marx was not only a member of that society described so graphically by Jung Stilling in vision, but he also belonged to several others, all of whom were more or less addicted to the practices of animal and mineral magnetism. The particular association to which I was first introduced constituted the German branch of a very ancient secret order, the name and distinctive characteristics of which neither I nor any other human being is privileged to mention, or even indicate more fully than I shall do in the following statements.

Many learned men, and patient students into life's profoundest mysteries, had transmitted from generation to generation the result of their investigations and the opinions deduced from their experiments. This society, which I shall call for distinction's sake the "Berlin Brotherhood," conserving the experiences of their predecessors, had evolved the following elements of philosophy: They believed that every fragment of matter in the universe represented a corresponding atom of spiritual existence; that this realm of spiritual being was the essence, force, and real substance of the material; but that both inevitably dissolved together, both

3

being resolved back into their component parts in the chemical change called death.

They acknowledged that the realm of spiritual being was ordinarily invisible to the material, and only known through its effects, being the active and controlling principle of matter; but they had discovered, by repeated experiments, that spiritual forms could become visible to the material under certain conditions, the most favorable of which were somnambulism procured through the magnetic sleep. This state, they had found, could be induced sometimes by drugs, vapors, and aromal essences; sometimes by spells, as through music, intently staring into crystals, the eyes of snakes, running water, or other glittering substances; occasionally by intoxication caused by dancing, spinning around, or distracting clamors; but the best and most efficacious method of exalting the spirit into the superior world and putting the body to sleep was, as they had proved, through animal magnetism. They taught that in the realms of spiritual existence were beings who composed the fragmentary and unorganized parts of humanity, as well as beings of higher orders than humanity. Thus, as man was composed of earthly substances, vegetable tissues, mineral, atmospheric, and watery elements, so all these had realms of spiritual existences, perfectly in harmony with their peculiar quality and functions. Hence, they alleged there were earthy spirits; spirits of the flood, the fire, the air; spirits of various animals; spirits of plant life, in all its varieties; spirits of the atmosphere; and planetary spirits, without limit or number. The spirits of the planets and higher worlds than earth took rank far above any of those that dwelt upon or in its interior. These spirits were more powerful, wise, and far-seeing than the earth spirits, whilst their term of existence was also more extended in point of time; but to no spirit did the Brotherhood attribute the privilege of immortality, and least of all to the fleeting and composite essence which formed the vital principle of man. Assuming that, as man's soul was composed of all the elements which were represented in the construction of his body, so his spirit was, as a whole, far superior to the spirits of earth, water, plants, minerals, etc., to hold communion with them, however, was deemed by the Brotherhood legitimate and necessary to those who would obtain a full understanding of the special departments of nature in which these embryotic existences were to be found. Thus they invoked their presence by magical rites, and sought to obtain control over them, for the purpose of wresting from them the complete understanding of and power over the secrets of nature. Whilst I found, by repeated conversations with my new associates, that every one of them emphatically denied the continued existence of the soul after death, they still believed that the soul's essence became progressed by entering into organic forms, and thus that our essences, though not our individualities, were taken up by higher organisms than man's, and ultimately formed portions of that exalted race of beings who ruled the fate of nations, and from time to time communicated with the soul of man as planetary spirits. They taught that the elementary spirits, like the soul essence in man, were dissipated by the action of death, but, like that soul essence, became progressed by existence in forms, and were taken up by higher organisms, and ultimately helped to make up the spirit in man.

Strange and even fantastic as the belief sketched above may appear to the sceptic, materialist, or spiritualist, permit me to assure all these differential classes of thinkers that these views have a far wider acceptance than the bare facts of history or biography would lead mankind to believe.

I have conversed with leading minds of the German schools in many phases of thought, and have found them unable to combat the facts I had to show, and compelled them to acknowledge the plausibility of my theory as an explanation of many of what would otherwise remain insoluble problems in nature. The society to which I was introduced by Professor von Marx was not the only one which cherished these views. In Arabia, India, Asia Minor, Hungary, Bohemia, Italy, France, Sweden, and Great Britain, secret societies exist where these beliefs are accepted, and some of the experiences I am about to relate occurred in the great Babylon of materialism, London, during a visit which I made with Professor von Marx to England.

The professor was exceedingly generous, and distributed his abundant means with an unstinted hand. One day, discoursing with me on the subject of his lavish expenditure, he remarked, carelessly, —

"There is that *mineral* quality in my organism, Louis, which attracts to me and easily subjects to my control the elementary spirits who rule in the mineral kingdoms. Have I not informed you how invariably I can tell the quality of mines, however distant? how often I have stumbled, as if by accident, upon buried treasures? and how constantly my investments and speculations have resulted in financial successes? Louis, I *attract money*, because I attract mineral elements and the spirits who rule in that realm of nature.

"I neither seek for nor covet wealth. I love precious stones for their beauty and magnetic virtues, but money, as a mere possession, I despise. Were I as mercenary in my disposition as I am powerful in the means of gaining wealth, I could be richer than Crœsus, and command a longer purse than Fortunatus."

"Is it not strange, my master," I replied, "that the specialty of your physical nature — namely, the power of attracting riches, as you allege — should not find a corresponding desire in your soul?"

"Not at all, my Louis; on the contrary, Nature is purely harmonious, and ever tends to equilibrium in all her strivings. Have you not remarked how often the possession of a special gift is accompanied by an indifference to its possession?

"Good singers, great musicians, and even poets, painters, and sculptors, rarely estimate their gifts as highly as the world that enjoys them. They are ever dissatisfied with themselves, and unless the world praises, applauds, and recompenses them, they find but little or no interior reward from the mere exercise of their faculty. And thus it is with all Nature's gifts. Abundance of strength in the physical departments of our being rarely accompanies unusual vigor of thought or profundity of intellect; muscle and brain seldom hold companionship; and so the magnetic attractions which draw unto my physique the metallic treasures of the earth fail to find any response in the magnetic attractions of my spirit, whereas, were I so constituted as to lack the force which attracts the service of the spirits of the metals, my soul would feel and yearn for a supply to the deficiency in a constant aspiration for money and treasure."

And that is why (as I then believed) Professor von Marx was rich, but did not care for or value his wealth, whilst so many millions, who do not possess in their organisms that peculiar mineral quality which, as the Brotherhood taught, was necessary to attract wealth, pine for its possession, yet spend their lives vainly in its pursuit.

It becomes necessary, for the benefit of any students of psychological mysteries who may peruse these pages, that I should here state, as briefly as possible, the specialties in my association with the "Berlin Brotherhood" which attracted them to me.

They believed (and with good reason) that the spiritual essence in man called *soul* is susceptible of acting a part independent, to some extent, of the body; that when the body is entranced, or subsides into perfect rest beneath the action of the mesmeric sleep, the spirit, becoming liberated from its control, acquires highly exalted functions, amongst which are the powers of traversing space, and beholding objects through the lucidity of spiritual light. Professor von Marx had detected, through certain signs familiar to good mesmerists, that I was a subject for magnetic experiments.

My power as a "clairvoyant" exceeded what he had anticipated; hence my services to the Brotherhood were highly appreciated. Ever since the practices of Mesmer had become familiar to them, they had delighted in pursuing them in support of their favorite theory, which was that the soul essence of man could appear, make signs, sounds, and disturbances, in places distant from the body; that at times, when these soul essences were dissipated suddenly, as in the action of violent death, they inhered to earthly things and places, and *for a time* could maintain a sort of vague, shadowy existence, which at length melted away, and became dissipated in space, to be taken up from the grand reservoir of spiritual essences in other souls. Now, the brothers insisted that these soul essences, which they called the "double goer," and more frequently the "atmospheric spirit," by its occasional appearances, both before and after the death of individuals, covered the whole ground of spectres, ghosts, apparitions, hauntings, and supernaturalism in general.

The fact that the "atmospheric spirit" often lingered round the earth after the death of the body, and could be seen, heard, and felt, did not militate against their theory that immortality was a fiction and that the soul died with the body. "It was *merely* the atmospheric spirit; a shadowy remnant of the soul," they said, "which had ever been seen or manifested in the realm of ghost land; and this was not a permanent, intelligent existence, but merely a temporary relic of the broken organism, like the perfume which lingers about the spot where the flower has been." By repeated and patient experiments with their magnetic subjects, they found that they could send the "double" or "atmospheric spirit" abroad in the somnambulic sleep, and that it could be seen, heard, and felt precisely like the spectres that were claimed to have been manifested in tales of the supernatural.

On one occasion, the society having thrown me into a profound sleep by the aid of vital magnetism, and the vapors of nitrous oxide gas, they directed my "atmospheric spirit" to proceed, in company with two other lucid subjects, to a certain castle in Bohemia, where friends of theirs resided, and then and there to make disturbances by throwing stones, moving ponderable bodies, shrieking, groaning, and tramping heavily, etc. etc. I here state emphatically, and upon the honor of one devoted only to the interests of truth, that these disturbances were made, and made by the spirits of myself and two other yet living beings, a girl and a boy who were subjects of the society; and though we, in our own individualities, remembered nothing whatever of our performance, we were shortly afterwards shown a long and startling newspaper account of the hauntings in the castle of Baron von L——, of which we were the authors.

In a work devoted to the relation of occult narratives I have in my library at this moment an account of the "manifestations," as they were termed, which occurred, on three several occasions, at a certain castle in Bohemia. The writer attributes these disturbances to disembodied spirits, but in the particular case in question, I insist that the atmospheric spirits of the Berlin Brotherhood were the authors of the facts recorded. As the experiments of these grave gentlemen were neither pursued in fun or mischief, but solely with a view to evolve the *rationale* of a psychological science, I must confess that they followed out their experiments without remorse or consideration for the feelings of others; and as we were all bound by the most solemn oaths of secrecy, there was little or no chance that a solution to any of the mysteries that originated in our circle could escape from its charmed precincts. I am now writing at a period of nearly half a century after the following occurrences; there will be no impropriety, therefore, in my recalling to any individual who may chance to retain a recollection of the event, the scandal that prevailed about fifty years ago in a town in Russia, concerning a nobleman much given to the study of occult arts, who was alleged to have put to death a young country girl whom he had subjected for some months to his magical experiments, and that for the purpose of proving whether her atmospheric spirit, violently thrust out of the body in the vigor of vitality, could not continue hovering around the scene of death, and make manifestations palpable to the sense of sight and sound. The popular rumor concerning this barbarous sacrifice was that the nobleman in question had seduced the unhappy peasant girl, and, after having perilled her immortal soul by his magical arts, he had ruthlessly destroyed her body for fear she should betray him.

Certain it was that the gentleman in question was charged with murder, tried and *acquitted*, just as it was supposed any other powerful nobleman in his place would have been. The results, however, were that strange and horrible disturbances took place in his castle. The affrighted domestics alleged that the spirit of the victim held possession of her destroyer's dwelling, and night after night her wild shrieks and blood-stained form, flying through gallery and corridor, "made night hideous," and startled the surrounding peasantry from slumber. Rumor added that the ghost, spectre, or "atmospheric spirit," whatever it might be, was not laid for years, and that the adept who had resorted to such terrible methods of gratifying his insatiate thirst for occult knowledge paid a tremendous penalty for what he had sought. Tortured with the horrible phantom he had evoked, his mind succumbed, and became a mere wreck. At the time when I commenced my experiences with the Brotherhood, this man, who had once been an honored member of their society, was confined as a hopeless lunatic, whilst his castle and estates were abandoned by his heir to the possession of the dread haunter and the destructive spirit of neglect and dilapidation.

It was by the command of my associates that I one

night visited, in the magnetic sleep, the cell of the lunatic; and being charged by the power of the Brothers with their combined magnetic force, I threw it on the maniac, and by this means, whilst his suffering body slumbered tranquilly, I returned to our "sanctuary" with his spirit; and from the records of that night's proceedings, I extract the following minutes of what transpired. He whose office I am not permitted by my *honor* to name, I shall call "Grand Master," and he thus questioned what was always called on these occasions the "flying soul" of the maniac: —

Grand Master. Did you kill the body of A. M.? Answer truly.

Flying Soul. I did.

G. M. For what purpose, and how?

F. S. To ascertain if the atmospheric spirit, being full of life, could remain with me. I killed her by a sudden blow, so as to let all the life out at once, and I drew out the spirit from the dead form by mesmeric passes.

G. M. Did you see that spirit pass?

F. S. I did.

G. M. How did it look?

F. S. Exactly like the body, only it wore an aspect of horror and appeal terrible to behold.

G. M. Did the spirit stay with you, and how long? Did it obey you, and act intelligently, or did it act a merely automatic part?

F. S. Mortals, know that *there is no death!* I did not kill A. M. I only broke up the temple in which her soul dwelt. THAT SOUL IS IMMORTAL, AND CAN NOT DIE. I found this out the moment after it had left the body, for it looked upon me, spoke to me, and reproached me. O God of heaven, saints and angels, pity me! It spoke to me as intelligently, but far, far more potentially than ever it had done in earthly being. It was not dead. It could not die; it never will die, and so it told me at once; but ah me, miserable! when I sank down aghast and struck with ineffable horror, as the spirit approached me, into a deep swoon, I entered the land of immortal souls. There I saw many people whom I had thought dead, but who were all still living. There, too, I saw the still living and radiantly glorious soul of my old pastor, Michael H——. Sternly but sorrowfully he told me I had committed a great and irreparable crime; that all crime was unpardonable, and could only be wiped out by personal, and not by vicarious atonement, as he had falsely taught whilst on earth; that my only means of atonement was suffering, and that *in kind,* or in connection with my dreadful crime; that, as the poor victim would be engaged during the term of her earthly life (broken short by my act) in working it out in an earthly sphere, so her magnetism, actually attracted, as I had deemed, to the spot where her life had been taken, would continue to haunt me, and repeat in vision the last dread act of murder until her life essence should melt away, and her spirit become free to quit the earth, and progress, as she would do, to higher spheres. Sometimes this stern teacher informed me I should see the real living soul of my victim, and then it would be as a pitying angel striving to help me; but still oftener I should see only the "spectre," and this would always appear as in the death-moment, an avenging form, partly conjured up from my own memory, and partly from the magnetic aura of my victim, and always taking the shape and circumstances of my dreadful crime. Mortals, there is much more to tell you of the awful realms beyond the grave, and the solemn connection between life and death, but more I dare not speak. Human beings will soon learn it for themselves; for the souls of the immortals are preparing to bridge over the gulf of death, and men and spirits will yet cross and recross it. Meantime ye are the blind leading the blind; deceiving yourselves with a vain philosophy, and deceiving all to whom ye teach it. THERE IS NO DEATH! I must be gone. Hark, I am called!

The minutes which follow, on this strange revelation of the maniac's "flying soul," add:—

"It would seem that the body was disturbed in its somnambulism, and the soul recalled; but we could have gained nothing by prolonging this interview, for evidently that soul had returned in its lucid intervals to the ancient and false philosophy in which it had in childhood been instructed, namely, the *mythical* belief in its immortality.

"The spirits of lunatics can be evoked, and always speak and think rationally when freed from the disordered body; but we note that they most commonly go back to the rudimental periods of their existence, and generally insist on the popular myth of immortality.

"Perhaps they are *en rapport* with the prevailing opinions of men, and are thus psychologized into repeating accepted ideas. There is nothing, however, to be gained from this experiment."

CHAPTER III.

In the college buildings occupied by the professors and employees attached to the university of which I became a student, resided a mathematical teacher, whom I shall designate Professor Müller. This gentleman held a distinguished place in the ranks of science, and was also one of the secret society associated with myself and Professor von Marx. He was a sullen, cold, ungenial man, and though esteemed for his scientific attainments, and regarded by our society as a powerful mesmeric operator, he was generally disliked, and was particularly repulsive to the "sensitives" whom he occasionally magnetized. Professor von Marx had always carefully isolated me from every magnetic influence but his own, and though I was consequently never required to submit to the control of Herr Müller, his very presence was so antipathetic to me that it was remarked my highest conditions of lucidity could never be evolved when he was by. He did not often attend the séances, however, in which I was engaged, although he belonged to our group, as well as others to which I was not admitted. Professor Müller's chief interest in my eyes was his relationship to a charming young lady, some years older than myself, but one for whom I cherished a sentiment which I can now only liken to the adoration of an humble votary for his saint; and truly

Constance Müller was worthy to be enshrined in any heart as its presiding angel.

She was beautiful, fair, and fragile-looking as a water-lily; gentle, timid, and shrinking as a fawn; and though residing with her stern, unloving uncle in the college buildings, and fulfilling for him the duties of a house-keeper, few of the other residents ever saw her except in transitory, passing glances, and none of the members of the university, save one, enjoyed the privilege of any direct personal intercourse with her. That solitary and highly-favored individual was myself.

I had made the acquaintance of the lovely lady on several occasions, when I had been sent from my friend, Herr von Marx, on messages to her uncle; and deeming, I presume, that my boyish years would shield our inter-course from all possibility of scandal or remark, the lonely fairy had deigned to bestow on me some slight attention, which finally ripened into a friendship equally sincere and delightful.

Constance Müller was an orphan, poor, and dependent on her only relative, Herr Müller. Young as I was, I could perceive the injustice, no less than the impropriety, of a young lady so delicately nurtured and possessed of fine sensitive instincts, being brought into such a scene, and subjected to such a life as she led in the university. She made no complaint, however, simply informing me that by the death of her father, a poor teacher of lan-guages, she had become solely dependent upon her uncle, and though she hoped eventually to induce him to aid her in establishing herself as a teacher of music, she was too thankful for his temporary protection to urge her choice of another life upon him, until she found him willing to promote her wishes. As for me, I lis-tened to her remarks on this head with strange misgivings. My own secret convictions were that the stern student of the occult had brought this beautiful young creature to the college with ulterior motives, in which his devotion to magical studies formed the leading idea. I may as well record here as at any other point of my narrative that, although I was deeply interested, nay, actually infatuated with the pursuits in which my clairvoyant susceptibilities had inducted me, I was never, from their very first commencement, satisfied that they were legitimate or healthful to the minds that were engaged in them. I felt the most implicit faith in the integrity and wisdom of Professor von Marx, as well as entire confidence in his affection for and paternal care of me; but here my confidence in any of my associates ended.

Somehow they all seemed to me to be men without souls. They were desperate, determined seekers into realms of being with which earth had no sympathy, and which in consequence abstracted them from all human feelings or human emotions.

Not one of them, that I can remember, ever manifested any genial qualities or seemed to delight in social exercises. They were profound, philosophic, isolated men, pursuing from mere necessity, or as a cloak to the stupendous secrets of their existence, some scientific occupation, yet in their innermost natures lost to earth and its sweet humanities; living amongst men, but partaking neither of their vices nor their virtues.

In their companionship I felt abandoned of my kind. Bound, chained, like a Prometheus, to the realms of the mysterious existences whom these men had subdued to their service, I often fancied myself a doomed soul, shut out forever from the tender and trustful associations of mortality, and swallowed up in an ocean of awe and mysticism, from which there was none to save, none to help me.

If the knowledge I had purchased was indeed a reality, there were times when I deemed it was neither good nor lawful for man to possess it. I often envied the peaceful unconsciousness of the outer world, and would gladly have gone back to the simple faith of my childhood, and then have closed my eyes in eternal sleep sooner than awaken to the terrible unrest which had possessed me since I had crossed the safe boundaries of the visible, and entered upon the illimitable wastes of the invisible.

And now, methought, Constance, the fair, gentle, and loving-hearted orphan, Constance, who so yearned for affection that she was content in her isolation to cling even to a young boy like me, was to become their victim; be inducted into the cold, unearthly realms of half-formed spiritual existences; lose all her precious womanly attributes, and with fixed, wild glances piercing the invisible, stare away from the faces of her fellow-mortals to the grotesque lineaments of goblins, the forms of sylphs, and the horrible rudiments of imperfect being that fill the realms of space, mercifully hidden from the eyes of ordinary mortals. Constance, I knew, longed for this knowledge, and whether prompted by the suggestions of her remorseless relative, or fired with the sphere of influence which he projected from his resolved mind, I could not tell; certain it was that she had obtained some clew to the pursuits in which I was engaged, and was perpetually plying me with questions and attempts to elicit information concerning them.

To this, though I felt as if I were betraying the interests of my beloved master, I invariably returned answers clothed in discouraging words and hints of warning. All would not avail. On a certain evening when I was my-

self off duty, but when a special meeting to which I did
not belong was held by the brothers, I saw Professor
Müller cross the college grounds, supporting on his arm
the closely-veiled and ethereal form of Constance. I
saw them enter a coach which was waiting for them at
the gate, and running hastily in their track, I heard the
professor direct the driver to set them down in that
remote quarter of the town where the meetings of the
Brotherhood were held. "Gone to the sacrifice!" I mentally exclaimed. "Constance, thou art doomed! sold to
a world of demons here and hereafter, — if indeed there
is a hereafter." Two evenings after this, as I was taking
my solitary walk in the college grounds, a quick step
pursued me; a hand was laid lightly on my shoulder,
and looking up I beheld Constance Müller, a transfigured being. Her eyes gleamed with a strange, unearthly
light; her head seemed to be thrown upwards as if spurn-
ing the earth and seeking kindred with the stars; her
cheek burned with a deep hectic flush, and a singular
air of triumph sat on her beautiful lips as she thus
accosted me: "Thou false page! how long wouldst thou
have kept the mistress, to whom thou hast sworn fealty,
imprisoned in the darkness of earthly captivity, when
realms of light and glory and wonder were waiting for
her to enter in and possess?"

"O Constance! where have you been?"

"Where I shall some day meet you, my young pala-
din, — in the land of light, for an entrance to which my
soul has yearned ever since I could look up from the
chill world of materialism, and feel that it must be
vitalized and fired by a world of spiritualism. Yes,
Louis, I know now the secrets of your nightly wanderings, — and I too can traverse space. I too can commune with the soul of things, and in enfranchised

4

liberty the inner self of Constance can roam the spheres of infinity and pierce the secrets of eternity."

"Alas!" I murmured, and then, unable to explain even to myself the unspeakable grief that filled my heart, I hung my head, and walked on silently by the side of the poor enthusiast.

For several weeks Constance Müller lived in the ecstacy of a pioneer who has discovered a new world, and deems himself its sovereign. I never could convey to her, in language, my own deep sense of man's inaptitude to commune with worlds of being at once foreign and repulsive to his mortality; but she saw, and in her wonderfully sympathetic nature appreciated the emotions I could not shape into words. In the glory of triumphant power over and through the invisible, however, the neophyte could not share the thoughts which some years of experience had forced upon me as convictions; but, ah me!. why should I have wished to hasten the *éclaircissement?* It came soon enough, or rather, too soon, too soon! I was never present at the séances in which Constance took part, nor were any of the other " lucid subjects " known to me, hence I never knew what transpired. The Brothers had many phases of spiritual communion among them, and though, thanks to the indulgent care of my teacher, I learned more than any of the other " sensitives " were permitted to know during their terms of initiation, I was aware that there were vast theatres of transcendental knowledge to be traversed, into which few if any mortals had been as yet fully inducted.

To every séance a formulæ was attached in the shape of oaths of secrecy, so tremendous that those who were sincere in their belief were never known to break them. That any part of the weird services conducted in these meetings should be subsequently revealed to the world is the best proof that the neophytes have ceased to be sincere or to regard their vows of silence as binding. At the time of which I write, I was deeply in earnest, and regarded the knowledge I had acquired as the most sacred that could be communicated; hence I never questioned Constance concerning her experiences, although I too well divined their nature.

As months glided on, I found most certainly that the spirit of this poor victim had been trained to become a "flying soul," and was, at most of the séances she attended, liberated for some purposes which I could only guess at.

Whatever these were, they soon began to affect her health and spirits. She pined away like a flower deprived of light and air. Frailer and more ethereal grew that slight, sylph-like form; more wan and hollow waxed the once tinted cheek and lips day by day.

Her large, blue eyes became sunken and hollow, and her curling locks of pale gold seemed like a coronet of sunbeams, already entwined to circle the brow of an eternal sleeper. At every séance she attended, her spirit, attenuating like a thread of long-drawn light, invariably floated away, as its first and most powerful attraction, to whatever place I happened to be in: sometimes poring over my books in my quiet little chamber; sometimes dreamily watching the ripples of the dancing fountain which played in the college square; not unfrequently wandering in the arcades of the thick woods that skirted the town; and at times stretched on the grass, watching, but never entering into, the merry sports of the youths of my own age, with whom, as companions, I had lost all sympathy. At home or abroad, alone or in the midst of a crowd, wherever I chanced to be, when the enfranchised soul of the beautiful Constance broke its prison bonds and went free, save for the magnetic spell of her operators, it invariably sought me out, and like a wreath of pale, sunlit mist, floated some two feet above the ground in bodily form and presentment before me. Accustomed to the phenomenon of the "double goer," this phantom neither surprised nor disturbed me. My spiritual experiences enabled me to perceive that during the few moments that the spirit of the "sensitive" was passing into the magnetic sleep, and before her magnetizers had yet full control of her, the instinctive attractions of her nature drew her to the boy whom she had already discovered to be her worshipper, the only being, perhaps, to whom she was drawn by the ties of affection, with which her loving nature was replete. All this I knew, and should have rejoiced in had not the phantom of the victim presented unmistakable tokens of being a sacrifice, and that an unpitied one, to the dark magians with whom she was so fatally associated.

In the vision of the "flying soul" of Constance, there was no speculation in the fixidity of the lustrous eyes; the form reposed as if on air, and the long, sunny curls would almost sweep the ground at my feet; but the look of hopeless sorrow and blank despair, which had grown to be a permanent expression on her waking features, was even more piteously depicted on the magnetic shade. She did not see me, touch, or know me, but the bruised spirit fled unconsciously to the shelter of the only presence that would, if it could, have saved her, and then passed away, to do the bidding of the remorseless men that had possessed themselves, as I then thought, of her helpless soul.

One evening, when we had been strolling out together,

and had sat on a lone hill side, watching the sinking
sun setting in gorgeous, many-colored glory over the
outstretched gardens, meadows, and plains beneath,
Constance broke a long silence by exclaiming in low
yet passionate tones, "Louis, you think the men who
have entrapped us, both body and soul, in their foul,
magical meshes, are good and pure, even if they are
cold and ungenial in their devotion to their awful
studies. Louis, you are mistaken. I bear witness to
you as the last, and perhaps the only act by which
I may ever more serve you on earth, that some of them
are impious, inhuman, and, O Heaven, how monstrously
impure!"

"Constance, you amaze me!"

"Do not interrupt me, Louis. I am injured past all
reparation. *You* may be snatched from the vortex
which pollutes the body and blasts the soul; but for
me, oh, would the end were come!"

The indescribable tone of anguish in which this
lament was uttered pierced me to the quick.

I threw myself at the feet of the beautiful lady, pro-
testing I would die to save her. For her sake, to do
her good or even to pleasure her, I would crush the
whole nest of magicians as I would so many wasps. I
would kill them, denounce them to the authorities, —
anything, everything she bid me do. All I asked was
to be permitted to save her.

To this wild rhapsody the low tones of the gentle
Constance only responded in stifled whispers, entreating me to be still, calm, patient, and to be assured that
neither I nor any other living creature could be of the
slightest assistance to her. "I have seen the end," she
added, when she had succeeded in calming me, "and I
know that, impatient as I am for its coming, it will not

be long delayed. I shall enter into the realms of light and glory, for these dreadful men have only abused my helpless spirit so long as it is imprisoned in my weak . body and its connecting forces; they have not touched its integrity, nor can they maintain their hold upon it one instant after it has severed the chain which binds the immortal to the mortal. When that is broken I shall be free and happy."

"Constance!" I cried, "is it then given you to know what new form you will inhabit? Surely, one so good and true and beautiful can become nothing less than a radiant planetary spirit!"

"I shall be the same Constance I ever was," she replied, solemnly. "I am an immortal spirit now, although bound in material chains within this frail body, and in magnetic chains still more terrible to the power of you base, bad men."

"Constance, you dream! Death is the end of individuality. Your spirit may be, must be, taken up by the bright realms of starry being, but never as the Constance you now are."

"Forever and forever, Louis, I shall be ever the same. I have seen worlds of being those magians can not ascend to, — worlds of bright, resurrected human souls upon whom death has had no power save to dissolve the earthly chains that held them in tenements of clay. I have seen the soul world; I have seen that it is imperishable. Louis, there are in these grasses beneath our feet spiritual essences that never die. In my moments of happiest lucidity, that is"— and here a strong shudder shook her frame — "when I could escape from my tormentors and the world of demons amongst whom they delight to roam, then, Louis, my soul winged through space and pierced into a brighter

interior than they have ever realized, aye, even into the
real soul of the universe, not the mere magnetic
envelope which binds spirit and body together. Louis,
in the first or inner recesses of nature is the realm of
force, comprising light, heat, magnetism, life, nerve,
aura, essence, and all the imponderables that make up
motion, for motion is force, composed of many subdi-
visible parts. Here inhere those worlds of half-formed,
embryotic existences with which our tormentors hold
intercourse. They are the spiritual parts of matter,
and supply to matter the qualities of force; but they
are all embryotic, all transitory, and only partially intelligent existences. Nothing which is imperfect is permanent, hence these imperfect elementary spirits have
no real or permanent existence; they are fragments of
being, organs, but not organisms, and until they are
combined into the organism of manhood, they can out-
work no real individuality, hence they perish — die,
that we may gather up their progressed atoms, and
incarnate their separate organs as the complete organism of man."

" And man himself, Constance? "

" Man as a perfected organism *can not* die, Louis.
The mould in which he is formed must perish, in order
that the soul may go free. The envelope, or magnetic
body that binds body and soul together, is formed of
force and elementary spirit; hence this stays for a time
with the soul after death, and enables it to return to, or
linger around the earth for providential purposes until
it has become purified from sin; but even this at length
drops off, and then the soul lives as pure spirit, in spirit
realms, gloriously bright, radiantly happy, strong, powerful, eternal, infinite. That is heaven; that it is to
dwell with God; such souls are his angels."

"Constance, you speak with assurance. How know you this — not from the Brotherhood?"

"The Brotherhood, Louis! Why, they are but groping through the thick darkness of the material world, and just penetrating the realms of force.

"I tell you those realms are only peopled with shadows, ghosts, phantoms.

"The hand is not the body, the eye is not the head; neither are the thin, vapory essences that constitute the separate organs of which the world of force is composed, the soul. Mark me, Louis! Priests dream of the existence of soul worlds, the Brotherhood of the beings in the world of force. The priests call the elementary spirits of the mid-region mere creations of human fancy and superstition. The Brothers charge the same hallucination upon the priests. Both are partly right and partly wrong, for the actual experiences of the soul will prove that beings exist of both natures, and that both realms are verities; only the elementary spirits in the realms of force are like the earth, perishable and transitory, and the perfected spirits in the realm of soul are immortal, and never die. Louis, I have seen and conversed with both, and I know I do not dream. Here, miserable that I am, I am bound to earth; my soul is imprisoned by the chains of force; I am compelled to minister to the insatiate curiosity of the spirits who cannot ascend beyond those mid-regions, and oh! the horror of that bondage would have bereft my soul of reason, had it not been redeemed by foregleams of the more holy and exalted destiny reserved for the soul in the blest sphere of immortality. Dear boy, ask me no more, press me no further. My sweet brother, dearly, fondly loved by Constance! when I am an enfranchised spirit, I will come to thee, and prove my words by the very presence of an arisen, immortal soul. Remember! "

During the months succeeding this memorable conversation, I only encountered the "flying soul" of the dying Constance once.

I understood that this recession of her spirit was from no decrease of the experiments, whatever they might be, that she suffered, nor yet from any cessation of her attraction to myself, but the bonds of earth were loosening, the vital forces waning, and I knew that the pale phantom was losing the earthly essence necessary to become visible even in the atmosphere of invisible forces. My beautiful saint would soon be taken from me, my earthly idol would be shattered; and oh! were it possible to believe her words, and think that she could still live in a brighter and better state of being, I might have been comforted; but driven from this anchor of hope by the emphatic teachings of the Brotherhood and their spirits, I beheld my earth angel melting away into blank annihilation, with an anguish that admitted of no alleviation, a pain at my heart almost insupportable.

I had been away for some months in England, pursuing studies of which I shall speak more presently. Professor von Marx had been my companion, and we had just returned, when one night, as I was about to retire to rest, and proceeded to draw the curtain which shaded my window, something seemed to rise outside the casement, which intercepted the light of the moon. The house in which I dwelt was on the borders of a beautiful lake, and too high above it to allow of any stray passenger climbing up to my casement. There was no boat on the waters, no foothold between them and the terrace, which was far below my window. I had been gazing out for some time on the placid lake, illumined by the broad path of light shed over it by the full moon, and I knew that no living creature was near or could gain access to my apartment; and yet there, standing on air against the casement, and intercepting the rays that streamed on either side of her on the mosaic floor of my chamber, stood the gracious and radiant form of Constance Müller. In the flash of one second of time I knew it was not her *atmospheric spirit* that stood there.

Radiant, shining, and glorious she now appeared, her sweet eyes looking full of penetrating intelligence into mine, her sweet smile directed towards me, and a motion of her hand like the action of a salute, indicating that the apparition saw and recognized me, and was all beaming with interest and intelligence. By a process which was not ordinary motion, the lovely phantom seemed to glide through the window and appear suddenly within a few feet of the couch, to which, on her first appearance, I had staggered back. Slightly bending forward, as if to arrest my attention, though without the least movement of the lips, her voice reached my ear, saying, "I am free, happy, and immortal." Swiftly as she had appeared, the apparition vanished, and in its place I beheld the visionary semblance of the old-fashioned room in the college building occupied by Constance Müller. On a couch which I well knew, lay the form of the once beautiful tenant, pale, ghastly, dead! The form was partly covered over with a sheet, but where the white dressing-robe she wore was open at the throat I observed clearly and distinctly two black, livid spots, like the marks of a thumb and finger.

The face was distorted, the eyes staring, and I saw she had been murdered.

Ghastly as was the scene I looked upon, a preternatural power of observation seemed to possess me, impelling me to look around the apartment, which I perceived was stripped of many things I had been accustomed to see there. The harp was gone, and so was the desk and books at which I had so frequently seen her seated. Looking with the piercing eye of the spirit behind as well as upon the couch where the body lay, I saw the black ribbon and gold locket which Constance had always worn round her neck lying on the ground as if it had been dropped there.

If there was any meaning in this vision, it would appear that this object was the point aimed at, for I had no sooner beheld it and the exact position in which it lay than the whole phantasmagoria passed away, and once more the shining image of a living and celestially beautiful Constance stood before me.

Again the air seemed to syllable forth the words, "I am free, happy, and immortal," and "I have kept my promise," when again, but this time far more gradually, the angelic vision melted out, leaving the pattern of the mosaic on the floor, gilded only by the bright moonbeam, and the diamond panes of the casement, shadowed only by the white jasmine that was trained over the house.

Moonlight reigned supreme, the shadow was gone; but ah me! it had been the shadow of an eternity of sunbeams. Never did I realize such a profound gloom, such an insufferably thick atmosphere, such "darkness made visible," as the absence of this radiant creature left behind. Whilst she stayed it seemed as if sorrow, evil, or suffering had never had an existence; life and being throughout was a mighty ecstacy: and now she had taken all the joy and sunlight out of the world, and that — forever.

The recital of the previous night's vision, every item

of which I faithfully related to Professor von Marx the next morning, found in him a grave, attentive, but still unmoved listener.

He did not seem to doubt but that Constance Müller was dead. He made no remarks upon the appearances which, I passionately declared, inferred that she had suffered death by violence. To all this he simply said, "We shall see"; but when I strove to convince him that the apparition of a soul after death, and that with all the signs of life and tokens of intelligence, must prove a continued existence, he seemed roused to his usual tone of dogmatic assertion. He repeated what he had often insisted upon before,—namely, that the life emanations called "soul" did often subsist for a short period after death, and appear as an organic form, but he still maintained that was no proof of immortality, since such essences soon disintegrated, and became as scattered and inorganic as the body they had once inhabited.

When I urged the words I had heard from the beautiful phantom, he insisted they were the reflections of my own thoughts, associated with the appearance of one who believed in idle superstitions, and to my plea that the dress of pure, glistening white in which the figure was arrayed could be no reflex of my mind, whilst the buoyant happiness that sparkled on her angelic face bore little or no resemblance to the sad, faded original, he replied that as the essence was pure and unalloyed by the earthy, so when I beheld the essence actually disengaged from the earthy, I should see it clothed in an image of its own beauty, light, and purity. I was silenced, but not convinced. Two days later Professor von Marx stood with me knocking at Herr Müller's chamber door. The professor himself opened it, and anticipated all we might have to say by informing us, gravely, that he had been unfortunate enough to lose his niece "by a sudden attack of putrid fever," which had compelled her speedy interment, the ceremony of which he had been just attending.

"I knew that Fräulein Müller was no more," replied my teacher, in a voice which, despite his philosophy, was something moved and broken, "and I called thus early, not to condole with you, for I know your resolved stoicism, but to ask if you are willing to let my dear young friend here make purchase of your niece's harp. You know the young people were much attached to each other, and Louis is anxious to possess this souvenir of his beloved friend." I could not speak; a choking sensation was in my throat, and I was astonished at the cool invention by which Herr von Marx was trying the truth of my clairvoyance; but I listened breathlessly for the reply.

"I had her harp, desk, books, and other matters which might have been rendered unsalable by the contagion of the fever, removed," replied Herr von Müller, with a slight shade of confusion in his manner. "I did not want a crowd of persons hovering around the sufferer in her dying moments, hence I had the apartment cleared in an early stage of her disease."

"Is there nothing my young friend could procure from this much venerated spot?" persisted my crafty ally.

"I do not well know," replied the other, completely thrown off his guard; "but if you desire it, you can step in and inspect the apartment."

Following the two strangely matched associates into the desolate shrine from which the saint had been removed, I gazed around only to see a perfect fac-simile of the scene I had beheld in vision. It was evident the quick, furtive glances of Professor von Marx were directed towards the same end as my own. Suddenly he stopped before a dark picture hanging on the wall, and standing in a line between me and Herr Müller, directed his attention to something which he pretended to call remarkable in the painting, thus giving me the opportunity to cross the room hastily, draw out a couch in the corner, and gather up from behind it *a black ribbon and gold locket,* which had lain there apparently unnoticed till then. Professor von Marx never lost sight of me for an instant, and no sooner saw me secrete my treasure in my bosom than he said abruptly, "Come, Louis, I don't like the atmosphere of the place. Herr Müller is right: the contagion of death lingers around; there is nothing left here *now* that you can desire to have. Let us go."

As we returned to our lodgings the professor silenced my deep and angry murmurs against the man we had just left by a variety of sophistries with which he was always familiar. One of these was the total indifference with which all the Brotherhood regarded the lives of those who were not of their order. It mattered little, he said, how poor Constance's thread of being was finally cut short, since it was evidently too attenuated to spin out to any much greater length than it had already attained; and finally, if I would persist, he said, in indulging in unrestrained and pernicious bursts of passion, I should mar the necessary passivity and equilibrium so essential to pure clairvoyance, and he should lose the best "lucid" in the world.

Before we parted for the night the professor asked me if I had ever seen or heard of Zwingler, the Bohemian.

"Who is he?" I asked, indifferently.

"You have never seen or heard of Zwingler? Then," he rejoined, "you have something to learn, another lesson to take, one, I think, that will help to dissipate your faith in the myth of immortality, and throw some light on the question of *apparitions.*

"Come with me to-morrow, Louis, to Sophien Stradt. There I will introduce you to Zwingler, and in his person to one of the phenomenal wonders of the age; and Louis," he added, after a moment's pause, as we shook hands at parting, "carry that ribbon and locket somewhere about you — poor Constance's jewel, I mean. We may find a singular use for it. Good-night."

CHAPTER IV.

To fulfil the promise which my teacher had made me of visiting Zwingler, we mounted several flights of stairs in an old house in Sophien Stradt, and at last reached a landing upon which many persons were congregated about and around an open door, through which I was led by Professor von Marx into a large apartment, shabbily furnished, and half filled with loungers, amongst whom I recognized more than one official of the constabulary force of the city.

Pushing his way through the assembled company to a sort of recess at the far end of the room, the professor addressed himself to a little, black-eyed, Oriental-looking individual, who was seated on a table, dangling his legs, and fidgeting restlessly about, whilst a grave official, in the habit of a notary, was taking down depositions or making notes from what the other was saying. The moment the little man set eyes on the professor, he sprang from the table, and seizing his hand with a sort of fawning, propitiatory air, which seemed more like the action of deferential fear than real cordiality, he cried, "Ah, my prince of the powers of the air! welcome! ever welcome to Zwingler, but more especially at this time, when a most wonderful phase of your art, that is to say, of mine, or the devil's or some of his imps', for what I know, has just been perpetrated through my innocent instrumentality." The little man whilst speaking manifested all the feverish excitement of an actor anxious to overdo his part, at the same time obviously desirous to interest his listener, as one of whom he stood in some awe. Without paying any attention to this speech, Professor von Marx, turning to me, said calmly, "Louis, this is Zwingler."

"Adept!" (to Zwingler) "a pupil of mine, for whose benefit I wish you to recite some little fragments of your experience;" then, seating himself upon the table from which the Bohemian had dismounted, and motioning me to a stool by his side, he proceeded, addressing the notary, to whom he had slightly nodded, "Well, Herr Reinhardt, what new discoveries has our lively little sleuth-hound been making?"

"Oh, nothing out of the common line, professor," replied the other, in a grave official drawl. "We 've caught the murderer of Frau Ebenstein; that 's all."

"That 's all?" cried the Bohemian, with a tone and gesture of almost frantic excitement. "That's all, is it? Slave of the dull earth and the duller prison watch and ward! All is it, to traverse nearly two hundred miles of ground, cross three rivers, plunge through marshes, scale mountain heights, pierce the forest, sink through the cavern's depths, and toss on the roaring rapids of the terrific Schwartz cataract; and still never to lose— no, not for a single moment—the scent of an invisible and unknown mortal, whom these eyes had never beheld, whom these hands had never touched, and of whom no sign, no symbol, no token in the realms of earthly existence could be found, except by me, Zwingler!"

As he spoke, he beat his breast, and elevated his glittering black eye to the heavens in an attitude of half-ecstatic frenzy.

5

The notary, without the slightest change of feature, continued to write, wholly unmindful of his rhapsody; but Professor von Marx, fixing his deep, piercing dark eyes upon the Bohemian, said in a calm, soothing tone, as if he were attempting to subdue a fractious child, "You are a marvellous being, indeed, Zwingler, and that all the world knows. Come now! there's a good fellow, tell·us all about it. Sit down — no, not there — there, at my feet; so, that will do. Now, relate the whole story; we will listen most patiently and admire most fervently," he added, speaking aside to me in Spanish. "Remember, I have not seen you for two months, and only yesterday heard that you had returned in triumph from your long pilgrimage. When I was last here, the tidings had just reached us that Frau Ebenstein, the rich widow of Baden Baden, had been foully murdered, her house sacked and plundered, and her destroyer—"

"An unknown," broke in the notary, as if impatient to recite details which were specially in the line of his duty, "an unknown, whether male or female also unknown, but supposed to be the former on account of blood-stained footprints, marks of a large thumb and finger on neck of the deceased, and a torn neckerchief, evidently a man's, part of which was clutched in the fingers of said deceased, and part of which was found beneath the couch, saturated with gore, and rent, as if in a violent struggle."

As the speaker proceeded, strong shudderings seized the frame of the Bohemian, though the hand of Professor von Marx, laid lightly on his shoulder, for a time subdued the spasms and quelled them into slight shiverings; but when the neckerchief was mentioned, the little creature's excitement was frightful to behold. He writhed like an eel beneath the touch of the professor, who at last, raising his hand, said quietly, "Now, Zwingler, proceed. Tell the rest in your own way."

"Yes, yes, I will tell," he cried. "I always do. When did I ever fail? Answer me that, prince of the air; answer me!"

"Never, my king of adepts; but go on."

"They brought me that neckerchief, then, mein Herren," he continued, as if addressing a vast assembly, but without looking at any of the loungers in the outer apartment, who now closed up about him; "and lo! as I clutched it, I saw.— yes, instantly, I saw a dark-browed, broad-shouldered Dutch serving-man,— the man of blood, the man who did the deed. I swear it! I saw him do it. I saw him and the whole act; and oh, how horrible it was! how cruel! how cowardly! and the poor, poor old Frau! I saw her too,— saw her struggle, plead, choke, die! All this I saw, — out of that neckerchief, mein Herren! Instantly, as I touched it, it came like a flash, a flash of darkness, but full of the scene I describe, and full, too, of all its horror. Gott in Himmel! Then it went as all scenes do after the flash I get of them as I touch the thing; after that I said 'Give me my shoes; I must walk far. Put me a cup to scoop up water with in my wallet, give me my staff, and let me go.' I had been hungry and was about to dine, but I hungered no more; no, not for seven long days did I touch other food than the nuts and berries close to the path streaked with the murderer's life, and the water of the rivers, streams, and cataract he had crossed; but I will tell you all. Listen! As I made to go, I chose my path as I always do, because a long black line seemed to stream out from the neckerchief I held in my hand, and point ever on the way I should go. It led me through the city; it pointed me

into a low inn where he had stopped to rest. I told them
such a man had been there. They shuddered, and said
to one another, 'Zwingler!' and then to me, 'He has
been and gone.' I knew it; but the way he had taken
was still pointed by the black line. I know what you
were going to say, professor; I *see your thought.* You
want to know if I see the line I speak of with my eyes,
my very eyes, or my soul's eyes. I reply, 'With both.'
My soul feels the line, and it draws me on, and seems
like a cord dragging at the object I hold, and pulling me
in the direction I must take to arrive at the owner of
that object. Sometimes I seem to see the line, and then
I do not feel it pull, but it never leaves one sense or the
other — sight or feeling — until I abandon the object or
find the person to whom it has belonged. Well, sirs,
thus it led me on, day and night, never suffering me to
get out of *his* track. It guided me through several villages and some towns, and wherever it was the thickest
and most palpable, there he had stopped to take rest or
refreshment, and there I said, 'Such and such a man has
been here'; and they answered with a shudder, 'Zwingler! he has come and gone.'

"I rested sometimes, but ever on the ground,—the
ground he had trodden; and then the black, vapory
cord seemed to coil up all around me like a misty garment. I tried to rest once on a bed he had occupied,
but O Heaven! all the scene of the murder was there.
I heard her shriek, I saw her struggle, and what was
still more horrible, it seemed to me that I was the murderer, and was actually doing the deed over again. I
fled from the place, and should have lost the track had
I not returned to it again, and started afresh from that
house.

"To one like me, professor, that house will always be

haunted; that is, until the murderer's shade melts away
from it; and it will do so in time. I answer your
thought again, you see, professor. It was near midnight, some time—I can not tell how long—after I had
started, that the black cord began to thicken and spread,
and at length to assume the shape of a man.

"It trembled and quivered, and at first was only the
indistinct outline of a man, but presently it grew more
and more dense, and now behold! It was the ghost of
the Dutch serving-man in full, walking just so far
before me, above the ground one foot, and ever looking over its shoulder at something coming after it.
That man went to a great many places in the town
I was now hunting through, for the ghost was at every
street-corner and in every alley, and lurking in all the
dark lanes and by-streets; and though I knew he must
be close at hand, by the density of the ghost, still he
had wandered and wandered, and lurked about in so
many places that I should have become confused had
not both senses been suddenly appealed to at once.
I saw him, and at last I felt him. I felt him, as it were,
tugging at the neckerchief in my hand, and striving—
O holy martyrs, how he strove!—to get it away from
me.

"Sirs, he was just then thinking about that neckerchief, remembering he had lost it in the murdered lady's
room, and wishing he had got it, and cursing his folly,
and mentally longing, longing to get it back. Lucky
for me he did think thus, for his thought, being set on
the neckerchief, pulled at it so frantically that it led me
straight to his hiding-place, and there and then, when
I saw him, and screamed that that was the murderer of
Frau Ebenstein, and the landlord and guests of the inn
cried 'Zwingler, Zwingler!' he uttered a great cry, and

fell as if he had been struck; and then it was they captured him and brought him thither."

"Ay! and the strangest fact of all this is, gentlemen," broke in the grave notary, unable to keep silence
any longer, "that this wretch had changed his dress
ever so many times, and when this wonderful Bohemian
here tracked him to his lair, he was disguised as a sailor,
and so disguised that none but the devil, or perhaps his
particular ally, Zwingler, could have found him out."

"Pshaw!" replied the Bohemian, scornfully, "what
know you burghers of my art? I do not track the
clothes of the man, but the man. His soul was in his
hand, on his neck, and in the neckerchief around it
when he did the deed. The sleuth-hound senses his
human game through the organ of smell. I sense it
through smell, touch, taste, sight, and hearing. I sense
soul through perception. Every thing, ·every place,
where soul has been, is full of it; and once give me a
link, a single thread of association, such as an object
the soul I would track out has come into contact with,
and the depths of the sea can not hide it, the mountains
can not cover it, the disguise of a monarch or the rags
of a beggar can not conceal the identity of the man
whose soul Zwingler would track out. But remember,
mein Herren, Zwingler tracks souls, not masking
habits."

The little Bohemian's slight form seemed to expand,
as he spoke with impassioned gesture and rapid utterance, into the proportions of a giant; and as he turned
away to reply to some question addressed to him by
one of his admiring auditors, the professor murmured
in my ear, "He has detected more criminals in this way
than all the constabulary of Germany. Give him but a
garment, a lock of hair, or even a rag that has come in

contact with a living organism, and he will track out its owner with a fidelity unmatched by the best blood-hound that ever ran." Then addressing the Bohemian, he said aloud, "Glorious Zwingler! as wise as you are gifted, tell my foolish young son here what you mean by a soul. He is eager to learn of you what soul really is."

"Soul is the life, my prince; you know that," replied Zwingler, half daunted, as he always seemed to be when addressing Professor von Marx.

"You think, then, soul is just the life principle and nothing more; that which keeps the man alive; is that so?"

"What else can it be?"

"But what is the 'black cord' you speak of, what the essence which clings to substances and enables you to describe or sense the person from whom it has flowed out?"

"The soul, of course, great master."

"Is the soul, then, a substance?"

"Is the air a substance, the wind a substance? You can not see or feel either until they come into contact with some other substance, and when they do, although invisible, you know they are something. The soul is finer than air, thinner and more ethereal than wind, and only some souls as fine and pure as mine can sense it. But when a Marx can sense the air, and feel the wind, a Zwingler can sense the soul and feel the substance."

"Admirable, my little philosopher! and now, one question more: What do you suppose becomes of the soul after a man dies?"

"Pshaw, learned master! why ask me so foolish a question? What becomes of the body after a man dies? Why not ask me that?"

"Why not indeed?" muttered the professor, glancing triumphantly at me. "But, Zwingler, if the form of a soul can appear whilst a man lives, can it not and does it not appear sometimes after death?"

"Does not the body appear too, if you look for it? Surely it does not all fade away at once, but decays and corrupts and at last disappears. No doubt soul and body both wear away, fade out, and melt into their original elements when they become separated, as at death. No doubt, too, some can see only the body, and some, like Zwingler, can see the soul as well; but both live only when they are together, and die when they are apart;" then contracting his singularly mobile features into a frown of impatience, he cried, irritably, "But why torment me, and make me talk about things which only you great professors understand? I hate to think of death! I loathe it! I—I—fear it! I wish I could live forever!" He was about to dart away, when Professor von Marx laid a hand gently on his arm; the Bohemian stood as if transfixed, and muttered submissively, "What more would you have of me, great professor?"

"Only to accept this slight token of my young friend's gratitude for your instructive narrative, adept," replied the professor; and as he spoke, Herr von Marx suddenly snatched from me the locket and ribbon of poor Constance, which I held as he had desired during the interview in my right hand, and which he now as suddenly placed in Zwingler's.

Before I could pronounce a word of protest against this unexpected and unwelcome transfer, the Bohemian clutched at the ornament with an action so fearfully spasmodic and full of terror that the words I would have uttered died on my lips. "Death again!" he mur-

mured, with a strangely piteous accent. "Ever surrounded with the faded blossoms of dead souls! But
ah me! this was a cruel death,—so young, so fair, so
innocent; and destroyed, too, by the hand of him who
should have been her protector! Herr Professor, I
shall not have far to go to trace the soul of him who
did this deed of blood."

"Hush, little dreamer!" responded the professor in
a low whisper; "your art is not wanted here. Stay!
I will change the token. Keep this, and be silent or
worse will come of it." So saying, he took back the
locket, returning it to me, and placing several gold
pieces in the Bohemian's hand, led me through the
crowd, who opened reverentially to permit the learned
and celebrated Professor von Marx to pass through.
At home again, and in our quiet lodgings, the ominous
silence of the last hour between Professor von Marx
and myself was thus broken:—

"What think you of Zwingler, my Louis?"

"What think you of the death, or rather *the murder*,
of Constance Müller, my master?"

"Ever harping on a worn-out theme and irrevocable
past, silly boy! Science must, will, and shall have its
martyrs, Louis, and woe to the progress of the race
when idle emotion erects itself to match the interests
of science. Enough, once and forever, of this. What
think you of Zwingler?"

"He fails to convince me that an apparition of a soul
after death is only an apparition."

"Then, what is it before death?"

"Ay! that is the question."

"Zwingler's mode of philosophizing is crude enough,"
replied Herr von Marx, "but the philosophy itself is
unanswerable. Like the lower elementary, and the

higher planetary spirits, the soul of man, the finest and most sublimated condition in which matter exists, inheres to all coarser forms, and thus it can be sensed, as Zwingler calls it, as a sphere, sometimes in a premonition of its approach, sometimes in the feeling of indescribable repulsion or attraction which we conceive for strangers even as we approach them. Sometimes it can be seen in bodily shape, apart from the body, as in the case of the 'double' or 'atmospheric spirit,' and sometimes it can be seen when it has separated entirely from the body, ere it is quite resolved back again into its original elements. And that is all."

"And that is all," I mechanically repeated, feeling, however, at the same time that the professor was merely reciting a lesson in a form of words familiar to him, whilst his spirit was strangely abstracted, and his manner vague and wandering as my own when I repeated his last words.

As the professor and myself relapsed into deep silence, a chiming us of very distant bells was heard in the air; a singular radiance stole through the dim twilight obscurity of our chamber, and settled about the table strewed with books, at which in the past morning I had been studying. That radiance at first appeared like a shimmering fire-mist; then it expanded, bent, curled, and at last seemed to weave itself into the proportions of a human form. Clearer, brighter, stronger grew the vision; at length the mists rose and parted on either side, disclosing the shining apparition and seraphic features of the dead Constance. Turning her head of sunny glory towards me, she smiled, then bent over the table, seemed to select with swift action a large Lutheran Bible from a heap of books, opened it, took up the locket and black ribbon I had laid down near it, placed the ribbon like a mark across a certain passage, pointed to it emphatically three times, then with such a smile as a mortal could scarcely look upon and live, she vanished from my sight, and all was darkness.

What followed, or how long I may have remained unconscious of life and being, after this vision, I know not; but my first recognition of passing events was the sound of Herr von Marx's voice speaking through the thick darkness of night which had fallen upon us, saying, "Louis, are you awake? Surely, I must have had a long sleep, for the night has stolen upon me unawares."

The janitor at this moment entered with lights, and placed them on a sideboard. The professor, rising from his seat, took one of the lamps, and advancing to the table held it over the open Bible, at the same time exclaiming in a voice of singular agitation, "Who has marked these passages?"

I advanced, looked over his shoulder, and saw him remove the ribbon and locket, only to disclose several deep black lines, drawn as if with Indian ink, beneath the following words, in different parts of the fifteenth chapter of the First Epistle of Paul to the Corinthians.

"There is a natural body, and there is a spiritual body."

"Behold I show you a mystery; we shall not all sleep, but we shall all be changed."

"Death is swallowed up in victory."

"O death, where is thy sting? O grave, where is thy victory?"

CHAPTER V.

BEFORE I had completed my educational term in Europe, I had the misfortune to lose my good father; but immediately after his death I received letters from my mother and our Hindoo connections, directing me to enter upon a course of study in a certain military school in England, where I was to fit myself for following my father's profession of arms in India.

Although I was greatly averse to this course, and would have preferred any other occupation rather than that of a soldier, I found the arrangements for my continuance in Europe were made contingent upon my compliance with these directions, and I had become so warmly attached to Professor von Marx, and his affection for me had become such an indispensable element in my existence, that I was willing to avail myself of any opportunity that would enable me to remain near him, if not absolutely so much in his society as formerly.

My mother informed me that honorable distinction and rapid military promotion awaited me in India, through the influence of my father's connections and the high estimation in which his noble services had been held, and she besought me not to blight all the hopes she had founded upon my compliance and good conduct, and concluded by referring me to the parties in Europe who would carry out her wishes by providing for my studies in the English military school. Professor von Marx seemed half amused as well as not a little pleased with the sorrow and reluctance I exhibited at the prospect of my separation from him. He told me his professorship at B—— had been accepted rather as a means of diverting attention from the more occult pursuits he delighted in, than from any necessity on his part to occupy himself in scholastic duties.

Being, as he said, free to come and go as he pleased, and having conceived an attachment for me which would render our separation mutually painful, while he advised me not to oppose the wishes of my friends in their choice of a profession, he completely reconciled me to my enforced absence from Germany by frequently visiting me in England, and spending much of his time in a quiet lodging near my school, where he occupied himself in his favorite studies, and enabled me to pass all my leisure hours in his society. Once more, then, we devoted ourselves to the experiments in which we had been engaged with the Berlin Brotherhood, and as I invariably spent my vacations at my beloved friend's residence near the college at B——, I troubled myself but little about the new views of life that had been opened up to me. My mother had consented to my remaining with Professor von Marx until I should have completed my twenty-second year; but as time sped on, and the attachment between myself and the professor deepened, the links which bound me to that strange man seemed to have become interwoven with my very heart-strings, and to contemplate rending them asunder was to me an idea fraught with indescribable anguish. After the lapse of many years of time, and with every youthful heart-throb stilled into the calm of waiting expectation until the mighty change shall come, even now I can hardly recall the life of indescribable oneness and magnetic sympathy which attached me to my singular associate without amazement that the identity of one human being should have become so entirely merged in that of another. In his presence I felt strong to act, clear to think, and prompt to speak; yet by some strange fatuity, it seemed to me as if acts, thoughts, and words took their shape from him, and without the least effort on my part to discover or inquire his will, I know that I lived beneath its influence, and derived my chief motives for speech and action from the silent flow of his thoughts. When I was absent from him, I became an indescribably lost creature. I was dreamy, uncertain, wandering; not so much a child as a being without a soul,—one in whom instinct remained, but self-consciousness lacked the pivot on which to revolve, and hence the wheels of mind vibrated and swung to and fro, searching for the sustaining power on which to anchor.

I can now discern the secret of this mystic spell, although I do not know that I have ever had the opportunity of observing a case in which one·soul had acquired over another an equal amount of control. The magnetic life of Professor von Marx had been infused into my system until I was a part of himself; his strong and persuasive will had pierced my very brain, until it had found a lodgment in the innermost seat of intelligence.

By a mutual understanding, though without any outward expression in words, I considered myself the adopted son of Professor von Marx, and I not only felt restful and happy in this tacit arrangement, but I vaguely speculated upon the possibility of my soul's becoming soon separated from the frail tenement it inhabited, and perhaps absorbed in the grander and more exalted entity of the being I so strangely idolized.

I do not know to this day how far the professor realized his magical power over me. He knew that I read his thoughts like an open page. He was able to conceal or reveal his will to me at pleasure, and without a word spoken. I knew when he willed to shut his thought from me, and at such times I was a blank.

When there was no such mental wall erected between us, all was as clear and lucid to me as if he were myself. I prepared myself to walk or ride with him, came and went as he wished, and all without a word spoken or a gesture made.

Professor von Marx was, I now know, fondly attached to me, and, I think, pitied my fearful subjection to his will even whilst he enjoyed its triumphant exercise.

This true gentleman was gravely courteous to the female sex, but never seemed to realize the slightest attraction towards them as companions. He understood them, as indeed he understood every one he approached; but though he never conversed with me on the subject, I perceived that he viewed the yielding and intuitive characteristics of the female mind with lofty contempt, and his intense and all-absorbing devotion to the peculiar studies he had adopted made him coldly indifferent to the attractions of female beauty. Eminently handsome in person, and polished though cold in manner, he might have commanded the adoration of even the fairest in any land. Why I alone, of all the human family, ever seemed to move his stoical heart to the least emotion can only be accounted for on the hypothesis that there was something of a reciprocal action in the magnetic processes which had so wonderfully bound me to him, and that in the absorption of his magnetic influence on my part, he involuntarily received in exchange influences from the elemental life which he displaced in my organism. Magnetizers not unfrequently imbibe some of the qualities of disease, or even the psychological tendencies of their patients, and call it sympathy.

When the term of my studies at the English military school ended, I accompanied my beloved friend on a tour through Europe and the East, which occupied us for many months, at the end of which, Professor von Marx informed me that his presence would be required for several months in London, upon business of importance connected with the interests of a certain society with which he was associated. As I had never visited the great British capital, my dear master promised himself much satisfaction from my introduction to a highly esteemed English friend of his, and the opportunity that would be afforded me for observing the progress of occultism amongst its votaries in England.

Dark, blighting, and inauspicious was the day when first Professor von Marx and myself established ourselves in an old-fashioned, time-worn mansion, a portion of which we were to rent during our stay in London. The fire blazed in the grate, and the mellow light of softly gleaming lamps lent a cheering lustre to the scene, however, as we sat, on the first evening of our arrival, in company with two guests to whom we had dispatched letters of introduction, and who had hastened to welcome us, at the earliest possible moment, to the British metropolis.

One of our visitors, a gentleman of most estimable character and high social position, was an old college companion of Professor von Marx, and it appears that in early youth they had been sworn friends, and associates in many of the societies to which the professor belonged. This gentleman, who subsequently enacted a most important part in the drama of my own fateful life, I do not feel at liberty to name, but for the sake of perspicuity I shall beg my readers to recognize his frequent appearances in these pages under the *nom de plume* of Mr. John Cavendish Dudley. The personage who accompanied Mr. Dudley was, like himself, a distinguished occultist, but his chief object in making us this early visit was to press upon us the hospitalities of his town and country residences; in fact, he was, as he expressed it, burning with impatience to renew his early intimacy with the esteemed friend of his boyhood, Felix von Marx, and he could scarcely be persuaded that the professor was immovable in his resolution to retain a private home for himself and his adopted son, as he called me, during our stay in England, and only to make occasional visits from thence to the houses of friends.

Mr. Dudley and his companion, Sir James M——, were very enthusiastic in their description of the wonderful séances they enjoyed amongst the occultists of Great Britain. They surprised us by citing the names of a great many persons highly distinguished both in the ranks of fashion and literature, who were members of the British branch of an association to which Professor von Marx had been elected an honorary member, and to which they both belonged. They assured us the professor's high renown as an adept of the most remarkable power, and mine as the famous somnambulist of the Berlin Brotherhood, had already preceded us, and our arrival was looked forward to with the utmost impatience by the students of occultism in Great Britain.

They expected much of us too, because they were led

6

to believe the German mind was more than ordinarily
capable of analyzing the unseen, and mastering the
mysteries of the imponderable. A few hours conversation with these gentlemen, however, convinced us that
in point of varied experience, their magical information
was not quite equal to our own, though they had visited
Denmark, Sweden, Norway, Iceland, and almost every
part of Scandinavia, carefully acquainting themselves
with the wild legendary lore of those regions, and
taking part in many of their singular ceremonies of
spiritual invocation.

In Lapland, Finland, and the northeastern part of
Russia, our new acquaintances had beheld so many
evidences of inborn occult powers amongst the natives
that they had come to a conclusion which the well-informed Spiritualist of modern times will no doubt be
ready to endorse, and that is, that certain individuals
of the race are so peculiarly and organically endowed,
that they live, as it were, on the borders of the invisible
world, and from time to time see, hear, act, and think
under its influence, as naturally as other individuals do
who are only capable of sensing material and external
things.

Moreover, our friends had arrived at the opinion that
certain localities and climatic influences were favorable
or otherwise to the development of these innate occult
endowments.

Experience had shown them that mountainous regions
or highly rarefied atmospheres constituted the best physical conditions for the evolvement of magical powers, and
they therefore argued that the great prevalence of super-
mundane beliefs and legendary lore in those latitudes
arises from the fact that intercourse with the interior
realms of being is the universal experience of the peo-

ple, not that they are more ignorant or superstitious than other races. Mr. Dudley had brought to England with him a *schaman,* or priest, of a certain district in Russia, where he had given extraordinary evidences of his powers. This man's custom was to array himself in a robe of state, trimmed with the finest furs and loaded with precious stones, amongst which clear crystals were the most esteemed.

In this costume, with head, arms, and feet bare, the *schaman* would proceed to beat a magical drum, made after a peculiar fashion, and adorned with a variety of symbolical and fantastic paintings.

Commencing his exercises by simply standing within a circle traced on the ground, and beating his drum in low, rhythmical cadence to his muttered chantings, the *schaman* would gradually rise to a condition of uncontrollable frenzy; his hands would acquire a muscular power and rapidity which caused the drum to resound with the wildest clamor, and strokes which defied the power of man to count.

His body, meantime, would sway to and fro, spin round, and finally be elevated and even suspended several feet in the air, by a power wholly unknown to the witnesses. His cries and gesticulations were frightful, and the whole scene of "manticism" would end by the performer's sinking on the earth in a rigid cataleptic state, during which he spoke oracular sentences, or gave answers to questions with a voice which seemed to proceed from the air some feet above his prostrate form. During my stay in England I was present at several experimental performances with this *schaman,* and though he could unquestionably predict the future and describe correctly distant places and persons, Professor von Marx and myself were both disappointed in the results which we expected to proceed from his very elaborate modes of inducing the "mantic" frenzy. Mr. Dudley accounted for the inferiority of his *protégé's* powers by stating that the atmosphere was prejudicial to his peculiar temperament, and though he had striven to surround him with favorable conditions, it was obvious he needed the specialties of his native soil and climate for the complete evolvement of the phenomena he had been accustomed to exhibit.

Amongst the distinguished persons into whose society Professor von Marx and myself were now admitted, we found several individuals of the magical type, who had been imported by earnest students from different countries, for the purpose of aiding their investigations. One of these mystics was a native of the Isle of Skye, and had been remarkable for his gift of " second sight." Panoramic representations of future events, with all the vivid imagery of well-defined persons and circumstances, would be presented to this man's waking vision, like a picture daguerreotyped on the atmosphere.

Another of the marvel-workers was a young Laplander, whose powers and methods of awakening them were not unlike those of the *schaman* described above, only that he seemed to possess an innate faculty of clairvoyant perception, which did not always necessitate the magical frenzy to call into play.

There were several other personages, all imported from northern lands, through whom our new friends attempted to conduct experiments; but it seemed that in each case the powers for which these weird people had been distinguished had either diminished or utterly failed them when taken away from the influence of their home surroundings. The islander from Skye had only beheld one vision since he had quitted his native shores, and that was the scene of a shipwreck, in which, as he affirmed, he was destined to perish, and for which reason he had steadily refused to return home, although his gifts as a seer were now suspended. It is a curious fact, and worthy of record, that this Skye man, having been placed in service as a gardener, was arrested for theft, convicted, sentenced to transportation, and after having been removed to the convict ship, finally perished in a gale, during which the ship, with all her hapless load of crime and suffering, was lost.

We, that is, my master and myself, saw little or nothing amongst the "magicians" whom our new friends had taken such trouble to surround themselves with, that equalled the experiences of our Teutonic associates, but our opportunities for enlarging our sphere of observation strengthened our belief in the following items of spiritual philosophy: first, that there are individvals who possess by nature all the prophetical, clairvoyant, and otherwise supermundane powers which are only to be evoked in different organisms by magical rites or magnetic processes.

Next, we found another and a still larger class, who seemed externally to have no extraordinary endowments of a spiritual nature, yet in whom the most wonderful powers of inner light, curative virtue, and prophetic vision could be awakened through artificial means, the most potent of which were the inhalation of mephitic vapors, pungent essences, or narcotics; the action of clamorous noise or soothing music; the process of looking into glittering stones and crystals; excessive and violent action, especially in a circular direction; and lastly, through the exhalations proceeding from the warm blood of animated beings. All these influences, together with an array of forms, rites, and ceremonials which involve mental action and captivate the senses, I now affirm to constitute the art of ancient magic, and I moreover believe that wherever these processes are systematically resorted to, they will, in more or less force, according to the susceptibility of the subject, evoke all those occult powers known as ecstacy, somnambulism, clairvoyance, the gifts of prophecy, healing, etc.

We derived another remarkable item of philosophy from our researches, which was that under the influence of some of the magical processes practised by our new associates, the human organism can not only be rendered insensible to pain, but that wounds, bruises, and even mutilation can be inflicted upon it without permanent injury; also, that it can be rendered positive to the law of gravitation, and ascend into the air with perfect ease.

Also, the body can be so saturated with magnetism, or charged with spiritual essence, that fire can not burn it; in a word, when the body becomes enveloped in the indestructible essence of spirit, or the soul element, it can be made wholly positive to all material laws, transcending them in a way astonishing and inexplicable to all uninstructed beholders. Of this class of phenomena, history has made such frequent mention that I feel justified in calling attention towards the array of evidence we possess on the subject. Let me refer to the "Convulsionaires of St. Medard"; the history of the "French Prophets of Avignon"; the still more recent accounts of the frightful mental epidemic which prevailed in the district of Morzine in 1864; the now well-attested facts of supermundane power enacted by the fakirs, brahmins, and ecstatics of the East, and many of the inexplicable physical and mental phenomena attributed to monastic "ecstatics."

Amongst the "Convulsionaires of St. Medard" and the possessed peasants of Morzine, one of the most familiar demonstrations of an extra-mundane condition was the delight and apparent relief which the sufferers represented themselves as experiencing when blows, violent enough, as it would seem, to have crushed them bone by bone, were administered to them. At the tomb of the Abbé Paris, and amongst the frenzied patients of Morzine, the most pathetic appeals would be made that sturdy, powerful men would pound and beat their bodies with huge mallets, and the cries of "Heavier yet, good brother! Heavier yet, for the love of Heaven!" were amongst the words that were most constantly uttered.

During the fearful struggle maintained by the brave and devoted prophets of the Cevennes against their oppressors, every history, whether favorable or antagonistic, makes mention of the exhibitions by which Cavillac and others of the "inspired" proved their ability, under the afflatus of ecstacy, to resist the action of fire.

Amongst a vast number of records concerning the mystical power of the spirit to act upon and through matter, we may cite the lives of some of those remarkable personages canonized by the Catholic Church as saints.

In the experiences of Saint Teresa, Saint Bridgetta, Saint Catherine, and many other "holy women," we are confidently informed that an actual "stigmata" was developed on their hands, feet, and sides, in imitation of the wounds attributed to the martyr of Calvary. Their foreheads were encircled by marks as of a crown of thorns, and drops of blood were seen to ooze from the stigmata at stated periods.

Of the Arabian fire-eaters and Hindoo ecstatics, I shall have more to say hereafter; for the present I close this long and discursive chapter with a few passages of explanation concerning the existence of magical practices and magical experiments in stern, gloomy, matter-of-fact old England.

Nearly all the English gentlemen to whom Professor von Marx had letters of introduction were members of secret societies, and, with one exception, pursued their studies in the direction of magic, deeming they could ultimately resolve the nature and use of all occult powers into a scientific system, analogous to the magical art as practised in the days of antiquity. The one exception which I refer to is an order that owes nothing of its working or existence to this age or time. Its actual nature is only recognized, spoken, or thought of as a dream, a memory of the past, evoked like a phantom from the realms of tradition or myth; yet as surely as there is a spirit in man, is there in the world a spiritual, though nameless and almost unknown association of men, drawn together by the bonds of soul, associated by those interior links which never fade or perish, belonging to all times, places, and nations alike. Few can attain to the inner light of these spiritually associated brethren, or apprehend the significance of their order; enough that it is, has been, and will be, until all men are spiritualized enough to partake of its exalted dispensations. Some members of this sublime Brotherhood were in session in England, and their presence it was which really sent thither my master and myself, at the time of which I write.

That there should exist within the very heart of rationalism and Christian piety, England, more than one secret society addicted to magical practices and superstitious rites, but above all, that the highest order of mystics in the world should be uttering its potent spells in the midst of the great modern Babylon, dedicated to the worship of mammon and pauperism, is a statement so startling and original that I expect few but the initiated into its actualities to credit me, and many of my readers, especially good, honest, matter-of-fact English people themselves, to denounce me as a lunatic or a modern Munchausen. I can only say, I write of that which I know, and of what many esteemed and reputable citizens, in their private experiences, know likewise; and if good, honest, matter-of-fact English people would only remember there might be realms of being both higher and lower than man's, links of connection and mutual understanding throughout the universe, and some few things more in heaven and earth than they (worthy folk!) dream of in their philosophy, the magicians of England would not feel compelled, for their credit and honor's sake, to make their societies secret ones.

As it was, the clairvoyants, seers, and weird subjects whom the societies procured for their experiments were generally employed in families, shops, or some simple ways of business, which effectually concealed their real characters. The magical experiments were conducted with the strictest reserve and caution; and it is only since the advent of modern Spiritualism, with its remarkable and wide-spread commonplaces in wonderful things, that the world has begun to discover that spiritual facts and experiences in Great Britain are several years older than the movement of the last quarter of a century.

It was some few weeks after our arrival in London, and one night just as I was taking leave of my dear master for the night, that the following conversation ensued between us.

"Louis, you have hitherto taken no part amongst these English magicians. I have secluded you from all exercise of your powers because — but you know the reasons, do you not?"

"Perfectly, my master: you wished me to have some rest, and to imbibe fresh force for future efforts; furthermore, you desired that I should have calm and deliberate opportunities for observation. Is it not so?"

"You understand me thoroughly; and now, what conclusions have you arrived at, from all you have witnessed?"

"Conclusions! O my master, I am more and more lost in an ocean of speculation; more wildly tost than ever before on the unresting billows of a shoreless sea! I realize the interference and all-persuasive power of invisible realms of being, but who or what they are becomes to me each day an ever-deepening mystery. I perceive each hour fresh evidences of a wonderful and mysterious fountain of influence in human beings, — ay, at times in the animal creation also; but who can fathom its depths, gauge its possibilities, define where it lies, or pronounce upon its destiny? The earth and the creatures that live upon it are all dual, and evidently maintain a dual existence; but I know no more the limitations of my own being than I do of the 'double goers' who flash before our eyes like tongues of flame or meteoric lights. Alas! alas! I think, believe, hope, and fear too much, and know too little."

"You shall know more; know—ay, even the absolute, soon, my Louis," rejoined the professor, with a deeper glow on his cheek and a more brilliant flash of his star-like eyes than I had ever seen before; then, after a strange, long pause, in which he seemed fixed and abstracted like one entranced, he drew a letter from his bosom, glanced at it, and heaved a sigh so deep that it almost amounted to a wail. That letter he turned over several times in his hand, gazing now on the large seal which closed it, now on the direction, which was in his own bold writing, and marked simply, "To my Louis." The painful sigh, the first and only token of deep emotion I had ever heard from this man, was repeated several times; at length he placed the letter in my hands, saying with an air of singular solemnity, "Keep this in the most secret repository you have, and never open it until a voice, the most authoritative to you on earth, shall say, 'The time has come. Open and read!'

"Good-night, Louis. Your experiences as a mystic in England are now about to commence."

"Good-night, my master," I responded aloud, adding mentally, "Would God they were about to close in the sleep that knows no waking!"

"The death-sleep of earth is the waking life of eternity," murmured a sweet, low voice, close to my ear. I started, and looked for the speaker. Professor von Marx was gone, and the luminous apparition of the beautiful Constance flitted by me like an electric flash, and vanished into the darkness, so much the more profound that she had been there.

CHAPTER VI.

No page of retrospect in my fateful life-wanderings excites in me more surprise than the inferiority of the results obtained through magical processes, when compared with those which seem to arise spontaneously as an organic peculiarity of certain individuals. Our English associates had studied with profound and scholarly research most of the arts of magic recorded by the mystics of the Middle Ages, the sages of classic lands, and the thaumaturgists of the East. Many of them were perfectly well versed in the cabala, with all its veiled mysticism and apocalyptic significance; some of them had been initiated into the rites of both ancient and modern freemasonry, and become affiliated with the most potential of the Oriental societies now in existence. Like Moses, Thales, Orpheus, and other sages of old, they had mastered the secrets of Egyptian wisdom, Chaldean astrology, and Persian chemistry; yet notwithstanding all their occult knowledge and the fidelity with which they strove to make it a practical power, they failed to achieve the feats common to the whirling dervishes of Arabia or the wandering fakirs of modern India, whilst the glimpses they obtained of the invisible realms around them were vague, unsatisfactory, and partial; indeed, many a good somnambulist would have regarded them with pity if not contempt, and any powerful "spirit

medium" of this day could have displayed more phenomena by aid of a dancing table in five minutes than
many of these really earnest students could have evolved
by magical processes in five times five years of profound
occult experiments.

The methods of the great majority of the magians I
was now introduced to may be briefly summed up as
follows: Their first aim was to secure the services of
such an one as they could discover to be a good *natural
magician,* — one whom the spiritists of to-day would
call "a good clairvoyant" or "medium," and we Teutons
style "a seer." This prerequisite obtained and the
society in session, they proceeded to form a circle on
the ground, prepared after the fashion prescribed by Cornelius Agrippa or some of the mediæval mystics. They
formed their book of spirits on the same approved pat-
terns, and carefully conformed to every item of the magical ritual or other formulæ declared to have been derived
from the magians of Egypt and Chaldea and practised
by such renowned mystics as Thos. Aquinas, Albertus
Magnus, Nostradamus, Count St. Germain, etc. I found
the practices of different societies varied but little, and
consisted chiefly in a due observance of days, hours,
times, and seasons, planetary, solar, and lunar phases.
Much reliance was placed on the fumigations said to be
appropriate to different days of the week, months and
seasons; in a word, our English associates had carefully
studied the formulæ of magic as taught in the writings of
Oriental and classical authorities, and faithfully endeavored to practicalize the directions laid down, as far as the
usages of modern society permitted.

To those who are unfamiliar with the occult subjects
I am now treating of, let me say with all candor, I
have faithfully devoted many years to the study of

spiritual mysteries; and both in my own person and that of my numerous associates of many lands have endeavored, by aid of all the light I could obtain, whether derived from ancient or modern sources, to discover what were the most effective methods of communing with the invisible world and penetrating into the actualities of other realms of being than those of mortality. The sum of all, to my apprehension, is that man, to obtain this boon, must be born *a natural magician*, or in more familiar phase, "a good spirit medium." Also that clairvoyance, clairaudience, seership, and all those spiritual gifts by which human beings can attain the privilege of communion with spirits, consist in certain organic specialties of constitution, naturally appertaining to some individuals, and latent in others, though susceptible of unfoldment by modes of culture. I believe that forms, rites, and invocatory processes, fumigations, spells, — in a word, the science and practice of magic, may be applied as means to aid in this communion, and are especially potent in enabling the operators to exercise control over lower orders of spirits than themselves; but I affirm that they are inoperative to open up the communion as a primary means, and that without the services of a good seer, clairvoyant, or spirit medium, magical rites alone cannot succeed in evolving spiritual phenomena. This I soon found to have been the general experience of our new associates in England. All their magical formulæ were subordinate in use to the one grand desideratum of a good *natural magician.* Professor von Marx once questioned, in his cold, sarcastic way, What was the use of magical ceremonies at all, so long as they could not effect any results without the required medium? and having secured this great desideratum, would not his or her presence render the rites unnecessary? Our friends generally denied this position, however, alleging that magical rites were the means of culturing and unfolding spiritual gifts; also that they were essential to the *orderly* intercourse with spirits, and enabled mortals to command them instead of being commanded by them.

In years of experience subsequent to the period of my first visit to England, I have found abundant reason to accept opinions composed of both sides of this question. The results of my experiments may some day be given to the world in a more practical form than these autobiographical sketches.*

To those unacquainted with the methods of invocation enjoined upon the high priest or chief magian of these rites, the following examples may not be uninteresting. After all the ceremonies of "purification," "ablution," and "fumigation" had been duly complied with, the chief magian proceeded to summon the spirit of the day, week, and season, after this fashion:—

"I conjure and confirm upon you, strong, potent, and holy angels, in the name of the most dreadful ADONAI, the God of Israel, and by the name of all the angels serving in the second host before TETRA, that great, strong, and powerful angel, and by the name of his star, and by the name of the seal, which is sealed by God most mighty and honorable, and by all things before spoken. I conjure upon thee, Raphael, the great angel who art ruler of the fourth day, that for me thou wilt labor and fulfil all my petitions according to my will and desire in my cause and business.†"

* The author has more than redeemed this promise in the publication of his magnificent work, " Art Magic."—ED. GHOST LAND.

† For a full and complete " Arbatel of Magic," together with the names of the angels of the various days and seasons, the fumigations proper to each, the modes of preparing the circle, robes, and *book of*

Invocations to Elementary spirits were given in a still more stringent and compulsory tone. The following will serve as a specimen thereof:—

"Therefore, come ye! come ye, Serapiel, spirit of the air, ruling on the fourth day! Angel of the southwest wind, come ye, come ye! Adonai commandeth. Sadai commandeth,—the most high and dreadful king of kings, whose power no creature is able to resist. Sadai be unto you most dreadful, unless ye obey and forthwith appear before this circle; and let miserable ruin and fire unquenchable remain with ye, unless ye forthwith obey. Therefore, come ye! in the awful name TETRA-GRAMMATON. Why tarriest thou? Hasten! Hasten! Hasten! Adonai, the most high, Sadai, king of kings commands!" etc. etc.

These words, lofty and sounding as they seem, can convey only the faintest idea of the fiery zeal and urgent ecstacy with which the Invocants were accustomed to pronounce them.

The more they could stimulate themselves up to the pitch of fervent ecstacy, the more potential became the results. On many occasions, where the officiating magian was in deep, tremendous earnest, and the assistants partook of his fervent zeal, I have seen the whole assemblage sink on their knees, and break forth into uncontrollable sobs, cries, appeals to Heaven, spirits, angels, and elementaries. I have felt the walls shake, the house tremble; beheld the floor riven apart; fiery tongues flash swiftly through the apartment, and forms of elemental spirits become visible to all. Hands have been seized; many amongst us have been thrown vio-

spirits, also for all the invocations and other formulæ of magical art, consult the author's elaborate work on " Art Magic," and the Heptameron of Peter d'Abano, page 360, " Art Magic." — ED. GHOST LAND.

lently on the ground, lifted up to the roof, and held suspended in the air. The entire scene has been one of the most tremendous and occult character, and though the experience of modern investigators with strong "physical force mediums" may supply abundant parallels of such scenes, and furnish what they deem to be a complete explanation of its marvels, there can be no question that the strong mental efflatus evolved by the scene, time, and modes of invocation combined to supply the powerful pabulum by which invisible beings effected such demonstrations of their presence.

These magical circles were always effective in the production of strong responsive action from the spirit world in proportion to the zeal, energy, and ecstatic fervor of the invocants; in short, it was the history of the Jewish Pentecost re-enacted in the nineteenth century.

It was the harmonious accord of the assemblage, the Pentecostal spirit in which they met, that supplied the invisible world with the force which exhibited itself in tongues of fire and a "mighty rushing wind." When our magians were most terribly in earnest, their spiritual respondents were most obedient and potential.

No doubt the specialty of certain human organisms present, always afforded the force necessary for spirits to work with. It is possible that our own spirits, too, stimulated to ecstacy by the efflatus of our earnest purpose, operated upon the inanimate objects around us, and served as instruments for the achievement of marvellous phenomena. I know that Professor von Marx and myself were never present at magical séances without obtaining results of a spiritualistic character. I believe we both furnished the pabulum by which spirits could come into contact with matter; but whether the wonderful phenomena we witnessed were the result of direct foreign intervention or the exercise of our own spiritual faculties even Professor von Marx himself could not always determine.

I know it would be proper in this place to anticipate the questions of some sincere spiritists concerning the character of the beings who were seen at those magical circles, and declare whether they were not, as most believers in spiritism would expect they would be, the apparitions of our deceased friends. On this point I answer emphatically in the negative, nay, more, I hardly remember at this period of my researches — certainly not in these invocatory séances — ever to have seen human spirits as the respondents in acts of magic. Human spirits were not summoned. Those magians did not practise that phase of the art they termed necromancy, to wit, *communion with the spirits of the dead.* Many of our English associates professed an unconquerable aversion to this idea, and Professor von Marx always discountenanced in me the belief that the spirits of the dead could subsist much longer than the period necessary to accomplish the disintegration of the body. No, we summoned the spirits of the elements, and they responded to us in all the varied forms in which these beings exist.* Sometimes we communed with bright planetary spirits; but those radiant beings were rarely visible to the whole circle; in fact, were seldom seen except by the clairvoyants and somnambulists, of whom there were several belonging to these circles besides myself.

If my readers would inquire what beneficial results, temporal or spiritual, man could derive from these weird communings, I frankly admit I am unable to

* See " Art Magic " on Elementary Spirits, Sect. 7, p. 102. — ED. GHOST LAND.

answer. Beyond the pursuit of knowledge or the attainment of power in some special direction, I do not myself realize any benefit from the achievement of intercourse with elementary spirits. Those beings appeared to me to be often malevolent and incapable of attaining to the perception of good. They seemed to look up to man as a god to be feared, propitiated, and served; but few of their species realized the good, truth, and beauty which belongs to pure reason and high exaltation of soul; hence they naturally resorted to mischief, torment, and deceit, as their protection against the superior powers of man, and except in a few instances of communion with the higher realms of "nature spirits," I never knew good, happiness, peace of mind, or virtuous inspiration result from these intercommunings. If to *know* the universe of being, and the nature and immensity of the existences that people it, be the object sought, the search is legitimate to the philosopher; but efforts to attain these communings stimulated by mere curiosity, a desire to obtain wealth, discover hidden treasures, gain power over the elements, and subdue enemies, although often measurably successful, invariably bring unrest, disappointment, and ultimate evil to the seeker, and I would earnestly warn mankind against the attempt, stimulated, as before suggested, by purely selfish motives.

I have had many pleasant interviews with the harmless and innocent spirits of the mines, and those who preside over and correspond to the air, fire, and atmosphere. Although rarely identified by mortals, and shy of holding direct communication with them, these classes of elementaries are still noble and exalted in their natures, constantly engaged in directing and inspiring students in the natural sciences, indeed they are so intimately related to human destiny that we breathe in their influence with every noble thought, and attract them, as sparks of intellectual fire, with every aspiration we cherish for scientific knowledge.

During our residence in London we were constant attendants and welcome visitors at a circle which for distinction I shall name the Orphic Circle. Its president and "Grand Master" was a noble gentleman whom I shall call Lord Vivian.

His methods were inspired by far loftier aims and regulated by much more pious aspirations than those of most other English magians. The seers, of whom Lord Vivian's society numbered several, conducted their experiments through the mirror and crystal, and the young ladies especially who attended these interesting séances, were particularly happy in attracting pure and noble planetary spirits in response to their call. On one occasion I attended a séance in London, when a mirror was to be presented to a fair young girl, whose acquaintance I made about twenty years before the date of my present writing.

The séance of which I am about to speak took place several years later than the period at which I first visited London, and I am anticipating the events of that time in referring to it; but as I may not have an opportunity of mentioning it again, and the scene in question has exercised a most potential influence upon all the succeeding years of my life, I shall plead guilty to the anachronism of recording its details in this place.

The party in question consisted of the master of the house, three gentlemen, distinguished occultists of the country, the young lady before referred to, and her chaperone.

The exercises commenced with a deep and heartfelt

invocation, the performance of some sweet part-songs, and the trance address of the fair somnambulist. This beautiful creature, like a Pythoness of old, rapt in ecstacy and filled with the divine efflatus, uttered one of the most sublime invocations for spiritual light, wisdom, and guidance to the source of all light and knowledge, I have ever listened to. How cold, lifeless, and insincere do the parrot-like prayers of hireling priests sound compared to the burning appeals and eloquent beseechings of these modern Pythia! If there was an angel in the high empyrean of the unknown heavens, he must have heard and answered the pleadings of this inspired girl. After the trance invocation our host, who was an adept of the modern magical school, unveiled the newly-made virgin mirror, and consecrated it in due form to AZRAEL, "the angel of life and death," whom the fair seeress had chosen as the guardian of her mirror. As its shining surface was disclosed to view, the lady, standing before it in a lofty attitude of rapt ecstacy, pronounced these words: "To Azrael, the shrouded angel, and his twin ministers of life and death, and to thee, O Father of spirits and Ruler of all life and being! I do hereby dedicate the service and consecrate the use of this mirror." When the spirit whom this invocation summoned, first appeared in the mirror, the seeress started, turned pale, and with an aspect of terror and aversion beckoned me to come and inspect the vision with her. What I then saw was as great a surprise to me as to the lady. There, distinctly outlined *on*, rather than *in*, the mirror, was the head and shoulders of a being whom for years I had been accustomed to regard as the presentation of my evil genius. It was a woman with a frightful aspect, full of malignity, rage, and ferocity. She wore a head-dress worthy of a Medusa. Her large, staring eyes glared hideously at the beholder; and according to the expression those malign features assumed, so had I been accustomed to expect the approach of the misfortunes of which this spectre was the invariable forerunner. When sickness was at hand, the hag would appear to me mocking and mowing like a wailing idiot; on the approach of discord, slander, or enmity, she would assume a grimace impossible to describe, but still graphically significant to a seer. Death, this hideous ghoul portended by opening wide her cavernous jaws and presenting within them a miniature resemblance of some victim whom she affected to devour. This ghastly image always appeared to me objective, life-like, and real. I have faced it in the street, in my chamber, in the midst of the gayest assemblages, in royal *salons*, and quiet solitudes.

Its appearance was an unfailing prophecy in the directions I have intimated, and I had become so accustomed to behold it that it created in me neither surprise nor alarm until I saw it appear as one of the legionaries of "Azrael, the angel of life and death," in my fair friend's mirror. I endeavored to calm her mind by explaining to her that it was but an image, representative of the action of mortal death, from which the angel Azrael sent shadows, some ghastly in their ugliness, others radiant with the promises of the better life to come. Whilst I spoke the mocking "image," as I had termed it, moved, smiled, or rather grinned, chattered at us, and shook her lean, skinny arms as if to assure us it was no *image* but a thing of life, one too which heard and understood my attempts to soothe my companion. "It is an elementary," she said, "and whilst it signifies all you say, it is still an actual existence, not a mere subjective image."

Once more I pause in my narrative to state that the seeress here alluded to has, since that time, been visited for a number of years — indeed, up to the present time — by the same apparition, in the same manner as I have described above, and with the same prophetic intimations. Banished almost instantly from the mirror by my will, I inquired what my friend would now wish to behold, as I doubted not the angel of the mirror would be ready to yield her a more agreeable and instructive vision. "Let me see whatever the wise and good guardian is pleased to display," she replied; when, after due invocation, soliciting Azrael to show us whatsoever would be instructive and prophetic, we both simultaneously beheld the following singular picture: Two forms arose in the mirror which strongly suggested the idea of the genii of night and day. They were apparently female forms, attired in flowing robes of black and white. Their long tresses were also the one of raven, the other of golden hue. Their faces were exquisitely beautiful, but sad, silent, and full of wonderfully pleading eloquence. The dark eyes of the one and the lustrous blue of the other were fixed upon us with a depth of sadness, pity, and sorrow which conveyed a whole history of prophetic meaning.

Between these figures was displayed an open book, upon the pages of which both the seeress and myself read *two words*. The lady informed me she had seen these spirits before, had been told that they were planetary spirits, the guardians of a mirror belonging to a friend whom she occasionally visited, and that the book which they thus presented was one which for ages they had been endeavoring to inspire some earthly scribe to write. She added, " These spirits seemed, when first I saw them at my friend Mr. H.'s, to beseech me to write that book; but it now appears as if they had transferred their plea to you, and I cannot but think the vision is significant of the prophecy that you are destined to write it." "If so then," I replied, "the first image is not meaningless, for the spirit of malignity as surely prophesies slander and malice in connection with what is to follow, as the beautiful legionaries of the stars prophesy that either you or I, or perhaps both, will become their scribe."

I give this example chiefly to illustrate the character of the intelligence which comes through the mirror and crystal in séances devoted to their exhibition. Whatever is thus presented is designed apparently by the guardian spirits of the mirror or crystal, to whom these objects are dedicated, to convey instruction, advice, warning, or prophecy. Some of the noblest communications I have ever received have been given by planetary spirits impressed upon the surface of the mirror, and some of the most startling and significant events of my life have been prophesied of by images, scenes, and representations rising up in the magnetic depths of a consecrated crystal. I do not claim that either of these instruments are essential to the unfoldment or exercise of clairvoyance; but where the power already exists, mirrors, crystals, a glass of water, or any polished, smooth, or untarnished surface seems available as a tablet for the use of the invisible artist, and a means of representation for scenic effects by attendant spirits.

Returning to the period when I first made the acquaintance of the English magians, I recall a special séance wherein I was myself the clairvoyant. Professor von Marx had as usual magnetized me by a single wave of his hand, and enjoined me to describe to those present various visionary scenes in which they were interested.

In the course of the séance I suddenly perceived the loathsome image I have just alluded to, — "the hag," as I was accustomed to call her, — crouching down close beside my beloved master, extending a long, lean, skinny arm, as if to clutch him, and gazing upon him with those distended jaws which to my shuddering apprehension prophesied the approach of death. My master at that moment seemed to be lost in profound abstraction. With folded arms he sat looking vacantly into the dim distance, his thoughts evidently centred on scenes far remote from his present surroundings. It was in this moment of abstraction, and in the absence of the intense and concentrated influence he was accustomed to throw around me, that I seemed to awake as with a sudden start from dreaming to reality, and piercing the mist of self-woven mystery in which he chose to enshroud himself and hide the realities of his being from me, I perceived a truth which he had not before permitted to dawn on my consciousness. He was unhappy, and his appearance betokened to my newly-opened vision the signs of physical decay and the fever of deep unrest. The pang of fear and anguish which thrilled through my frame touched his. He recovered from his state of abstraction with a slight shiver, turned an anxious, inquisitive glance upon me, rose, laid his hand lovingly on my shoulder, and instantly caused the clouds of reserve once more to roll down between us. The spectre vanished. Professor von Marx resumed his seat, carelessly waved his hand to recall me from the magnetic state, remarking, "Enough, my Louis; you are weary." To the external eye all was as calm and serene as ever, and our relations to each other had not in the least degree altered; interiorly, however, I had received a revelation which not even the will of this all-powerful controller could oblit-

erate, and with this cherished independent secret stored
away in my soul, arose the determination to effect a
change in our circumstances. Under the pretence that
the air of the metropolis affected me unfavorably, I induced my beloved friend to set out with me on a tour
through North Britain, purposing amidst the breezy hills
and in the pure atmosphere of Scotland and Wales, to
obtain that rest and renovation for him which he fondly
deemed I needed for myself.

My purpose is not to invite my readers to a perusal
of my personal adventures, but to a retrospect of such
scenes alone as may tend to throw light or bring evidence to bear upon the mysteries of spiritual existence.

When I write of myself it will only be in illustration
of that realm of mind whose varying emotions should
become the field of more profound exploration and analysis than has yet been bestowed upon that all-important
subject. I pass by then, our wanderings through many
memorable scenes, and only pause to record one illustration of spiritual interposition, in connection with events
which are still well remembered at the place where they
occurred. Professor von Marx's reputation as a man of
letters, and the report that he was accompanied by one
of the seers of the renowned "Berlin Brotherhood," procured us far more hospitable attention in our quiet rambles than we desired to attract. On one occasion we
were so earnestly entreated to become the guests of a
nobleman whose estate lay in the heart of the wild Tro-
sachs, that we felt unable, without positive discourtesy,
to resist his urgent invitation that we would remain with
him for a few days.

We arrived at our place of destination early in the
forenoon, and after partaking of a lunch characterized
by all that profuse hospitality for which the "kindly

Scot" is so justly celebrated, our host proposed that we should accompany him and one or two of his friends on a ride through some of the most romantic points of the neighborhood. In this excursion we visited many interesting places, frequently leaving our horses in charge of the grooms, whilst we explored on foot mountain-passes whose savage wildness might never have been disturbed by the invading presence of man.

It seemed almost impossible for me to wander amidst these lovely glens, vales, and woods, climb mountains of rarest grandeur, and gaze over outstretched panoramas of gorgeous loveliness, without yielding to the spiritual efflatus which Nature in her profuse displays of scenic beauty ever inspires. Every foot of ground, too, was historical. Every wooded height was crowned with a castle or old manorial building, memorable as the residence of kings or princes, heroes or statesmen. We gazed upon gloomy fortresses which had once held captive the fairest and noblest of Scotland's peers and princes. Every scene was redolent of wild and thrilling memories. We passed through deep glens, or penetrated into the heart of mountain defiles, where the best blood of the land had drenched the ground, and lingered in many a fairy nook, imprinted with tragic legends of violence and wrong. Every towering crag or peaceful glen, every deep defile or shady grove, was stamped with thrilling memories. To one who like me, lived on the borders of the unseen world, and whose clairvoyant sight revealed unbidden, a thousand pictures of interior life veiled to the outer eye, this land of mighty deeds and romantic associations opened up a page of wondrous revelation.

Oftentimes when solitude and silence brooded over the glowing landscape to the eyes of my companions, to me the air was thick with visions. I beheld flying armies, dying heroes, captive princes, persecuted martyrs, and all the weird phantasmagoria of life in its stormiest and most unresting moods. And these visions must not be classed as the result of a mere overheated imagination or creative fancy. The spectral forms of the long ago are indelibly fixed in the " astral light," which is the spiritual atmosphere of the universe; and what seer can pass amidst those scenes where these thronging phantoms most abound, without perceiving, through the rifts and rents of matter, the myriads of forms which hang on the gallery-walls in an imperishable world of spiritual entities? Nothing that ever has been is lost to the vision of the seer; nothing that now is, can be hidden from his piercing gaze; nothing that shall be is wholly veiled from his prophetic glances. Involuntarily, though perhaps shudderingly, he finds his spiritual eyes are open, and he is compelled to gaze upon the innermost of life's awful mystery whether he will or no. No hand, not even that of his own tired spirit, can draw the curtain between his vision and that of the solemn scenes inscribed by the actors in life's wild drama upon the indestructible page of the astral light. Nature in her external loveliness afforded me but half-revealed glimpses of her meaning in each scene I looked upon. It was the array of phantom images that came trooping up before my soul's eyes, filling each spot with the living, dying, dead; with fierce battle-scenes, romances, intrigues; with all the stirring events, in short, which make up the wild legend of Scottish history, that I beheld, loading my spirit with the fatal burden of involuntary seership, filling my heart with anguish for the woes of poor humanity, and isolating me alike from human sympathy and human companionship.

Lost as I was in the absorption of this fatal gift of second sight, I could rarely contribute much to the entertainment of my companions. Professor von Marx was scarcely more sociable, for he was divided in his wish to gratify our host and his friends with his fluent strain of conversation, and his anxiety to watch the waves of thought which rolled in upon my soul, the full details of which he could master without the interchange of a single word between us, when he willed to do so. Meantime there was a markedly restless manner in our host and his friends, which could not escape the keen perception of the professor. They seemed to fence round some subject, which they were equally desirous yet unwilling to introduce. At length they asked abruptly what Professor von Marx thought of the nature of obsession,— whether he had ever had any experience in that direction; and if, as he openly taught, the obsessing power did not proceed from the undeveloped spirits of human beings, how he would account for the strictly human tendencies (evil though they might be) manifested in the conduct of the obsessed. Professor von Marx replied that he believed, though he could not prove the fact, that the obsessing power was to be traced to the elementaries. He claimed that these beings exist on every grade of the ladder which reaches from the lowest depths of inorganic matter to the highest stages of organized being; that many of the kingdoms of elemental existence were near enough to man to share his thoughts and inspire him with their own ideas. Meantime, he argued, in many notable cases of obsession, familiar enough to those who have studied the subject, a large proportion of the control seemed to influence its unfortunate victims to the commission of acts strangely in accordance with *animal* natures.

He cited a number of cases in which the obsessed exhibited the strongest tendencies to bark, whine, cry, and whistle, leap, crawl, climb, roll their bodies up into the distorted resemblances of animals; in fact, to imitate by every possible method the habits of animals rather than human beings. It was in the midst of this discussion, and just as we had reached a romantic defile which wound its way partly through the mountains and occasionally opened up on the shores of an enchanting lake, that we all began to observe the unusual agitation and restlessness of our horses. They were rugged Highland steeds, strong, docile, yet sufficiently spirited to bear us safely over the most toilsome mountain roads. The pass we had now gained was intersected by numerous streams, which in many places swelled to torrents, and pouring over vast masses of piled-up rocks, formed cascades of exquisite beauty. Our horses had passed through many such scenes before in that very day's excursion; they had forded several streams, and in the midst of the foam and roar of the cascades had never before exhibited the least signs of terror. Now their obvious reluctance to proceed was marked and obstinate. The evening was fast deepening around us; already we were beginning to view the scene through the haze of what the Scotch poetically term the "gloaming," and our host informed us of his intention to shorten our path by passing through a certain district which he had previously fixed upon as the scene of our next day's excursion. A nest of villages, through which we were to make our way, lay outstretched on the distant plain, at the foot of the mountain we were crossing, and presented a most inviting picture of rural peace and tranquillity. It was just as these village houses came into view, and whilst we were passing through the last portion of a very rugged defile, that my horse, which was somewhat in advance of the rest, became actually unmanageable, rearing, snorting, and plunging with all the signs of frantic terror.

From early childhood I was accustomed to the management of a horse, and had been taught to govern the wildest and most untrained animals of Arabia. In the present instance however, my past experiences were utterly unavailing. Even when I had dismounted, and strove by every ordinary method to soothe the frightened creature into tranquillity, I could scarcely prevent him from plunging into the depths of a foaming cataract to which he seemed drawn by some irresistible attraction. Looking curiously around to discover the cause of this unaccountable action, I saw, or fancied I saw, amidst the vortex of foaming waters towards which the frantic creature was impelled, several dark bodies plunging and tossing, in the semblance of human beings.

Deeming it impossible that any one, however hardy a swimmer, could live in the revel of those wild waters, I stooped down to examine them more closely, when I distinctly saw a long lean arm and misshapen skinny hand stretched out towards my horse's bridle as if to drag him forward into the cataract. At the same moment the animal gave a tremendous backward plunge, and as he dragged me with him from the torrent, it seemed as if I was suddenly losing my senses, and passing into the condition of deep somnambulism. Never in my life did I experience so powerful or malignant an influence as that which was now sinking me into helpless unconsciousness.

The more dim and shadowy the outer world grew to my sense of sight, the more real and horrible became the objects revealed to my interior senses. The air, the earth, the waters, appeared to be thick with grotesque and hideous semblances of half man, half beast. Creeping, crawling, flying, and leaping things, of all shapes and sizes, held goblin carnival around me. The outer world was receding, and I passed into a veritable realm of demons. I scarcely dare even now recall the full horrors of this vision, nor should I have attributed to it any objective reality had I not witnessed the terror of the poor horses, and connected the whole scene with subsequent incidents. I was aroused from this palsy of horror by the voice of Professor von Marx, whose tones, though modulated almost to a whisper, so as to reach my ear alone, sounded like thunder, as he murmured, "Louis, Louis! rouse yourself, or you will let the demons of hell get possession of you!" My strength and composure returned with the touch of my master's powerful hand. Even my poor horse owned the spell of his resistless influence; for I found it standing, with drooping head, and sides flecked with foam, and at my side; and though trembling violently, it was no longer restive or intractable. "You have forgotten your Eastern training, methinks," said the professor half reproachfully, as I looked at my poor steed. "No training will avail here," I replied in the same tone. "Through this accursed spot I will not attempt to lead this suffering creature."

There was no time for further discussion. In a single instant a thick, vaporous mist fell upon us, enveloping us in its damp, slimy folds as in a wet garment. It rolled, surged, and filled the atmosphere for a moment, just as I have seen the air grow instantaneously thick and almost impenetrable in the murky folds of a London fog; but before we could comment to each other on this remarkable phenomenon, the mists rose, curled, and separated into ten thousand fragments, and with slight, sharp, detonating sounds, exploded into the well-known appearances called will-o'-the-wisps, or as the country folk of England call them, "Jack-o'-Lanterns." Truth to tell, the appearance of these phosphorescent lights in a place where no marshy ground existed, and where, as our whole party affirmed, they had never been seen before, in no way tended to reassure us. As for me, I saw around these glimmering lights, which danced, flitted, wheeled, or floated by hundreds on every side of us, the opaque bodies and grotesque outlines of the elementaries, not as before in distinct resemblances of animals and men, but in a vague, undefined burr around each shimmering flame, which was situated, as my shuddering fancy suggested, just where the nervous centres of their strange life might be supposed to inhere. Sometimes fierce, malignant eyes glared at me through the fast-deepening gloom, when the sudden start and unmistakable terror of my poor horse, which I continued to lead, proved either that he shared with me the goblin sight, or my hand communicated a sense of repulsion to the sensitive animal. Soon after leaving the village, the phantom lights disappeared, one by one, and we reached our home without further interruption.

That night, after retiring to rest, the same vague sense of terror that had beset me in the glen at the moment of my involuntary entrancement again took possession of me, and again seemed to threaten a magnetic control as hateful to my feelings as it was strange and unusual. I felt that an unknown presence filled my apartment, and a nameless horror threw its chilling influence over every nerve. I had frequently visited the realms of the elementaries at the command of the Berlin Brotherhood or my dear master. In the service

8

of these adepts I had penetrated, clairvoyantly, the interior of the earth's crust, its rocks, caverns, mines, oceans, rivers, forests, and atmospheres. My all-potential master had taught me how to summon and control elementary existences, as well as to penetrate the realms they inhabited. In all departments of Nature, my wandering spirit had explored, and communed with the countless spheres of graduated being that peopled the interior of Nature's wonderful and teeming laboratories. Whilst I was sustained by the potency of Professor von Marx's magnetism, and maintained my relations of a superior being towards these elementaries, they could neither control nor distress me; but now, by the effect of some strong magnetic influence, of which I had not been forewarned, the mysterious dwellers of the innermost had overpowered and almost mastered me. Arrayed against me, in unconquerable force, these malignant beings had now subdued me with a facility as new as strange in my experience. Even the fear with which they oppressed me I felt to be dangerous; and conscious that a mustering of these evil genii was even now pervading the suffocating air of my apartment, I arose hastily, dressed myself, and determined to seek Professor von Marx's apartment.

Just as I had gained the door which led into the corridor I was intercepted by a gigantic form, which seemed to loom up in the semi-darkness of my chamber as if it had arisen from the ground, and at the same moment a strong arm drove me back, and laid me, prostrate and breathless, on a couch near by. Being more astonished than frightened by this sudden apparition, I turned my gaze steadily upon it, and was able to master all the minutiæ of its appearance.

The figure, as I have said, was gigantic in height,

and of vast proportions; but as it seemed to be entirely shrouded in some envelope of a gray and misty nature, I was unable to determine whether it wore the human form or not. At first it loomed up before me like an irregularly-shaped column, but as I gazed, I could perceive the substance or material which enveloped it change, flutter, collapse, and expand, after the fashion of smoke or mist. It seemed, too, as if an atmosphere less dense than itself surrounded it, and occasionally emitted a luminous radiance through the apartment.

No word was spoken; no sound broke the deathly stillness as I reclined on the couch, where the force of that shrouded thing had cast me.

At first a sense of terrible helplessness possessed me, and I felt oppressed even unto death by the power of a crushing nightmare; but after the pause of a few breathless moments, the unknown stirred, and extended a part of itself—a robe or some attachment belonging to its columnar proportions—towards me in the attitude of protection. Following upon this motion others ensued, and then it seemed as if wreaths of mist were rolling through the apartment, and folding up like cloudy drapery around the quivering mass that stood erect at my side. All this I saw, and as it seemed with my natural eyes, for on this occasion I retained all the normal faculties of my waking state, and can never recall the slighest sensation either of dreaming, trance, or magnetic efflatus. Presently the mists which had filled the chamber cleared away, and with their dispersion the scene also changed. I beheld no more the walls, ceiling, and furniture of my sleeping-room, but I found myself gazing upon the interior of an old Gothic church.

I looked around, and could distinctly trace, aye, even read, the brass tablets on the walls, the inscriptions on many an ancient monument, and note various forms of marble statuary, some broken and defaced by time, others in a fine state of preservation. I saw no organ or instrument of music within the fane, but there were finely-carved stalls and a magnificent pulpit, the steps of which I perceived had been worn by the traces of many feet in by-gone ages. A splendid railing parted off the altar or communion-table from the body of the church, and behind it stood three men in black dresses, such as I learned afterwards were worn by ministers of the Scotch Kirk. Before the screen or railing, kneeling in long rows on the steps and ground, was a crowd of women and children clad in the ordinary dress of the poorer classes of the land; behind these again, and filling up the entire body of the church, was a crowd of earnest, sorrowful-looking men, who seemed to be regarding the kneeling figures with the deep sympathy of interested kindred. It appeared to me as if this vast concourse was gathered together to witness some ecclesiastical ceremony in which the kneeling women and children played the part of penitents. One of the ministers appeared to be addressing them in a style of stern exhortation, though I could not hear the words he spoke. At length I felt the approach of a new presence. A sound came soughing through the air like the rush of heavy wings. I could feel the wind stir the hair on my temples, when the same demon crew rushed by that I had seen in the glen a few hours before. There they were in swarms and myriads, dreadful-looking shapes, with gleaming eyes and faces distorted with the wild joy of their frantic revel. In an instant the whole host of demons swooped down on the kneeling crowd, and vanished, immersed as it seemed, in the bodies of their victims. I saw them no more, but in their places the women and children themselves assumed the attitudes of the fiends that possessed them. They sprang up with whoops, yells, and shrieks of perfect frenzy. Some rolled on the ground, foaming at the mouth, others beat their breasts and tore their hair, uttering piteous cries and choking sobs; some stood erect, with clasped hands and upturned eyes, in silent prayer; and others danced around them, uttering mocking execrations that made the blood of every listener curdle.

Little children began to scale the walls and columns, run along the giddy heights of window-sills, and suspend themselves, coiled up like squirrels or monkeys, on cornice, roof, or pinnacle.

The whole scene was one of fiendish import, horrible to hear, witness, or think of; yet it was not such a rare spectacle to me as many an unaccustomed reader may suppose. I had often witnessed cases of obsession before, in some instances falling upon whole communities, in others attacking only solitary individuals.

The scene, shocking and loathsome as it was, I knew and felt to be a real picture; and so feeling, I looked with ever-deepening interest to discover from whence the deliverance would come. Yet come indeed it did, and thus it was: Whilst the ministers shouted forth their prayers and exorcisms, mingling up passages of Scripture and fierce cries for civic help in a strange jumble to which no one listened; whilst the excited friends and kindred of the possessed rushed from one to the other in the vain endeavor to subdue them into modest behavior by tears and supplications, in the midst of this pandemonium, another phase of the phantom-scene transpired. I saw two fair and gracious beings float into the midst of the demon revel, clad in robes of glistening white, and leading by the hand a young man, in whom I at once recognized the exact presentment of myself. The dress of this wraith, although resembling the one I then wore, was still remarkable from the fact that it seemed to be composed of some glittering substance, from which streams of light radiated in every direction, enveloping the phantom in an aura of wonderful brightness. As these figures appeared upon the scene, the disturbance instantly ceased. The cries died away; the children dropped down from their fantastic perches, and crept to their mothers' arms; every one subsided into the attitude of repose, and as if an enchanted wand had been waved over the wild revel, a deep, holy calm seemed to have been diffused on all around.

Whilst I was gazing in delight upon this happy change, I noticed that a strange blue mist began to rise from the forms of the obsessed. At first it appeared to be a mere thread-like vapor, but gradually it extended in volume until it filled the church, and in the midst of its rolling waves I saw the forms of the elementaries shooting up in air with the same wild shrieks, hisses, and grimaces with which they had borne down on their victims. Upwards and outwards they soared, an obscene host, before whose approach the walls, ceiling, and windows seemed to melt away, or become soluble, permitting the dark shapes to pass through as if they had been air; and they sped, screaming and gibbering, into the heavy-laden atmosphere, where they were at last lost in masses of rolling clouds.

Directly the elementaries disappeared from the building, I beheld the noble and erect form of Professor von Marx entering it. He wore his college robe and cap, and carried in his hand a knotted staff wreathed round with a serpent, similar to one I had seen him use in certain invocatory processes. This staff he laid lightly on the heads of the lately obsessed ones, when instantly they arose from their semi-entranced positions like beings restored from the dead. With a slight start, as if awakening from slumber, the victims proceeded to arrange themselves in ranks before the altar, taking their places beside their husbands, fathers, and children with the calm and modest deportment of pure-minded matrons in attendance upon a religious ceremony. The ministers opened their books, and began to read. A dimness now crept over the scene, no longer emanating from the phantom worshippers, but stealing in insidious wreaths from the gigantic figure at my side. The couch on which I reclined rocked and reeled; enclosing walls seemed gradually to grow up around me; the church, with its tablets, sculptured ornaments, and silent congregation, melted out of view. My last memory was of a gloriously radiant face bending over me, loving eyes gazing tenderly into mine, and a sweet, distant, chiming voice murmuring as if from afar off, "He giveth His beloved sleep."

It was nearly noon before I felt able to join my host and his friends on the following day.

My dear master, with his usual kind solicitude, paid me an early visit, and listened to a detailed account of my previous night's vision. On this, as on every other occasion when I related to him my extra-mundane experiences, he never wounded me by doubt or denial of my statements. Many points of my narrative drew from him instructive and philosophical comments, and when I had concluded, he informed me that we were expected to accompany our host to the villages he had designed to pass through on the previous night, and he further

intimated that he somewhat anticipated I should find a
commentary upon my previous night's vision in the proposed excursion.

The place we were to visit had a barbarous Highland
name, which I am now unable to recall, but the main
incidents I have to relate are too well known to the
inhabitants of that district to need more particular indication.   Once more we passed through the weird glen
we had traversed the night before, and once more I
experienced the approach of involuntary somnambulism;
but being now on my guard, I was able to conquer the
tendency, and we arrived without interruption at our
destination.

This was a beautiful village, nestling at the foot of a
range of mountains, covered as usual with sweet purple
heather, and crowned with the ruins of a fine old castle.
On our arrival, our host intimated his intention of carrying us to the house of the minister of the place, by
whom he said our visit had been expected at a much
earlier hour.   My attention, however, was irresistibly
attracted to a fine old Gothic church, which stood on
an eminence surrounded by a grove of trees, and about
the open doors of which were gathered an immense
concourse of people.   Without waiting for guidance or
consultation, I felt impelled to dismount, throw the
horse's reins to a groom, spring up the eminence, and
push my way amongst the throng into the church.
Every one made way for me as I advanced.   Whether
they were impressed by my impulsive action, my foreign
appearance, or some other inexplicable cause I know not,
but the jostling crowds drew back as I approached,
and parted a way for me, through which I sped on until
I reached the scene of action.   This I doubt not my
readers will already be prepared to learn was the exact

counterpart of my last night's vision. There were the same brass tablets and marble monuments on the walls and floor; the same carved stalls and pulpit; the high Gothic windows of stained glass, casting their many-colored reflections of saints and apostles on the checkered marble aisle below. There, too, was the same gilded screen parting off the communion-table from the body of the church. Behind this dividing line stood the three ministerial men, in black, that I had seen in my vision. They each held open Bibles in their hands, and were occupied, like their phantom presentments, in hurling exorcisms, prayers, passages of Scripture, and wrathful denunciations against a frenzied mob of women and children, who, with sobs, shrieks, wails, fierce laughter, wild oaths, and frantic gesticulations, were enacting in its hideous details, the exact counterpart of the scene I had beheld in vision twelve hours before.

Turning my eyes upwards I beheld, as I expected, little children running along the dizzy heights of the windows and cornices, mewing like cats, barking like dogs, or coiling themselves up like serpents in nooks which would hardly have afforded foothold for a squirrel. One ecstatic was actually suspended in the air several feet above the ground, and her distracted husband, clinging to her feet, was vainly endeavoring by main force to drag her down to earth. Sobs and supplications, mingled groans and prayers, wild laughter and bitter wailings, resounded on every side of me. Had I been myself and in full possession of my normal faculties, I should have stopped my ears and fled from this *inferno* as from a pest-house; but the spirit was on me, and though in full possession of my sense of observation, every other faculty was under the dominion of a bright and beautiful band of planetary angels, who accompanied and impelled me on, and who from my boyhood had guided, counselled, and influenced me, under the spell of the deep magnetic trance. Awake now, and fully aware of their blessed presence and ministry, I passed amidst the demoniac rout as if I had myself become a spirit. I can not recollect that I touched the earth or realized the slightest sense of weight or hinderance to locomotion.

I moved silently through the maddened groups, and they fell at my feet, clasping and kissing my hands, addressing me as "the angel of deliverance," and hailing me as the "sent of God."

I do not recollect that I spoke in words, but I *thought* pity for these sufferers, and sent up thanks to an unknown God that they were to be free from their tormentors. I know that the same flight of demons that I had witnessed in vision rose through the groined arches and Gothic roof of the church; and when my part was done, and the stilled multitude, like rebuked children, subsided into their places, hushed, quiet, and prayerful, I too stood aside, moved by the angel presence that attended me, and just as I expected, Professor von Marx and his friends came forward and took my place. At once assuming the post of authority that belonged to him, my noble master moved amongst the quiet and humble throng, laid his powerful hands upon them, and murmured a few words of encouragement in their ears. The effect of his action was no less magical than that which had attended mine. The women started up and began to arrange their dishevelled hair and disordered dresses with modest haste. Many of them blushed, and dropped the peasant's courtesy of the country, thanking "the good doctor" for their recovery. One little child, whose shrieks had been most frantic and whose actions resembled only those of a tiger, humbly murmured, "Forgive me, mother dear! I have had a sad, drear dream, and I fear I've been very naughty."

Amongst this primitive and superstitious people it is almost unnecessary to say that the obsession which had thus fallen upon them had been attributed wholly to the power of witchcraft.

The cure now so suddenly wrought in their midst, however beneficial its results, could not fail to suggest the same weird influence. Of this the laird we were visiting was perfectly aware. He hastened therefore, to whisper in the ears of some of the church officials, who had been amazed witnesses of the scene, that we were celebrated German doctors; that our cures were effected by means of concealed but very potent drugs; and that, as warm Lutherans, they might rely upon our methods being strictly orthodox and in accordance with the doctrines of ecclesiastical practice.

Fearful lest our inveterate heterodoxy might in some unguarded moment display itself in contradiction to these whispered explanations, our good host hurried us away, and it was on our return to his hospitable mansion that we learned the material details of the circumstances in which we had been unpremeditated actors.

About four months ago, it appeared, a young girl in the parish, who had always been more or less the subject of strange dreams, visions, and tendencies to epilepsy, became suddenly frightened by what she insisted upon declaring to be the apparition of " six fairy people," who came into her chamber through the window, and after performing sundry pranks in her presence, laid their hands one after another upon her mouth, and declared that she should not again taste food until she

came forth at midnight, to dance with the fairy people.
After this strange narrative, the girl began to pine
away, refused food, and for several weeks lived entirely without any sustenance; fits of deep somnolency
attacked her; and to use her parents' simple phraseology,
"She began to die while yet she lived." All at once she
revived from this lethargic state, and at the recommen-
dation of a neighbor, she and three girls of her acquaintance stole forth one night at the full of the moon to
keep tryst with the mysterious "good people," who a
month before had invited her to one of their midnight
gatherings. Without deeming it worth while to repeat
the wild tale of glamour the romantic adventuresses
brought back from their midnight escapade, it is enough
to relate that from that time forth they began to manifest all the signs of obsession, the excess of which has
been described in the foregoing pages. Unfortunately,
their aberrations were not limited to themselves. At
first their little brothers and sisters, next their mothers,
and finally, scores of young people and females of their
acquaintance, fell under the same dreadful ban. Even
the domestic animals associated with them seemed to
share their fatal propensities; they ran wild, changed
their natures, and in some instances died beneath the
effect of *the spell*. Priests and mediciners exerted their
powers in vain. The fell disease only increased in proportion to the efforts made to quell it; and finally our
host, fearing that the superstitions of the country people,
once aroused, would induce them to lay violent hands
upon some helpless persons suspected of being instrumental in promoting the witch mania, and hearing of
our projected tour to the north, determined to try if
genuine spirit power would not do for his afflicted
neighbors what material science and superstitious piety

had failed to effect. He confessed, in fact, that he had pressed his hospitality upon us as much in the hope that our occult knowledge might devise means of relieving the district as in admiration of Professor von Marx's high reputation and standing in a certain society to which he belonged.

The result was achieved with even more success than had been anticipated. Our host had · purposely drawn us towards the scene of the visitation on the first day of our arrival, but without informing us of the real motives which prompted him. The effect of our near proximity to the possessed village upon our unfortunate horses baffled him at first, and made him fearful of trying further experiments, especially when, during the night which followed our visit to the glen, he was informed by his grooms that the horse I had ridden during the day *had actually died of fright.* "I prayed," said the good old man, "to the Father of spirits to send his angel to guide us through this wilderness of terror. Long and earnestly did I pray, and when the gray of the morning came, I fell asleep from sheer exhaustion, and dreamed I saw myself and you, my friends, leading the Israelites of old through an awful wilderness, but I saw moreover, that we were guided by a *pillar of cloud*, which moved before us, and by this I knew that my prayers were answered, and that the angel of deliverance was at hand." Some months later we heard from our venerable friend that no signs of the demon fever had ever reappeared in his district, and that none of his young clanswomen had again seen fairies or stolen forth by moonlight to attend their midnight revels.

CHAPTER VII.

IN this day of universal enlightenment there can be few if any readers of these pages who have not heard, read of, or witnessed some cases of obsession similar to that described in the last chapter. The well-informed student of psychologic phenomena must be aware that I have understated rather than exaggerated the worst features of such scenes, whilst I refer those who are unfamiliar with the subject to the graphic accounts of obsession in different countries, and occurring at different epochs of time, given by William Howitt, Dr. Ennemoser, Schuberth, Horst, Upham, and other writers on spiritualistic subjects. By these eminent authorities descriptions have been given of the *convulsionnaires* of St. Medard, the nuns of Loudon, the preaching epidemic at Sweden, etc., before the thrilling horrors of which my brief sketch of obsession in the Scotch Highlands becomes tame and lifeless. Perhaps one of the most forcible and striking instances of this demoniac fever on record occurred as recently as 1864, when a wholesale obsession seized upon the quiet and peaceful inhabitants of Morzine, Switzerland, which lasted for a period of over four years, and included in its ravages more than a thousand of the best disposed, most pure, pious, and inoffensive dwellers of that district. William Howitt has given a fine magazine sketch of this terrible visitation, which he justly entitles "The Devils of Morzine." Whether this caption be regarded as referring to the unhappy victims or the power that controlled them, it is certainly a most appropriate definition of the condition in which hundreds of hapless persons appeared during the reign of the demoniac fever which infested Morzine for several years.

I know it is the favorite theory of the modern spiritists, especially in America, to attribute all extra-mundane visitations, good, bad, or indifferent, to the spirits of deceased persons. I have conversed with many very intelligent clairvoyants who have described apparitions which manifested themselves in the form of dogs, cats, bears, tigers, and other animals, and all these appearances they assured me, were but the representation of human beings under low conditions of development. The same persons have informed me, they often saw different individuals surrounded by toads, lizards, serpents, and vermin, but that such objects had no real objective existence, but were projections from the evil tendencies of the parties, whose thoughts engendered them. They have cited Swedenborg's doctrine of correspondences in support of their opinions, urging that the great seer assures us it is the invariable tendency of evil thoughts to clothe themselves in the shape of the animals to which they correspond. It is wonderful to note with what ingenuity and ceaseless stretch of the imagination such reasoners argue for the crystallization of thought into forms. In their philosophy the varying appearances of the human spirit are sufficient to account for all the ground once occupied by supernaturalism. The Good People or Fairies of England and the Pixies of Scotland are simply the spirits of small children clothed in green.

Pigmies, Gnomes, Kobolds, etc., are the souls of the early men, who of course, were very small or very large, in accordance with the size of the phantoms they are to account for. In the same manner, Sylphs, Undines, Salamanders, and all the weird apparitions of every country, clime, and time are disposed of on elastic human hypotheses. In the opinion of these philosophers there never was, will, or can be any other than human spirits, and the whole boundless universe must look to this little planet earth to furnish forth the material for its population. There can be but little doubt that this is a relic of that materialistic theology which made a man of its God, and taught that the sun, moon, and stars were but heavenly gas-lights, fixed in a crystal firmament for the especial purpose of illuminating the path of the sole end and aim of creation, MAN. Those who plead for the existence of human spirits only, are wonderfully ingenious in showing how they can enlarge themselves into giants, contract into dwarfs, expand into winged, horned, crooked, rounded, or elongated animal substances; and all this mobility of representation is designed, they assure us, to signify certain passions or states of spiritual growth and development.

In the cases of obsession at Morzine, Sweden, Scotland, France, etc., also in the reports of trials for witchcraft, especially in New England and Scotland, it is notorious that the reputed witches and wizards were accused of mimicking the actions of animals. In all cases of obsession, too, this is one of the most marked features of the frenzy. Little children are seized with the passion for climbing, mewing, barking, and coiling themselves up into all sorts of animal shapes. The records of witchcraft and obsession both present these repulsive features as an invariable rule, and those who claim that nothing but the action of human spirit influence is manifested in these, the lowest and most revolting phases of spiritism, fail, to my apprehension, to account for this invariable tendency. It is contended that the demons of the Jewish Scriptures, whose obsession of human beings is so often referred to, could be acccounted for on the ground of epilepsy and other conditions of physical disease to which Eastern nations are peculiarly liable.

Without being able to combat the opinions of so many respectable witnesses and sound thinkers as abound in the ranks of American spiritism (the chief supporters I find, of the human spiritual theory), I would yet submit that there is a vast array both of direct and circumstantial evidence favoring a belief in the interposition of other than human spirits, especially in the cases of obsession, witchcraft, and all other forms of spiritual manifestation, where demoniac wickedness, animal tendencies, and malignity towards the race are demonstrated.

I neither venture to offer my own testimony as a clairvoyant nor that of the thousands of seers and seeresses who in all ages of the world have professed to see and commune with the elementaries, as irrefragable proof of their existence. Swedenborg and the American spiritists generally have undoubtedly a certain amount of truth on their side when they plead for the representation of man's basest passions in the form of animals; in fact it is rather in the tone of speculation than certainty that we should question whether this theory covers the whole ground of apparitional manifestations.

In another place I shall present more extended views concerning the existence and gradations of elemental

9

life, for the present, it must suffice to say, the visions narrated in the previous chapter have been faithfully described, and their results conform so closely to the experiences of a vast number of seers, who have like myself, witnessed the underlying causes for obsession, the source of which is in the invisible world, that I have no shadow of doubt in my own mind concerning the exact nature of the influence at work in the case I have related. The theory of ancient magians and mediæval mystics will be found in harmony with those of the Brotherhood from whom I first derived my opinions concerning the existence of the elementaries; and as I have before dwelt upon this subject, I shall simply add in this place that whilst I now believe the undeveloped spirits of humanity are actively engaged in stimulating every scene of human folly and error which re-enacts their own misspent lives, I am still assured such occasions offer opportunities for the intervention of the lower orders of elementaries. I conceive, moreover, that those beings exert a more constant and important influence upon humanity than we have dreamed of in our narrow philosophy, and that the demonstrations of this momentous truth will form the next phase of spiritual revelation to this generation.

Let me conclude these remarks by suggesting in brief the theories presented to us by certain of our spirit teachers, concerning the physical philosophy of obsession. The conditions that furnish opportunities for this affection are sometimes peculiar to individuals; at others, to communities. In the former case, it is generally the result of a highly mediumistic temperament, in which some disturbance of the nervous system has arisen, rendering the subject unusually negative and open to the control of strong, brutal spirits, who desire to re-incarnate themselves again in human bodies, or elementaries, who are attracted by sympathetic states of the physical system they wish to obsess. In nearly every instance, the subjects best adapted to this terrible affliction are delicate and sensitive persons, young children, pure and simple-minded women, those in fact, whose physical and nervous temperaments are negative and whose minds are receptive to the influence of others.

When obsession affects an entire community as in the case described in the last chapter, it may generally be attributed to epidemic states of the atmosphere. Solar, planetary, and astral changes are forever transpiring in the grandly permanent yet grandly varied march of the universe. That these changes must affect the earth, itself the subject of every beam of light that can reach its surface, the simplest review of the sublime scheme of the sidereal heavens will show. Yet more potential by far than the merely mathematical astronomer can perceive, are the influences which solar, planetary, and astral conjunctions exercise upon the receptive earth. We must also glance at the opinion which the study of astrology combined with astronomy inclines us to arrive at, which is, that all diseases, mental, moral, or physical, that bear upon man in the form of epidemics are produced in the first instance by malignant conjunctions of the bodies in space in relation to the earth. Tides of atmosphere, especially equatorial currents, are the carriers and distributors of these malignant influences. Hence arises the war spirit which so often marches from land to land in regular tidal waves. In the same line of atmospheric influences are borne the subtile elements of criminal propensities, popular opinions, fashions, tastes, customs, an epidemic of genius, mechanical skill, physical susceptibility to certain dis-

eases and all manner of plagues.   One susceptible organism is first attacked; then by the force of sympathy
in mental, and contagion in physical states, a whole community or district succumbs, until the prevailing influence is fully spent, when a reaction sets in.   I have cited
the experience of Professor von Marx and myself in the
Scotch obsession chiefly to show how available the all-
potential force of spiritual and animal magnetism may
become in such affections, and how much more rapidly
endemic disorders, especially of a nervous or spiritualistic character, might yield to such influences than to the
ordinary methods of cure.   In my own case I attribute
the marvellous effect produced upon the demoniacs
by my presence, to the operation of the beautiful planetary spirits who poured their divine influence upon a
human multitude through the instrumentality of a human
medium.   Professor von Marx's influence was more direct
and physically potential, for he infused his own powerful
and healthful magnetism upon the afflicted ones by direct
contact.   I doubt if every case of obsession could not be
thus instantly and effectually cured, could the right elements of spiritual and human magnetism both be brought
to bear upon the subject.

I well remember being in London, some years ago,
when a most malignant and fatal form of Asiatic cholera
was raging through the city.   The season was that
of summer, the temperature immensely high, and the
deserted city seemed wholly abandoned to the ravages
of the fell plague.   Going forth into the silent and
woeful streets, one bright morning, when not a single
particle of vapor flecked the deep azure of the sky, and
not a cloud was visible, I beheld with open spiritual
eyes an enormous column of black vapor hanging in
seething, murky folds, horizontally extended and stretch-

ing for miles across the infected districts of the city.
Curious to ascertain the nature of this columnar mass
I gave myself entirely up to the magnetic afflatus, and
presently perceived that the column was composed of
millions and tens of millions of living creatures generated in the atmosphere by a certain potent but malignant conjunction of the earth and the stars. I realized
that this conjunction had converted the unparticled
matter of the atmosphere into particled and finally
organic conditions, and though the organisms thus produced were far too attenuated to come within the range
of any instruments yet known to science, they were and
are perpetually in course of formation, and when operating, under malignant planetary and astral influences,
they impressed, as in the instance under consideration,
a diseased and pernicious influence on the atmosphere
through which they were swept, and wherever they
were borne they left their tracery behind in the form
of pestilence.

I can scarcely hope to be believed by those who have
not had the same opportunities of observation and analysis as myself, but for the truth's sake I will here leave
a record behind, which may be accepted and understood
in future generations even if rejected now.

It was during the prevalence of the great cholera
plague to which I refer that I was invited by a few
gentlemen, who were in sympathy with my mystical
studies, to join them in a select party, the aim of which
was to make astronomical experiments under peculiarly
favorable circumstances. I do not feel at liberty to
mention the names of those who graced our little gathering; it is enough to state that they were all distinguished for their scientific attainments. At a certain
period of the night we adjourned to an observatory,

where we were to enjoy the rare privilege of making observations through an immense telescope, constructed under the direction of Lord Rosse. When my turn arrived for viewing the heavens through this wonderful piece of mechanism, I confess I beheld a sight which for a long time held me breathless. At first I saw only the glorious face of the spangled firmament, with that sense of mingled awe and reverence which never forsakes the mind of the most accustomed observer when he exchanges the view of the black vault of midnight, with its thinly-scattered field of distant lamps checkering the heavens, for the gorgeous mass of divine pyrotechnics which bursts upon the sight through the dazzling revealments of the magic telescope. Breathless, transfigured, whirled away from a cold, dim, cloudy world to a land—not of fairies or angels, but of gods and demi-gods—to skies burning and blazing with millions of suns, double suns, star roads, and empyrean walls, in which the bricks and mortar are sparkling suns and glowing systems, miracle of miracles! I hold my breath and tremble as I think, for the sight never grows old nor familiar to me, and every time I have thus gazed, it has only been to find the awe and wonder deepen.

Absorbed as I was in contemplating the immensity and brilliancy of this ever new and ever gorgeous spectacle, in about forty seconds from the time when I first began to look through Lord Rosse's telescope, I found a singular blur coming between the shining frame of the heavens and the object glass. I was about to draw back, deeming some accidental speck had fallen upon the plane of vision, when I was attracted by observing that what I had deemed to be a blur actually assumed the *shape of a human profile*, and was, even as I gazed,

in the act of *moving along in space between the glass
and the heavens*. Fascinated and wonder-struck, I still
retained the calm and fixed purpose of continuing my
observations, and in this way I saw, yes! I distinctly
saw, a gigantic and beautifully proportioned human face
sail by the object-glass, intercepting the 'view of the
stars, and maintaining a position in mid-air which I
should judge to have been some five miles above the
earth's surface.

Allowing for the immense magnifying powers of the
instrument, I could not conceive of any being short of
a giant whose form would have covered whole acres
of space, to whom this enormous head could have
appertained. When I first beheld this tremendous
apparition, it seemed to be sailing perpendicularly in
the air, intercepting the field of vision just between myself and the planet to which the glass was pointed. I
have subsequently seen it four times, and on each occasion, though the face was the same, the inclination of
the form must have varied, sometimes floating horizontally, at another time looking down as if from a height,
and only permitting a partial view of the features,
greatly foreshortened, to appear. Still again I have seen
it as at first, and finally, it sailed by in such a fashion as
to permit the sight of an immense cloudy bulk which
followed in the wake of the beautiful head, the whole
apparition occupying at least a hundred séconds in
passing the glass, during which period the sight of all
other objects but this sailing dense mass was entirely
obscured. On the occasion I at first alluded to, I
became so fixed with astonishment and doubt, that I
should not have mentioned what I saw had not the
figure returned and from the side where it had disappeared I beheld it slowly, gradually, *unmistakably*

float by the object-glass with even more distinctness. than at first. This second time I could perceive as unequivocally as if I had been gazing at my own reflection in a mirror, the straight, aquiline cast of features, the compressed lip, and stern expression of the face, the large, glittering eye, fixed like a star upon the earth beneath, and long lashes, like a fringe of beams, falling upon the side of the face. A vast curtain of streaming hair floated back from the head, and its arrangement seemed to imply that the form was moving at an inconceivably rapid rate through a strong current of opposing winds. When I had fully, unquestionably satisfied myself that what I had seen was a reality, I withdrew from the instrument, then requested one of the company present to examine my pulse and report upon its action. "Moderate and firm," was the reply, given in a tone of curious inquiry; "but you look somewhat pale, Chevalier. May we not know what has occurred to disturb you?" Without answering, I proceeded carefully to examine the glass, and to scrutinize all its parts and surroundings, with a view of endeavoring to find some outside cause for what I must else have deemed an hallucination.

I was perfectly familiar with the use, capacity, and arrangement of the telescope, and as neither within nor without the instrument, nor yet in the aspect of the cloudless sky could I find the least possible solution to my difficulty, I determined to resolve the occurrence into the convenient word I have just used, and set the matter down as hallucination. But my friends were not so easily satisfied. Some of them were personally acquainted with me, and fancied they perceived in my manner a thread of interest which they were not disposed to drop. At last, one of them, an old and very venerable scientist, whose opinions I had long been accustomed to regard with respect, looking steadily in my face, asked in a deep and earnest tone, "Will you not tell us if you have seen anything unusual? We beg you to do so, Monsieur, and have our own reasons for the query." Thus adjured, but still with some hesitation, I answered that I certainly thought I had seen the outlines of a human face, and that twice, crossing the object-glass of the telescope.

Never shall I forget the piercing look of intelligence interchanged by my companions at this remark. Without a word of comment however, the one whose guest I had the honor to be, stepped to a cabinet in the observatory where he kept his memoranda, and drawing forth a package, he thus addressed me: "What you may have seen to-night, Chevalier, I am not yet informed of, but as something remarkable appears to have struck you in the observation you have just made, we are willing to place ourselves at your mercy, and provided you will reciprocate the confidence we repose in you, we will herewith submit to you some memoranda which will convince you some of us at least, have beheld other bodies in space than suns and planets." Before my honored entertainer could proceed further, I narrated to him as exactly as I could, the nature of what I had seen, and then confessed I was too doubtful of my own powers of observation to set down such a phenomenon as an actuality unless I could obtain corroborative evidence of its truth. "Receive it, then, my friend," cried my host, in such deep agitation that his hand trembled violently as he unfolded his memoranda, and raising his eyes to Heaven, gleaming through an irrepressible moisture, he murmured in deep emotion, "Good God! then it *must* be true."

I dare not recall *verbatim* the wording of the notes I
then heard read, as they were so mixed up with details
of astronomical data, which have since become public
property, that the recital might serve to do that which
I then solemnly promised to avoid, namely, whilst pub-
lishing the circumstances I then heard of, for the benefit
of those who might put faith in them, carefully to sup-
press the names of the parties who furnished me with
the information. My friends then (five in number on
the occasion referred to) assured me that during the
past six months, whilst conducting their observations at
that place, and by aid of that as well as two other telescopes of inferior power, they had, all on several occasions, seen human faces of gigantic proportions floating
by the object-glass of their telescopes, in almost the
same fashion and with the same peculiarities of form
and expression as the one I had just described. One
gentleman added that he had seen three of these faces
on one night, passing one after the other, their transit
occupying, with slight intervals between them, nearly
half an hour. For many successive weeks this party
had stationed themselves at distant places, at given
periods of time, and determined to watch for several
consecutive nights and see if the same phenomenon
could or would appear to more than one observer at a
time. The memoranda which record the results of this
experiment were indeed most startling. Take the following extracts: —

"*Tuesday*, June 4, 18 . Third night of watching.
Took my station at the glass at 11.30 P. M. At 2, or
just as the last vibration of the clock resounded from
the observatory, the first outline of the head came into
view. This time the form must have been directly
perpendicular, for the sharp outline of the straight

profile came into a direct line with the glass, and enabled me to see a part of the neck, and clear the top of the head. The figure was sailing due north, and moved across the glass in 72 seconds," etc. etc.

Memoranda 2d. "I began to despair of success as three days had now elapsed without any interruption of the kind anticipated in my observations. At 10 minutes and 3 seconds to 2, I began to experience an overpowering sense of fatigue, and determined to close my observations at the moment my chronometer should strike the hour. 2.30.— The giant has just appeared; his head came into view exactly as the clock was striking 2, and placing my chronometer directly before me so as to catch the first glimpse of the time when he disappeared, I find that his transit occupied exactly 72 seconds. Attitude horizontal, position of head, a direct and magnificent profile." Note No. 3 simply states: —

" *Tuesday,* June 4, 18 . Titanus came into view at 2 o'clock precisely, sailed by in 71¼ seconds, upright, and face in profile, moving due north," etc. etc.

Some of the observations recorded by the spectators of this phenomenon were full of emotion, and as the venerable gentleman who first questioned me read over the comments this strange sight called forth, my companions were so deeply moved, and manifested such intense feeling on the subject of what they had seen, that the reading was several times interrupted, and one of the party remarked, he believed he should be disposed to shoot any one who should presume to cast doubt or ridicule on a subject which had affected them all so deeply.

For the next fortnight I enjoyed the privilege of spending a considerable portion of each night in that observatory. Twice the strange phantom sailed before

my view in one week. By permission of my friends,
I changed my station and continued my anxious
watch with another instrument. On the second night
I beheld the Titanic head with even more distinctness
than before, and three of my fellow-watchers shared the
weird spectacle with me from different posts of observation. One week later, although greatly fatigued by my
long and close vigils for so many nights, I determined
to avail myself of a final observation with one of
the most superb instruments ever constructed. For
many hours my exhaustive watch was unsuccessful; but
just as I was about to take my leave of the enchanting
fields of fiery blossoms that lay outstretched before me,
two faces of the same size and expression, the one
slightly in advance of, and measurably shading the
other, sailed slowly, very slowly into view. They
passed on with such an unappreciable, gentle motion
that I could almost have imagined they were stationary
for some seconds of time. Their appearance so completely surprised me at the moment when I was about to
retire that I omitted to take note of the time they occupied in passing. The companion who shared my watch
had pointed his glass a little more to the east than
mine, and I had but time to murmur an injunction for
him to change it as the figures came into view. He
saw them, however, just as they were passing out of the
field of vision, and exclaimed, with a perfect shout of
astonishment, " By heavens! there are two of them!"

Some years after this memorable night I received a
letter from one of my associates in this weird secret,
according to me the permission I sought, namely, to
publish the circumstances I have related thus far, but
carefully to withhold the witnesses' names. In answer
to my query whether my correspondent had again seen

the tremendous phantom of the skies, he replied in the
negative, adding, "Call me superstitious or what you
will: the whole history lays us open to ourselves and to
each other, to such wild suggestions and inconceivable
possibilities, that no hypothesis can seem so improbable
as that we should all be correct. I will venture to hint
to you, *one of us, you know*, that I have somehow always
connected the apparitions in question with the prevalence of the cholera. It was immediately in advance of
this pestilence, and during the time when it raged, that
we all saw them. Since that period we have never
again beheld them, that is, none of us who now remain
on earth.

"These appearances ceased with the pestilence, and
came with it. Could they have been the veritable
destroying angels, think you? You, who are a mystic,
should be able to answer me. I, with all my materialism, am so terribly shaken when I recall the terrific
reality, that I endeavor to banish its remembrance whenever it recurs to me."

Again, I have anticipated the experiences of later
years, and been guilty of wandering from the line of
narrative which the march of events prescribes. I feel
as if I should attempt too to render the explanations
of the foregoing circumstances which my astronomical
friends looked to me to supply them with, but looked,
as the reader may do, in vain.

It seems to me as if a vain and egotistical fear of a
sneering and sceptical age, keeps many others besides
my astronomical associates silent on the occurrence of
events 'which are chiefly remarkable because they are
unprecedented, and which encounter jeers and denial
chiefly from those who strive to measure eternity by
the foot-rule of their own petty intellects. The buffets

of such small wits as these have done me the good service of making me at last wholly indifferent to their opinions; hence I have in this instance, and shall in many more throughout these papers, record what .I KNOW TO BE TRUE, without fear or favor.   I can not always explain what I have seen, heard, and taken part in, but the favorite motto of a very dear friend has now become my own, and "the truth against the world" will be the ruling inspiration in the dictation of these pages.

CHAPTER VIII.

"Come, Louis! let us leave all this. I am tired for you,—tired of seeing you exhausted in body and mind to please insatiate marvel-seekers; tired of beholding every nerve kept on the stretch, and a young life ebbing away to feed the curiosity of those who little know or heed that they are looking into the realms of the invisible through the telescope of your weary eyes. Come, my Louis! we will leave these festive scenes, where your very being furnishes forth the feast, to go and regale ourselves upon the fair face of Nature." Thus spoke Professor von Marx as I lay on a couch where I had sunk in sheer exhaustion some hours before, worn out indeed both in body and mind with the repeated séances, undertaken to gratify the numerous kind entertainers who besought us to "come and take rest" at their hospitable mansions in some charming retreat, which they converted into a scene of fashionable saturnalia, where crowds of visitors were invited to meet and stare, and not uncommonly to sneer at also, "the great German occultist and his young somnambulist, who were so very wonderful and so very entertaining, and all that sort of thing."

Thoroughly sick of being lionized, and solicited, the professor to talk philosophy and put fine ladies into becoming trances, and I to raise up Undines and Sylphs,

and predict which would be the winning horse at the next
" Derby," I joyfully obeyed the behest of my dear master to depart with him that evening on "urgent business,"
which would compel us to decline all further invitations,
and leave the world of fashion for parts unknown.

We did not travel very far at first, for I was too thoroughly depleted to endure the fatigue of a long journey
anywhere. Professor von Marx either desired me to
realize practically, or else had to learn the lesson himself, that the aims for which spiritual forces are employed determine in a great measure the recuperative
powers of the body that is their vehicle. So long as I
was occupied as the seer of the noble professor, and the
high-toned and powerful adepts with whom I had been
constantly associated on the Continent, my soul was
fed with intellectual inspiration, and my physique was
vitalized by life-giving magnetism. I frequently passed
whole days without food, whilst engaged in these sessions, yet I never experienced the slightest sense of
fatigue, weariness, or hunger.

I lived in a state of semi-ecstacy, my whole being
sustained to its fullest capacity of reception, both mentally and physically.

In my dear master's presence I felt an influx of strength
and spiritual power impossible to describe. I should not
dare to relate to those who have never experienced their
exalting and ecstatic possibilities the phenomenal evidences of magnetic force too which these séances evolved.
It is enough to affirm, it was as natural for the seers on
such occasions to ascend in air, and float there at will, as
to remain attached to the earth, in fact the token which
a closed circle of adepts were accustomed to receive that
their magnetic aura had combined in the required degree
was the levitation of their seers, and their suspension

in air for given periods of time. But let it be remembered that my companions were all intellectual men, and isolated in the grand purpose of their researches; they could at will send forth the spirits of their seers to traverse space, but they never exerted this stupendous power on trivial occasions or for the mere gratification of selfish aims.

Their sole aspiration was to discover and gauge the forces of the unseen universe and penetrate into the profoundest of Nature's mysteries. They were often cold, hard, stern, and remorseless in the pursuit of knowledge, but in their presence the minds of their seers could not fail to grow and expand into lofty aspirations and soar away above the frivolities and petty aims in which most young people are educated.

Of all their seers, too, I believed they loved me the most. Combined with their indomitable purpose of wresting from Nature her secrets at any cost, there was a special gentleness and appreciative respect in their dealings with me, which made the bond between us unusually kind and sympathetic, and thus I was kept completely isolated, I might say sacredly reserved for the most exalted purposes of research and aspirational effort.

Let the character of these séances be compared with the littleness, selfishness, and frivolity of the fashionable crowds by whom I had been recently surrounded, and the effect of the latter upon me may be measurably appreciated. It required but a few weeks of such a life to convert me into a forlorn, worn-out invalid, and to assure my dear master the stern restrictions he had laid upon the very thoughts no less than the lives and habits of the persons whose magnetisms were permitted to become incorporated into the systems of his sensitives

10

were justified by the practical though bitter experiences of his best-beloved somnambulist in fashionable English society.

How well he understood both the nature of my sufferings and their cause, I one day learned by hearing him addressing a party of ladies and gentlemen who had been pleading for another séance, "just one more, before the cruel professor took his charming young mystic away, to bury his talents amongst German boors or plotting Illuminée." Addressing these butterflies in his gravest tones, I heard him say, "Spiritual forces are sacred elements which should not be tampered with, and unholy, impure, or sensually-minded individuals can more safely play with the lightnings, or hurl burning coals at each other's heads, than deal with or touch the lightnings of life, or palter with the fires of soul. My Louis," he added with terrible emphasis, "is almost dying of such play; and I take him hence at once to save the remnant of his — to me — most precious life." I fear I may not succeed in impressing my inexperienced readers with the force of these positions. I narrate them as they occur, faithfully and truthfully, but to an age that has been accustomed to regard occult power as a mere hap-hazard endowment requiring no culture, no conditions, and spiritual gifts, as a mere source of amusement or curious experiment, to be exercised at will in any company or under any circumstances, I shall never write understandingly, and my views will be regarded as overstrained or rhapsodical, and my narrative as exaggerated if not actually untrue. Still I re-echo the above-quoted words of my beloved master, and confident that in a succeeding generation, if not in this, their import will be duly recognized and acted upon, I proceed with my narrative.

After passing through many a lovely scene, and halting as our inclination prompted us at little wayside inns in the most rural and unfrequented spots we could find, Professor von Marx and I determined to make a tour through the lake district of Cumberland. Whilst we were lingering in this enchanting region, we were induced to make a detour of several miles from our projected route, for the purpose of visiting the humble dwelling of one Frances Jones, an abnormal personage, known in that district as the "Welsh fasting girl." This case, which had attained considerable celebrity, presented most of the general features which accompany protracted fasting, namely, long-continued fits of somnolence and occasional intervals of remarkable lucidity, during which the girl delivered trance addresses of wonderful beauty and exhibited striking powers of clairvoyance and prevision. Professor von Marx was not prompted to make this visit by the motives of vulgar curiosity which attracted crowds of persons to the residence of this phenomenon. He knew how long I could myself subsist without material sustenance; he had witnessed the extraordinary effects of renewed life and vitality I had exhibited by sleeping for some time on beds of fresh flowers or sweet-scented herbs; above all, he had frequently seen me maintain a protracted fast of several days, without experiencing hunger or weakness, by simply placing me in the magnetic condition at stated periods, and surrounding me with a strong circle of powerful magnetizers.

The professor and his associates had demonstrated to their entire satisfaction the triumph of spiritual forces over material in my case, and were prepared to carry their theories forward into still more extraordinary results, when opportunities were favorable for their experiments. It was, therefore, with a view of analyzing a case which might present some kindred features that Professor von Marx and myself set out upon this visit.

We found our subject sitting upright in bed, with her eyes firmly closed, and her form and face by no means emaciated, though somewhat pallid from her frequent isolation from the light, which at times affected her unfavorably. Just as we arrived she was "in one of her fits," as her rustic parents informed us; that is to say, in one of those crises or periods of her disorder when she was impelled to utter her singularly beautiful improvisations, one of which she was pouring forth in a strain of remarkable eloquence to a crowd of gaping country folks as we entered the cottage. Directly Professor von Marx crossed the threshold the girl stopped speaking, and beckoning to him with an authoritative air, took his hand, laid it on her head, and with looks of ecstacy which transfigured her face into an almost angelic expression, murmured, "Great master, you are welcome! Speak, and I will answer you."

Question. Tell me truly, is it Frances Jones or the spirit of another who addresses me?

Answer. I am the voice of one crying in the wilderness, Prepare ye the way of the Lord!

Q. Whose voice cries?

A. Him that cryeth now as of old.

Q. You call yourself John the Baptist, then?

A. Thou sayest it.

Q. Who and what is the Messiah you predicate?

A. The outpouring of the Spirit on all flesh; and behold (pointing her finger at me) even there, is one of the prophets of the new dispensation. Thou knowest it, and he can tell thee all thou hast come here to inquire.

Q. Not all; I wish to hear from your own lips a description of your case.

A. Ask him; he knoweth.

Q. By what means are you sustained in life?

A. I am fed by the angels, and live on angels' food; I hunger not, neither do I thirst.

Q. You speak now as Frances Jones: where is the spirit who first addressed me?

A. He moves these utterances and inspires these answers.

Q. Was he a man or an angel?

A. If I should answer thee thou wouldst not believe me. Thou art of the sect of Sadducees, who say there is no spirit or angel. I cast not my pearls before swine

The professor here smiled at me significantly, but continuing to address the patient, he rejoined, —

Q. Can I do you any good by the touch of my hand?

A. Thou hast done all that was required of thee; *the closed gate is unlocked by thy hand,* and in due course of time the angels of restored health will reopen it and walk in. Now depart in peace. Thy seer will tell thee the rest.

At this point the invalid sank back upon her pillow with a slight convulsion, which, passing rapidly away, left her features calm, pale, and tranquil, when her ordinary deep sleep fell upon her, and her parents assured us it might be many hours ere she would reawaken. Before we quitted the cottage I informed my master what I had clairvoyantly perceived in this case, namely, that a partial paralysis had attacked first the great solar plexus, then extended throughout the ganglionic system, finally impinging in the same partial way upon the cerebro-spinal nerves. The medulla and cerebellum were more powerfully affected than the cerebrum, and the pneumagastric nerve was more completely paralyzed than any other of the cranial system. I observed that the processes of evaporation and absorption remained untouched, and acted with their usual force; hence, she could receive such nourishment as imponderable elements afforded her, and her assertion that she partook of angels' food was not altogether irrational.

It is certain that little or no waste of tissue could ensue in a state which was entirely one of passivity. Though the vital functions were in operation, they proceeded so slowly that there could be little more waste or evaporation than the process of absorption might renew; hence the absence of emaciation or any evidence of that decay which might have been the result of inanition. It seemed that a certain periodical condition of activity set in at stated times, and kind Nature used these opportunities to attempt a renovation of the paralyzed system; then it was, that the invalid became clairvoyant, uttered her remarkable trance addresses, and with eyes closely bandaged to exclude the light, which distracted her sensitive brain, the poor girl cut out paper flowers and made little drawings, which were sold by her poor relatives. I perceived that this young creature was surrounded by crowds of spiritual beings, who fed her with the emanations of plants, vegetables, and the magnetism of some of those who visited her parents' cottage.

I also saw that the strong and potential magnetism of Professor von Marx, had, through the hand which he placed on her head, infused new life into her system, by virtue of which the paralytic condition of her frame had in truth been " unlocked." Recuperative action once commenced, I had the pleasure of perceiving that nature would do the rest; that the real source of cure was already infused, and that with ordinary care this girl would be restored in two months more. I mentioned this promise in my clairvoyant vision to her family. Professor von Marx at the same time generously supplied them with funds to supersede the necessity of their appealing to the charity of inquisitive strangers, and I had the satisfaction of learning some months later, that a gradual and apparently spontaneous cure had set in from the time of our visit, until this poor sufferer had become completely restored. I understood that her faculty of trance-speaking and clairvoyance ceased with her recovery, in a word, spirits found no more a vehicle for the reception of their influence, and her own normal activity furnished no longer the conditions for abnormal control. I have since witnessed many cases of long-protracted fasting, accompanied by somnolent states and periodical conditions of clairvoyance, and I very much doubt if the physical causes would not be found in every instance measurably the same, had scientists the same opportunities for analyzing the obscure realms of causation as clairvoyance afforded to me.

It was a few days after our visit to the "Welsh fasting girl" that Professor von Marx and I, sitting in the porch of a rustic inn-door, observed a tall and stately female approaching us, attired in the humble peasant garb, with the scarlet cloak and hood which distinguishes that singular class of vagrants known as "gypsies." Dressed as we were, simply in sportsmen's costume, and lodgers at an humble wayside public house, we did not expect to attract the attention of those shrewd wanderers whose favors are most liberally tendered to the wealthy; but our new visitor evidently deemed she was in the right track when she approached us, for she advanced with an air so decided that we felt as if we were fairly captured before she had spoken a word. Fixing her lustrous black eyes with the most piercing expression upon me, she asked in a sweet voice, and with a far more polished mode of expression than ordinary, if I did not want my fortune told. "See what you can find out for my father first," I replied laughingly, pointing to the professor, who sat by my side.

"He is no father of yours, senor," said the girl decidedly, "nor does he come from the same land, or own one drop of the blue blood that flows in your veins."

Now, if there ever were two human beings, who, without the slightest tie of consanguinity between them, closely resembled each other, those two persons were Professor von Marx and myself. We were constantly taken for father and son by those who first met us; and whether from our peculiar interior relations to each other, or because Nature had formed us out of the same mould I know not, but certain it is that it would have required some direct evidence to the contrary, to convince any stranger that we were not what we called each other, namely, father and son. As such we had been known in our rural wanderings of the last few weeks, and in those characters we had charged the single groom who attended us, to represent us at the inns where we stayed.

This striking proof of our new acquaintance's discernment then, awakened our curiosity, and induced us to let her proceed with her proposed delineation of our future. As far as the past was concerned, she gave a perfectly correct account of myself, my family connections and characteristics, but when she came to depict the future she gazed at me with such deep and pitying earnestness that her eyes filled with tears and her sweet voice became broken with emotion. Her mode of speech changed, too, from the rambling monotone of her craft to a fine sonorous rhyme, a sort of lofty "rune," in which she prophesied for me a life of deeply tragic import, and sorrows which God alone knows how truthfully she foreshadowed. At length she paused in her sad, wild song, — indeed I interrupted her, — for I felt she spoke the truth, and yet I would rather not have heard the sad page rehearsed in those hours of fleeting sunshine and gladness.

When it came to Professor von Marx's turn she absolutely refused to give him one word. He could neither bribe, threaten, nor coax her into a prophecy, and though her own bright eyes fell before his still more lustrous and penetrating glances, I saw the unbidden moisture trembling on her long lashes, as she resolutely reiterated she had nothing to tell him.

Professor von Marx was in one of his satirical, if not gay moods, and snatching the little hand with which she was waving him off, he exclaimed, "What, not one word, my pretty Gitana? not if I cross this hand of yours with gold instead of silver?"

"Not for the wealth of the Indies!" she cried, in a harsh, frightened tone, as she fiercely drew her hand away. Then, as the color died on her flushed cheek, and the wild expression of her dark eyes became subdued before his resistless glance, she murmured in a beseeching tone, "Master of spirits, spare me! I dare not speak now."

"Enough, enough!" he replied, waving her off and throwing into her hand several pieces of silver, which she as hastily pushed back. "You are wiser in holding your tongue, Gitana, than you are in loosing it; but take your money, — nay, *I command you!*" The girl slowly and reluctantly dropped the money into a bag at her side, and was turning away, when the professor recalled her in a half-laughing tone, by saying, "We shall see you again, my fair Zingara; we are coming to board with you a while. What is your name, my princess?"

"Juanita," replied the gypsy, in a low, humble tone.

"And you are a queen in your tribe, Juanita, is it not so?"

"I am, senor," replied the girl, proudly.

"I thought so," rejoined my master. "Well, good-by for the present! We shall soon meet again."

The gypsy turned submissively away without a word and that night, in obedience to my wayward father's will, we left our groom and baggage at the inn, and the professor, carrying a small valise in his hand, led me, by an instinct peculiar to himself, over moss and fell, moorland waste, and through mountain-passes, until we had traversed a distance of nearly seven miles, and at length, a little before midnight, we came in sight of the lonely field where outstretched tents marked an extensive gypsy encampment.

Juanita, who was indeed the veritable queen or leader of the tribe which we were about to visit, seemed, by the same instinct that had guided us, to be fully prepared for our coming. She had ordered two tents to be got ready for us, and already our savory supper smoked upon the wooden platters laid out for our entertainment. The red fires were smouldering in dotted heaps over the wild heath; a few lanterns still burned at intervals on the crossed sticks that upheld them. Most of the encampment were asleep, but the beautiful Juanita welcomed us as expected guests, with that natural grace which belongs to the dispenser of hospitality everywhere. Professor von Marx took her aside and spoke a few earnest words, to which she listened with a downcast and reluctant manner. He then gave her money, which she received in the same subdued way, although at first she strenuously endeavored to return it. When the interview closed, she waited on us at supper with the grace and condescension of a captive princess, and showed us to our tents, in which beds of fragrant heather, covered with the skins of deer, were already prepared for us. My tent, I observed, was adorned with bouquets of sweet wild flowers, the professor's with some curious skins and a few stuffed lizards and reptiles.

"The girl's a witch," said the professor, as he observed these significant arrangements, "and has read us like a book."

Before parting for the night my master gave me to understand he had long been seeking an opportunity for me to spend some days in this rough tent-life. "I want to bring you down from heaven to earth," he said, — "to make you sleep on the earth, and partake of earthly things; it is only in this way I can hope to keep you upon the earth as long as you ought to remain." My master's expectations of benefit to an overtaxed frame were speedily realized. Deep and unbroken slumbers visited me under the greenwood tree, such as I had not known for many years. Relieved from the artificial restraints of conventional life, and subject to the rough but appetizing fare of these wanderers, I became positively rugged, and delighted my watchful and anxious companion by the length of my daily rambles and the keen enjoyment with which I entered, for the time being, into the rough sports of my entertainers.

Everything was so new, free, and enchantingly natural that I began to contemplate the tent-life as my future destiny, and actually set myself to studying the manners, customs, and language of these vagrants, with a view to my adoption in their respectable ranks. Whilst the charm of this recuperative and healthful change lasted I sought to excuse to myself the aimless life of indolence I was leading, by endeavoring to discover if this singular people cherished amongst themselves any legendary opinions concerning their own origin. Existing everywhere, but everywhere as a solitary, marked, and isolated band of fugitives; never at home, though everywhere familiar; always strangers, though they might be in the very country of their birth; realizing more completely than any other created beings the awful legend of Cain, "A vagabond and a fugitive shalt thou be on the face of the earth"; homeless, nationless, unconnected with any other races than those so widely scattered over the world, yet ever bearing in their physiognomy, character, language, and customs, peculiar traits which never forsake them and at once distinguish and isolate them from all other living peoples,— who can solve the problem of their exceptional and incomprehensible destinies?

Except in respect to the peculiar characteristics which must accompany very poor nomadic tribes, I have never found amongst the Bohemians of France and Germany, the Zingari of Italy, the Gitanas of Spain, the Gypsies of England, etc., any marked criminal tendencies or specialties that seemed to explain the world-wide ban of proscription that has followed them for at least the eight hundred years during which they have been known as a separate people. I found on this occasion, as on many others, when, in later years I spent a few days of free, wild, untrammelled life amongst the Gypsies, that the great majority of them, though shrewd and crafty enough in some respects, were stolidly ignorant and indifferent concerning their origin or national existence.

Juanita was one of those rare and exceptional beings whose appearance amongst such hordes, serves to stamp them with an air of romance and throw around their name and fame those captivations of ideality which have rendered them so celebrated in poetry, music, and romantic literature. Juanita was the reigning queen of a large tribe composed partly of Spanish and partly of English gypsies, over all of whom she, a Spaniard by birth and descendant of a former king of the tribe, ruled with undisputed sway. She was but twenty-five years of age, beautiful as a poet's dream, impulsive, passionate, poetical, and proud, with a natural tone of refinement and sensibility in her nature, come from whence it may, which would have graced an Andalusian princess.

This beautiful and wayward being, deigned to select me as the special object of her favor during our *escapade*, and by way of disposing of Professor von Marx, for whom she conceived a corresponding aversion not unmixed with awe, she assigned him a guide and companion, in the person of her young brother Guido, a fine, intelligent lad some ten years her junior, with whom the professor took long rambles and soon became fast friends. It was our daily custom to make our simple sportsman's toilette, by a fresh bath in the flowing river which skirted the encampment. Our breakfast was partaken of in the large common tent to which Professor von Marx on our first entrance, had paid such a footing, as should ensure the foragers of the party a quiet holiday and total cessation from their ordinary methods of replenishing the larder, during the whole time of our residence amongst them. The morning meal disposed

of, the men betook themselves to their petty trades as
itinerants, the women to their domestic duties and the
care of their children, of whom there were the usual
bountiful supply.   The professor wandered off with
Guido, and sometimes joined a hunting party, which, in
less choice phraseology, might have been termed by the
more conventional name of *poaching*.   Meantime I wandered off with Juanita to gather flowers and mosses,
visit the most romantic nooks and glens of a wild and
almost savage district, and hear this beautiful creature
pour out rapid and singularly sweet poetical improvisations concerning that beloved Andalusia of which she
informed me she was a native, though descended as she
sometimes claimed from "a long line of Moorish kings."
At night we returned to the tents, where the professor
won all hearts by romping with the little ones, playing
at rough sports with the boys, cards with the English
gypsies, whom of course he always allowed to beat him,
and making himself generally delightful to young and
old, and such an astonishment in my eyes, that he would
often burst into a fit of uncontrollable merriment as he
caught my looks of amazement at his thorough trans-
figuration.

I was not less popular with these ragamuffins than
my plastic master, for besides being the chosen friend
of their proud and authoritative ruler, I sang them songs
which I will venture to affirm obtained more rapturous
encores and genuine applause than ever greeted a *prima
donna assoluta*.   Besides my *volks lied* and Italian *can-
zonets*, Juanita and the Spanish gypsies made sweet
music with their guitars and lutes, and some of the
English girls sang glees with a simplicity and sweetness
that was wonderfully touching in this moon and star lit
auditorium.

One old crone of the English tribe, whose *forte* was story-telling, and who varied our evening camp-fire amusements by legends which would have done honor to Munchausen, traced back for me the history of her people to one of the Pharaohs. She also detailed graphic accounts of some of her former states of exist-ence, she being, like others of her compeers, a decided " re-incarnationist," and finally gave me to understand that though she then performed the humble duty of tend-ing the gigantic cauldron from whose savory steams the promise of a real gypsy feast was to be derived, she well remembered the time when she was " one of the highly trusted officers of a certain mighty Pharaoh, by whose orders the great pyramid of Egypt had been erected, under her supervision."

In their natural gifts of improvisation, prevision, and spontaneous clairvoyance, no less than in certain physiog-nomical peculiarities, these people continually reminded me of some of the still existing low castes of Hindostan.

There can be no doubt that their nomadic lives and constant intercourse with Nature in her ever-varying moods, are all aids in unfolding the interior perceptions of these dwellers in tents; still there are vestiges of Oriental tendencies in their fervid imaginations, alle-gorical modes of expression, some of their customs and religious beliefs, which plead strongly for an inheritance derived from the far East in many successive genera-tions. Their language, too, although containing whole vocabularies of slang phrases and thieves' jargon, still partakes of the Sanskrit character, and there are some words which I found to be pure and unadulterated Sanskrit. A vague traditionary belief exists amongst them all that they originally came from the East, were a once "mighty people," but had become degraded and scattered. To my mind they have never been anything but a degraded people. I am more and more inclined to the opinion that they came from one of those low and oppressed castes of India which were driven forth and scattered upon the face of the earth under Mohammedan rule and oppression.

The most accomplished amongst them were astrologers, and I found that their calculations and methods were purely Chaldaic. Juanita was as well skilled in this art as any person, save one, I ever met with. That one was a distinguished Arabian physician, a member of the "Berlin Brotherhood," an admirable astronomer and mathematician; in fact, he was professor of astronomy at the scene of my boyhood's studies, and from him I learned the Chaldaic method of calculating the stars, one that had never been published to the world, and was only imparted under certain conditions to adepts. Yet here in the wilds of Cumberland I found it substantially known and practised by a poor Gitana, who could neither read nor write. "See, senor mio," she would cry, " I can not *tell* you how I know these things, but I will *show* you." She would then find a flat stone or smooth piece of wood, and chalk thereon maps of the heavens, dividing the stars by lines and connecting them in squares and figures with an accuracy which perfectly bewildered me. Substantially I repeat, her method was that of the Arabian philosopher, and yet this untaught girl worked out with her fingers and piles of pebbles a scheme that she could have obtained only from Chaldaic sources, and those of the most occult and secret nature. Juanita informed me she had derived her knowledge from her father, like herself a ruler in his tribe, and that he again had obtained it by direct succession from a long line of ancestors.

"Now, Nita," I said, "tell me the names of the stars
you have figured out here, and then, *show* them to me
on the heavens"; for I wished to see if this was mere
routine work, or whether the girl really understood what
she had drawn. Fixing her dark eyes on the shining
field of light above our heads she began, in a high strain
of poetical imagery, to describe the famous legend of the
astronomical religion, pointing out correctly every con-
stellation of which she spoke, but to my utter amazement giving to those shining bodies, not the ordinary
astronomical names, but their cabalistic titles and history, and reciting some of the myths in this connection
that I have never seen anywhere detailed, except in the
ancient "Zohar" or "Book of Light." More and more
perplexed by this sibyl's strange lore, I endeavored by
every means I could devise, to ascertain how she had
gained her extraordinary knowledge. I found then, what
I had before suspected, that the gypsies were not, as
has been generally supposed, conformists to the religion
of any country in which they chanced to sojourn, but
that with all their slang habits and reprobate style of
life, they were genuine fire worshippers, and cherished
amongst them the Sabaen system with the real ardor of
Parsees. More than this I could not learn; but as Nita
would go into ecstacies over certain stars which she
delighted to liken to my eyes, ending by christening me
her "star-beam," I determined to change the conversation by inviting her to teach me the art of palmistry, —
"that art, you know, Nita, by which we first became
acquainted," I said. "Palmistry!" replied the girl, with
a scornful laugh; "there is no such thing as palmistry
in the sense you mean it, senor; we don't really tell
fortunes by the lines of the hand. See, she added,
snatching impulsively at my hand and pointing to its
11

undefined lines, "you have no lines here, like *working*
people. Such a hand tells nothing, save of the menials
that work for you. No, no, senor; it was your eyes that
told me all your sad, wild history. When I look at the
stars they tell me a thousand times more than those
charts of my fathers; so it is when I look at your eyes.
There I read your history, your soul, your mind; past,
present, future, — all linger in those dark depths so
plainly, so clearly, that I could see, did I dare to gaze
long enough, — ay! see the day when the earth will
grow cold and chill because the lustre of your life
will be quenched out of it."

"Never mind that day, Nita, — would to heaven it
were to-morrow! — but tell me yet more plainly how you
see all this."

"How should Nita know? It comes; it rises up to
my mind and trembles on my lips before I know the
words that are spoken. Mark you, senor, I have two
ways of knowing. I first look into the eyes, and
there I see the soul, — see its joys and sorrows, its
weary travail and happy hours; I see its loves and
hates, and many of the paths it has taken the body,
and many more it will have to follow. As to the hand,
I feel, not see its meaning. Few hands are so difficult to read as yours, senor, for your heart is locked
away in the keeping of yon dark Master of Spirits,"
pointing off, as she spoke, towards Professor von Marx,
of whom she still retained an unconquerable fear; "but
with most persons whose hands I touch, their modes
of life, past, present, and future, come up with the
heart's blood, and thrill through my fingers just as if
I could feel out the words which tell the tale. This,
too, is the way Marianna and Louise" (alluding to two
other sibyls of her tribe) "tell fortunes, senor mio.

Mother Elsie is blind, you know, yet she tells better than all of us, and she tells everything by the touch, and sometimes when she lays her withered hand on a stranger's head or a lady's dress, or even touches the glove or handkerchief that an inquirer has touched, she knows just as much as if the whole story were read out from a book. Don't you know this is true, senor?"

"Quite so, Juanita. I have tested this Mother Elsie, as you say, and she can tell very wonderful truths; but still you have not told me *how* Mother Elsie can do this, or how you can read my life in my eyes or feel it in my hand. That is what I wish to know, Juanita."

"Because Elsie is a Gypsy and I am a Zingara, senor," replied the girl, simply.

"You refuse to tell me then, Juanita," I replied, assuming to be piqued at her reticence. "I thought you would have told everything to your friend; you promised you would."

A passionate burst of tears and the wildest protestations of devotion, sincerity, willingness to lay down her life to please me, etc., followed, making me feel condemned and humiliated for questioning the simple earnestness of this poor, untaught child of the forest, and measuring *her* utter guilelessness by my own worldcraft. It was evident to me, as it had become to Professor von Marx, though he took other means to arrive at his conclusions, that these wanderers were naturally gifted with strong clairvoyant and psychometric perceptions, varying in degree, of course, with their different endowments, and that where these powers existed, they resorted to the fascinating gaze, or the touch of the hand, merely as a means of entering into *rapport* with their subjects, even as the old woman above alluded to — one

of the most celebrated pythonesses of her time — found
the contact of some object which had been touched, necessary to open up her psychometric perceptions. These
methods are familiar enough now amongst well-informed
spiritists; but in the earlier days of my investigations,
I was unceasing in my endeavors to find a deeper
philosophy than Nature herself afforded me for the
exercise of spiritual powers. My search was and ever
will be in vain. As to the astrological lore existing
amongst these people, that still remained a mystery.
The possession of such knowledge involves scientific
attainments, not natural endowments; and from whence
they derived their information except, as Juanita insisted,
by inheritance from their ancestors, I was at a loss to
discover.

The poor girl had no more to tell, that was evident.
She was beautiful, intelligent, and highly gifted beyond
any one that I have ever met amongst her class.
Transplanted into a fairer soil, she might have graced
the royalty of a nation instead of a tribe of vagabonds;
but she was a Zingara, and the laws of fate which bound
her to her destiny were as absolute as those which had
set the ineffaceable mark upon the first fratricide. During
the fortnight we spent amongst her people, I learned
one *trait* concerning them which merits more consideration than is usually allotted to it. The gypsies, as a
race, are everywhere acknowledged to be irrepressible
thieves, and their approach in any neighborhood has
proverbially been recognized as the signal for drawing
bolts and bars against their inroads. Some of their
biographers have even gone so far as to assert that
they live entirely by plunder, and that their assumption
of practising itinerant trades and fortune-telling, are
only so many pretences to facilitate their access to

the houses or pockets of the wealthy. Whilst emphatically disclaiming the character of an apologist for this distinguishing feature of gypsy life, I must be allowed to urge that the people in their innermost natures regard themselves as Ishmaelites, and the whole human family as their natural enemies. They conceive themselves to be in some way outcast from their nation, land, inheritance, or place amongst men. Regarding mankind ever as their oppressors, they deem they are as much justified in plundering from the rich and highly favored of earth, as God's chosen people of old deemed themselves righteously employed in spoiling the Egyptians. I learned this questionable piece of morality through the unlimited confidence reposed in me by the fair Juanita, who was better informed of her people's secret opinions and idiosyncrasies than any one of her generation perhaps. I learned, also, that whilst they dared not openly avow these opinions, they were in reality unquestioned articles of faith with them, as much so as gratitude is towards those who favor or oblige them.

I have been repeatedly assured that the smallest article of property belonging to any person or persons who treated them well was as safe and exempt from spoliation, though it lay in their path, as if it had been guarded by bolts and bars. "Our honor and gratitude are the best bolts and bars mankind can use with the gypsy folk," said one of their old patriarchs, in enlarging upon this subject; and in truth they gave us a practical proof of their good faith, for though Professor von Marx and I had brought with us some few toilet appendages of value, and left these, like our money, wholly unguarded in our tents, often scattering small coin amongst the children with tempting profusion, we never found a single article touched or a penny abstracted; more than this, we had occasion to send several times to the servant we had left at our inn, and though the external appearance of some of our messengers would have furnished a ready passport to any jail in the land, and our groom, according to order, frequently left them in tempting situations for petty plunder, we never found them fail in the strictest fidelity to their trust, or guilty of committing the slightest act of peculation whilst thus engaged in a confidential capacity.

I have already said we had commenced our residence in the encampment upon certain conditions, and I am bound to add that during the whole period of our stay, the neighborhood enjoyed complete exemption from the ordinary predatory habits of the gypsies, as a strict furlough was observed, and not one foraging party of an illegal nature issued from our peaceful ranks.

The evening at length arrived when our Gypsy life was to terminate.

The Zingari were instinctively aware of this, although we had made no formal announcement of the fact. Our groom was ordered to be in waiting with the horses at a short distance, and old and young, from the cooking crones to the crowing babies, hung around us with a half-respectful, half-sorrowful fondness, which showed what a depth of human kindness still lingered in those outcast hearts, and how readily noble instincts and gentle sentiments might be enkindled in the rudest natures under appropriate influences. When all was done, many mutual kindnesses exchanged, and many slight presents forced upon the youngest and oldest of the tribe, the hardest task of all — at least for me — still remained. No word of our intention to depart immediately, had been spoken to the fair queen, whose stately form I silently pointed out to Professor von Marx as she lingered by the river-side, some half mile distant from us, gathering the wild flowers with which she had been accustomed to adorn my tent. " Well, what of her? " asked the professor, brusquely. Somewhat confused by this direct question, I ventured to suggest, in a low voice, that it might be as well to take advantage of her preoccupation, and depart without further leave-taking.

" What!" cried my master, with an unusual burst of merriment, — " steal a march upon our gypsy queen in the fashion of deserters, Louis? Shame upon you for so recreant a proposal! No, no; that will never do. Besides, Juanita is too much of a sibyl not to know that the hour has come when she can sing her siren songs no longer in the ears of her young Telemachus. But fear not, craven cavalier as you are! The gypsy queen will speed our departure, not oppose it."

" I think not," I answered, with some hesitation. " But why this haste, father? Could we not wait till to-morrow? "

" To-morrow!" rejoined the professor, sternly. " To-morrow may be too late. We have lingered too long already. Know you not that this Juanita is the peerless beauty of her tribe, and that there is not an unmated youth in the gypsy universe who does not look to her with some vague foreshadowing that he may yet secure her as his especial prize? Come away, foolish boy, and that right speedily, unless you calculate to live, with a dozen bullets in your body from the rifles of as many vagabond rivals."

" The bullet is not yet forged, my father, that can harm my life. My hour is not come."

" Trust not too much to destiny, Louis. These half-and-half savages know you bear a charmed life, but

they are not altogether unacquainted with the arts of
'Gramarie.'*   Do you know that some amongst them
have been melting up the silver we have been so lavish
in dispensing, and forming bullets with it? and do you
know what silver bullets are used for in the black art?

"To destroy those whose lives are deemed invincible
with baser missiles," I replied, carelessly.   "I have no
fear; but how did you learn there was such a murderous plot on foot, father?"

"Oh, by using my eyes and ears, and listening to
the voice of a certain little bird called *reason.*   But
come! we lose time.   I give you one half hour to make
your *adieux,* — and then for a swift horse and a midnight ride!"

A few minutes more and I was by the side of Juanita, of whom, during this conversation I had never lost
sight, as she gathered flowers by the river half a mile
off.   No one had been near her nor did she change her
attitude until I reached her, when, stooping to address
her as she sat on a mossy stone, she murmured in her
sweet, sad tone, "Juanita *will sing no more siren
songs in the ear of Star-beam.   The hour has come when
he must go, and the gypsy queen will speed his departure,
not oppose it.*"   The professor's very words! but how
on earth could she have heard them at half a mile's
distance?   Then raising herself from the ground and
slowly turning to gaze on the figure of my master, who
still stood on the hillside and in plain view, she said,
with a stern pride peculiar to her lofty moods, "O cold-
hearted, insolent man of the world! Dost thou then
think that the gypsy would turn to sting the hand that
has fostered him? Dost thou know the wanderer so
little as to deem that under the shadow of his own tent

* Magical art, or sorcery.

he would murder, in treachery and cold blood, the guest he has broken bread with?"

"How is this, Juanita?" I said, gravely. "Do you then know that I am in danger from some of your people, and yet you have not warned me of it?"

"Danger!" cried the girl, fixing her full, fearless eyes upon me, with an indescribable expression of mingled tenderness and reproach. "You, senor, in danger? Know you not," she added, sinking her voice again almost to a whisper, "*that you bear a charmed life, and that the bullet is not yet forged which can harm you? Your hour is not come.* Nevertheless I am not unmindful of what is around us; but oh!" she cried, her voice raised to a pitch of enthusiasm and her cheek deepening to the richest crimson, "Juanita has thrown around her Star-beam a spell from which every danger will fall away, and every bullet will turn back harmless, save to him who speeds it against thee. My people may pursue the sunbeams that have dazzled their poor eyes, accustomed only to look upon the humble light of the glow-worm; they may, with insensate envy of a beauty and nobility they can never attain to, hunt for thee after thou hast left behind, the boundaries which even our rude hospitalities make sacred and which would shelter thee from harm, shouldst thou stay amongst us forever: but my spell extends farther than that,—farther than the bullets of envy can ever reach; and thou mayst go on thy way harmless forever from any wrong that Juanita or her people can work thee."

Poor Juanita! I left her with a path in life to tread the more lonely and desolate, because the sun had shone across it, for once, all too brightly; a destiny the more unendurable because glimpses of a better lot had flashed like streaks of lightning before the eyes that would look on their brightness no more.

Three days after we had quitted the gypsy encampment a strange accident befel us. We were wandering on the shores of a beautiful lake, and had halted to rest beneath the shelter of an overhanging precipice, where rugged projections shielded us from the afternoon sun. Just as we had placed ourselves in reclining position against the rocks, an immense mass from the portion above and beyond our heads, was suddenly dislodged, and fell with a tremendous crash on the pebbly shore, burying itself with enormous force to a considerable depth in the loose ground at our very feet, and enclosing us in a narrow chasm between itself and the rocks against which we leaned. Simultaneously with this astounding descent, a shower of bullets was launched against us, which, being intercepted by the descending mass, dashed upon it in every direction. At the same moment the discharge of several rifles rang in our ears.

The whole of these motions were so coincident one with the other that for some time we were unable to separate and arrange each in its proper order. When we had succeeded in extricating ourselves from our newly formed prison and took note of the different points of our situation, we found the following series of striking coincidences. The rock above us had no doubt been long upheld in a very threatening position. Had we not retreated beneath the alcove to which it formed a sort of roof, at a certain moment, it must have crushed us to death, as we should then infallibly have been standing in the immediate line of its descent. There in fact, we had remained up to the minute before it fell, when the inviting character of the nook induced us to retreat within its pleasant shade. Yet again, it was evident from a comparison of the rifle-sounds that we had heard, and the shower of bullets that beat against the descending rock, that but for that friendly catastrophe, the said bullets would have found their lodgment in our recumbent forms. That they were aimed against us was unmistakable from the fact that nothing but the intervening rock separated them from us, and their flight could only have been directed at the same instant, or possibly one second earlier than the fall of the rock, seeing that the bullets reached its sides and surface at the same moment that it touched the sand.

"The bullets were evidently aimed by the hands of assassins, Louis," said my master, after carefully inspecting the whole scene.

"And the rock thrown down by those of our guardian angels," I added.

"Or the 'atmospheric spirit' of the fair gypsy queen, perchance," said the professor, smiling; "for see! here are the traces of her subjects' work," gathering up and showing me a handful of the flattened bullets, which were made of pure silver.

"You see, father," I remarked; "we bear charmed lives."

"Even so," answered the professor, gravely; "but it may be as well in future, to avoid visiting powder magazines with lighted torches in our hands."

CHAPTER IX.

THE LETTER.—THE LIFE TRANSFER.

TIME sped on, oh, how swiftly! The changing seasons with all their succession of varied beauty, alone reminded us how protracted had been our intended holiday, and how weeks had lengthened into months since we had determined to live—for a brief period at least—for ourselves alone and revel in scenes of enjoyment which we each secretly believed were means of restoration to the health and well-being of the other.

I love to recall these wanderings, for they constituted the happiest period of my life, and they form, even now, the oasis in a stormy·wilderness, around which the most cherished memories linger.

Nature was to me an ever new, ever wonderful page of revelation. At the wave of my powerful master's hand, my external senses would become closed, suffering my liberated soul to go free and my spiritual senses to explore that wonderful arcanum of life locked up in forms, colors, odors, and sounds, of which the external world gives but the faintest reflected shadow. With clairvoyant perception I beheld on every side, the myriad tongues of many-colored fire which played around or shot up from rocks, stones, gems, crystals, shells, grasses, flowers,— in short, from every form of mineral or vegetable life. Under the wondrous achromatic glass of spiritual sight, the life of the·universe became revealed to me, and I found there was not a blade of grass or a sand grain, any more than a crawling worm or mighty man, that was not vitalized by an element which to the sense of sight resembled flame, and which in operation was life, with its varied graduations of power, eliminating motion and vital heat. How gloriously beautiful creation appeared to me under the transfigurating light of clairvoyance! I ceased to wonder that the ancient seer was a fire-worshipper, beholding in all luminous bodies the deific principle, and in the sun, as the centre of life, light, and heat, the god of earth, to which his knowledge of the universe was limited.

In addition to the marvellous powers of discernment which clairvoyant sight afforded me, I also realized special faculties of perception through the spiritual senses of touch and smell. Every thing in being I found to be endowed with an individual character of its own, and it soon became apparent to me that, either by sight, smell, or touch, the human soul could come into contact with the soul of things, and thus recognize its special individuality. As sound could only be produced by the collision of two bodies in space, so the sense of hearing afforded a mixed revelation of two or more characteristics; hence I observed that sound represented the harmonious relations of things to each other; sight, smell, or touch, the individual character of the thing itself, and its grade in the scale of creation.

I could at that time have readily made charts in which the universe of created forms, organic and inorganic, each in its place in the scale of being, could have been ranged under their distinctive shades of color, their corresponding odors, and the density or rarity of each substance as defined by touch. Let me add that touch, like sound, was often composite in its impressions, all things in creation being so liable to come into contact, and all things that collide leaving upon each other an appreciable taint of each one's peculiar qualities. It is thus that the psychometrist is able to realize so correctly the characteristics which have surrounded or come into contact with any object under examination. The airs which sweep over the face of the rock, charge it with the characteristics of all the elements that are in the atmosphere, but organic life, and human life in particular, as the highest, most potential, and comprehensive of all elements, inheres most powerfully to the inanimate objects it comes in contact with; hence, after some weeks devoted to the culture of my sense of touch, I found I could correctly analyze the characteristics of every human being that had recently passed through any room or scene I chose to examine, determine to a certainty the mental, moral, and physical status of any individual whose glove, handkerchief, etc., was presented to me, in a word, "psychometrize" all things in nature, and by the sense of touch alone realize their hidden qualities or most secret potencies.

I cannot commend these occult studies to any one in pursuit of happiness or contentment. The knowledge I enjoyed was often ecstatic, wonderful, startling, and suggestive; but where it concerned the revelation of human character, and dug up from the mine of inner consciousness the secrets which were wisely hidden from ordinary view, the revelation was nearly always painful, serving to expose to my wounded sight, petty meannesses and interior stains, which lowered human nature in my eyes and rendered me so painfully sensitive to the spheres and atmospheres of every place I entered that I was

obliged to put a strong guard upon myself, ere I could
endure the revelations which public rooms, conveyances,
or streets impressed me with. Yet in the midst of the
pain, sorrow, and isolation which these revealments
brought me, there were hours of unspeakable recompense. I often beheld such sweet stores of natural
beauty and goodness hid away under unlovely exteriors
that whilst I was on the one hand, shocked and dis-
couraged, I would be on the other transported with the
discovery of the brightest mental gems.

It was this interior perception which made me admire,
yet resolute to shrink away from the poor gypsy girl. It
was this which one day wafted to my sense of smell such
a perfume as is exhaled from a bed of the choicest clove
carnations. Looking about me to discover in what human
form this glorious emanation originated, one which my
interior perceptions assured me must proceed from a
generous and unselfish nature, I traced its source to
a poor, old, threadbare street-porter, who stood waiting
for employment at the corner of the square I was passing through, and whose appearance was about as un-
attractive as any which the motley city could have
offered. Determined to verify or dissipate my fancy,
if such it was, I entered into conversation with this
person, and subsequently made many inquiries concerning him. Generosity, benevolence, and unselfish-
ness were the characteristics wafted to my spiritual
sense from this poor bundle of rags and wretchedness.
Take the following description rendered me of this
old man by a tradesman of the neighborhood who knew
him well.

"You would scarcely believe, sir, that yon forlorn
old man was once *a gentleman,* and quite wealthy. He
had a large family of extravagant sons and nephews,

upon whom he spent his means so liberally that he reduced himself to abject poverty on their account. He was so good to the poor, too, sir, — ay, and he is so still, — that when he gets a shilling he can not keep it. He runs errands now for many a gentleman who has sat at his table, and who would provide better for him if he did not lavish all that is given him on others. He should not be in rags, for he often has decent clothes given him, but he will strip them off his back to give to a poor neighbor, and go in rags that he may still help his dissipated and profligate family."

How many sweet airs from the unknown paradises of the human soul have swept across my spiritual senses in this manner, bringing to light hidden virtues the world knows not of, and — alas for the *per contra!* — how many foul and noisome exhalations have warned me from the sphere of perfumed fops and jewelled dames, whose attractive exteriors concealed the rank weeds of vice and base passions! I have met in my career with several persons who partook of this faculty of discovering character by the sense of smell, — one dear friend in particular, who suffered so keenly from the involuntary revelations this subtile gift occasioned, that she besought her spirit guides to quench the power, and remove from her a source of interior perception that rendered her daily intercourse with her fellow-mortals at times unendurable.

When we are known for what *we are*, not for what *we seem*, in the realm of spiritual truth and revelation, we shall find the number of every living creature, and in that mysterious figure we shall discover the peculiar color, sound, smell, and touch which appertains to each, and recognize that all and each are revelations which contain the whole in the part; also we shall learn that the color of the odic light which lingers in the photosphere of every human being, the perfume which the soul exhales, the mystery of the impression conveyed by the touch of the hand, and the tone which vibrates through the air in which we move or breathe, are all exact revelations of what we are and who we are; that all these things are known to the angels, and can measurably be felt, if not clearly defined, by every sensitive whose spiritual perceptions are more or less unfolded.

Oh, wondrous revelation, world of fairy lore, angelic teaching, heavenly inspiration! How blest and happy I was when living in this unseen realm, — this universe of shining truths and spiritual entities! Will these pages ever fall beneath the piercing eye of spiritual lucidity? If so, it will discover how I fence about the dividing line which separates me from this period of unmixed happiness and the bitter, bitter to-morrow that awaited me. One there is who will read these lines understandingly, and to her deep, pitying sympathies I appeal, with the agonizing cry of "Not yet! not yet! Let me linger a while ere the flaming sword drives me forth from the paradise of my vanished youth and early gleams of life-rest."

Wandering with my much-loved father in woody dell or over moorland wastes, sometimes encamping for the livelong night beneath the canopy of glittering stars and solemn, queenly moon, within the shelter of some ruined fane, through whose green, ivy-mantled towers and sculptured arches the celestial lamps looked in with soft and holy lustre; sometimes reposing on grassy banks in deep communion with the soul of Nature, or stretched on yellow sands beneath the beetling rocks that overhung the ever-sounding sea, we lived for a few brief months on earth, yet not of it. Sometimes we sat for hours, our open books unnoticed, listening in deep, abstracted mood to the tinkling stream or hoarse cascade, but ever recognizing in every sound, in every voice of Nature, from the sighing breeze to the crashing thunder-peal, the story of creation sung by unseen intelligence.

Happy days, and hours of divine entrancement! How I love to roll the misty veil of fading memory back, and gaze again on your sunlit pictures, the bright realities of which are fled, all fled forever!

Professor von Marx had been summoned to London on business, and as he did not expect to be absent more than a few days it was agreed that I should remain in our quiet north-country inn, from whence we had projected a tour into Wales. I insisted that he should take with him our only attendant, and leave me to the enjoyment of that deep, undisturbed repose which I prophetically felt was to be the last moment of hush and stillness I should ever know again on earth.

A few days after his departure my dear father wrote me word that he wished me to join him in London, as he was likely to be detained longer than he had anticipated, and could not endure to have me absent from him. I was staying at a very remote village, distant many miles from the railroad, which there was no means of reaching except by a stage or private conveyance.

Having secured my place in a coach which was to leave at night and connect with the train which started for London the next morning, I proceeded to beguile the hours that must intervene before I could leave, by a final ramble in the beautiful scenery of the neighborhood.

Towards evening, some three hours before that fixed for my departure, I sat down on the banks of a winding stream, broken by rapids and miniature cascades, to watch the glory of the approaching sunset.

On the opposite side of the river was a high bluff of rocks which shut out the land view in that direction, but away to the west, hill and plain, valley and moorland, were beginning to be bathed in a flood of crimson and purple radiance reflected from the glowing sky. Whilst my whole soul was imbued with the soothing tranquillity of this lovely scene, there suddenly crept over me a shuddering chill, an indefinable sense of dread, which completely obscured the surrounding landscape and impressed me with sensations of unaccountable fear and loneliness.

I closed my eyes and leaned back against the trunk of the tree beneath which I was sitting, when a whirr as of rushing wings sounded in the air, and the *hag* whom I had so often beheld as the precursor of evil tidings, flashed before my eyes, and with a mocking, gibing expression, terrible, hateful, fearful to behold, swooped close against my face, and then as suddenly swept on and was gone. In a few moments this well-accustomed yet ever-terrible apparition was succeeded by a thought which pressed upon me with overpowering urgency. *The letter* which Professor von Marx had given me some months before, seemed to rise up to my mind in a form so vivid that the impulse became irresistible to draw it forth from the lining of my vest, where I had placed it for special safety, and, holding it in my hand, turn it over and over again, with a sentiment of deep and newly-born interest. At this moment it seemed to me that I heard a chorus of voices in every imaginable tone, crying, "Read your letter! Read — your — letter — letter! Read! Read! Read!" I knew it was imagination, and yet those voices sounded very real in my ears. Some of them were hoarse and rough, others shrill and piercing, faint, near, distant yet close.

I was under the influence of a spell, and determined I would break it. I was about to replace the letter in my vest when, in the midst of those weird voices so uncertain in their origin, one I never could mistake, one whose tones were the echo of my life's deepest meaning, even the voice of my dear adopted father, repeated my name, calling to me evidently from the high bluff on the opposite side of the river.

Raising my eyes in amazement to this point of view, and in answer to his again reiterated sharp cry of "Louis, Louis! Look up!" I beheld Professor von Marx standing on the very edge of the rock, and leaning over its rugged sides towards me. In equal astonishment and delight I responded, "Dearest father! is that you? Have you then come to fetch me?" Then rising hurriedly I looked about to see in what part of the narrow river I could find a ford so as to cross and join him, but again I was arrested by the voice of the professor distinctly pronouncing these words: "*Open and read your letter! The voice most authoritative to you on earth commands you. At once! Now!*"

With such a quick, imperative wave of the hand as I had never disobeyed, the professor turned away, and I saw his retreating form pass over the heights and melt away into the gray horizon. Perceiving that he was going around the hill in order to cross the river at a rustic bridge some half a mile below the spot where I then stood, and would soon join me, I, who had never yet questioned or resisted the commands of that potential voice, resumed my seat against the tree, and opening the letter read the contents, which were as follows: —

"It is now some months, my Louis, since the vague, unsatisfactory character of the researches to which I have devoted my span of life have begun to pall upon me, and

strike like ice-bolts into my tired spirit, freezing up its
energies and palsying its powers. The realm of being
which alone responds to my piercing inquisition is too
embryotic, and too far beneath the perfected intelligence
of man, to feed his yearning aspirations or furnish his
higher nature with healthful communion. Dragged down
to merely rudimental states, and groping amidst the chaotic spheres of twilight intelligence, I am weary, life-
sick, baffled! When I would reach higher and ascend
beyond myself, my soul only stretches away into the ocean
of the unfathomable, where I find no compass to steer by,
no pilot to guide me, and whether I stand in the gray mists
of a coming morning, whose sunny light shall yet dispel
all mystery, or linger on the edge of a vanishing day,
whose evening shades will deepen into a rayless, never-
ending night, I know not. I wander on in the midst of fog
banks which skirt a shoreless sea, and the future has now
become for me a problem too urgent and too terrible to
wait for longer. I must solve it or perish eternally. But
whilst my soul trembles on the verge of the unknown, the
sharpest pang it feels is not for myself but for you, child
of my love, being upon whom my all of heart-love or
human affection is anchored! For you, darling companion, whom I have led into the same unfathomable abyss
of mystery and unrest which destroys my own peace and
almost wrecks my senses. To think that I have guided
your young feet into the wild and awful solitudes of unlighted gloom in which I am lost myself is now my bit-
terest thought, my keenest pang of self-reproach. But
Louis, spark of sunlight! the only one that now sheds
warmth or light upon a starved and imprisoned nature,
to you at least, I can and will make reparation. Even
whilst I write I know that the end is for me fast approaching. Louis, I am dying; and whether death be

the sleep that knows no waking, no return, the worm of
slow decay, or something I cannot comprehend of continued life and consciousness, know it soon I MUST and
WILL.   Think not I shall hasten the time of this tremendous unfoldment by the coward's act of rushing from
this life, or shaking off the mortal coil so hard to bear.
No, I scorn self-murder, nor will I commit any act of
rash impatience.

"In one sense alone can I speed the great *dénouement*,
and that is in acting out to you my intended reparation.
Louis, I WILL GIVE MY LIFE TO YOU.   I am now engaged in constantly projecting, by the power of my will,
the life and force by which I am, in magnetic tides upon
you.

"I know it is in the power of the adept to part with
these living waves and send them ebbing to the shores
of another's life at will.

"In this mysterious transfer *my life can become
yours*, my being can incorporate itself with yours, and
the effects will be seen and felt when I am gone, in the
increased power and prime of your noble manhood and
the enlarged capacity of your unfolded spiritual nature.
My strength shall supplement your gentleness; my powerful manhood shall uphold your dependent youth; my
commanding force shall inspire your attractive beauty;
and this great and wonderful work is on the very eve
of accomplishment.   The woof of destiny is nearly spun.
Day by day I keep the force of my will so exercised
upon you that you can not, shall not see the fading process of my life's transfer to you, or note how thin and
attenuated the cord becomes which binds the waning
spirit to the dying form.

"In the hour when the last process of transfer is to be
made my body will be far away from you.   I shall leave

you a while alone, so that your glance of tender pleading may not recall me to the life I loathe, or stay my fluttering spirit on the shores of the mystic ocean in whose silent waves it must sink forever or rise to swell thy young life's barque with the freight of my new-born soul and its resurrected powers.

"I shall leave thee during the process of the mighty wrench, my darling; then shall I gather up the broken threads of life, weave them into one mighty chain of purpose, and throw the last links around thy neck, my Louis, to anchor there my liberated soul. Louis, I die that you may live. To you I give the fires of parting life, to you dispense the spirit's mystic breathings. If I live again, or the essence of my soul is not all dissipated into viewless ether, it will be *as a part of you.* I will my life to you, whilst yet I can send it forth in living fires to illuminate the temple of your spirit. I will to you whatever may be left of the smouldering flame when the breath of the destroyer shall have put it out for me. Perchance that dying flame may yet retain some spark of consciousness, which, added to your own, shall vitalize your frame, give double manhood to your character, clear from your spirit's eyes the scales of earth, lift up your soul to loftier heights than mortal ever reached before, and raise you above those grovelling elementary spheres in which we have been doomed to wander, to the shining realms of sunlike nature, in which the cause of causes must inhere. On earth farewell, my loved one! When these lines have met thine eyes thy father will be no more. Either thy soul and mine must be united in the mystic bonds of a dual life, or else the fires of mine will be extinguished in eternal darkness. One with thee or nothing!

"FELIX VON MARX."

The letter dropped from my palsied hand.   Grief, fear, doubt, and confusion filled my distracted brain.

The sudden perception of my beloved friend's failing health, that glimpse of his real condition which a moment of abstraction on his part had permitted me to catch when we were last in London, that glimpse of a possibility too dreadful for me even to dwell upon, yet that which had induced me to urge this country tour, — all this recurred to my mind like a torrent overleaping its barriers and rushing in upon an overwhelmed plain with resistless force.   At length stole over me the stupendous reality that this beloved friend, this more than father, *the master of my life and being,* was no more. By this time, even at the moment when I held that awful letter in my hand, he must be dead, — or rather *gone,* gone for ever! and oh, for what cause!   Dead that I might live!   What new and horrible mystery was involved in this confused and wild idea of a life transfer? At another time this one thought alone would have swallowed up all others, and compelled me to turn upon myself with loathing and aversion, — living whilst he was dead! living because he was dead! — but now all my visions of the occult were swallowed up in the one tremendous reality of my irreparable loss.   Struck, stunned, helpless as I felt, I buried my face in my hands, cast myself frantically down on the grass, and gave vent to the anguish of a breaking heart in choking sobs and scalding tears.   In the midst of my frenzied grief it was no surprise to me to feel a gentle touch on my shoulder and a caressing arm thrown round my neck.   The capacity for new emotion was dead within me, and the heavens might have been shaken down to earth without awakening one sentiment of surprise or adding to the intensity of my feelings.   Yet I heard again *his* voice, the voice dearest to me in creation; I felt again *his* touch, the touch of those lips through which my own life breathings seemed to have exhaled. That touch was surely on my cheek, and I heard him murmur in such accents as recalled his hours of deepest tenderness, " One with thee forever! Weep no more, my Louis. There is no death!" Mechanically I raised my streaming eyes to gaze upon the speaker. A flash, a radiant stream of light, the vision of those dark, lustrous eyes fixed for a second only on me, looking into my soul; then a radiant fire-mist seemed to hover round me; a blazing star shot up from the earth on which I knelt, sped meteor-like through the sunlit air, paling the glory of the western sky, then vanished in the heavens and left me — alone!

Upspringing from the cold, dark earth, the sunlight gone, and a rayless night now closing fast around me, I sped to our empty cottage. I knew he was not there. He had not been there,—I knew that, too. He would never come again, there or anywhere.

A moment's pause to think out where I was, and then I was on the road to London. Oh, that weary road, that endless night, and the next long, weary day! Changes there were to make and hours to be sped away,— oh! would they never end?

Somewhere upon that endless desert road I left my youth and boyhood, — left them behind forever, and as once more I entered gray old London, I returned a man, matured in a few short hours of anguish into untimely manhood.

The streets were cold and empty, the night had begun to fall, and the dim, pale lights served only, as it seemed, to show me what a strange and sickening void had overspread the once gay city.

I made my way to what had once been our home, but the familiar faces of the domestics who admitted me had grown strange and altered in my eyes. I asked no questions, spoke no words, and none addressed me. I think now, though I scarcely knew it then, that some one said, in a low and pitying tone, "It is the poor young Chevalier. How could he have known it?"

Mechanically I ran up the stairs, stood before the door of our common sitting-room, and turned the lock; but I retreated without entering, for I knew *he* was not there. I moved on to another door, and now with throbbing heart and finger pressed on my hushed lip, softly, softly I trod. Stealthily I entered,—entered like one who feared to disturb a sleeper. I knew my step would never wake him more: he slept the sleep that knows no waking. Something like a prayer stole through my bewildered brain, "Would God I were sleeping with him!" Professor von Marx was dead. He lay all cold and white, with burning lamps at the marble brow and stirless feet, pale white flowers on the paler hands, and a frozen stillness everywhere. Professor von Marx was dead; and yet a still small voice, in the well-remembered accents of the speechless dead, rung through the hush and gloom of that solemn place, and seemed to murmur, "One with thee forever! Weep no more, my Louis. There is no death!"

CHAPTER X.

THERE is an instrument whose manifold uses few of earth's children really appreciate until they are compelled by necessity to use it. Should the gardener desire to open the earth for the reception of the precious seed, he takes this instrument to break apart the stubborn clods withal; when the plant he sows has grown to be a stem, he uses it to prune the branching shoots and trailing tendrils. The mineralogist applies it to sever the rough quartz from the pure gold or shape the precious gem. The reaper uses it to cut his sheaves; the housewife to slice her bread; the butcher to prepare his meat; the cook to carve it; the surgeon uses it to cut, to probe, to amputate, to cure; the assassin uses it only to kill: and thus from a single blade of steel all of life's uses for good or ill may be evolved; nay more; these multitudinous uses can not be performed without it, and though in one single instance it may kill in the hands of crime, the knife that prunes and trims, dissects and amputates, and ministers to every form of art and science, may surely be esteemed as very good, even if its name is "sorrow." And yet it takes a life of many bitter trials to realize the manifold uses of this same keen knife, sorrow! I know this lesson now, though it has cost me many a year to learn it. I did not know it as I sat, a helpless, lonely being, more than a child in years, but far less than a man in self-reliance, beside the silent, rigid form of him that had been my idol, my very life, my more than self, the inspiration that had made me — anything! I had been in the presence of death many times before, and despite all the lessons of the Brothers, tending to render me callous to the sight, it had always affected me painfully, depressing me physically, and filling my mind with a sense of blank mystery which derived no satisfaction from the doctrines of annihilation insisted on by my philosophic associates; but when the subject of these revulsive emotions was my more than father, O Heaven! as I look back now on the dumb anguish of that terrible hour, the hour I passed in such awful stillness and mystery with the best beloved of my life, I pity myself, and could almost weep for the miserable being, then too deeply sunk in despair to weep for himself. But at length that dreadful hour of silent watching ended; with its close, two fixed ideas took possession of my mind: the first was that Professor von Marx was no more, — utterly, irretrievably dead and gone, gone forever; the next, that I, too, must die, for life without him would not be wretchedness merely, to me it seemed an impossibility.

Accustomed to act upon rapid flashes of thought, the future with all its bearings seemed mapped out before me the moment I roused myself to quit the chamber of death. My spiritualistic readers may question why I did not derive hope and comfort from the vision which had, in the semblance and tones of my beloved friend himself, apprised me of his decease. I answer, I could not at that time derive either hope or consolation from such a visitation. Facts make their impression on the mind in proportion to its tendencies and receptivity for special ideas. My mind had been bent into materialistic forms of belief. I had been constantly censured for indulging in any of the "vagaries" of religious aspiration; taught to regard immortality as the attribute of the elements only, and the apparitions of the dead, like those of the living spirit, as magnetic emanations from the body, which might subsist for a brief period after death, but which could maintain no continuous being when once the body became broken up by the process of natural disintegration. Even the many flashes of wondrous light, irradiated as they were, too, with intelligence, which had appeared to me in the semblance of the beautiful Constance, I had been taught to regard as subjective images only, projections from my own fervid imagination, taking shape in the "astral light," where the impressions of all things that ever had been, remained imperishably fixed. This was my creed at the time when I silently stole down the stairs leading from the death-chamber, and passed out into the quiet street. It was deep night in London. A pale spring moon shone fitfully through the rifts and rents of a stormy sky. The air was chill and blighting, and my neglected attire was not calculated to protect me against the damp, chill winds which moaned around me. I was all alone on earth, for though dim memories of friends and kindred flitted through my mind, they were all shut out by the one engrossing thought of *him.* A vague idea possessed me that some one on earth might be sorry for my loss and miss me; but I could not centralize this idea on any one in particular, save on *him,* and he was gone.

Professor von Marx had succeded so far in filling up my whole being with himself that I perceived nothing real, nothing tangible in existence but his image; and now that he was no more, quenched, nothing,—what remained for me but to become, like himself, no more, quenched, nothing? With a rapidity truly astonishing to those who have not studied the philosophy of extraordinary mental states, I ran over the different methods by which I might arrive at the bitter end, but I rejected at once all that might incur, even for my worthless remains, publicity or curiosity. I would not be pitied or mouthed at, speculated over or talked about. In my utter desolation, I shrank even from the possibility of human sympathy or contact with pitying mortals when I was dead. I would hide away, die in secret, where none could find me. I finally determined I would starve myself to death, and thus gain time to see the world passing away and myself fading out of time before I was launched upon that ocean of oblivion, which had swallowed up my better self. One more thought of him I permitted my mind to indulge in ere I abandoned myself to my fate. Strange to say, that thought was not one of tenderness or regret: it was a sentiment of reproach, — reproach that one, to whose mighty will destiny itself seemed to bow down, should have thus forsaken me; or rather I inwardly questioned why he did not take me with him, — he who so loved me, he who alone of all mankind could understand me! It was but a few short weeks ago that, in his half-dreamy, half-satirical way, he had affected to predict for me a splendid destiny. "Young, rich, and handsome Louis!" he said. "Youth, wealth, and beauty, — are not these the conquering graces before which the world bows down?" Alas! alas! Did he even then contemplate casting me on the world, reliant on those adventitious aids to guide the stumbling feet that he had led so blindly? With what a strange mixture of anguish and bitterness did the memory of those cold, speculative words return to me now! Oh! did he know me then so little as to deem that any possessions could be aught to me when he was gone? Gone! Ay! that was the word that put all questioning to rest forever. On I sped, — past the quiet rows of houses and through the silent streets; on through miles of dreary suburbs, where the ugliness of waste places and half-built roads became softened in the gloom of midnight; on through lanes and fields, — I scarce knew where, yet by an instinct that seemed to propel my eager steps, I pursued my way until I had left the city and all its hateful wilderness of slumbering life behind, and penetrated to the woods that skirted the north of London. I believe I was traversing one of those suburban districts known as Hampstead or Highgate. I had been driven there some months before, and was greatly attracted by the beauty and retirement of those woody heights, which at the time I write of, nearly thirty years ago, were almost in the country.

I had no idea of the distance I must traverse to reach that spot, or the direction in which I should go, yet I wished to be there; and ere the deep pall of night yielded to the gray dawn of morning, I had attained my goal, and sinking on the ground beneath the shadow of a deep and almost pathless wood, I felt as if I had arrived at my last earthly home. Being unaccustomed to steady walking for any great distance, the excessive fatigue I had undergone, no less than the stunned condition which succeeded to the anguish of the preceding hours, induced a deep sleep, from which I did not awaken till the sun was high in the heavens, so high indeed, that I perceived the day must be far advanced.

Unlike most persons who awake from the first sleep that succeeds some mighty sorrow to a gradual consciousness of the truth, I awoke at once to the mental spot from which I had sunk to sleep. There might have been but one intervening second between the great agony with which I lay down and arose again, to take up the burden just where I had dropped it.

Instinctively noting the features of the place where I had sought shelter, I perceived it was not the deep retirement I desired to find. The woods were thick 'tis true, but they resembled more a grove of trees whose pleasant shade might attract suburban loungers to my retreat than a lonely spot where a hunted hare might die in peace. That was no place for me; and quick as the thought occurred, the action followed on it. I started from the ground and determined to make my way yet farther on, — on to a safer solitude, one where no wandering foot of man might track me. I arose stiff, weak, and weary. At first I could scarcely drag my tired limbs from the spot where I had lain; but as I moved, I gained elasticity of limb, and strengthened by my will and feverish purpose, I walked on for several hours, walked on in fact, till night again overtook me, I passed through many pleasant places, country roads, and shady lanes. I left behind me handsome villas, nestling cottages, and homes where happy people seemed to dwell, where children's voices and merry village tones resounded through the air. I passed them all, like a spectre as I was, shrinking from sight, sound, or companionship. The very echo of a human voice drove me away.

Some wretched tramps in fluttering rags, with lean and hungry faces, passed me on the road, and looked wistfully into my face. An old and white-haired man, with very threadbare clothes, was tottering on amongst them, and fixed on me a pleading glance. One human feeling still remained within my seared heart, prompting me to throw my purse amongst them. How glad they seemed! How I hastened on with wavering steps to escape from their noisy thanks! Did they know that the youth "so young, so rich, so handsome," looked upon them, so old, so poor, so hideous, in their rags and poverty, and sighed to think he was not one amongst them? Undoubtedly they belonged to each other. There were fathers, sons, and brothers there perhaps; friends at the least they must be. But who and what was I? Father, brother, friend, — all, all were gone for me.

On, on I sped, — on till night again overtook me. On the banks of a deep and sullen river I reached a thick and extensive wood. Pushing my way through the tangled underwood, a few steps brought me to a deep and rugged dell, whose gloomy depths seemed as if they had never been traversed by human feet. The solitude and utter desolation of this wild haunt were all I sought.

Here I would stop and wait for the destroyer. Another long, long night, but not as before a restful one. Aching in every limb and racked with feverish thirst, I spent that weary night in pain unutterable. The morning came, and with it a new and strange sensation. The gnawing pangs of hunger now beset me. It was two days and nights since I had tasted a morsel of food, and this sensation of racking hunger was something new and urgent. I knew it was a part of the programme, a scene in the drama I had set myself to enact; but I had not considered, for indeed I did not know, how painful it would prove.

As the sensation deepened, my spirit seemed to pass out in the old familiar way and take note of many distant scenes, but only of those where hungry people were.

13

I saw none but those who were hungry, because I suppose I was attracted to no others. I saw beggars, little children, old men and women; poor laborers who had nothing to eat, and would not have till a long day's work was done. All were hungry, sad, and sullen. I saw those English work-houses where the wretched inmates were always hungry, besides a great many little children who looked eagerly and longingly into the shops where provisions were kept. Many a little, emaciated, pale creature I saw crying for bread; and besides these, my unresting spirit seemed drawn as by a spell to the interior of wretched huts, up to roofless garrets, and down into noisome cellars, where miserable people lingered,—people of both sexes and all ages; but all were, like me, so very hungry! All of them had little or nothing to eat; and the multitudes I saw thus, seemed to me to be more in number than I had deemed of the whole human race. It was a ghastly yet wonderful sight this, and awful to know that in one vast, rich, and mighty city were hungry wretches enough to constitute a nation.

Presently I began to speculate upon the different effects which this one great pang produced on different people. Some of those whom I gazed upon were merely restless, then fretful, irritable, angry, sullen, savage: all these were stages in the great woe, but only the first stages. The next was a fierce, wild craving, and after that the natures of these hungry ones became wild and brutal, whilst all the nervous force of the system concentrated about the epigastrium, and then they were all hunger, just as I was all despair. Kindness, pity, shame, honesty, and virtue,—all were merged in the intolerable sense of urgent hunger; but this was an advanced stage of the pang, and was very terrible to witness.

The physiological conditions of these people too, were opened to my clairvoyant vision as I flitted amongst them, a phantom drawn to them by the irresistible ties of sympathy. Had I been at the ends of the earth, and there existed but one hungry creature at its centre, I should have been infallibly drawn to that one, so potential is the strength of spiritual sympathy. How strange, yet orderly and strictly natural, I found to be the routine which ensues in hungry systems! First there was the sense of demand, the want which a craving stomach makes known to the intelligence, for the sake of its own repair. Then came the mustering of the gastric and salivary juices, promoted by the thought of food. These secretions flowed in tidal currents to the salivary glands and gastric follicles, and if there was nothing to act upon, they began to dry up and become inflamed, and this it was that produced that gnawing sense of pain which attended the first stages of hunger, and communicated to the nerves an intense degree of irritability. In the next stage I perceived that the mucous membrane lining the digestive apparatus was in a measure consuming itself; also I saw how the entire force of the nervous system mustered to the point of suffering, and manifested sympathy with the epigastric regions.

Hour after hour I traced by involuntary but inevitable clairvoyance the entire progress of this ghastly phenomenon, want, acting upon hundreds, ay, thousands of victims in and about the happy, well-fed, rich, and splendid Babylon of the world, — London. I noticed as a curious fact in the physiological results of starvation that whilst the tissues of the body generally, wasted, dried, and consumed themselves, the nerves never wasted, never failed; on the contrary, their power of sensation grew more and more acute with every moment's bodily pang. Still more, I perceived that the ganglionic nerves which supplied the nutritive system attracted to its aid the force of the cerebro-spinal nerves, so that — mark it well! — there could be little or no other sensation than that which arose from the intolerable sense of hunger and thirst; and thus it was made plain to me why poor wretches under the influence of this sharp pang are rarely moral, kind, or gentle. The nervous force which should be distributed through the intellectual and emotional regions being all absorbed by the fierce cravings of the digestive system, there can be no operation for the affections, the reason, or the morals. And yet again let me pause and remark upon another singular and noteworthy revealment of these clairvoyant wanderings. I saw the entire chain of connection between the brain and every fibre of the body; noted how conclusively motion and sensation, waste and repair, were all represented on the brain, and I marvelled why no *brain metre* had as yet been invented, first as a means of detecting disease in remote parts of the system, and next as a gauge by which physical conditions could determine corresponding states of the mind. In the starving miserables from whom all the nervous force was abstracted from the brain to the stomach, there were no cranial nerves in operation, save the pneumagastric, and these acting upon the surrounding fibres in the cerebellum, necessarily prompted the appetite to revenge, destructiveness, acquisitiveness, and all the lower animal instincts.

Methought had I been destined to a continuous life, I should forevermore have felt the deepest sympathy for the poor and hungry. I pictured to myself how glad I should have been to have fed the ghastly multitudes

I saw, and how unreasonable it was for society to expect gentleness, piety, humility, and kindness, where the gaunt demons of want and poverty held their sway.

Would that every legislator in the lands of civilization could have shared the perceptions of my wandering spirit in those dreary hours of suffering! Surely one great change would ensue in the laws of nations, making it a crime in legislation to permit any human being in the realm to go hungry, whilst for any citizen to die of starvation should be a blot sufficient to expunge the land where it occurred from the list of civilized nationalities. I think it must have been towards the sixth or seventh day of my terrible probation that the character of my wanderings changed. I had lost count of time, and being racked by intolerable thirst, I thought I might assuage that dreadful craving, and yet not prolong much my hours of torture. I made out then, to stagger to the edge of the river, and by dipping boughs of trees into the water, and laying my burning head upon them or applying them to my lips, I found the fearful sense of thirst in some measure allayed. It was so soothing to bathe my hands thus in the cool river that I lay down very close to it, and but for fear some one might find and recognize the poor remains floating on its surface, gladly would I have made it my winding-sheet, and thus have ended the awful struggle at once. Firm to my proposed plan, however, I contented myself with the luxury of the dripping boughs, and when I found sleep overtaking me, I crept back again to the shelter of the secluded dell. I believe there were several heavy storms of rain and hail, drenching the ground and adding racking pains to my fast stiffening limbs, but my resolve never failed, though physical tortures began to increase upon me. A time came, however, when these terrible pangs became subdued, indeed at times I almost forgot them; besides, let me add, the sense of hunger I endured, unlike that which afflicted the poor, was voluntarily incurred. I bore my sufferings willingly, because I did so in the hope of release from still greater misery. The sentiments of rage, envy, indignation, and bitterness, which would add such additional anguish to the pains of hunger in the starving poor, were not present in my case; on the contrary, every pang that racked me was a response to my insatiate yearning to die and be at rest.

But I have said there came another change, and this it was. With the last minimum of my strength I had collected and surrounded myself with dripping boughs dragged through the cool river, and on these and my handkerchief, steeped in water and pressed to my parched lips, I laid myself down in the deepest recess of the wood I could find, to take my last, long sleep. Then it was that a sweet and restful sense of dying stole over me. Bright and wonderful visions too, gleamed before my eyes. In every department of being I saw the spirits of nature. With involuntary lucidity I gazed down into the earth beneath me, and beheld whole countries peopled with grotesque forms, half spiritual and half material, resembling in some respects the animal and human kingdom, but still they were all rudimental, embryotic, and only half formed. I saw the soul-world of earths, clays, metals, minerals, and plants. In those realms, were beings of all shapes, sizes, and degrees of intelligence, yet all were living and sentient. Everywhere gleamed the sparks of intelligence, the germs of soul, semi-spiritual natures, clothed with semi-material bodies corresponding to the varieties of the mineral, vegetable, and animal kingdoms, with all their infinite grades of being. Some of these spirits of nature were shining and beautiful, like the gems and metals; some coarse and unlovely, like the earths and roots; all were endowed with some special gift corresponding to the plane of being which they represented. In moistening my hands and face with the dripping boughs I seemed to be brought into rapport with the countless myriads of watery spirits, and throughout all departments of elemental life, recognized a sort of caricature representation of the births, deaths, kindreds, families, associations, and wars that pervaded the human family. Later on in time, though how long I never knew, I saw sweet and lovely lands filled with a sweet and lovely people mirrored in the shining air and nestling amidst the flowers and grasses; in fact the air became translucent to me. I saw immense realms filling up the spaces of our gross atmosphere, which were permeated with a wonderful number of countries, each formed of finer and more sublimated vapors, gases, aromal essences and ethers than the other. In some of these realms, the flowers, bloom, and essences of earth, became spiritual emanations, which crystallized into far rarer and more beautiful flowers, blossoms, and airs than any which earth could display.

The lower strata of these aërial regions were filled with very small, sometimes grotesque, but generally beautiful people. Some of them were no taller than the daisies and buttercups of the field, some were as high as the bushes, and some towered up to the tops of the forest trees. Most of them were fragrant, flower-loving, merry beings, whose incessant habit of singing, dancing, leaping, and sporting in the sunbeams, filled me with joy. Many of these were short-lived races bubbling up with the ecstacy of a life which began and ended with the power of the sunbeam; others lived long vegetable lives of many centuries, haunting the woods, groves, and forests, and seemed especially interested in all that belonged to sylvan lives and pursuits. I again repeat that all these elementary tribes were divided off into different strata of atmosphere, or inhabited different parts of earth, filling every space from the centre to the circumference, where new planetary existences commenced. All were endowed with varying degrees of intelligence, special gifts, powers, and graduated tones of life and purpose, and all appeared to me first as a spark, spear, tongue, or globe of light, pale, ruddy, blue, violet, or of different shades of the primal hues, and all at length assumed the forms of pigmies, giants, plants, animals, or embryotic men, according to the particular grade they occupied in the scale of creation, or the tribe, species, and kingdom to which they corresponded.

I learned many, many things of the immensity and variety of being which seem either impossible to translate into human speech or which " are not lawful to utter." I perceived that HEAT WAS LIFE, FLAME ITS SUBSTANCE, AND LIGHT ITS MANIFESTATION. I mused upon the contending theories of the philosophers concerning the sources of light and heat, and I know now, though perchance I might never be able to prove my knowledge, that the true source of light and heat were in the *life* and restless motion of the living beings that pervade the universe. The thought struck me, reflected from the teachings of conventionalism, that the sun must be the source of all the light and heat that permeates the solar system. Directly the shadows of this opinion crossed my mind, my spirit was lifted up into the spheres of responsive truth, and lo! instantly the sun became revealed to me like an orb of molten gold. Oh, what a wonderful and glorious sight this world of ecstatic being presented to me! I beheld it full to repletion of swelling, glittering seas, rivers, fountains, lakes, and streams, all dancing in the radiance of many-colored illuminations from the internal element of molten light. I beheld forests, groves, hills, vales, high mountains, and unfathomable caves and dells, all crystallized out of living light, all imprisoning prismatic rays, not of one, but of countless shades of color.

The air, though translucent beyond our conception of the most attenuated ether, was still shimmering with the billions of glittering creatures that floated in it and disturbed its shining waves as they moved. Vast firmaments, spangled thick with suns and systems, swung over all, a crystal arch, in which immensity seemed to be outspread. From these glorious galaxies of worlds, countless meteors were being forever thrown off, sailing through space like chariots of fire.

The movements of the sunny worlds on high were plainly discerned too, and instead of a silent, moveless plain of stars, like that which overarched the earth, the wheeling, whirling stars were rushing on in their several orbits, shooting, darting, speeding round and round some vast and unknown centre, on a glorious scale of heavenly pyrotechnics which dazzled the straining eyes into wondering ecstacy. In lower air were sailing cars and airy ships, carrying the rejoicing people of these sunny realms from point to point in space, whilst some were floating by their own resistless wills, upheld by a perfect knowledge of the laws of locomotion and atmosphere. Thus they swam, sank, ascended and sustained themselves on waves of air like happy birds, and oh, what a gracious race, what a nobly-created form of life they revealed to me! Tall and elastic, sunny-haired, blue-eyed, with slender, majestic forms, vast, globe-like heads, and lovely, placid faces, all attired in robes of snowy white, azure, or sun hue. Their cities were full of trees, flowers, and spire-like towers, with glittering domes and minarets crowned with metallic ornaments. These cities were divided off by white, smooth roads and shady trees, and a wealth of flowers that made the senses ache to inhale their perfume. Vast palaces of art and science were there devoted to the study of the universe, not in *part*, but *all*.

.Thus these children of the sun comprehended fully music, rhythm, speech, motion, chemical, astronomical, and geological laws. In short every form of art or science was known and taught in these vast and gorgeous cities. Labor was rest and exercise; work was knowledge put in practice, and food was the simple gathering-in of rare and precious plants and herbs and fruits that grew by nature where the beings of nature might demand them. Oh, what a glory it was to live upon this happy, happy orb,—to be a child of the gracious sun! I thought by only looking on this radiant world all sorrow vanished, and its very memory could never come again.

Before the vision closed I perceived that for millions of miles in space, beyond the surface of the sun world, were glittering zones and belts of many-colored radiance, forming a hazy rainbow, a photosphere of sparkling fire-mist visible to the eye of spirit alone, all crowded up with lands and worlds and spheres peopled with happy angel spirits of the sun. But ah me! I veil my presumptuous eyes as I dream again of these heavenly regions, and thoughts, thoughts like scintillations from the mind of Deity, fill up my throbbing soul as the memory of this wondrous world of heaven and heavenly bliss recurs to me now. The awful glory vanished, and when the gorgeous panorama faded, I knew where the light of our poor, dull planet's day-beams came from. I saw that the magnetic oceans flowing from this radiant sun sphere, combining with our earthly magnetism, created by mutual saturation that freight of heat and light, motion, and all impon-derable force, the sum of which was LIFE. I saw that the light and heat and life which permeates all being, is evolved by galvanic action generated between the pho-tospheres of the parent mass, and circumferential satel-lites. Hence at those points which in the revolutions of time are turned from the central orb, no galvanic action is proceeding; the result is lack of action, lack of galvanic force, hence darkness, night. Life *per se* is motion, motion is light and heat. Light and heat are magnetism; and this causes the action and reaction ensuing between the negative photosphere of the earth, and the positive photosphere of the sun. This simple scheme, so like a schoolboy's lesson, pervades all the billions upon billions of marching and countermarching worlds, bodies in space, and all that in them is, in the boundless universe.

Recalled at length from these blinding, wildering vis-ions, by my own near approach to the mystic gate where human life ended, and all beyond was veiled to me in shadow land, the weary, dying body put in its claim for sympathy and thought, and I was about to make a last instinctive effort to drag myself again to the river's bank, when my attention was attracted by a strange, chiming sound, such an one as had often before warned me of a spiritual presence. This time however, I fancied I heard a peal of very distant bells, such bells as ring out from some great city in majestic strains of

joy and gladness; very distant, and subdued by distance to the sweetest tones, melting almost to echoes;
still they rang in my dull and heavy ear. Then came a
more distinct sound, like the rushing of mighty wings,
and then, though my eyes were closed, I could see
through their heavy lids, vast sheets of corruscating
light, darting like gigantic fans over the entire quarter
of the heavens which lay to the north.

At first I thought—if thought it could be called that
resembled a faint light streaming over a pathway where
the clouds of death were fast mustering—that a great
display of the splendid aurora borealis was illuminating the scene; but in a moment the light became collected from space around, and centred on a radiant figure
that stood before me, in size gigantic, in form like that
of a man, in substance a fleecy mass of fiery glory.
"I am Metron, the Spirit of the North," this being said,
speaking in the same chiming tone as the distant joy-
bells, "I am thy guardian spirit, chief of the Elemen-
tarics amongst whom thy soul hath roamed so long.
Thou hast not dreamed nor fancied what thou hast seen.
When all shall be revealed in the light of spiritual reality, matter shall prove to be the phantom, spirit the substance of creation. The visions of the body are dim,
uncertain, changeful; those of the soul are real, although
often broken and refracted through the prismatic hues
of matter. Thou hast drunk at the fountain of the real,
for the first time in thy life, alone and unaided by
another's will. A little while, another brief season of
probation ended, and thou must live and walk, learn and
know, by spirit teaching alone.

"I am he to whom the task of guiding thy spirit
through the first stages of the universe has been intrusted. Lean on me, beloved one; and now for a sea-

son, rest and sleep be thine! In the hours that shall be, when thou livest again and art thyself alone, call on me, thy guardian spirit, — and Metron, Spirit of the North, will ever answer."

Darkness, cold, death-damps, and deep, deep stillness succeeded. What do I last remember? Let me try and think.

A voice, sweeter, softer, tenderer far than Metron's, whispered in my ear, "Louis! my darling, suffering Louis! All will soon be over now, and then thy rest will come." .

Did I speak? Did I answer then? I know not. If I did the words must surely have been, " O Constance, let me die and be at rest forever! " *

---

* Nearly the whole of the foregoing and succeeding chapters were rendered into English by the author himself, and although submitted to the Editor for correction, have been left untouched, the Editor finding it difficult to modify the author's peculiar style of constructing sentences, without marring their intention. — ED. G. L.

CHAPTER XI.

On, to awaken free from pain, from care and toil, and sordid strife for bread! To feel no grief, no cold or heat, no thirst or hunger! nevermore to weep or know what sorrow is; to look on all life past as an empty dream, whose gloomy shadows can nevermore return! No more bereavement, bitter separations, injustice, cruelty, or wrong! No more heart-ache, not even a sob or sigh!

To feel no sense of weight or bonds to earth; to float or wing on high in air; to speed like the lightning's flash through space, or sail like a bird on the buoyant waves of ether! To see the dull, round globe far, far below, with its canopy of clouds and its creeping myriads, insect-like, swarming upon its surface, all left behind! To look up through happy tears and melting fire-mists to the spangled heavens, so dim to earth, so gorgeously bright to you! To feel kind hands about you, tender arms enfolding you, and hear the tones of well-remembered friends, long-lost, almost forgotten, whispering sweet words of welcome in your ear; to gaze around and see a brilliant, happy circle of loved and loving friends, companions, kindred, beckoning you home, home, home forever!

No more parting, no more death or sadness! Oh, to be there! On, on through upper air! On, on, still higher, beyond the night and darkness, beyond the stars! Up higher yet! up through soft airs and sweet perfumes, up to the realms of never-setting sunlight, up above mountain heights, where glittering domes and towers and palaces are flashing in bright, prismatic, many-colored rays, and spanned by a thousand arching rainbows.

To look down far, far beneath, and see white cities and long, bright roads, embowered in spicy groves and waving trees, and outstretched, flowery plains, all full of busy, happy, lovely beings, radiant with joy and life. Still to speed on, borne on in an airy car whose swift and rocking motion stirs the pulse, quickens the breath, and makes the wild heart leap for very gladness! On, till you reach the lovely, lovely land far higher than the highest thought can measure, far off in space, forever removed from earth and night and gloom; the land where home is, and home the spot you most desire to reach; the place you long for, wait for, where all you love wait for you. Oh, glorious ride! Oh, life of a thousand years pressed into one sweet hour! And such was my awakening, such my flight through space, such the rest a tired spirit and broken heart encountered. Vain would be the effort to speak of things and scenes and modes of life for which earth has no language, mortal being no parallel. Some few points alone of this better land I may describe in human speech. Let me recall them. Music! Every motion there has its own sound, and when vast numbers of tones combine in harmony, — and all is harmony there, no discord, — that combination forms music. Hence music is speech and sound; but when it is designed to represent ideas, recite a history, tell a tale, or explain the marvels of creation, masses of symphonic music are performed; and as each tone is in itself an idea, every separate tone has a special meaning, and the whole combined form a language in which the highest glories of the universe can be revealed. There is no music in heaven without a real meaning; hence the listener or performer finds in music volumes of ideas.

As I listened to the sweet yet awful symphonies that greeted me when I paused, all glowing with life and joy and love at my radiant home, I heard the song of life with all its deep, inner meaning. I heard and understood that poor, weak, trembling mortals are never out of the hands of creative wisdom. The tones of Nature sang of her eternal Author, Finisher; an all-sustaining, all-protecting Providence; told of his goodness, wisdom, power; instructed us to trust and lean on him; spoke of the grand design in suffering; the beauty, symmetry, and order of creation, when the finite being begins to understand the infinite. Home! Can I convey by that precious word any realization, however faint, of the rest and peace of a heavenly home? I fear me not. Home was the place where my loved ones clustered, to which all their divergent wanderings tended back again. Home was the place where all my special tastes found expression, where I might stay, rest, grow, exchange glad greetings with all who sought or loved me,—a place to think in until I grew ready for another advance. Every spirit has a home, a centre of love, rest, and ingathering of new powers and forces, a place where all one has loved, admired, most wished or longed for, takes shape, and becomes embodied in the soul's surroundings.

Sometimes the spirit gravitates, as mine did, to some lonely, church-like hall, a stately, silent place of inner rest and contemplation, and there the past resolved itself in shadowy pictures on the walls, and came and went like dissolving views, mapping out the minutest event or thought or word of my past earthly life, all which I found was fixed in the astral light, of which that temple was a Scripture page, forever. Oh, wonderful alchemy of spiritual existence! As I read again the panorama of my life, that ineffaceable record which every soul must read and read again, the past returned with its appropriate judgment. Many events which at their time of action I had felt regret for, even remorse, I now beheld as an inevitable sequence to other acts, stepping-stones, without which my life would have been incomplete. Deeds on which I had prided myself, now showed the littleness or petty egotism from which they sprang; sorrows which had wrung my spirit, appeared as blessings; and thoughts I had lamented once, I now perceived to have been effects inevitable. I saw and knew myself to be a chemical compound, made up of what I had been, or what had been done, said, and thought. All things appeared in judgment, and, stranger yet, all that I had, all that I possessed, enjoyed, or saw, nay, the very air I breathed, was tinctured by myself, and I saw, felt, heard, and enjoyed only, as my inner nature colored my surroundings. All things were real around me, but my capacity to know and use them sprang from my inner self. O Heaven, keep our earthly record fair, or woe betide us in the immutable procedures of the land of souls!

In another scene I may not fully speak of, I learned that our souls and all their faculties are magnetic tractors, drawing to themselves only such corresponding things and persons as assimilate with them. If the faculties are all engrossed by unselfish love, loving friends will answer. If the spirit reaches out for beauty, light, or special knowledge, the answer comes in kind, and sur-

11

rounds the soul with beings and associations kindred with its yearnings. Base passions, vicious habits, and criminal propensities find no responding satisfaction in spirit land. They are all outgrowths of earth and earthy things, and cast the soul down to those lower depths that permeate the earth and chain it to the scene of its affections. In spirit land, ideas are all incarnate, and become realities and living things. Nothing is lost in the universe. All that ever has been, can be, shall be, are garnered up in the ever-present laboratories of being. Glorious privilege it is to roam through the endless corridors of time, and still to find an eternity beyond to grow in! THE SPHERES! what may they mean? What mortal tongue or pen can fitly speak of them? IDEAS ARE SPHERES. There are ten thousand million spheres, all rounded into complete worlds, and all are the habitations of those who cherish the special idea which rules the sphere.

The spheres are not permanent, but the temporary homes of those who pass through them. They are the garners into which are gathered up the sheaves of earth, there to rest and gain experience, until they become distributed and amalgamated into the bread of eternal life. There are spheres of love, where tender natures cling to one another, until they are drawn by higher, broader aspirations, out into broader planes of thought. There are spheres of every shade of mental light, ideality, thought, and knowledge; spheres of special grades of goodness, intellect, and wisdom. In all and each is a special meed of happiness, but also in all and each are prevailing impulses to branch out farther, press on, and grow, so that every soul partaking of the special characteristics of every sphere in turn, may glean and gather in at last the good of all, and thus become a perfected spirit.

WORLDS IN SPACE, yes, worlds, — thousands, millions of them; world within world, the finer permeating the grosser, the grosser filling up the space of the still more dense, until at last I saw no finite lines, no end to the infinitely fine, the infinitely dense.

I saw the concentred scheme of the whole solar system with earth and its zones and belts of spirit spheres, countless in number, various in attribute. Myriads of rare and splendid beings sped through the spaces, piercing the grosser spheres invisibly to all but their own grade of being. Myriads of duller, grosser beings lived in these spheres, unconscious that they were permeated by radiant worlds, all thronged with glorious life, too fine for them to view. Each living creature was surrounded and enclosed by the atmosphere to which he belonged, and this restrained his vision to the special sphere in which he dwelt. Yet the finer realms of being could view at will the grosser; for now I found the secret of will: 'T IS KNOWLEDGE PUT INTO PRACTICE, and the knowledge of the highest is power, and power is will. Thus is supreme will resident alone with the Unknowable, the Being who knows all. In these spheres that so lock and interlace with another, I saw that the lowest and nearest earth were dull, coarse, barren spheres, dreary and unlovely, where dark and unlovely beings wandered to and fro, seeking the rest and satisfaction earth alone could give them. No homes were there, no flowers, no bloom, no friendly gatherings, no songs or music; the hard, cold natures of the wretched dwellers gave off no light, no beauty, harmony, or love; yet all felt impelled, *obliged* to toil. Toil was the genius of the place, yet whatever labors were performed, became instrumental in digging up the spirit, and breaking the clods of hard and wicked natures.

Every occupation seemed to come perforce and must
be done, yet all seemed destined to help re-make the
nature, open up new ideas, new sources of thought, and
impel the hapless laborers to aspire after better things
and higher states. I saw the flitting lamps of spirit
hearts, bright missionary angels, who filled these leaden
spheres with their gracious influence, and yet though
often felt, were unseen by the dull-eyed inhabitants,
except as stars or gleams of shimmering radiance. Ah
me! I fain would linger on the awful, grand, and wise
economy of being, but the seal of mortal life is on my
lips and on the minds of those I write for: who but the
death-angel can break it? I hasten to the conclusion of
my own brief pilgrimage. My noble father, my gentle,
loving Constance, and hosts of the dead of earth, the
angels of a better life, were around me.

At length, in the midst of my great egotism of joy, a
fearful pang shot through my mind as a dim remembrance came of one *who was not there.* Stronger and
stronger grew the thought, till again he filled my being,
and I loathed myself because for a season I had forgotten him, — my more than friend and adopted father;
but oh! where was he now, and why not with me?
Where was that dearest one of all, for whom I had
given my life? The pitying angels who thronged around
me showed how their wish that I should rest and gain
strength and life and light in the land of souls had intercepted thoughts of him before, but now the answer came,
and all too soon.

The spheres I had seen were not the all of earth,
though countless to me in number. Myriads there were
within the earth itself, where lingered bound and captive, vicious spirits, the ignorant, dull, idle, and criminal,
who had not done with earth and who must learn, per-

haps for ages, all that belonged to their human duties, ere they could pass the threshold, and enter on the life of the upper spheres; and yet beyond again, below, beneath the earth, inhered an *anti-state* of mortal being, vast realms where dwelt the spirits of nature. Here were millions of ascending grades of life, ranging from the vital principle of growth in the rude stone, to the shining spirits of the fire and air, who only waited to pass through the last stages of progressive life and death ere they should gravitate to earth and inherit mortal bodies and immortal souls. Crowds of aspiring spirits filled these realms, who were not men, but who looked to man in inspirational dreams and trances as to the angel which led and called them upwards.

I had seen these elementary spheres through the films of earthly magnetism, and then they seemed bright, some resplendent as in the tales of fairy-land; but now, beholding them through the pure alchemy of spiritual truth, I saw that they were destitute of all the warmth and life and beauty that humanity confers. It was in the midst of the sad and barren realms of elemental spirit-life that I saw at length my beloved and imprisoned friend and adopted father. I knew it all at once and how it was. He had on earth sunk his bright intellect down to these elementals instead of drawing them up to him by his own aspirations for a higher life than man's. He had descended below man to seek for causation instead of ascending above him; and now, oh hapless fate! he had gravitated to where he had chained his spirit. He could not look through the radiant realms of upper air and see me, but he felt the streams of pitying love I poured out upon him, and stretched his weary arms towards my spirit home in tender sympathy. Spirit-life, glory, peace, and happiness ended for me then. There was no more rest for me in heaven so long as I knew there was work to do for him. A strange and striking picture of life and what I could do was now unrolled before me. I saw myself on earth again, once more in the midst of suffering and pain. I saw the soul of my dearest friend clinging around me like a tender parasite. For a brief period I saw my life and his commingle like two quivering flames or uniting rain-drops. For a season the spirit of my father, thus drawn back to the earth by the magnetism of one so very, very near to him, almost himself in fact, would be released from the lower elemental spheres, and resuming its life functions through my mortal body would shake off the old errors, strike out into new paths of light, rise to its natural home in spirit-life, and, looking through the windows of my soul's eyes perceive the glorious truth of spiritual immortality. My spirit should be the ladder on which his soul should rise from the elementary spheres through earth again to his home in the better land. This was to be my destiny and his.

I saw it all and cried, " Speed, angels, speed me back to earth again! Haste! help me to release the imprisoned soul of him I love so dearly! " But this was not all. I learned that I too had been robbed of my soul's manhood; that I had not lived my own life, but that of my erring friend. His spirit had usurped the rights of mine; his will had superseded mine and left my soul a mere nonentity.

I must return to live again on earth then, —return for what seemed in earthly measure many long and weary years, but still I must undergo their pains and penalties, first for the sake of my dearest friend, and next for my own. My destiny was all laid out before me, — the rugged paths my bleeding feet would tread, my heart's deep love, bereavement, desolation. The cold world's slights and sneers, the keen tooth of ingratitude, the harsh sting of injustice, — all, all were mapped before me like a baleful battle-scene intruding on some lovely landscape whose peace and joy it ruined.

I felt an unbidden tear steal down my cheek whilst I bowed my head and murmured, "Thy will, not mine, be done." I knew that will was good. I had seen the glory, goodness, wisdom of the scheme, the perfect order in disorder, the good which sorrow brings, the triumph over evil, wrong, and death.

I knew God lived and reigned. I felt his bounteous hand and all-sustaining presence upholding every creature he has made, though their blind eyes cannot perceive his tracks. I knew that I could trust his eternal wisdom, and when the darkness should thicken round me, the thunders peal, and my blinded eyes could discover naught but ruin, he would be strong to save. The angels bade me take for my life's watchword, GOD UNDERSTANDS, and I knew it was so. And now the fading light of the spiritual sun receded from my view; the joy-bells rang more faintly; the crashing symphonies of heavenly music resounded in dim echoes; gray mists, descending thicker, faster, deepened into night, and closed around me. The stars came out above my head, as descending still, I floated down through the murky atmosphere of earth, upborne in the arms of loving spirit friends, and cheered by their whispered promise, "Ever with thee!" At length I reached this cold, dull, lonely orb; arrived at last on earth.

They bore me to the solitary wood, the dreadful dell of mortal agony. Torches flitted through the darkness of the night, and at length, half concealed by trees and underbrush, I saw a rigid, pale, distorted form, a scarcely living creature, on which some kind and tender beings lavished human cares, and gentle eyes were raining tears of pity. At first I turned from the spectacle with loathing, but even then a voice, though far and distant, reached my ear, whose appealing tones cried, "Help, Louis! Louis, help!" It was *his* unresting soul that pleaded. That cry broke forth from *his* imprisoned spirit and wailed through the sad night air in accents of wildest anguish. I paused no longer. I know not how, save that I acted by a mighty effort of resistless will, but in one instant I ceased to be a freed and rejoicing spirit. Minutes of dull forgetfulness succeeded, then keen pangs awoke me; the gates of life rolled back amidst my sobs and sighs, to let the spirit in, and gentle voices murmured, "He lives! Thank Heaven, he lives! and we are yet in time to save him."

CHAPTER XII.

[In the Introduction to this work, the editor has already explained the necessity of incorporating some portion of Mr. John C. Dudley's Diary into the "Ghost Land" papers. Without the continuous thread of narrative afforded by Mr. Dudley's interesting journal, there would be a hiatus in the record of several months, which the reader will readily perceive could not be filled up by the Chevalier de B——, and yet this would leave a most important part of the history in a bald and unfinished state.

Neither the Chevalier nor Mr. Dudley have been very exact in the order of chronological data. The editor, however, being quite familiar with the narrative, is enabled from personal knowledge to state that the extract from Mr. Dudley's diary with which the following chapter commences, refers to the period when Professor von Marx and his pupil first visited England together, and antedates by several months the catastrophe narrated in the last chapter but one.—ED. GHOST LAND.]

March 10, 18 .—Good news for the occultists of Great Britain! Just what we wanted, in fact, and that is, the infusion of a new element into our effete, lifeless ranks. Although not one of us has half digested the good things we have been receiving for years, we have long been on the tiptoe of expectation, waiting for something new. Well, unless my expectations are strangely disappointed, we shall have just the dish of excitement our *blasé* palates have been hungering for; for lo! I shall have the welcome task of announcing at the Orphic circle, of which I am the recording secretary, the advent of the great Professor Felix von Marx, the Cornelius Agrippa and Nostradamus of the nineteenth century, accompanied too by a peerless somnambulist, one whom the *Illuminée* of Germany exalt as the rarest and most gifted seer in the world.

I don't very well like the tone of von Marx's letter
though, for he declines to accept of my hospitality, old
and dear as are the ties of friendship that bind us; nor
yet he adds, will he consent to parade the gifts of his
Seer before the craving wonder-seekers of England.
The boy he says is tired, and needs entire cessation
from magnetic influences, besides they are coming to
London as he assures me, chiefly to find out what we
can show them; to determine what progress we have
made in the black or white art, as the case may be, and
learn whether the Teutons are not surpassed in magical lore by the countrymen of Roger Bacon, Dee, and
Kelly.   Well, no matter what they come for, I for one,
feel my heart leap with joy at the prospect of clasping
hands once more with my dear and well-tried friend,
Felix von Marx.   Let me recall the circumstances of
our early intimacy.   At the university of W——, Marx
and I were sworn chums.   We had but one heart, one
purse, and one lesson between us.   The heart was our
joint-stock property; the purse was mine, the lesson
his, for he did all my learning for me.   What a bright
and glorious scholar he was!   Took all the prizes, and
never had any rivals; I suppose because nobody dared
to compete with him.   What he ever found to take a
fancy to in such a dunce as me, unless indeed it was my
unbounded admiration for him, I never could understand; but I suppose we loved each other on the principle of positive and negative agreement; certain it is
we were never apart, not even in the tremendous mysteries in which von Marx had been initiated before I
knew him, and which he, like a true friend as he was,
determined I should share with him when we became
such constant associates.   Heavens! what awful things
we did at that K—— association.   If but half our

doings had been known to the jealous German government,—our fly-by-night excursions, our Asmodeus inspections of any house or castle we chose to enter spiritually, our *Polter Gheist* performances, sending our spirits out to knock about the pots and kettles of old fraus and pelt their pretty frauleins with rosebuds and spiritually written *billets-doux!* methinks we students of the occult, in secret session in our upper room at W——, would have been deemed fitter subjects for fine and imprisonment than many a political plotter or distinguished conspirator, hosts of whom were constantly under arrest, whilst we continued to cut up our capers unmolested and unsuspected.

It was a hard matter for me to quit the university at W—— and my dear friend Felix, when my father at length recalled me for the purpose of placing me at that dull old anti-German, anti-spiritual, anti-everything that is progressive, Oxford College, but when after two years of useless waste of fees to professors who could teach me nothing, and "fags" who could cram nothing into me, my father thought the time had come for me to make "the grand tour," how gladly did I remember my promise to von Marx, and at once propose him to my respected sire as the tutor most fit to accompany me. In vain I argued that though von Marx was in reality a shade younger than me, he was a perfect octogenarian in learning and experience. My father had inquired about him, found he had just been appointed to a professorship in Oriental languages, but that, taken on the whole, he was a strange, mystical sort of a fellow, and anything but a fitting mentor for me. The subject was still *in petto,* when a brilliant diplomatic opening occurred for me in our minister's suite to Russia.

No sooner was I installed in my new dignity than I

discovered the immediate necessity of my having an under-secretary. Now Professor Marx was a splendid linguist, and besides the Oriental tongues, was a complete master of the Russian language. He could give intelligible expression to more consonants in one word of seven syllables. in fact than any one of his generation. The result was, I proved to my father's entire satisfaction, that if I did not succeed in securing the services of Professor Marx as my under-secretary and instructor in the Russian language, my whole diplomatic prospects would be blighted, in fact, likely to come to a premature end.

My father appreciated the force of my logic. The case was stated to the professor, who, as an act of friendship, felt bound to sacrifice himself. His salary, fixed at double the worth of his professorship, his ragged college gown and cap exchanged for a neat suit of Khamschatka dog, behold us smoking cheroots and plotting occult séances at our elegant quarters in the Grand Square of St. Petersburg.

I had always loved the mysterious, doted on ghost stories, and though I shrank away with inexpressible terror at the idea of their realization, I ever returned to their study again, and cared for nothing so much as the wild, the weird, and the wonderful. Now, if there ever was a born Adept, with all the natural qualifications for a magnetizer, biologist, healer, astrologer, in a word, for a master of spirits and spiritual things, that Adept was Felix von Marx. As to me, my occult powers were my natural inheritance. My sainted mother, then in heaven, had been a seeress, my honored sire, still on earth, was a devoted student of astrology. Coward as I was—I am bound to own it—in the ghost-seeing line, I never could get out of that invol-

untary and much dreaded accomplishment. When quite
a little lad, I was regularly worried with ghosts. My
father spent the autumn months generally at a fine old
castle he owned in the north of England, and there
these phantoms took such an extraordinary fancy to me
that they walked with me, talked with me, met me in
every gallery and corridor, made me come and go,
fetch and carry just as if I had been a young sexton,
and naturally belonged to the dead. I saw, moreover,
sprites and fairies by the score; heard the mermaids
sing and the tritons whistle; in a word, there never was
a boy more admirably adapted to be a good magnetic
subject, never an operator more completely *au fait* at
putting me through the spiritual kingdom than Felix.
Of course we gravitated together as naturally as the
magnet and its armature, and though, now I was in
office and had attained to the dignity of a diplomatist,
I declined to be put to sleep like a fractious child or
sent out of my body as a *Polter Gheist* to scare honest
peasants out of their wits with throwing stones and
making noises invisibly, my love for the practices of
mesmerism and magic only increased with my years
and the fine opportunities which association with my
accomplished secretary afforded me. I found Professor
von Marx had made immense strides in occult knowledge whilst I had been wasting my time in learning the
arts of *impolite* dissipation at Oxford. He had visited
the East, where he was born, and had there picked up
so many awful scraps of magic lore that I began to be
almost afraid of him.

Whilst we were deep in our plans for the prosecution
of occult study, however, I suddenly realized the truth
of that excellent proverb, "Man proposes and God
disposes," in the very awkward fact of my falling des-

perately in love. The object of this unexpected awakening, was a charming young widow, the relict of a certain old German Margrave, the Prince de K——, who
had left his fair lady with a fair fortune, by virtue of
which double accomplishments madame, the princess,
became the cynosure of all eyes, and the target at which
every bachelor in the land aimed his arrows. Of course
I should have had little expectation of carrying off such
a prize, with so many odds against me, had not the lady
conceived a very agreeable plan of perfecting herself in
the Russian language. She was visiting for the season
at the house of some very distinguished relatives of her
late husband's in St. Petersburg, and having frequently
met us in the diplomatic circles, and noticed, as she
courteously observed, the immense facility with which I
acquired the throat-splitting language of the country
under the admirable tutelage of my secretary, she inquired in the most insinuating manner whether my
studies could not be conducted in her *salon*, by which
arrangement she could have the advantage of participat-
ing in them. I was enchanted. To me the whole thing
was plain. The princess had in this delicate way, hinted
at her wish to enjoy my society untrammelled by the
frivolous crowd who usually surrounded us, and thus
I should be able to get the start of all my rivals, and lay
siege to the fair widow's heart at my leisure.

The only difficulty was, to enlist that cold-hearted
Mephistopheles of a secretary of mine in the scheme.
I did not dare confess the real motives that prompted
me, for I could by no means venture to meet the tremendous sneer with which I knew he would meet my
avowal of being in love. At length I conquered his
stubborn prejudices against "the attempt to teach a
woman anything but folly," by assuring him I was so

situated that if I did not continue my studies in the Princess K——'s private apartments I might be recalled to Europe at any moment. Von Marx could not, as he affirmed, see the force of this position; but at length, finding his friend's heart strongly set on the matter, he complied with the best grace he could. Thus it was arranged that I and the princess should read Russian three times a week in her elegant *salon,* where, by aid of coffee, chocolate, German poetry, and Italian music, I managed to get through a deal of covert flirtation with the fair widow, whilst the professor, ensconced in a distant easy-chair, pored over the pages of Cornelius Agrippa or Jacob Behmen.

At length the time arrived which I deemed ripe for my intended declaration. Taking advantage of my secretary's being laid up with a sore-throat, and presenting myself one day in his stead, Russian books in hand, ·—volumes, by the way, of which hitherto we had not found a convenient opportunity of cutting the pages, — I began to open my battery, and with a rush of enthusiastic courage, stimulated by the absence of my secretary, I laid my name, fame, fortune, life, etc. etc., at the feet of the adorable princess. The result of this outbreak was a polite request on her Highness's part that I would discontinue my visits in future. I was in despair. I would instantly go mad, hang, drown, shoot, or freeze myself to death; I would cut somebody's throat, exterminate the human race, and by way of preliminary, I smoked ten cigars and wrote the princess a series of letters once an hour for three days. Each missive ended, like my cigars, in smoke. At length and just as I had made up my mind to confide in von Marx and urge him to plead for me, that gentleman called me into his apartment, lighted a cigar, begged me to do the same, and then, putting a letter into my hands, asked me to read it and tell him what I thought of that. What I thought of that, indeed! Great Heavens! what should *that* be but a deliberate offer of herself, her name, fame, fortune, etc. etc., from the Princess K—— to Professor Felix von Marx! Rage and astonishment choked my utterance at first, whilst prudence and self-respect urged me to keep my own counsel at last. Recovering my composure, I began to congratulate my friend on his good luck. Of course I was glad, I was delighted, I should dance at his wedding *furiously;* in a word, I was "only too happy," I said, "to see him so very happy." But as I spoke, with a sardonic grin worthy of a demon, I could not help remarking that my friend appeared most particularly unhappy. With a comical mixture of discontent and perplexity, he declared he could not imagine what the deuce the woman could want him for, but the worst of it was he did n't know how he was to get out of it.

"Get out of it?" I exclaimed, in high indignation. "What! when the handsomest woman in St. Petersburg lays her fortune at your feet?"

"But I don't want the woman, nor her beauty nor her fortune either," replied the cynic.

"But my dear fellow," I rejoined warming with the idea that my idol was to be slighted and insulted by being called "a woman," "you can't treat a lady of her exalted rank and character in that way. You must have her, you ought to have her, you *shall* have her, or—I'll know the reason why."

"Whew!" cried my friend, with a long whistle. "Am I to be married against my will, and to a woman I don't care two straws for?"

I saw I must change my tack. Professor von Marx was just then the handsomest young fellow I had ever looked upon. Tall and finely formed, any Grecian sculptor would have laid violent hands upon him for a model. With what I had so often heard the ladies describe as "those lovely black, curling, waving locks," tossed carelessly over a noble brow; a pair of large, splendid dark eyes, that went right through everything, especially that frailest of all things, a woman's heart; with a classic mouth, fine teeth, and what every female authority declared to be "such a duck of a moustache, and such a love of a pair of whiskers," but above all, with a sort of indescribable, Oriental, magical kind of spell-like way about him that nobody seemed able to resist; who could compete with him? On the other hand, how could I, a slim, genteel youth, with narrow shoulders and a stoop, blue eyes and a cough, a small crop of straw-colored hair on my face and an equally slender allowance on my head, the latter of a stubborn character too, which no *frizeur* had ever been able to twist into curl,—how could such an one enter the lists with a von Marx and hope for success? Oh, if my father had only been an Arabian sheik or my mother an Eastern sultana, there might have been a chance for me! But as it was, and with the fatal experience of the princess's choice between a poor Adonis and a rich gawky,—as I in my humility deemed myself,—I saw there was no chance for me in future, unless I got von Marx married right out of hand. Besides, I loved the dear fellow in one way as much as I adored the faithless fair one in another way, and the only balm my wounded spirit could receive was to see them united. This done, I would seek an early grave, and—"die in peace." How I managed it I cannot tell,—whether by coaxing, scolding, or fairly badgering my friend into the match, I know not. Certain it is, I did succeed; and after laying out before

15

Felix all the opportunities he would enjoy of following up his favorite pursuits as the husband of the rich and fashionable Princess K——, I finally saw the knot tied by the chaplain of the embassy, and Professor von Marx and his illustrious bride departing for one of her charming castles on the Rhine, at which spot I promised to join them as soon as I could get released from my now irksome official duties.

It was three years before I was able to redeem this promise, and when I did, it was in company with the dear and lovely lady who had discernment enough to discover in the slim, genteel youth, whose many disadvantages I had so humbly pitted against the splendid von Marx, the dear companion by whose life-long love every other female image has been displaced, always excepting the admiration I share for her, with three fair duplicates of herself, who now call me their loving father.

When I and my beloved bride reached H——, and I had placed her to rest in the pleasant apartments provided for us, I hurried off to the castle where my servants had learned the Princess von Marx was then residing. Great was my chagrin to find neither my friend nor his lady at home. Her Highness was out at the hunt the domestics told me, and the professor,— they did n't know, but they thought I should find him at the neighboring college. "At the college!" I repeated. "That is odd. What could he be doing there?" They did n't know, but they believed he was there; if not, they did n't know where he would be.

Hurrying away, with strange misgivings in my mind, I applied to the chief janitor of the college, and learned that von Marx was professor of the Hebrew and Arabic languages in that institution, and might be found in his own rooms in such and such a direction.

Professor von Marx a teacher, and occupying shabby rooms in a third-rate college, whilst his illustrious consort was residing in a neighboring castle and amusing herself with a hunting party! There was " something rotten in the state of Denmark" with a vengeance, I thought. I soon reached my friend's quarters, entered without ceremony, found him in, and received such a greeting as assured me whatever else was changed, his early friendship remained. In all other respects I found him a sadly altered man. He seemed to have grown taller and thinner, though he still retained his unparalleled grace and symmetry of proportion; his air was as commanding as ever, but it was tinctured with a deep and stern sadness which added many years of age to his manner; his face though as noble and handsomer than ever, was pale and care-worn; his brow was contracted with an habitual frown, and there was a fixidity in his expression which almost made me shrink from him. His dress, though still gentlemanlike and clean, was worn and threadbare, and the furniture of his room was beggarly compared to that which in old times we used to share together. In the corner of the room was a rude, evidently home-made cot, shaded with a pure white coverlet, on which were strewed wild flowers, and beneath which slept a beautiful child, the father of whom unmistakably stood before me.

Subdued in an instant to the tone of my friend's altered circumstances and appearance, I could only take his hand and stammer out, " How is all this, Felix? Let us sit down and talk it all over like dear old times, you know."

And talk it over we did, and for a few hours the dear old times seemed to come back to my friend's wounded spirit.

It was an old story von Marx told me,—the story of a marriage which was not made in heaven, and wherein the hapless couple were yoked, not mated. The princess was a gay, frivolous butterfly, utterly incapable of appreciating anything in her talented husband except his remarkably handsome person. He was a stern, devoted student of the occult, who found neither sympathy nor companionship in his fashionable wife; thus before six months had worn away, both had bitterly repented,—the one her infatuation, the other, the astonishing facility with which he had suffered himself to be " entrapped."

Their lives of unceasing discord were, it is true, interrupted for a time by the birth of a lovely boy, upon whom the unhappy father lavished all that wealth of affection of which he was so capable, could any one have found and governed the secret of its source.

After two years of mutual bitterness and recrimination the ill-matched couple agreed to separate, and in so doing Professor von Marx retired, as he had for some time lived, entirely upon the proceeds of his writings, translations, and lectures. He refused to accept the smallest portion of his wife's wealth, and finding he could not obtain possession of his idolized child by amicable arrangement with his lady, he actually carried him off by force, and held him under an unceasing watch and ward by the same means.

He had gladly accepted the offer of a small professorship in the poor college of H——, and was now lingering in that vicinity awaiting the tardy decision of the law in respect to his boy, whom the princess sought to reclaim.

Such was the sum of a history which occupied in the relation many hours of the night. I heard it with great pain, not only on my friend's account, but on that of my wife also. The princess and herself had been school-mates. Educated at the same convent in France, they had conceived a girlish affection for each other, and I knew my dear companion, with the zeal of her warm, loving nature, would be sure to take her friend's part in the impending dispute.

For several weeks we lingered in the neighborhood of II——, vainly endeavoring to effect a reconciliation between a couple who had nothing in common with each other to be reconciled about.

With the old sophistry of appealing to their sense of religious duty, we endeavored to convince them they had taken each other " for better or for worse," and ought to endure the worse if worse it were. The princess declared the professor had no more sense of religion than a stock or a stone; the professor swore that the princess's religion was all carried in the feathers of her church-going hat; in short, our efforts were as fruitless as nature intended them to be. At length the time arrived for the decision which was to award the little fellow, who was the only tie of mutuality between them, to one or other of the parents, and the law, by what hocus-pocus I know not, decided to bestow him on the mother. The professor had left his pearl of price in the college building in charge of a trusty friend, but before he returned from the court to defend his rights, as he certainly would have done unto the death, by force of arms, a party of German Jagers surrounded the place of the child's con-cealment, carried him off, and placed him in his mother's castle, under the protection of half a regiment of well-armed domestics. Deep if not loud were the curses which the bereaved father uttered, when he returned to find the little cot, which he had made and adorned with his own hands, empty, and his idol gone. Were those curses vented on empty air alone, or did they take effect in the realm where evil wishes are registered by evil though unseen powers? Within twelve hours after the young boy was removed to his mother's castle, reaching out of a window to call piteously on what he insisted upon declaring was the form of his father in the court-yard below, he escaped from the grasp of his attendant, and screaming, "Coming, papa! Erny's coming!" he sprang through the open window, fell nearly sixty feet into the court below, and was instantly killed. Professor von Marx soon after inherited, by the death of a near kinsman, a small independent fortune, and a title of nobility to which he was the next heir.

The title he repudiated, the fortune he claimed, generously offering to divide it with his late partner, who with equal liberality declined the proffer.

This was the last communication the ill-assorted pair ever held, the professor having, as he has since assured me, never heard of or sought to inquire for his lady again. The princess is still, as I hear, a gay *habitué* of many an European court; the professor, one of the most celebrated writers and lecturers on metaphysics of which the age can boast. Openly, he devotes himself to the duties of a professorship at the university of B——, but privately, he has addicted himself to the incessant study and practice of occult arts, in which, throughout the secret societies of the East, Germany, France, and Continental Europe generally, he is acknowledged to be one of the most skilful and powerful adepts that ever lived.

In a correspondence with me which has never been interrupted, he has of late years made frequent allusions to his deep interest in a young Austrian boy of

noble birth, who was placed by his parents for education at the college of which von Marx is still a
professor.

This child, he once wrote me word, was born, the
very day on which his own idolized Ernest, then only
two years and a half old, died. "Born one hour after
the tragic event, this child," he added, "strange to say,
resembles me so closely in appearance, that every master and student in the university remarks upon the likeness. Day by day this weird resemblance increases,
and if the dreams of the re-incarnationists had any
foundation in truth, it might have been supposed that
the spirit of my precious Ernest had passed into the
form of the infant born in a far distant land at the self-
same fateful hour that my Ernest died. I know these
are worse than idle dreams; still I have pleased myself
at times by indulging in them, just as a weary man of
the world might take up at some odd hour a fairy tale
and linger over the page of fiction which once constituted his childhood's delight." *

* Since the editor of these papers has become intimately acquainted with
the Chevalier de B—— she has frequently heard discussed, the extraordinary resemblance between him and his adopted father, named in these
writings "Professor von Marx." A fine portrait of Professor von Marx
is to be seen in a certain German collection of oil paintings, in which it is
almost impossible to trace any dissimilarity between that and a portrait of
the Chevalier de B—— at the same age, save in point of costume. This
remarkable resemblance has been frequently cited to the editor and the
author also, in confirmation of the re-incarnationists' theory that the soul
of the dead child Ernest had passed into the new-born form of the Chevalier, the period between the decease and the birth being only one hour,
and the parties, though originally strangers to each other, having been so
singularly brought together in later years. The author has requested the
editor to record here his utter disbelief in this theory, or indeed in the doctrine of re-incarnation at all. He himself is a firm believer in the existence
of special types of physique prevailing throughout all the kingdoms of
nature. He conceives that he and his adopted father belonged to the
same peculiar type of being, and that the resemblance first instituted in

Perhaps these circumstances may account for the extraordinary fancy which the stern and otherwise ascetic professor has conceived for the young Chevalier de B——. I am advised that his personal adventures, marriage, and paternity have never been revealed to his *protégé*, to whom, as he claims, he can veil or disclose his mind just as he pleases. Despite this boy's high birth, his family have it appears, consented to his adoption by the great and learned Professor von Marx; and this then is the prodigy, whom the professor declares to be the finest seer and the most perfect ecstatic upon earth, and whom I hope soon to welcome as my honored guest.

My dear wife and our three charming girls are not, I regret to say, in sympathy with my spiritualistic pursuits; in fact, they profess to be quite scandalized at the idea of their beloved husband and father being a "magician," a practiser of the "black art," a regular Zamiel or Ashmodi. As to my two boys, they are such a rough-and-tumble pair of young profanities that I don't dare to trust them with any higher ideas on spiritualistic subjects than a mild ghost story or two about Christmas or New Year. Take it on the whole, however, my happy household are all agreed to disagree. My magical pursuits moreover, are all conducted in other scenes than my own home, and whatever friends I do introduce there, are ever warmly welcomed by my wife and children. Professor von Marx is of course, well known to my wife, though not altogether her special favorite. With true womanly feeling she espoused the female side of the matrimonial dispute; nevertheless she was in

the architecture of Nature, was deepened to a perfect fac-simile by the formative process of magnetization during a period of many years, also by the strength of the attachment subsisting between the parties, which tended to mould even the expression of their features into similarity.

the habit of saying to me privately, that any woman
who was bold enough to offer herself in marriage, deserved just whatever treatment she might receive; so,
take it for all in all, she did n't know that the fault was
wholly on the professor's side.

March 29. The long-looked-for guests have arrived,
and I have just returned from my first visit of welcome
to them.

The changes which years have wrought in my friend
Felix von Marx, seem to have intensified rather than
altered his marked characteristics. In form and face
he is still superb, but his manners are even colder,
more resolute and self-centred than in the days of
yore, when I and all around him bent before his indomitable will. His friendship for me still remains undimin-
ished, but the yielding points of his nature seem to be
all called forth by his *protégé*, to whom his manner
always becomes softened when he either speaks to or
even looks towards him. My long and curious study
of mesmeric subjects, natural somnambulists, sensitives, etc., has been fruitful of a rich and strange experience, and inspired me with much curiosity concerning
the young man for whom Professor von Marx and the
German mystics generally, make such high claims.
How then can I permit my pen to record my first
impressions of this paragon, and own that I was disappointed in him? Yet such is the actual fact. Perhaps I placed my expectations of personal gratification
too high; but to me, he is unapproachable; I am
troubled in his presence, troubled even when I think
of him, and yet I am lowered in my own estimation
for being so. In external appearance he so wonderfully resembles his adopted father, that it would be
difficult for strangers to believe there were no ties of

relationship between them; the only perceptible differences in these gentlemen are in respect to age and the fact that all the sterner features of Professor von Marx's expression are softened in his ward by an excessive sensitiveness.

The professor's almost insupportable penetration of glance is subdued in this boy's magnificent dark eyes, by a dreamy, far-off look, which speaks unmistakably of the spiritual mystic. They are truly perfect types of a high magian and his subject, but that of which I complain—if indeed I have any right to use such a word—is the entire absence of pleasure, earthly interest or sympathy in this young man's manner. He received me as if he were in a dream; answered when I addressed him, as if by an effort to recall himself to my presence or remember where he was. His sweet and beautifully modulated voice, sounded a long way off, and his entire *personel* was so statuesque and unearthly, that I could have almost imagined I was a boy again, and shivering under the old superstitious awe which used to possess me when I deemed I was in presence of a spirit, or, in more homely phrase, thought I saw a ghost.

I noticed, moreover, the wonderful, I may truly say the unspeakable, understanding that subsisted between these strangely-matched persons. Professor von Marx seldom addressed a word to his friend during the whole interview, yet the latter frequently rose, handed him a book, some papers, or other matters he required, without any other than a mental request. He evidently understood and obeyed the least thought in the professor's mind, and on more than one occasion turned towards him, and by silent looks replied to his unspoken thoughts. Through the same extraordinary process of soul intercourse, the professor would fix his questioning eyes upon his ward, and obtain an answer without one syllable being interchanged between them. I have often seen and wondered at the remarkable *rapport* which existed between my own mesmerized subjects and myself. I have seen still more positive evidences of pure, mental transfer between the *Lucides* of the celebrated Baron Dupotet, MM. Billot, Deleuze, and Cahagnet, also with a number of my English associates, whose honored names. I withhold in view of my anonymous style of writing; but I never beheld any system of soul intercourse so perfect as that which existed between these unrelated Teutons, nor so complete an adept in mindreading as this young Chevalier.

· After a short experience of the singular influence diffused by this speechless intelligence, I began to comprehend that it was the source of the troubled feeling which possessed me, and involuntarily I began to speculate upon the possibility of the young mystic's reading my mind with the same facility that he did his father's. This thought not only disturbed me, but awoke these spontaneous reflections within me: "I wonder if he knows I don't like him," and, "I wish to heaven he would leave me alone with my friend." No sooner did these *mal-à-propos* ideas fill my mind than the Chevalier arose, and with a flushed face, and for the first time during our interview, a furtive smile playing around his lips, he bent to me courteously, apologized for his indiscretion in obtruding his presence "so· long on dear friends who must be so very glad to renew their old, confidential intercourse with each other," and before I could stammer out any protest against his obvious interpretation of my secret wishes he was gone.

The professor, who seemed more at home and like his old self when his sprite was gone, laughed outright at my confusion, and cried cheerily, "Never mind, John! Louis knew just as well as you did that you wished him at the deuce, so of course he retired; but don't let that worry you, old fellow. The fact is, this boy feels rather than sees or hears what is going on around him; but now tell me candidly, what do you think of him?"

Once again I began to stammer in that ridiculous way of mine, when my thoughts are a long way off and want collecting, but the professor saved me all further trouble by giving me such a complete word-picture of what I had actually thought in the Chevalier's presence that I started up fairly aghast, and cried, "Come, come, Felix, this will never do! It is bad enough to be obliged to say many things we don't always think, but when we only think things and don't say them, and yet have them all said for us in this remorseless way, 'pon my life! I don't know what is to become of us. Felix, I am getting to be fairly afraid of both you and that weird friend of yours."

"Well," replied von Marx, coolly, "if you will venture upon the enchanted isle, and place yourself at the mercy of a Prospero and Ariel, why you must take the consequences; but come now John, let us talk as of old, and somewhat more to the purpose. You have had great experience as a magnetizer since we met, conversed with many of the best and most philosophic of Mesmer's followers, both here and on the Continent, besides enjoying the opportunity of analyzing the idiosyncracies of some hundreds of 'sensitives.' Tell me, then, what do you think of them as a class?"

"Felix," I replied, "I will answer you in the words of Geiblitz, that fine old writer on mental philosophy, whose works you and I used to pore over so constantly at W——, and whose description of this very class I was so enamoured with that I committed several pages to memory. Geiblitz says: —

"Now, as copper and zinc would not form a galvanic battery if the acid which consumes the metals acted on both alike, neither would the thunder roll or the lightnings flash if the two clouds that met in mid-air were equal in force and polarity, one with the other, so would there be no exhibition of soul galvanism, or mental lightnings, if the body in which they shone was all equilibrium, and the person was well composed and evenly balanced. Methinks all history shows us that the ecstatic or seer must be an inharmonious being. Something ails him which disturbs his balance or sets the measure of equilibrium at odds, before he can admit another mind to govern him.

"'Thus it was with the great fabulist, Æsop, who was an idiot in all things but the strong point of allegorical composition which, to my mind, was pure inspiration. So also with Robert Nixon, the Cheshire prophet, who was also foolish, yet subject to that high inspiration which prophesied through his lips. Again, with Chetwynd, the fool of the great Saxon monarch, and many others, who, although so silly as to be marked with the fool's cap and bells, yet when the spirit spoke through them, did give utterance to prophecy and wiser things than most other men. And if the intellect be well composed, then must we look to find a lack of balance amongst the moral qualities; for example; Cagliostro and Kelly, both being great seers and governors of spiritual things, were yet knaves. Bohemians, Gypsies, and Zingari are all thieves and cheats, yet they know the future better than many wise men, and can see farther with their soul's eyes than most men with their telescopes.' In short, Felix," I continued, seeing that my quotations were beginning to be more dangerous than apt, "you and I, at a very early period of our investigations, came to the conclusion that fine sensitives or high magnetic subjects must be unevenly balanced or lack equilibrium somewhere. They must be either fools like Nixon, and therefore good subjects for the control of others, knaves like the Bohemians, and in constant rapport with the elementaries, or sick sensitives like St. Bridgetta, St. Catherine, and other saints of great renown, who floated in air, bore the stigmata, prophesied, read every mind, and — and — were, in a word, so highly endowed with spiritualistic gifts."

"How about Jesus of Nazareth, Appolonius of Tyana, and Joan of Arc?" said the professor, dryly. "Were they fools, knaves, or sick sensitives?"

"Well," I replied, taken something aback, "Jesus was undoubtedly very sensitive, as his susceptibility to human suffering and pain demonstrated; Appolonius was said to be an epileptic, though I can't vouch for the fact; and as to Joan of Arc, we know she was a very melancholy young person, remarkably fond of the sound of bells in her youth, besides being very pious, which I regard as a sign of a morbid temperament, to say the least of it."

"Well, well!" interrupted von Marx, impatiently. "Set your brains no more to wool-gathering to find out similitudes. My Louis is at once the purest being in the world, and endowed with the finest and most comprehensive intellect, but he is just as fragile in physique as your argument would need to prove him. But for the constant and steady infusion of my magnetism, his soul would long since have escaped from so frail a tenement as he bears about with him. Will that satisfy you?"

"Felix," I said, looking steadily into my friend's troubled eyes, "tell me; is it a normal or healthful life for one human being to live upon the magnetism of another? I know *it can be done*, but is it in the sweet and natural order of creation?"

"No, John," replied my friend, sadly, "it is not, and I have often felt it was not. But when do we enter upon any new and untried path and see the end from the beginning? When do we determine how far we may drift before necessity or some strong impulse forces us to stop? I commenced magnetizing this adopted child of mine, first, for the sake of continuing my experiments, then because I and the Berlin Brotherhood found in him a rare and unusual combination of splendid powers. We all know that the most passive mentality, or that which in ordinary life would be mere imbecility, often supplies the best, because the most unsoiled tablet for the inscription of a foreign mental power. We have also proved that the same aromal life principle which clusters in excess about the cerebellum, and makes its subject sensual, acquisitive, or destructive, furnishes in many instances the potency by which the elementaries and earthy spirits can control mortals; hence we so frequently see fools and knaves endowed with those spiritual gifts which plead for the intervention of the dæmons, but here we have an exception to all such experiences. Here is a being of the noblest and least guileful character that ever lived, and yet so intellectually bright, that he acquires knowledge with magical intuition. Ere he had been our subject long, I am well convinced if our society had been one of the fanatical kind that were likely to be entangled in religious absurdities, we should have exalted this boy into a new Messiah, hailed him as a tenth incarnation of Vishnu or a modern Buddha.

"Delighted with my prize, and somehow always associating him with that little one whose cot I made with these hands, — John, you remember, — I gradually drew him away from all other influences than my own. I have watched the dawning of his noble manhood as an astronomer would watch for a new planet. I put my life upon him, trained the tendrils of his lonely being to cling around me with all the wealth of a passionately loving nature concentred on one object.

"Many a time when the life had nearly ebbed away, and the thread which bound him to mortality became so attenuated that my earth-dimmed eyes could scarcely discover it, by a mighty wrench of will, by the throbbing of my whole heart's love poured out upon him, and the vials of my own life drained to supply his, I have succeeded in dragging him back to me, keeping him alive, and seeing him grow into a spiritual, physical, and intellectual beauty that knows no peer on earth. John, do you remember the story of the German student, Frankenstein? He made a monster, I an angel. His was the story of a myth, mine that of a scientific truth. Is there no gain to the cause of science in the success of my singular experiment?" The strange man paused, wrought up to the most intense pitch of emotion, and gazing at me with an almost imploring expression, asked, "Have I not cause to love him, John?"

"Ay," I replied, with equal emotion, "you cannot fail to do so; still you have not answered my question, Is such a life as his normal, healthful, right?"

"No," he answered, firmly, "and never will be whilst — "

"Whilst what?" I asked, eagerly.

"Whilst I live," he half whispered; "but enough of this now. I know he is not a creature of earth, but he is mine, all my own, the angel side of myself, and I will yet think out a bright destiny for him, or wreck myself body and soul in the attempt."

I was subdued, awed, by the depth of this strong man's fierce love for the creature he had made, and whilst I was not less struck by the obvious return the young man gave in his deep and absorbing affection for his adopted father, I could not for the life of me realize the angelic excellence of which the professor boasted. To me there was something wanting in this singular being's nature. He was too unsympathetic, too anti-human for an angel; too dreamy, exalted, and visionary for a man. I almost felt as if he either lacked a soul or was so much of soul that he had no business with a body. He was a problem I could not solve; in fact, the whole visit left such an uncomfortable feeling upon my mind, that I began to half surmise my dear wife was right, and that in meddling with matters too high for us, we poor mortals are apt to get out of our depths.

One thing was certain: a train of speculation in which I had been indulging prior to the advent of my friends, fell to the ground with a crash. The truth is, I had heard that the young heir of the great Professor von Marx was of noble birth, wonderfully handsome, and altogether a most eligible *parti;* hence, with what my eldest daughter, Sophia, called, my inveterate spirit of match-making, I had already got up a little imaginary romance between this *preux chevalier* and a certain fair Lady Rosa, a dazzling creature whom I strongly affected, and who had always promised to marry only just that particular person whom dear Uncle John should select. Now, this was not the only lovely creature I had destined for my interesting young foreign guest, but now, whew! before I quitted the presence of this young mystic, or could shake off the remembrance of his soul-haunting, far-away-looking dark eyes, I came to

the conclusion I might as well expect the north star or
one of the Pleiades to come down and woo the Rosies
and Sophies of fashionable life as this unearthly Chevalier
de B——.   With my old habit of putting my reflections
into shape I mentally exclaimed as I passed down-stairs,
" I 'll wager that this young fellow has got a spirit
bride somewhere off in one of the planets.   Perhaps he
might deign to chant a sonnet to a Sylph or serenade an
Undine; but as to his falling in love with any of the
pretty butterflies that call me dear papa or darling old
uncle, pshaw!   I 'll go and put all the girls on their
guard against him, or else they will be throwing away
their hearts upon a streak of moonlight."

" Have no fear of that, senor; your butterflies are all
safe from me," said the sweet voice and soft Italian
accent of the Chevalier, close to my ear.

Turning round in the entrance-hall hastily to face this
audacious mind-reader, I encountered — nothing!   Save
for the Irish porter who held the hall-door open for me,
not a creature was within sight or hearing.   Quitting
the house with a little more than my ordinary precipita-
tion, I hurried into the street hoping that in a strong
current of east wind, I might at least be free to think or
resolve never to enter that weird house again, unless
indeed, I could leave my thoughts at home, or in some
distant scene which the wizard's spell could not reach.

That afternoon, having retired to my library, and according to custom being about to compose myself to take
half an hour's *siesta* before dressing for dinner, I was
startled by the noiseless opening of the door, which, by
the by, I generally locked on such occasions.   Looking
up in surprise, it being against the rule of that charmed
scene even for my own daughters to enter without knocking -at the door, I beheld, in a maze of astonishment

which kept me speechless, the young Chevalier de B——. Speaking in an earnest, pleading tone, which somehow filled my eyes with an irrepressible moisture, he said, "Dear sir, there are some beings on earth who are not yet born into actual humanity. It requires for them a great change, most commonly a great sorrow, to effect that new birth in which the true union between body and soul takes place. One man may know many births and deaths in the course of a single life pilgrimage, and I am one of those who must be born again, conceived in sorrow and born through great anguish, before I can be really the man my too fond father deems me. To be a man I must be endowed with the passions of one, — with vices as well as virtues, and criminal as well as noble tendencies. As yet, the humanity which makes a full-grown soul is lacking in me, and I am not good, because I am not bad; not virtuous, pure, or noble, because I have no opposite propensities to rise above. My poor father has not created an angel, only endowed this frail form with a spiritual essence which yet lacks parts and passions. But O dear sir! the hour approaches when I shall be born again through a maternity of great sorrow. In that hour I shall stand in direst need of a human friend and helper: will you not be that friend? The world of spirits pleads with you for me, their child and servant."

At the conclusion of this extraordinary speech, every syllable of which seems to me to have been indelibly engraven on the tablets of my memory, he extended his hand towards me. As I was about to grasp it, my eye was arrested by the sight of the word ISABELLA inscribed in finely-formed, crimson letters across the palm of his small, white hand. This was the name of my deeply-cherished and long-lamented dear mother. I had often prayed that if the soul was immor-

tal, could live, love, and know those they had left on
earth, especially if they could minister to them, this most
tender mother might be permitted to give me some sign
which should convince me of the stupendous fact of her
immortal being. No response had ever before been
vouchsafed to my soul's deep aspiration, but even as I
gazed on that familiar name, and saw the letters melt or
fade slowly away in the outstretched hand before me,
the thought was irresistibly borne in upon my mind
that here was the proof I sought. I have since, during
the modern dispensation of Spiritualism, seen many a
name of the beloved ones gone before, inscribed in fleshly
characters upon a medium's body. I had heard of such
stigmata appearing amongst my friends the French
magnetists, but never had I witnessed aught so wonderful, aught that took so deep a hold upon my inmost
convictions of spiritual identity before. As the letters
faded, I rubbed my eyes, started, rubbed them again, and
with my characteristic slowness was about to seize the
young man's hand, and make a speech, assuring him of
my eternal friendship and devotion to him, under whatever circumstances he might command it, when lo! he
was gone. I rushed to the only door in the room, and
found it locked on the inside just as I had left it.

Returning to my library table I found a volume of
Shakespeare unclasped; open at the play of "The Tempest," a leaf turned down, — a liberty I never allowed
with my books, — and a deep pencil-mark drawn under-
neath these lines of the fair Miranda's: —

"Believe me, sir, it carries a brave form, — but 't is a spirit."

And thus began our campaign with the Prospero and
Ariel of the nineteenth century, Felix von Marx and his
adopted son, the Chevalier de B——.

CHAPTER XIII.

February 10, 18 . On looking over the fragmentary entries that my diary presents during the last few months, I am painfully conscious that the records are not of a sufficiently consecutive character to weave into the body of this narrative, at least not without more revision than I have now time or opportunity to bestow on them. During these eventful months there has been so much that has been new and marvellous to us all; even we, who have been accustomed to witness the exhibitions of abnormal spiritual powers through our clairvoyants and somnambulists, as well as at our magical séances, have been so startled at the extraordinary phenomena introduced amongst us by our German friends, that we seem to have commenced a new era in our experiences, and I feel the necessity of recording our testimony with more than usual care and caution. Strange rumors too are abroad that new and wonderful disclosures are being made to mortals amongst the matter-of-fact, commercial Americans, and by what can we suppose? Actually, it is affirmed by *spirits in person!* spirits of the dead, or rather the spirits of those the world *calls dead*, who, so say these floating rumors of a *waking* "Arabian Night's Dream," are not dead at all, but alive, and as inhabitants of a progressed world, have found a way to telegraph to the friends they have left as bereaved mourners, assuring them they are all in life, in the full possession of their faculties; see us, know us, love us still, and come into communication with us by sounds and signals that they find the means of making, through those very persons who were formerly our somnambulists, seers, and mesmeric subjects.

May not this be the secret of the young Chevalier's wonderful and abnormal surroundings? He and his father claim that all we see and hear is the work of the elementaries whom they command, and planetary angels who attend upon them and signal to them through this youth's trances and the professor's magical power over spirits.

We are all lost in conjecture. Whatever be the new dispensation dawning upon us, if something still more potent than magnetism, still more occult than somnambulism, be at hand to startle us from our dreams of earth and earthly things, then must this magical friend of mine and his strange companion be its heralds. For my part I can not see whither we are drifting, scarcely can I discern my way amongst the scenes of mystery that are now deepening around me. Professor von Marx is very jealous of his young seer's gifts. He himself is reticent and fearfully sensitive. The wonderful powers these men possess should be at the command of science, yet they are all limited to our most secret sessions, and scenes which, if reported, would scarcely obtain credit, even with those·who best know and trust me, are permitted to pass by like the phantasmagoria of an unquiet dream with hardly a record. How true it is that the greatest gifts seldom accompany the best dispositions to use them!

These German magicians, whose impulses are as erratic as the visions that they produce, have now been absent some months. They left us as suddenly as they came; their purpose was to travel through North Britain, as I understood, but now I learn that after making some visits among our associates in Scotland and Wales they have disappeared altogether.

February 25. Letters have been received from Professor von Marx. He is coming back to London for a few days, and sends me word he wishes to join our next meeting of the Orphic Society on Friday night. How did he know we had called a special séance for Friday night? but pshaw! why do I question? He knows everything, and what he does n't know the Chevalier can tell him. No matter, he will be dearly welcome to us all. He leaves his son in the North, he writes me word, rusticating in a quiet village for the benefit of his health. Of course they won't stay long apart; however, I will now go to his lodgings and find out when to expect him.

March 3. Professor von Marx has now been with us nearly a week. He attended one séance at the Orphic Circle on the evening of his arrival, and by desire of our guardian spirits, we are to have another session to-night. Great results are promised us, but, I scarce know why, there is a singular depression on my spirits, and one which seems in a measure to affect our whole society. Let us hope that the to-night's séance will serve to disperse the clouds.

MINUTES OF THE PROCEEDINGS AT THE ORPHIC CIRCLE HELD
MARCH 3.

Present the usual number of members and officers, the neophytes, Estelle, Sarina, and Marcus, two Brothers from Malta, and one honorary member, Professor Felix von Marx. John C. Dudley, Recording Secretary.

After the customary preliminaries of opening our session, and the business arrangements had been disposed of, it was announced that this was an "open meeting"; at which visitors might be introduced, whilst the proceedings should be subject to general discussion, or if desirable to publication. [I may here state that our society was a private, if not absolutely a secret one, hence our sessions were only canvassed openly, or the phenomena occurring therein reported beyond our lodge-room, when we received intimation from our guardians (planetary angels) that the meetings were to be "open ones." The séance called for the 3d of March, and one which was announced to follow, were to come under this category and be open to reports of what might transpire.] Considering the high expectations with which we had come together that evening, our session was less animated than we had anticipated. Professor von Marx was unusually sad and abstracted.

Amongst other subjects, we discussed reservedly, but somewhat pointedly, the reflex action likely to be produced upon a magnetizer by his subject. We were led to consider this subject all the more earnestly, by the obvious depression and restlessness manifested in Professor von Marx's manner in the absence of his beloved *protégé*, the Chevalier de B——. The professor took the ground that no such reflex action could ensue if the operator was well-composed and self-centred. Lord L—— and Sir Peter S—— were in favor of the reflex hypothesis, and I cited the professor's own change of manner and deep anxiety, now that he was absent from his best subject, in contrast with his invariable composure and self-possession when, as in earlier visits, his friend was present with him at our circle. Von Marx acknowledged the disturbing effect of the Chevalier's absence upon his mind, but added in a tone of stern self-reproach, that it was ever a failing in the true adept to cherish human affection, and that the intense emotion which was expended on personal interests, always marred the procedures of deliberate science.

Our experiments with the neophytes on this occasion were less satisfactory than usual, and they evidently felt the oppression cast by the overpowering influence of the professor's disturbed mind. We exchanged greetings successfully with the circle at L——, and neophyte Alexander's "atmospheric spirit" visited us from M——.

We had some interesting visions in the mirror, but the crystal spirits could not obtain force enough to appear. At the usual hour, when our "Rulers" were accustomed to give us some spontaneous phenomena by way of climax to our meeting, we asked, through our best *lucide* present, Mlle. Estelle, if the Chevalier de B—— could not visit us. Starting hastily from his seat, and speaking in violation of our usual order, the professor exclaimed, " No, no! I would not have it so,— that is —I beg pardon of all present, but·I would prefer to waive this visit."

Instantly the *lucide* became demagnetized, the "Rulers" vanished from the mirrors, and the lights became quite dim, the fires, sunk in the braziers, and the whole scene bore testimony to our visitor's indiscretion.

Recovering his composure in a few minutes, the professor apologized for his irregular action, and reluctantly assented to our wishes. The formulæ, which I am not at liberty to describe, by which an "atmospheric spirit" or "flying soul" is summoned, being gone through, the professor produced, as if by a strong effort, a piece of a waving lock of black hair cut from his beloved pupil's head, and with still more hesitancy than usual, submitted it to the fire of the brazier. As the leaping flame seized on the beautiful lock, von Marx, as if repenting such a sacrifice, drew it hastily away. A small portion of the crisped hair however, adhered to the brazier, but no sound of invocation moved the magician's lips. The lights were again sinking, and the neophytes shrank back, trembling and disturbed, when a blast of cold air rushed through the apartment, a deep-drawn sigh resounded in our ears, and the lights flashed up for a moment disclosing what seemed to be the form of the Chevalier de B—— extended on a visionary couch, apparently in a deep sleep. It was the first time the apparition of a slumbering "flying soul" had been amongst us, and as the Chevalier had often thus spiritually visited and communicated with us before, we attributed his present entrancement to the professor's failure in fulfilling the conditions of evocation. Yet we all beheld him plainly, and sympathized with the professor as he bent over his adopted son's form with apparent sentiments of rapt interest and admiration.

"Waken him!" whispered Sir Peter S——. "We would speak with him."

"Not for worlds!" murmured the professor, extending his arms towards the vision. "He will waken all too soon. Sleep on, my Louis, and — farewell!"

In an instant a strange, distant cry seemed to resound through the apartment, and the form of the sleeper started up and seemed to cast itself into the professor's arms. Something of an indescribable character that I have never seen or realized in any other presence than that of these Germans, then seemed to cast a spell over us all, preventing us for the moment, from seeing, hearing, or collecting our thoughts. It has often been repeated in the presence of the Chevalier de B——, and is the nearest approach to my idea of "*glamour*," or that which the Hindoos have a word for signifying *illusion*, I ever experienced. It lasts but a few seconds, and on the occasion I write of, came and went like the lightning's flash. When it was dispelled, the couch, the "flying soul," and the professor himself were all gone. Nothing could restore composure to our *lucides* after this, and our circle broke up after arranging with our guides to meet again on the following night. Lord L—— was instructed to notify the absent members, also to invite Professor von Marx's special attendance, he having promised to be present at our next séance.

How shall I record the events which immediately succeeded my last entry, or attempt to hand down to posterity statements so entirely out of ordinary human experience that I could scarcely hope to obtain credit for them did I testify to their truth on solemn oath before the world? Although at the present time modern spiritualism, with its array of well-attested marvels, has become a fixed fact, and at the time when these lines will meet the public eye, the details I record will have become the accepted belief of millions, still the circumstances which surround my narrative present an air of incredibility, which the matter-of-fact, commonplace methods of the Spiritualists are wholly lacking in. I write of apparitions, phantoms, sounds, and motions which appealed to unaccustomed witnesses; came upon us with all the awful paraphernalia of magical surroundings, and at a period when our hearts were possessed with an overwhelming dread of revelations from the world of spiritual existence. The Spiritualists now meet in jolly parties, and hail their spiritual visitants with fun and frolic, hence the very same manifestations which custom has invested with the prestige of a fashionable amusement were, in the time of which I write, surrounded with a halo of preternatural light, borrowed in part from the occult reputation of supernaturalism, but still more colored by the stupendous interests and heart-felt sympathies which were awakened in our spiritual séances. Bear with me, then, my readers, whilst I relate to you a scene whose weird horrors would *now* be received calmly and with the same meed of applause which you would bestow on a successful operatic performance, but which, at the time of its occurrence, excited such terror and deep agitation in every witness's mind that nothing that has ever occurred since has sufficed to efface its terrible memories.

Let me recite the narrative from the ordinary extracts in my diary, which read as follows: —

March 5. Meeting in session and duly inaugurated. Present: twenty members, all our officers, and the four Lucides of the month.

One hour passed away after the opening of the session, but Professor von Marx did not appear. At 10 P. M. our *Lucides,* without a word exchanged, and as if by a concert of action, rose and assumed their places at the four quarters of the lodge as if we were not in open but secret session. All four were deeply entranced. Soon after this movement, they sang a sweet and exquisite improvisation, at the close of which they joined in a well-known hymn, their fine voices attuned to such a pure and rich harmony, that every heart present felt its resistless spell. It was not until the singers had ceased, that we perceived, by the dim light of the four altar lamps, Professor Marx was amongst us. He had entered noiselessly and unseen by any one; in fact, how he had entered was a mystery, the séance being conducted with doors locked and guarded. The professor had not taken his usual place amongst the members, but stationed himself in one of the seats assigned to visitors, although there were none admitted that evening.

Before we had time to greet him or remark upon the suddenness of his appearance, he addressed us, speaking in a singular, far-off tone of voice, which affected every listener with an indescribable sense of awe. His words were, as far as I can remember, to this effect: "My time is short, my power to address you limited. My beloved one is in fearful peril. *Summon him not, nor inquire his fate for nine days.* When that time expires, I will come again and direct you what to do. I have fearfully wronged him, and it is for you, John Dudley, to help me make reparation. I have tampered all too presumptuously with the sacred forces of a human soul, and ere I can find peace or rest, I must redeem my error. Aid me!" He paused, yet a spell was on us all so strong, that not a creature moved or a voice replied.

As for me, my tongue clove to the roof of my mouth. A nameless horror possessed me, and though I looked fixedly at the speaker, and could trace distinctly, even in that dim light, every line of his pale and anxious face, my eyes seemed blighted, and I would have given much for the power to turn them away and fix on them some other object. As he paused, he bent his eyes upon me, and so pleading, wistful, and yet piercing became their expression, that I felt as if I could not endure that glance another moment, when lo! he slowly melted out before us into thin air. As he disappeared, the room shook violently, every object rocked as in an earthquake; the lights flamed up, then sank, and seemed on the point of expiring; deep sighs, and one or two low moans resounded through the apartment; the air was suffocating. "Great Heaven! what is all this?" cried one of the members.

"Let me be gone; I cannot stay in this dreadful place!" said another. In a moment there was a general movement towards the entrances; the veils were thrown aside, and the whole of the party were hurrying back and forth through the room with restless and irrepressible agitation.

Whilst I sat in my place staring vacantly at the spot from whence the "atmospheric spirit" — as we deemed the apparition to have been — had disappeared, one of our *lucides*, in her natural tone, said hurriedly, shaking me by the arm at the same time, "Mr. Dudley, Mr. Dudley, arouse yourself! That was no 'flying soul,' but Professor von Marx's spirit. For Heaven's sake, hasten to the professor's lodgings, though I fear me it is too late. *He is dead!* I feel sure he is dead, and the poor young Chevalier is abandoned."

March 6. Yes, Professor von Marx is dead! Our circle broke up and dispersed immediately after the scene last recorded, and accompanied by our president, the venerable Lord V——, I hastened off to the professor's lodgings, which were at a considerable distance from my residence; in .fact, close down by the river side. It occupied some time before my servants could be summoned, my carriage brought round, and Lord V—— and myself set down at the old mansion which my friend had selected as the retreat of himself and his adopted son.

It was near midnight then, when we reached the house, but we found the domestics all up and in the utmost perplexity and consternation. The professor had desired to be called at six o'clock that evening to dress for dinner, but when his valet reached him in fulfilment of his orders, he found him cold and rigid, as if he had been dead some hours. Medical aid had been summoned in vain. The proprietor of the house had despatched messengers to me, but as I had been dining out, and was subsequently engaged at our lodge, I could not be found, and there was no means of apprising me of the fact save through the extraordinary apparition which we had so recently witnessed. "Apoplexy," "heart disease," etc. etc., these were the medical verdicts on a case which none could understand and no science account for.

March 10. My position is becoming most embarrassing. The people with whom Professor von Marx lodged, inform me the poor young Chevalier arrived the night after his father died, and passed up the stairs without speaking a word to any one. How long he remained they cannot tell, but in the morning they found he had left the house and gone no one knows whither. It is a mystery to us all to discover how he heard of his friend's decease. I had despatched special messengers to him with the sad tidings, but they could not have reached him before the very night when he appeared in London. Taking into account all the mysteries by which we are surrounded, I don't feel at all sure that the individual seen was really the Chevalier in person. How do we know but what it might have been only his "atmospheric spirit," or what the Germans call the *Döppel Ganger?*

For my part I am so bewildered with the attempt to find my way amidst these dark and occult paths, that I become lost, and uncertain how far we are justified in lifting the awful veil which divides the realms of spirit and matter. Half my time I know not by what or whom I am surrounded, or how to discriminate between the real and the phantom people that flash before my eyes.

Remembering the mysterious charge we have received, I dare not seek for this poor young man before the prescribed nine days elapse, and yet I am filled with the deepest anxiety on his account, and long to tender him the consolations of friendship and sympathy. More difficulties yet beset me. Professor von Marx has left his entire property to his adopted son, and named me as his guardian and trustee. His will is clear and lucid, and was evidently made for the hour, suiting so well the present crisis that it would seem as if he had foreseen and provided for the very moment of his decease.

March 11. No tidings yet of the Chevalier, and the singular emphasis with which the apparition demanded a nine days' suspension of all inquiry, paralyzes any attempt on my part to discover what has become of him, yet my business advisers urge me to seek out the young heir without loss of time, and my best friends begin to wonder why I take no steps in this direction. Urgent advice and suggestions to "act promptly" pour in upon me from all quarters, and even my servants are regarding me with furtive and suspicious glances. I suppose every one will soon begin to set me down as crazy,—an opinion that I shall not, I fear, be very undeserving of, unless something occurs to relieve my mind from the terrible anxiety that now possesses it. The hardest task I have yet had to encounter is to resist the pleadings of my dear wife and children, who constantly urge me to institute inquiries for the missing heir, whom, they persist in believing, has been "made away with," through the same magical arts that have (as they allege) destroyed the unfortunate professor. It would be in vain for me to attempt combating such an opinion, absurd as it appears; equally impossible for me to explain why I am determined to commence no search until after the nine days have expired.

We have called two special meetings of the Orphic Circle, but alas! the visions seem to be closed. Our *somnambules* are themselves so much disturbed and their minds so agitated by the prevailing excitement, that they are unable to come into those conditions of passivity necessary to procure reliable visions. They all seem to concur in the opinion, however, that the Chevalier is still living, and destined, as they predict, to grow out of his present semi-earthly condition and attain to a high and noble manhood.

March 15. This night completes the prescribed season of inactivity, and at 10 p. m. the Orphic Circle will meet to advise with, whatever powers may be pleased to attend us, upon the necessary steps to be taken for the discovery of our unfortunate young friend. Amidst all manner of annoyances, estranged looks, covert reproaches, and open rebukes, I have faithfully adhered to the commands of the mysterious phantom and abstained from all attempts to discover the Chevalier's retreat. I only know that he left his country retirement and appeared at his former residence in London. At neither place have any tidings been heard of him since; and his unaccountable absence from the funeral of his adopted father, which we delayed until yesterday, leaves us no longer a shadow of hope that he will voluntarily appear amongst us.

To-night, the ninth since the apparition of Professor von Marx at our circle, must decide how far we can look for help from the invisible world; if that fails us, to-morrow's dawn will see me surrounded with every instrumentality that human effort can afford, to make our search successful.

Many days have elapsed since I made my last entry, but the events that have crowded so thickly upon me

17

have prevented my fulfilment of that which has now become to me a solemn. life duty, namely, to record as plainly and truthfully as language can set forth the facts of spiritual intervention in human affairs, and to draw the mysterious and awful veil which has hitherto shrouded those realms of power and influence, from which the invisible springs of human action mainly proceed.

On the night of March 15 our session commenced at 9 P. M., and our lodge was opened with the usual formalities. Our four neophytes were stationed by the altars, each with the mirror and crystal appropriate to the time. The four lamps which sufficed to dispel the darkness of the lodge were lighted, the braziers duly served, and the fumigations carefully attended to. After the opening hymns had been sung and the invocations commenced, the lamps began to flicker with the usual unsteady motion which indicates responses from the spirits summoned, and in a short time they went out one after another, leaving the room only faintly illuminated by the colored fires from the braziers.

Around the central altar we now perceived that the crystals were beginning to be covered by bright corruscations of sparkling light. With sensations of unwonted awe and breathless interest, we noticed also, that small tongues of flame and globes of pale light loomed through the darkness at different parts of the hall, sailing around, and gradually disappearing near the altar. At length we observed that the whole apartment was becoming lighter and lighter.

From whatever source the illumination proceeded, it completely overpowered the light of the braziers, until it gradually filled the whole place with a soft, hazy twilight. Then it was that we discovered around the cen-

tral altar, a circle of crouching, dark forms, who, with
veiled heads and misty robes, seemed to be supported
on seats faintly outlined, and stretching away, row after
row and circle after circle, until they reached from the
first or inner circle, up to the remotest portion of the
roof, completely filling our vast lodge-room and ascending as it seemed even beyond the roof, in the form of
an ancient Roman amphitheatre. This spectral company, although clearly outlined in the mysterious twilight of the room, obscured but did not conceal the
other persons or material objects present, which shone
through them as if they had been merely shadows.

I find on comparing notes with the other members of
the circle, the appearances I have thus briefly described
were realized by all pretty much alike. Let it be remembered, however, that what I have attempted to depict in
cold, matter-of-fact language, can never be thoroughly
realized except by the awe-struck witnesses, nor could
any word-painting, however vivid, do justice to the
tremendous and harrowing impressions produced on
every mind by the presence of this immense company
of formless, nameless shadows. I might live for centuries ere the memory of that solemn and terrific scene
could be obliterated; I might behold death and carnage, the red battle-field, or mortal catastrophe in its
direst form, yet nothing could ever equal the insupportable horror of that phantom gathering. I recall it now,
with sentiments of dismay which no time has served to
diminish. Presently, in the midst of the awful stillness,
there came a sudden movement amongst the spectral
forms; with one accord they all rose to their feet, and
as they did so, a soughing, sighing sound filled the apartment, like the uprising of a vast multitude, accompanied by the rushing of a mighty wind. It was evident

that something or somebody had come into their midst, whom these shrouded phantoms rose to receive. During what ensued, they all remained erect and motionless, yet still dimly visible in the peculiar and unearthly glare that illumined the lodge. Then, without perceiving any other form or realizing who spoke, except from the tone and substance of what follows, a voice, which all present recognized as that of Felix von Marx, speaking from the circle of braziers which surrounded the central altar, addressed us thus:—

"My Louis is dead; he lies in the wood by the side of the river on the road to which I will direct you through Estelle, and from whence you, John Dudley, must bring him to your home. Take him to your heart, and do your duty by him as a man, a friend, a father. Your course towards him will be inspired, and all your actions guided by those who have his soul in charge. They will give you the daily bread of wisdom so long as he tarries with you. In the life that has passed for him, for me, I have greatly wronged him, — filled his soul with mine, clothed his spirit in my own, consumed, absorbed, and killed him. His spirit has fled in yearning after mine, but during the dread hour of mortal death, the Father of spirits has permitted his angels to repair the mighty wrong, allowed his soul to gain another birth, struggle into a new life, attain another being; moulded anew by pain and anguish, the crushed germ of his new-born soul has been revived by pitying angels. The body sleeps now, but the spirit hovers near, upborne in the hands of ministering spirits, who weave afresh the vital cord that binds him to mortal life, and when you have rescued the suffering frame from its grassy death-bed, the reunion of the new-born soul with its earthly tenement will be effected. Rescued to be a revelator in the new dispensation, spared to take his place as a builder in the temple of the new religion, his real life-work must begin under your fatherhood, John Dudley; and the Lord and Master of life, the Father of all, do so to you, and more also, as you do to him, my victim and my child. Now speed away, and hasten! hasten!"

The voice ceased, or rather the last accents seemed to die off in a prolonged and singular wail, hushed by the soughing sound before described, as if the vast concourse of moving phantoms were about to resume their crouching attitudes, but no, they sank down, down, with a long, subsiding sigh, until they melted into the ground beneath our feet. The lights streamed up from the braziers; the veils of separation and banners that floated from the walls stirred and waved as if moved by a strong wind; sweet odors streamed for a moment through the room; a few distant chords of music rang through the air, then all was still, and everything resumed its place and aspect, as if the whole past scene had been nothing but an unquiet dream.

By the time the hour of midnight had sounded from the city clocks, Estelle, our best clairvoyant, Lord V——, and myself were seated in my barouche, with four of my best horses in harness. The night was wild and threatening. Heavy banks of clouds from time to time obscured the moon and cast their murky shadows across the path which our flying horses traversed. Our clairvoyant, in a deep magnetic trance, directed our path at every turn in the road. I myself sat on the box and drove, Estelle being placed by my side, two outriders following, to render such service as we might require. We traversed Hampstead Heath, and guided ever by our admirable somnambulist, we struck off several times from the direct road, until towards morning, after five hours' ride, pursued without pause or interruption, we reached the banks of a deep and sullen river, and began to near the outskirts of an extensive wood.

So frequent had been the divergencies we made under our somnambulist's direction, that I had lost all track of the road we pursued, and the spot we had now reached was entirely strange to me. On gaining the point in question, Estelle gave me a peremptory sign to stop, and for a few moments her attitude of breathless silence induced me to fear she was losing the mysterious thread of influence that had guided us thus far. My doubts were soon dispelled however, and a new-born hope set my heart wildly throbbing, as the young girl hurriedly bade us alight and give our carriage and horses in charge of the grooms, who were to wait for further orders. Then crying, "Follow me!" she sprang forward into the wood, moving with a pace so swift and a step so light, that it was with the utmost difficulty Lord V—— and myself could track her through the darkness by her white garments. As we advanced, struggling painfully forward amidst the tangled underbrush and overhanging boughs of half-fallen trees, we saw a distant light sailing through the air and descending towards the ground, where it seemed to hover for a few seconds, then sunk rapidly and became extinguished. At the same moment a cry from Estelle warned us to quicken our pace, and obeying the impatient waving of her white handkerchief, we stumbled and groped our way on until we reached the edge of a ravine, at the side of which, a few steps below the path, we found Estelle, awake, in her normal state, and with tears streaming down her cheeks, kneeling on the ground beside the cold and lifeless form of him we came to seek. His garments drenched with rain, whiter than snow, with staring, open eyes fixed in the awful glare of death on the silent stars, with stiff, thin hands clutching as if in agony, masses of earth and up-torn grass,— there lay the piteous form of the once beautiful and highly-gifted heir of the great Professor von Marx.

Speculation was idle; pity gave place to rapid action, sympathy and grief to quick resolve. Raising the dead form, for such it appeared to be, in my arms, with Lord V——'s help I carried him from the dreary wood to the carriage, and ere noon of the day which was just then dawning, I placed him beneath the shelter of my own roof. I brought back to my anxious wife and children a sad and piteous spectacle 't is true, a mere skeleton, with scarcely a shadow of the brilliant grace and beauty that had once distinguished him; but I knew the invisible powers that had rescued him could restore the life they had so miraculously saved. I knew that the future called him, and the hand of waiting destiny could raise him from the very bier. I was neither surprised nor excited, therefore, when the physicians I had summoned, reported that the faint fluttering of the still throbbing heart, gave promise that my cares and anxieties would yet be rewarded, and Professor von Marx's solemn trust of fatherhood had not been bequeathed to me in vain.

CHAPTER XIV.

May 18, 18 . Many weeks elapsed before I had an opportunity of making another entry in my diary. Meantime spring had almost ripened into summer, and the ward in whom I had become so strangely and involuntarily interested, was restored to life and partial strength, and at the request of my pitying wife and daughters, became established as an inmate of my own home. These dear members of my family, although unyielding in their prejudices against my "magical practices," had always manifested a deep interest in the young Chevalier de B——; in fact, they had so won upon his reticent nature by their kind and womanly attentions, that he was completely familiarized amongst them, and proved an ever-welcome visitor in my wife's *salon.* His high intellectual culture, passionate love of music, exquisite voice, and skilful performance on several instruments of music, completed the charm with which nature had endowed him, and few persons could have supposed that there was any subject of divided opinion between the ladies of my household and their fascinating visitor.

On the sad day when I brought the wasted form of their favorite to rest for a while beneath my roof, my wife insisted upon his being given up to her tender care. The time came at last, however, when this gentle nurse, no less than all his other attendants, myself included, began to regard his convalescence with a mixture of equal astonishment and perplexity.

We could not disguise from ourselves the startling fact, that the unfortunate Chevalier, whilst regaining his usual composure and lucidity of manner, had obviously lost sight of his own identity. That his external appearance should long retain traces of the terrible sufferings he had undergone was naturally to be expected; but the look of mature age which overspread his haggard face and worn form, did not pass away with returning strength.

Although little more than twenty years of age, he might have been taken for a man of forty. His voice, naturally sweet and melodious, assumed a deeper tone, and his accent, strongly marked by his mother's native Italian, now betrayed the same German intonation peculiar to his adopted father's. Day by day some fresh token of a wandering mind, fixing itself into the very self-same grooves of identity that had distinguished Professor von Marx, became more and more strikingly apparent. He would frequently perplex his kind nurses by entreating them to tell him *where Louis was, and why he had* deserted his unfortunate father now that he was so weak and helpless. At times he would startle me with the same supplication, always addressing me as his "dear old friend John," and speaking of himself as if he had been the real Felix von Marx. Sometimes he would ask whether there was no letter yet from Louis, and speculate, with an anxiety distressing to witness, on the causes which prevented his hearing from him.

I was greatly embarrassed how to answer him, but he would generally save me the trouble by running off from the subject in his wandering way, saying, "I know I have been very ill, distraught I believe in my mind, but I am nearly well now and able to understand all you may have to say to me. Tell me then, about my darling. You know I left him at R——, and thought to have joined him just as I was taken ill. How long is it since then? Tell me, John!" I would commonly answer him in the same strain, saying, Louis had gone on a visit to our mutual friend Lord V——, and that he had only been ill a week or two. Louis would soon return, etc. etc. Sometimes these stereotyped replies would quite satisfy him, though repeated many times a week; at others he would try to think, and murmur dreamily, "I thought it was a very long time ago and that I had been travelling through many strange countries, of which I have no distinct recollection." As time wore on, the impression that he was Felix von Marx deepened upon him, but the strangest part of all was, not alone his perfect assumption of all the professor's peculiar traits of character, but his entire renunciation of all ideas and habits which had formerly distinguished himself. The Chevalier's accomplishment in and love of music gave place to the professor's indifference, amounting to dislike of the art. Even the sweet voices of my daughters, which the young man had been accustomed to join, and listen to with rapt delight, now displeased him, and he would hastily quit the room when they began to sing. He would accompany us in riding or driving as far as his feeble strength permitted, but he shrank away with dislike, almost fear, from the presence of strangers or visitors, and desired only to spend his time in solitude and deep abstraction. He frequently spoke of his intention to go and seek Louis, but he seemed unable to fix his mind upon a permanent idea, and was easily persuaded that the same week or two since he had been taken ill, was all that had elapsed, and that Louis was coming home to-morrow or next day. As if to compensate me for the deep anxiety I suffered on my poor ward's account, a change arose in the feelings of my family which brought me unmitigated satisfaction.

The strange tidings from America about the marvels of spirit communion, came faster and thicker, and wonderful narratives were in circulation, concerning the system of telegraphy by which the world of spirits was bringing assurance of their continued existence to the minds of their earthly friends. Although the report of these marvels formed a prominent theme of discussion at many a fashionable assemblage and amongst our numerous visitors, I never promoted or made the slightest allusion to them in my own family; perhaps I never should have done so, had I not one day been timidly sounded by my youngest darling, Blanche, who after beating about the bush for a considerable time in her own pretty, insinuating way, proceeded to pour out a remarkable narrative, the sum of which was as follows:—

It seemed that my daughter's German maid had lately been much disturbed by unaccountable noises, which kept her awake of a night, and finally induced her to ask the housekeeper to change her sleeping apartment. On mentioning the cause of her request, the housekeeper gravely informed her she would obtain no relief from a change of rooms, as she herself as well as several of the other domestics had experienced the same strange annoyances; that the sounds in question were to be heard all over the house, in a word, according to the *gouvernante's* theory, the strange sounds were *the new thing* that had come across the ocean from America, and no one could prevent or hinder them.

When this piece of philosophy began to be discussed in the servants' hall, it turned out, as the housekeeper had said, that strange knockings and odd motions of furniture, had been noticed all over the house. Some of the servants attributed the trouble to the goblins that their master and Professor von Marx had been so busy in raising; others, to the work of the late professor's ghost; but all agreed that they had something to do with the poor young Chevalier, as they were most frequently heard around the apartments occupied by him and his Arab servant, and they finally agreed to refer the whole matter to Lady Emily L——, my wife's sister, a staid widow lady now on a visit amongst us, and one whose strong sense constituted her a high authority in such occult difficulties. When Lady Emily heard the various statements concerning the disturbances now prevalent, she did not, as had been expected, deny their credibility or rebuke the narrators for their superstitious opinions, but she quietly informed the housekeeper and German maid, that her nieces as well as herself had experienced the same disturbances; that she had lately been much occupied in reading accounts from America on similar phenomena, and certain tracts on the subject had explained the method by which mortals could put themselves in safe and direct communication with these haunting spirits; she ended by advising that her nieces and herself, assisted by the worthy housekeeper and two of the most intelligent of the ladies' maids, should form a circle on the approved American fashion and see what would come of it.

At first the bold investigators nearly scared themselves into fits by their rash experiment, for no sooner had they seated themselves on the prescribed plan around their circle-table, than that hitherto well-bred and inanimate article of furniture, began to leap, dance, slide, kick, and behave in such a generally frantic manner, that the astounded sitters retreated from it in horror, and ended by summoning a footman to carry the demoniac piece of furniture away into parts unknown.

After recovering from the first shock of this astounding exhibition, the pioneers returned to the charge with another table, and then another and another. At last, finding that as soon as they put themselves in position, every article they laid hands on behaved in the same unruly manner, they concluded to consult some of their acquaintances who, as report alleged, had already taken their first degrees in the mystery of spirit rappings and were known to be holding nightly circles with immense success.

From this point it is unnecessary to trace the unfoldments of the great secret with which my Blanche had come charged. Her gentle mother — at first strenuously opposed to such terrible doings — had finally been initiated as one of the sisters, and become classified as an excellent impressional and seeing medium. My eldest daughter Sophie, was the writing and drawing medium of the band, and had already filled up several quires of foolscap with "communications from the seventh sphere." Blanche was a tipping, rapping, personating, singing, playing, and every other sort of a medium. Lady Emily and the housekeeper were "developing mediums," and two German, one Spanish, and one French lady's maid, were rapping and seeing mediums. In short, I was informed that my entire household had become hand-and-glove with the spirit world; that circles in our own family, as well as in those of several of our acquaintances, were in full headway, and that they had at length thought it fit and proper that they should ask my permission to carry on their investigations, as well as my advice as to their best modes of procedure.

Without even hinting to my fair informant that I deemed her application came a little late in the day, much less apprising her that a certain cousin Harry, an Oxford B. A., had kept me fully informed of the whole matter from first to last, I assumed a grave air, declared the thing had become serious and must be immediately looked into; that it was my duty as a county magistrate and the father of a family to take the whole thing into custody and join the next séance they were to hold, which turned out to be that very night. It would be unnecessary to pursue this subject further at the present time, save to state, that I found several good test mediums in my family, as my dear little Blanche had stated; that then and for some two or three years subsequently, my dear ones enjoyed a heaven upon earth in the bright and consoling communion of loved ones gone before, and that it colored their whole lives and tinctured their opinions with a liberal element, which has happily never failed to exert its elevating influence over them.

One day, when I was more than ordinarily concerned at the increasing hallucination of the Chevalier, I determined to ask our spirit friends what course they would recommend me to pursue with him. It seemed to us all, a remarkable circumstance that amongst the number and variety of spirits that had identified themselves through our mediums, Felix von Marx had never manifested. I had often asked for him, but without success, and what was still stranger, none of our spirit friends seemed able to give any account of him. They all concurred in stating that they believed he was "still in the earth sphere." Pesenting my special request for advice to one of our trusted spirit guides, we received the following message: "Bring the Chevalier here." I was doubtful whether he would come; the spirits were sure of his compliance. The matter was soon decided, for I tendered my invitation to the Chevalier, who at once, and with something of his old yielding manner, rose and followed me without a word. No sooner had he taken the place assigned him at the circle, than a letter came fluttering through the air, passing his face and falling on his hand. On opening the sheet we found written in ink not yet dry, the words, " Send for Ernestine — you know who, for you have been writing to her this morning." The letter was unsigned, but addressed to "John C. Dudley, Esq., —— Square, London." Now, although I had long since given up being astonished at anything, I was considerably startled now: first, at the only direct writing I had ever received from a spiritual source;. next, at the intelligence conveyed. The truth is, in a recent conversation with my ward, he, under the fixed impression that he was Felix von Marx, stated that in the early days of his married life he had purchased and presented to his wife a piece of valuable land, the lease of which would run out just about this time, and as she would be liable to lose her interest in it unless she took certain legal steps which he referred to, so he wished I would do him the favor to write and advise her of what was requisite to be done. Never was I more completely astounded than by this address. I knew, if I knew anything, that the Chevalier was entirely ignorant that his father had ever been married, whilst the information he gave about the property was equally unknown to me. Directly after Professor Marx's decease I had inquired for the address of his widow the Princess Ernestine, and informed her of her loss, at the same time mentioning the disposition her late husband had made of his property. The princess by letter, expressed her entire approval of the professor's will, and when I again wrote to her to inquire whether any such business transaction as that the Chevalier had described, really took place, she entered into a full account of the matter, described it in the same terms as those employed by the Chevalier, and announced her intention of seeing me when she came to London, which, she added, she expected to do in a few days on special business. She gave as her town address a certain hotel in Bond St., and it was a note addressed to her Highness at that hotel that I had actually been engaged in writing in the morning. I had been interrupted before I could finish my letter, and having put it in my desk under lock and key, I had the best reason to believe no human being was cognizant of its existence, although, as I now found to my astonishment, there were other eyes than those of humanity on our most secret actions.

Our séance soon closed, and this was the first and last time the Chevalier ever joined us; in fact, after he had taken his place amongst us, his entire absence of mind rendered all that passed a complete blank to him.

The next day I drove to the hotel to which the Princess von Marx's letters were to be directed, and on reaching it, learned to my great surprise and gratification, that she had already arrived, although she was not prepared to receive visitors. Sending up my card, with the pressing request that she would favor me with an interview, I found myself admitted to the illustrious lady's presence before I had well made up my mind how to prefer the strange request I had to make to her. I found her Highness composed enough to compensate for my blundering ways, so I let her rattle on until it suddenly occurred to me I ought to have opened the interview by condoling with her on her widowed condition. Before I had got half through the speech I deemed it proper to make on this point, the princess interrupted me with a grave assurance that she quite appreciated the depth of my sympathy, but for her part, her chief concern was in the idea that poor Felix must be such an *unprogressed spirit*, in fact, she could not rest until she had learned something of what sphere he was in. Unprogressed spirit, spheres, and all that sort of thing! What did I hear? Why, this was the spiritualistic dialect to which I was now becoming thoroughly accustomed, and if my ears did not deceive me, the Princess Ernestine must be a Spiritualist. A few leading questions soon settled that point. The princess *was* a Spiritualist, an ardent one, of course, — nay, she had actually made a visit to London for the sole purpose of consulting a celebrated American medium who had lately arrived in the city. Thus was my way made clear for me, and my difficult mission more than half accomplished. As delicately as I could, I explained to her the singular and tenderly intimate tie which had bound her late husband to his young *protégé*.

I then proceeded to detail the awkward dilemma in which I and my whole family were placed, by the strange hallucination of my ward, whom the princess pronounced at once to be "obsessed" by that violent and determined late spouse of hers. Interrupting me before I could explain the object of my mission, this very impulsive lady launched out into the peculiar nature of obsession, the special tendencies of that very obstinate person, Felix von Marx, and the certainty that there was but one way of exorcising him, or in other words, getting rid of him, and that was by boldly confronting him in

18

her own person. She *naïvely* enough assured me, if it were von Marx's spirit that possessed the victim, there was no surer way of disposing of him, than to bring him face to face with his wife; adding, she was quite satisfied he could n't stay in her presence a single moment, but would only be too glad to relinquish his prey, after which of course he would retire to the particular sphere to which he belonged. "You see, my dear friend," urged the lady, in a torrent of eloquence which proved how deeply she was immersed in the subject under consideration, "von Marx can not be anything less than the most obstinate of all spirits, just as he was the most determined of all men. Now, my plan is this: I 'll present myself before him, announcing my intention of remaining there for life if it be necessary. Of course he will go, he can not but choose to do so, and thus your friend will be delivered from his tormentor and I shall have my chance to retaliate; that is, of course, I don't mean that, only to aid this most unprogressed of spirits to make atonement for past offences."

When the lady had talked herself out, I at last had an opportunity of putting in a mild suggestion. I availed myself of it, by informing her my principal object in soliciting her interference was, with a view of finally testing the truth of the sad proposition as to whether the young man was or was not obsessed by the spirit of 'his adopted father.

As the Chevalier was not only a stranger to the person of the princess, but had never even heard of her, it occurred to me, any intelligence that might be manifested by bringing him suddenly into her presence, must prove decisive of the real condition of his mind. Of course Madame had ulterior designs, to which my proposition was but subordinate. However, I mentally determined to let matters shape themselves, provided I could only succeed in procuring the interview and testify its results as above suggested. As the princess was perfectly willing to accede to any arrangement that could favor the design which now possessed her, namely, that of helping her late husband "to become a progressed spirit," it was agreed that she should accompany me back to my residence that very evening, so that by taking the Chevalier, as well as the whole of my family by surprise, we might make any test of intelligence all the more confirmatory.

After an early dinner, which I partook of *tête-à-tête* with my old flame, but in which anxiety for my ward colored our whole conversation, the princess was good enough to take a seat in my carriage and accompany me to my house, which we reached about eight o'clock in the evening. Ushering my fair visitor into my library, which led out by French windows on to a broad stone terrace overlooking the garden, I went out in search of my wife, to whom I proposed to mention the fact of the princess's arrival. Just as I had passed on to the terrace, my wife and the Chevalier, with whom she had been walking, approached, and I immediately returned for the princess, whom I thus allowed to encounter the Chevalier without a moment's preparation on either side. The pale and haggard face, bent form, and pleading eyes of the unfortunate young man, would have commanded pity from the least interested observer, but when the singular and almost preternatural resemblance that existed between the professor and his *protégé* is remembered, the start and faint cry of the princess on beholding such an apparition, might easily be understood.

As to the Chevalier himself, the wild glare which lit

up his eyes and the look of horror which transfigured his whole expression, fixed us all in anxious expectation. The deep flush which at first mantled his worn cheek, turned to a frightful pallor as he exclaimed in accents of deep agitation, "Ernestine! Ernestine! in the name of heaven and our dead child, why have you come hither to torment me?"

"Is it you, Felix?" the lady murmured, in low and trembling accents.

"Is it Felix von Marx?" he asked, in those tones of bitter scorn which I had so often heard from the professor, but never before from the gentle lips of his son. "Is this poor, shivering wreck the Felix whom you took on that bright, fatal summer day, O Ernestine! when I sold you my peace and liberty for a mess of pottage?"

I had heard from von Marx that this very expression, wrung from him in one of his most acrimonious matrimonial disputes, had been more violently resented by his lady than any other reproach that had ever fallen from his lips. To hear it now repeated by one who was not even in existence when it had been first uttered, and who never by any possibility could have heard it applied in such a connection, was so startling to myself, my wife, and the princess, that the insult it conveyed, passed us all unnoticed; meantime the Chevalier, assuming a more dignified and less passionate tone, now addressed the lady with grave courtesy and begged her to retire with him for a few moments, then bowing to me and my wife, he motioned the lady with an air of deep respect to accompany him to the end of the terrace where he seated her, standing leaning against the stone balustrade to the end of the interview. As they retired, my wife, who was by this time thoroughly convinced my theory of obsession was correct, remarked in a frightened

whisper how strange it was that throughout the whole
scene the young man should have spoken in the Russian language. Now, we were both aware that though
von Marx spoke this tongue with perfect facility, he had
in vain tried to induce his son to learn it. Its harsh
guttural tones were so distasteful to him, that he always
declared he could not study it, yet he had used it in
addressing the princess, and that with the fluency and
correctness of a native. Madame von Marx assured us
also he had maintained their protracted conversation
entirely in that language.

What the substance of that interview was we never
heard. The lady wept abundantly as it proceeded, and
when at last the Chevalier, bowing to her profoundly,
passed us and retired, Madame, whom we immediately
rejoined, was so much affected, that it was some time
before she could recover her composure. She begged
us not to press her for details, but assured as "that
weird stranger" had spoken to her of matters which
none beside God and her late husband could have
known, and that had she not previously been convinced
of the truth of Spiritualism, *the unmistakable presence
of Felix von Marx's spirit in a human body, whilst his
own was mouldering in the grave,* must have converted
her. We decided that it would not be safe to subject
our visitor to a renewal of these exciting scenes, hence
the princess determined not to see him again; besides,
the test which we had sought, was fully rendered, and
now the only question that remained was what steps we
should pursue to release the victim from his terrible and
unnatural bondage.

If my readers can apprehend the scope of my strange
narrative, if they do not deem it an idle and senseless
fabrication rather than a statement put on record for the

sake of illustrating one of the most momentous and solemn of problems in mental science, they will perceive with what stupendous difficulties my path was now environed.

My good name had already been injuriously associated with vague and, of course, utterly unfounded rumors concerning the nature of the occult practices in which I was known to be interested. Despite the extreme reticence of my wife and daughters on the subject of our spiritual investigations, the tidings had gone abroad that I had succeeded in perverting them from the faith of their fathers and "inveigling them into the absurd and blasphemous pretensions of the new sect calling themselves Spiritualists."

These pernicious reports were sufficiently calculated to prejudice us in the opinion of our large circle of acquaintance and painfully affect the sensitive natures of my dear ones at home.

The sudden death of the celebrated Professor von Marx had excited much injurious comment, and sufficed to cast an ill odor on all who were supposed to be engaged in the occult pursuits to which whispered rumor attributed his mysterious demise; but the most distressing of all my perplexities was the condition of my unhappy ward. Here was a young foreigner of high birth, distinguished appearance, and heir to property of which I had been left sole trustee. This gentleman had first disappeared and then reappeared under the most mysterious circumstances, and the deep seclusion in which I was now said to hold him, served to swell the tide of prejudice that was mustering against me. The faithful Arabian who attended on my ward could speak no English, but my other domestics converted even this circumstance into evil testimony, alleging that he was stricken dumb to all but his master under the influence of a spell."

The strange sounds and sights that had of late possessed my house, and the report that the Chevalier was obsessed by demons, were other items of public gossip against which I found it impossible to make headway.

My lawyers urged an immediate settlement of Professor von Marx's estate, but my ward was in no condition to assist me in doing so. Meantime my large circle of *very dear friends* testified by the frequency and length of their visits, the deep interest they took in my private affairs. They manifested this disposition more especially by their reiterated inquiries for my " charming ward," and their pressing requests that Mrs. Dudley would bring him with her to this assembly or that *soirée*, nay, at times they propounded the direct question to my wife and daughters, why the Chevalier never appeared in public any more. To all these impertinences my poor girls could only plead their guest's ill health and his inconsolable grief for the loss of his friend.

At length a rumor began to spread, from what source I know not, that Professor von Marx was not really dead, but that his pupil was, and a hint was even dropped upon the propriety of exhuming the body to ascertain its identity.

The poor princess, shocked at the various evil reports that were in circulation, fled away to the Continent, postponing her intention of helping her late husband's spirit out of purgatory, until matters were more favorable for the experiment. My dear wife and children bore up more bravely under our various trials than I had a right to expect; still we all realized that though the ominous words " witchcraft " and " magic " were gone out of fashion, and we could no more become obnoxious

to the sorcerer's doom of fire and fagots, there were yet
two words of scarcely less evil import whispered against
us, and these were "Spiritualism" and "infidelity," whilst
the fire and fagots of public opinion might be made
scarcely less scorching than the flames of the ancient
auto-da-fé.

I am now writing not so much for my own time or
generation, as for myself and posterity. I wish to leave
a record behind me which will serve as a mile-stone on
the road of spiritualistic discovery which later generations will assuredly traverse. I wish too, in thus recalling the bitter experiences I have passed through, to
analyze some of the mysteries of their causation, and
endeavor to profit by the lessons they have afforded me
through a candid examination of their different points.
Let me add then, to this page of confession, that the
most insoluble problem that now beset me, I found lurking within the depths of my own consciousness, that is
to say, I felt entirely uncertain concerning the propriety, or even the righteousness of my own past course.
What had my researches into these awful realms of
spiritual existence, brought to me and mine? I asked.

Visions of horror, scenes which make the blood
curdle to remember; phantoms from realms of which
I knew nothing, and association with beings whose
nature was revolting to my poor, weak humanity. My
friend too was dead, and in the midst of all the revealments which the weird phenomena around me brought,
I could learn no tidings of his immortal being, except
such as filled me with new horror and dismay. The
dreadful hallucination of the young Chevalier, that is,
if hallucination it was, rather than a still more fearful
reality,—all this, added to my own doubts, fears, and
present struggles with public opinion, formed such an

array of calamity that, light-hearted and trusting as 1 generally was, I felt as if I must soon sink beneath my burdens, unless indeed, something came to help me endure, or relieve me from them.

It was in the depth of this Gethsemane that my dear girls became mediums, and furnished to their afflicted parents just the very bread of life for which they were famishing. The proofs of immortality these happy, blessed séances of ours brought us, were irresistible and conclusive. The tokens of spirit presence, guardianship, and continued protection became to our wounded spirits a perpetual strength and consolation.

Wise, reasonable, just philosophy was rendered us for the difficulties by which we were surrounded. Professor von Marx's excessive absorption in occult practices was represented as the cause of the great wrong he had done to his beloved *protégé*, rendering him a mere parasite on another's life, and filling him with a foreign magnetism which destroyed his individuality, and made him a mere fragile, helpless instrument of another's will. It was to this cause that our spirit friends attributed the Chevalier's desperate attempt at suicide and his present obsession.

As to the shafts which public opinion levelled against us, we were warned that the path of the reformer and innovator ever runs in the grooves of martyrdom, and that if we would be found worthy to become participants in new revelations of truth, we must endure the fires of persecution from the disciples of the old. We were promised a speedy deliverance from all the pains and penalties that now beset us, although the way was not yet clearly mapped out; and thus when I began to compare the sufferings which ignorance and misrepresentation put upon us with the vast boon of knowledge, consolation, and exalting communion which we enjoyed by the new revelation vouchsafed to us, I concluded the jewel we had obtained was more than worth the cost, and we who were recipients in this precious truth, whilst we felt the necessity of shielding it from vulgar comment, and reserving our pearls lest the swine of calumny and prejudice should destroy them, still united in the resolve that we would continue to bear our cross so long as we realized that Calvary was the footstool of Paradise.

CHAPTER XV.

"Felix von Marx has, in his earth life, taken himself out of the hands of loving spirit ministers, and sunk down to the sphere of elementary spirits, from which he can only escape by a resumption of the natural order of being, an order he has striven to reverse. He has entangled the soul and body of his adopted son in the same fatal meshes of error, and both must pay the penalty of new birth and resurrection, through pain and sorrow, before they can come into the order of nature, where the love of spirit friends and kindred can minister unto them.

"A little while longer and this beneficent change will be accomplished. In the spheres ruled by sub-mundane and super-mundane being, this great revolution has originated, and from thence the restoration must also come. Human spirits can not yet intervene or aid them. We can but hover near and seize upon every favorable opportunity to sustain and strengthen them, until their restitution is effected. The All-Father when he placed mortals on earth, wisely dropped a veil between the past and future, the higher and lower realms of being, sufficiently opaque to shield the dim eyes of mortals from too much light, — knowledge too high or vast for their frail natures to apprehend. The daring souls who lift that veil and penetrate into the awful realms beyond are like swimmers who venture into the billowy wastes of which they have no soundings. Von Marx and Louis de B—— are in the midst of these fathomless abysses of sub-mundane and super-mundane knowledge. We cannot help them yet, but God, the Father of spirits, can. He sees, knows, and pities, and will redeem them from the depths, and bring them into the paths he destines their feet to tread. Meantime His providence works through human means, and these you must employ to fulfil his designs.

"Once more the agencies of magic must be set in motion to redeem its victims. Call together then, the Orphic Circle, and there you will receive the help you solicit, the guidance necessary for your future action, and the direction we cannot give, but the spirits who govern there can."

Such was the communication rapped out to me, letter by letter, at one of our own family séances in answer to an urgent appeal on my part for guidance concerning my future course in connection with the Chevalier de B——. In obedience to the suggestions of the communicating spirit, one in whom we had all learned to repose implicit confidence, I determined to resume my place amongst the members of the Orphic Circle at their next regular meeting. I had not joined my companions for nearly four months, and the announcement of my intention to do so induced them to call a special séance at an earlier period than usual. On the night in question I left my invalid guest in his own apartment, whither he had retired, declining to accompany me, as he complained of an unconquerable tendency to sleep; indeed, he had sunk into a profound slumber before I left him, and I heard him desire his servant not to awaken him till the following morning.

After our lodge had been opened with the usual formulæ, the scene began to resemble that which transpired on the night of Professor von Marx's death. There was the same uncertainty and waiting expectancy in our minds; the same restlessness of feeling amongst our neophytes, clairvoyants, and members. The lamps flickered and became extinguished spontaneously several times, although the indescribable feeling of awe that pervaded our assembly induced the wardens to relight them, contrary to our custom. All at once, sheets of lightning flashed through the room in every direction, finally extinguishing every other light and followed by the most tremendous peals of thunder, I think, I ever heard.

This awful crash announced the bursting of a long-. expected storm, which had been brooding over the city all day. For more than three hours the wildest commotion of the elements succeeded, indeed, for many subsequent years, the violence of the tempest that raged that night was not forgotten by those who witnessed it. At first we felt relieved by the opening of the storm without, deeming that the sensations of oppression we had experienced might be thus naturally accounted for, but very soon the feeling of nameless awe returned, and at length we perceived in the incessant glare of the lightning which filled our otherwise dark lodge-room with sheets of livid flame, a tall figure standing beside the central altar with one foot on the lowest step. At first we were disposed to think one of our own number had assumed this position under the efflatus of the magnetic trance, but the repeated flashes of the electric fluid illuminating the stranger's features, at length revealed to all present the unmistakable similitude of Felix von Marx. We noticed too, that the figure was arrayed in a professor's robe, whilst the college cap, which formed a portion of the costume, was distinctly visible, lying on the white cloth of the altar. Let me here remark, without any wrong done to a Society many of whose sessions and underlying principles, the members hold themselves sacredly bound to keep secret, that the apparitions which we had been accustomed to invoke, and those described by our seers, clairvoyants, and neophytes, *were not the spirits of the dead,* or at least not so regarded; hence this unmistakable apparition, manifest to all present, and so clearly identical with one whose mortal remains we had ourselves committed to the grave, made a deeper and more profound impression upon us than a thousand spectral forms of the " flying soul" or the spirits of nature, whether in or out of the crystals and mirrors. We *knew* that on that night no stranger could by any possibility have entered the hall, nor had any one been present when the doors were locked and guarded, save the members and officers of the Society.

Several minutes of fearful suspense elapsed, and then the truth began to flash upon us, that the apparition of von Marx was not alone. Seated on the ground were a circle of dark, shrouded figures, such as we had seen some months before, only this time there was but one circle, and this seemed to enclose the altar and surround the tall stranger on every side but one, and in that opening, on the side of the altar opposite to von Marx, stood a female form veiled and enveloped in a luminous white, sparkling mist, through which we could dimly discern the outlines of her form. As this beautiful apparition with all the other phantom surroundings became visible, it seemed as if we, the watchers, would be turned to stone. My blood began to freeze in my veins, my eyeballs to start from their sockets, and a horror such as I had never believed could possess a mortal without bereaving him of life, stole over me and threatened me with speedy dissolution. Had no relief come I am certain I should have expired; and the sensations I then felt, I was afterwards informed, were shared by most of my companions. I have seen as well as heard much of spiritual phenomena since that time; beheld what is called by mediums "materialized forms," that is, human souls clothed again in the panoply of substantial fleshly bodies; but all these sights paled before the spiritual actuality of this dreadful phantom band, these dead alive, through whose impalpable forms we could see the opposite wall, the glare of the lightnings, and each other; these beings, who diffused around them that aroma of horror, from which our sentient humanity shrinks back; between whom and us exists an invisible barrier, which none can pass and live. But relief came at last. A slow and solemn strain of music filled the hall, commencing at first in soft and distant echoes, then it grew stronger, firmer, and more distinct, until *it came amongst us*, and was evidently accompanied by the soft but regular beat of marching feet. *Something* then passed me by; I felt the wind of moving bodies, and I saw my companions stir and turn their heads to look in the line of an invisible procession, which all could *feel* though none might see it. We also felt that the line of march was towards the altar. We saw by the unceasing glare of the lightning, the crouching forms look up and the tall stranger draw back to make way for the invisible host.

A space was cleared in front of the altar, which presently became filled up with a dense mass, and whilst a succession of rapid flashes kept the lodge in a continu-

ous livid light, we saw a bier covered with white drapery, on which seemed to lie the sleeping form of the
Chevalier de B——. Then the female figure extended
across the bier a staff wreathed with a shining serpent.
This she pointed towards the male figure, who took it
from her hand, and bent his head as if acknowledging
a gift. The music ceased, and we heard a voice issuing,
as it seemed, from the spot on which von Marx stood,
although his lips moved not, nor did he appear to
speak.

The voice said, "The life transfer has been made;
man's work is ended, and God's has begun. The woof
of two lives is spun anew; one regains his spiritual, the
other his mortal birthright. God's will be done on
earth as it is in heaven."

Then the tone changed, and from the direction of the
female form came a voice, sweeter than ever tone of
music rung in mortal ears, saying, "Behold, I show you
a mystery; we shall not all sleep, but we shall all be
changed; for the trumpet shall sound, and the dead
shall be raised incorruptible." If more was spoken, our
deafened ears lost it, for peal after peal of thunder
shook the hall, distracting us by its crashing vibrations.
A few seconds of thick darkness prevailed, and when
next the streams of electric fire filled the hall, it was
empty; at least, the phantoms had vanished, although
we felt their dread presence passing us by, pressing
against some of us the bier they carried, and heard
amidst the pauses in the heavenly artillery, the beat of
the rhythmical march and the faint vibrations of distant
music, swallowed up again by the peals of the rolling
thunder. Muttered exclamations of horror and the
flare of matches followed. Some one in mercy to the
rest had relighted the lamps, enabling us to look at each

other's wild and haggard faces and stagger forth from that place of dread and glamour.

For four weary days and nights I and my distracted family watched by the cold, rigid, and lifeless form of our unhappy guest. No morning of awakening life had come for him, and the physicians pronounced that the vital spark had fled; nay, they urged, with what all who loved him felt to be indecent haste, that the formulæ of interment should proceed at once. My mediumistic girls insisted that life still remained, and that he would revive to thank and bless us; in fact, the grief and indignation of my wife and loving children at the conduct of the strangers around us, was only equalled by the fear and inhumanity they displayed. The medical men shrugged their shoulders, sneered at the tender assiduity of the poor ladies, and muttered prophetic remarks about lunatic asylums. My dear wife sat holding the sleeper's lifeless hand, bathing it with her tears, but, like myself, felt uncertain in what direction to yield credence.

Deep as was our concern for our cherished guest, there were other points in our situation of an equally distressing character. During the entire four nights and days of our sad watch, an array of terrors beset us difficult to describe. The air, the ground, the walls, and every place and thing around us, seemed to be charged with unearthly sounds and spontaneous motion. Sometimes we sat listening to the pattering of little feet, or the regular beat of a marching host. The whining tones of small animals, the rustling of silk, flapping of wings, or a succession of low knockings, greeted us everywhere; strange birds flew through our halls and galleries, and rushed past us in our very chambers; indistinct forms flitted hither and thither by day as well as

night. At times the noises deepened to an indescribable
uproar, in which the ear found no special tone to distinguish, and then soughed away to deep sighs, or distant
moans. When neither sight nor hearing was affected,
the scene became still more ghastly and oppressive in
appeals to the sense of touch; some object would press
against us, or so disturb the air, as to. cause vibrations
in all things around us. Towards evening and in the
gray of the dawn, we heard on each successive night,
the sound of solemn music, which would alternately
advance and recede, like a band of performers who came
towards the place wherever we might happen to be,
passed through it, and then retreated from it. These
strains were not only delightful to the ear, but wonderfully soothing to our excited minds; they seemed to
convey an element of consolation and a message of
peace, very cheering to us and entirely free from the
ghastly prestige of all the other manifestations. At the
earnest request of my faithful associates of the Orphic
Circle, who rallied around my afflicted family with true
fraternal kindness, we had placed the poor Chevalier on
a bier, surrounded with burning tapers, and a profusion
of the sweet, fresh flowers in which he so passionately
delighted. On several occasions the tapers would flicker
and go out spontaneously, but as we never left the
sleeper alone, the watchers were careful to relight the
tapers at the very instant they were extinguished.

Before the fourth night had set in, several of our
domestics had left us in irrepressible terror. Those
who remained, though they had grown old and attached
in our service, expressed their deepest horror of the
scenes enacting around them, but pity for our distress
overcame their fears, and provided they were permitted
to move about in groups, they determined not to forsake

us. The Arabian, who had attended the young Chevalier from early infancy, throughout this whole dread period remained unmoved. He never left the chamber where his beloved master lay, and if we had not brought him his daily mess of rice and other simple articles of food, he might have starved ere he would have quitted his solemn charge.

The heroine of my now diminished household was my precious Blanche. This brave young girl rallied the drooping spirits of the domestics, and assembling them together at morning and evening, read them passages of Scripture and made them join her own pure voice in singing solemn hymns. Each night, accompanied by my old and well-tried butler, she passed through every room in the dreary mansion, inspected its fastenings, and by her cheerful voice and noble example, stimulated the timid domestics to exert themselves in guarding the house from the possible inroad of marauders. These precautions were by no means unnecessary. All sorts of wild reports had gone abroad concerning the state of our distressed household. For two days the door was beseiged with curious inquirers, who sought under any pretence to gain admission, or learn tidings of what was passing within. It would seem that the reports of those who left us were rather discouraging to the idly curious without, for after the first two days of our mournful watch and ward, our house was quite deserted, and even the tradesmen who presented themselves with goods at the servants' entrance, handed them in and fled away, with signs of terror as marked, as if the place had been infected with some dreadful pestilence.

Looking back upon this most trying period of my life, I am amazed to recall my own power of self-gov-

ernment and composure. Like my youngest daughter,
I felt that my mission was to cheer and strengthen
others, and in the effort to do this, my own fortitude
and self-reliance rose to the rescue. I never before,
perhaps I might own with compunction, never since,
have prayed so heartily, never felt a more complete reliance on the great, good God, to whom I knew all subordinate agencies, however powerful or wicked, were
eternally subject.

My faith increased with every new trial, and at last I
felt able to endure whatever more might come, and only
marvelled what the worst would be. I must not omit to
mention that there was one phenomenon which, though
calculated to inspire the most dread of all others, filled
us with sentiments of hope and courage, for which we
could not account, even to ourselves. This was the
unmistakable sound of Felix von Marx's voice, speaking
from the empty air, speaking above, about, around us,
we knew not from whence, but ever sounding with a
tone so clearly human, kind, and encouraging, yet firm
and commanding, that all our fears vanished directly his
accents met our ears. Sometimes he uttered only the
one word "John," sometimes "Dear John," or "I am
here; fear nothing." On one occasion my little Blanche
startled our dreary hall with one of her bright, ringing
peals of laughter, her delight was so great, as she heard
the full, rich, well-remembered tone crying, "Good little
Blanche, well done!"

On the fourth evening this consoling voice repeated
many times in clear and cheery accents, "All 's well!"
Towards midnight, worn out as we were with a distress
that knew no parallel, oppressed with long watching,
the desertion of the world without, and the increasing
prevalence of the awful disturbances within, I insisted

that my dear girls should retire with their weeping mother to rest, and that no one should watch with me that night, but the faithful Arabian, and my Orphic brother, Sir Thomas L——. Before parting for the night, I dismissed my tired domestics with a short prayer and kind benediction. I then assembled my family, including Sir Thomas and the Arabian, in my library, which adjoined the room where the bier was laid. There met together, I read to my sobbing listeners the beautiful sixty-ninth Psalm, which commences thus: "Save me, O God, for the waters are come in unto my soul." Just as I had reached the pathetic words, "I am become a stranger unto my brethren and an alien unto my mother's children," I was struck dumb by hearing the voice of von Marx crying in sharp, clear, distinct tones, "Louis, Louis, awake!" Instantly there was a movement in the death-chamber; a deep-drawn sigh, then another and another. Other sounds followed, echoed by the beating of every throbbing heart; then — the sound of a foot-step. It advanced nearer, nearer yet. The half-closed door between the rooms was gently moved, then pushed open, and the Chevalier, dressed in his ordinary costume, as we had laid him on the bier, very pale, but moving with a firm step and erect bearing, stood in our midst. The light of reason was in his fine eyes; the smile of recognition on his lips. Extending to my wife and myself each, a cold hand, which we warmly clasped to our hearts, he said in his own natural voice and sweet Italian accent, "My dear friends, I have had a long, long sleep. I see you thought it was to have been my last; but your wayward Louis is not dead yet you see, and will live for many years to thank and bless you for all your kindness."

CHAPTER XVI.

Sept. 30, 18——. Five months have elapsed since I made my last entry, and now it is the glorious period of ripe autumn, when Nature summons all her reserved force to cast a spell of loveliness over the scene, ere she closes up her summer housekeeping; when woods and hill, forest and glen, are adorned in the richest liveries of the fading year; when the green earth, blue sky, and the many-colored foliage of the woods, combine to clothe the scene in a wealth of harmonious beauty, unknown to any other season.

I am reclining on the velvet turf which covers the side of a lofty mountain overlooking the boundless expanse of the ocean. The purple mists of an autumn sunset, crown the swelling hills of the distant landscape, and linger amidst the shady dells which checker the lovely scene. Far out at sea the white sails of many a fishing-boat gleam over the crested waves and relieve the expanse of heaving waters from the deep loneliness of an ocean view.

At the mountain's foot is the broad expanse of my own domain, the park and grounds of my old ancestral home, and by my side, stretched like myself on the mossy turf, is the object of my last eight months of incessant care, the Chevalier de B——.

A greater change than that between my town residence and the sea-side home in which we now luxuriate, has come over my esteemed but singular guest. All of youth or youthful manners, thoughts or habits, have wholly disappeared in him. He speaks and acts like a man of mature life, yet he is not yet twenty-one years of age. Although he has become almost restored to his ordinary share of health and strength, the cataclysms of the past, have robbed him of that vigor and elasticity which should mark his time of life; and whilst regaining the singular beauty of person which formerly distinguished him, there is a weary air, and a sad, far-away expression in his fine face, which never brightens into mirth or lights up with joy. He never speaks of Professor von Marx, and whenever I chance to mention his name, he listens with a shiver, and shrinks away from the subject with such evident distress, that I have come to regard that once dear and familiar name, as tabooed between us. The passive submission which once distinguished his manner, has now changed to a stately, dignified demeanor, which speaks of fixed purpose and firm will. Though kind and courteous to all, affectionate to myself and family, and deferential to the opinions of others, there is a wall of isolation built up around him, which none can surmount; a lonely abstraction which repels all human sympathy and silently rejects all confidence. In his days of convalescence, I communicated to him the details of Professor von Marx's will, his generous bequest of his small yet sufficient fortune to him, and his desire that I should become his guardian and trustee. He listened to the financial details with some show of impatience, carelessly alluded to his own resources, which he supposed were already sufficient for his simple requirements; but he seemed too indifferent even to converse upon a topic so important to most young men as the bequest of an independence. Somewhat piqued in my own mind by what I could not for the life of me help considering as ingratitude for the poor professor's fatherly care, I remarked, perhaps rather coldly, "My dear old friend's chief sources of income, were derived from the exercise of his brilliant talents; still, the bequest of every shilling he died possessed of, proves his desire to convince you that his affection for you survives beyond the grave. Don't you think so?" With an expression of anguish such as I have rarely seen upon any human countenance, the young man gazed at me for a moment, then crying in a choking voice, "Oh, hush! hush! if you would not kill me or drive me mad," he buried his face in his hands, over which the tears streamed fast and thick. I was shocked at the effect of my unkind remark and strove to atone for it by blundering apologies; but I soon found I had unstopped with reckless hand the vials of a grief too deep for utterance, and one which, thus renewed, bore down all the barriers of self-control, which the silent mourner had been laboring to erect around him. His form shook with convulsive sobs; he threw himself on the ground, tearing up handfuls of earth and sod, in his wild and uncontrollable grief. I was fairly aghast, and knew not what to say or do in such a crisis, when, for the first time for nearly five months, I was equally startled and rejoiced to hear the low, deep tones of Felix von Marx's spirit, murmuring clearly in my ear, "Leave him to me." I retreated, and never again ventured on such dangerous ground, except to speak of such business arrangements as were absolutely essential to be discussed. When I again mentioned the topic of my guardianship, he thanked me, with many expressions of grateful appreciation, but stated, as one that had formed a resolution from which there could be no departure, that he should be glad to stay with me for one year; he then proposed to take his leave, having determined to visit Madame his mother, now his sole surviving parent in India. I was a little taken aback at the quiet air of determination with which this plan was announced, and asked him if he desired to spend that intervening year in college, or some seat of learning, where he could cultivate his wonderfully intellectual powers by study.

"No, no, no! my friend," he replied, with that nervous haste which always seemed to possess him, when any allusions were made to his past life. "I shall never study again, at least not in schools or colleges. My future studies must be conducted in the hard school of life, but not in books. I cannot read! I cannot read! I shall not need to do so either." And read he did not. I never saw him open a book whilst he remained with me, yet his conversation upon every subject except his own past life, was brilliant and masterly. He played and sang exquisitely, yet he never glanced at a note of music, nor do I know when or how he had learned that art. Except in his preparation for his military career, none of his acquirements were of a scholastic character, yet their compass and range was immense. He could solve a mathematical problem and speak with the utmost correctness of geometrical proportions, yet sound him on the methods by which he had arrived at his conclusions, and he became confused, and said he had not studied enough to answer. He would discourse brilliantly on geological formations and was never weary of descanting on the grandeur of the universe, but when pressed to answer some question of mere detail, he would gaze wildly at the questioner, and complain that such subjects troubled him. In ancient lore, especially on the foundations of theology, astrology, and ethnology, I have heard this strange being discourse by the hour. With eyes fixed on some far-distant object, and seemingly unconscious of the interest and admiration he excited, he would pour forth a stream of eloquence on the most occult subjects. Color, form, tone, earth, heaven, the marvels of astronomy, the superb architecture of the universe,—everything, in short, that a long life of profound study would have informed others of, this young man described in words that burned into the listener's consciousness, and when the tides of thought ceased to flow, he would stammer, stare wildly, seem worn and exhausted, and sink back into his usual abstracted isolation. Nothing ever seemed to distress him so much, as the attempt to find out whence he derived his knowledge, or how he had acquired such a vast fund of information. I have seen others of his stamp since then; trance mediums gifted with a similar influx of inspiration, but the type was new to me when I first saw the Chevalier de B——, nor do I ever remember any somnambulist as highly gifted as him.

When he announced his intention to stay with me for one year, he added, "I will remain for your good, my best and truest friend, as well as for my own. I can tell you some things that will interest you; you will help this shivering, unstrung, frame of mine, to grow into strength and manhood."

These were the very words he was speaking at the time marked in my diary at the opening of this chapter. We had never held any séances of the Orphic Society since the memorable night of the Chevalier's resuscitation. The great shock we then experienced, and the cares which had since engrossed me with my invalid ward, had determined us to adjourn until the winter. During my young friend's convalescence all my butterfly acquaintances had returned; congratulations poured in upon me, and my weird reputation changed for a character of "unmixed firmness and benevolence"; meantime, I had deemed it prudent in my intercourse with my singular charge to avoid all allusion to his past life or occult subjects generally. How to deal most tenderly with this fearfully sensitive nature was my sole care, and in so doing, I utterly disregarded the advice of my Orphic associates, namely, to take every opportunity of cultivating his remarkable powers of clairvoyance, or, as we had now learned to term it, mediumistic gifts. My daughters and many of their young acquaintances still held spirit circles, and I often joined them with my dear wife, when we derived such happiness as the earth and earthly things could not bring, in communion with our beloved angel guardians. To the Chevalier I never spoke of these séances. I believe he knew of their occurrence, but he never mentioned them to me, and generally absented himself from the house when they were in session.

Unearthly sounds had not wholly ceased, nor did the flitting forms of unknown beings altogether disappear from our old, time-honored residence, but these mystic sights and sounds were chiefly confined to the apartments occupied by the Chevalier and his Arab servant, and into these charmed precincts I was the only member of the family that ever penetrated. I know I heard thrilling, mystic voices more than once, in conversation with my strange ward when I approached his rooms; sometimes, too, I saw unmistakably, a beautiful, luminous female form hovering in the moonlight when I had lin-

gered with him alone after the night had fallen; but as
he never entered with me on the topic of the inner life,
and I would no more have dared broach it to him than I
would have trodden on a wounded foot, the subject was
entirely dropped between us until the evening that again
introduces us to — whoever my readers may chance to
be. On this occasion my guest, raising himself on his
arm and fixing his dark, luminous eyes on mine, said,
" Mr. Dudley, why don't you renew the Orphic séances
with which you were so interested? "

" Why don't I renew them? " I said, taken aback by
the abruptness of the question. " Because — because —
I have been engaged in other matters; besides, you see,
we are away off in the country, and our lodge is in
town, you know."

" What does that matter? " rejoined my companion,
with that impetuosity which I had begun to associate
with his most abnormal conditions. " The place matters -
little, except when it is favorable or otherwise to the
work in hand. Mr. Dudley, summon your companions,"
naming over rapidly several gentlemen, near neighbors
of mine, whom I knew to be interested in occult pursuits, but of whose secret predilections I had no reason
to think the Chevalier had been aware. " Call them
together and establish a lodge-room in the midst of yon
glorious grove; the grove behind that hill, I mean. It
is your own property, and you can take measures to
secure it from interruption."

" I like your idea," I replied, " but you know we have
none of our *lucides* or clairvoyants within reach, nor
shall we be likely to meet with them again till winter."

" You will need none," replied the Chevalier in his
far-off, dreamy way.

I did not question him then, for I was beginning to

understand this "mystic" better and better every day. I only asked, therefore, when he thought we might begin.

"One week from now."

"Be it so. The plan shall be put in operation."

For the next six days I busied myself incessantly with gardeners, woodsmen, and carpenters. I had a space cleared in the centre of a thick grove of pines which grew in the bottom of an amphitheatre, surrounded on all sides but one by precipitous rocks difficult of descent. The fourth side was bounded by a lovely little lake, on which I was accustomed to have boats plying for the enjoyment of my family and visitors. As the lake and the whole of the surrounding ground was on my own estate, there was no fear of any strangers gaining access to our romantic lodge, especially when I issued orders that no boats should ply at the time when we were in session. As our meetings were fixed for the evening, I had lamps hung up in the trees around the open space, and a temporary shed erected in which to keep our instruments of music, etc.

The arrangements were as nearly as possible modelled after our lodge-room in town.

There was but one of our London members living near me, and that was a fine old French gentleman who might have formed a not unapt representative of Scott's "Last Minstrel." He was a poet "improvisatore" and divine harpist. Several of our other members were musicians, singers, and members of an amateur madrigal club, to which in my younger days I had myself belonged. Here, then, were all the elements required for our séances, save always the *officiating priest*, about the identity of whom I at first speculated with some anxiety. When the appointed evening arrived, however, I at once understood that my young friend, penetrated with gratitude for the services I and my family had been the happy instruments of rendering him in his hours of severest trial, had determined to devote the one year of his residence with me to the gratification of my dearest wishes, — namely, the interpretation of the divine order of being, the profound mysteries of nature, and the grand arcana of creation, as revealed by the inspiration of the noblest spiritual influences, through his own entranced lips.

For one entire year I and a choice circle of friends were the highly privileged recipients of these sublime truths, conveyed to us partly in our woody amphitheatre at N——, partly in a London lodge, which we had fitted up expressly for these sacred meetings, from which all but an assemblage of kindred minds were excluded.

From the first séance, I had fortunately secured the conditions by which they could be reported. The memoranda transcribed from the phonographic notes of one of our party, who kindly devoted himself to this service, are still in my possession, and may one day be given to the world. Much of the ideality they abound with has become filtered through the utterances of other inspired media during the new dispensation, but never have I read, heard of, or imagined a scheme of divine order so grand, so just, complete, and beautiful in all its details, as that furnished us by the inspiration of this highly-gifted mystic.

In my plain and homely phraseology I may venture to say I think more highly of myself and my kind, the world I live in, the scheme of which I am a part, and the God who created and sustains me, as I find all these elements of being described and explained in these sublime trance-addresses; and now, if I have dwelt long, fondly, and perhaps with too much minutiæ of detail, upon the strange events which have served to carve out the remarkable character of whom I have written, nay, if I have seemed to exaggerate his excellences almost to the rank of a hero of romance, it is not because I am moved by the deep affection which he has won from me and all around him, not, as many cursory observers have declared, because we who knew and loved him were "under the spell of his many attractive qualities," but because I perceived in him, as in all sensitives, mediums, and mystics, idiosyncrasies which if carefully studied and classified, would serve as the basis of a new phase of mental science, and one of which the world stands very much in need.

Looking back upon my intercourse with the Chevalier de B——, I find one of the most noteworthy and interesting examples of abnormal power and spiritual inspiration it has ever been my lot to encounter, but I have also found one of the most striking evidences how far the practices of animal magnetism and human psychology can be abused and perverted from their true use to become an instrument of ruin, mental imbecility, and even madness.

Happily, my experiences with this gentleman bore witness also to the *per contra* of this fatal position, and showed how healthful and elevating pure spiritual influences and high inspiration may become, when exercised upon a self-centred mind and freed from the intervention of powerful human influences.

I need scarcely offer to the intelligent reader and comments on the history of this young man's subject tion, and the final subversion of all personal identity to his erring but devoted friend, Felix von Marx. The history conveys its own moral rebuke and lesson.

The narrative of the "life transfer," mysterious and unprecedented as it is, I solemnly affirm I have detailed word for word and incident for incident exactly as it occurred, as far as I myself apprehended it. The terrible visions and spectral scenes at the Orphic Circles only partially explain the mystery of their origin and meaning, but because their awful demonstrations were shared with me by many other witnesses, who urge me to place them on record, I have fulfilled this task as faithfully as an earnest desire to narrate the truth and nothing but the truth could inspire me to do. I can scarcely expect to obtain credit for my statements, not because they are more remarkable or startling than the wonders which are now transpiring amongst us every day in the annals of the modern spiritualistic movement, but because they did not occur in a commonplace way, and because there are urgent reasons why I cannot openly and publicly vouch for their reliability. I know the lack of authenticity which attaches to an anonymous writer, and one so deeply interested in his subject as I have been; still I am *compelled* and *impelled* to write. I put my narrative into the great cauldron of Time, confident that the base metals of error and misapprehension will ultimately be fused away, whilst the grains of true gold will be gathered up and become current coin in the generations that shall be; and now, for the present at least, my journal in connection with my much esteemed friend, the Chevalier de B——, must draw to a close. Well and nobly has he paid me with gems of inspiration and heavenly truth, for all I endured in his behalf during our seasons of great trial.

The time came at length when his highly prized ministry was to cease amongst us, and young and old in my household, mistress and maid, master and servant, looked sorrowfully and with heavy hearts to that to-morrow when we should see his face no more.

The day came when I was to depart for America, my friend to India;—I, on a mission hardly known to my family, scarcely acknowledged to myself: to search into the realities of the much-vaunted American spiritualis-tic movement by a tour through the United States that I designed should occupy me one year; my friend to enter upon those stormy scenes of public life which have made for him a name and fame which few would, or ever will associate with the dreamy, unearthly mystic whom Felix von Marx delighted to call his "moody sprite," his "well-beloved Ariel."

"God bless and keep you, and good angels have you in charge, my Louis!" I muttered, between the spasms of nose-blowing and eyes-wiping, as I stood waving a very damp handkerchief on the wharf from which a splendid East Indiaman was setting sail on the day when I took leave of my friend,—he whom I would so gladly, so proudly have called my *son*, had Fate so willed it.

"We meet again this day ten years hence, my kind and generous friend," cried the Chevalier de B——, returning the salute.

I watched the white signal waving in the breeze as long as my blurred eyes could keep the noble form of my friend in sight, and when at last I stood staring at vacancy, and suddenly remembered what a spectacle I was making of myself to the booby wharf-men standing by, I turned away, murmuring, "Ten years! It is a long time to wait, but he will surely come."

PART II.

THE ADEPT.

PART II.

INVOCATION: THE SOUL'S LITANIES. *

THOU who dost dwell alone,
Thou who dost know thy own,
Thou to whom all are known
From the cradle to the grave,
  Save, oh, save !

From the world's temptations,
From tribulations,
From that fierce anguish
Wherein we languish,
From that torpor deep
Wherein we lie asleep,
Heavy as death, cold as the grave,
  Save, oh, save!

When the soul, growing clearer,
Sees God no nearer,
When the soul, mounting higher,
Sees God no nigher,
But the arch-fiend Pride
Mounts at her side,
Foiling her high emprize
Sealing her eagle eyes;
And when she fain would soar,
Makes idols to adore,
Changing the pure emotion
Of her high devotion,

* The beautiful lines here quoted were selected from a spiritual journal, entitled *The Principle*, and sent by the editor some years ago to the Chevalier de B——, who has ever since adopted them as his favorite expression of prayerful aspiration; he also deems them the most appropriate possible prologue to the second part of his autobiography. — ED. GHOST LAND.

To a skin-deep sense
Of her own eloquence,
Strong to deceive, strong to enslave,
    Save, oh, save !

From the ingrained fashion
  Of this earthly nature
  That mars thy creature ;
From grief that is but passion,
From mirth that is but feigning,
  From tears that bring no healing,
From wild and weak complaining,
  Thine whole strength revealing,
    Save, oh, save !

From doubt where all is double,
  Where wise men are not strong,
Where comfort turns to trouble,
  Where just men suffer wrong,
Where sorrow treads on joy,
Where sweet things soonest cloy,
Where faiths are built on dust,
Where love is half mistrust,
Hungry and barren and sharp as the sea,
    Oh, set us free !

Oh, let the false dreams fly
Where our sick souls lie,
Tossing continually!
Oh, where thy voice doth come,
Let all doubts be dumb,
Let all words be mild,
All strifes be reconciled,
All pains be beguiled!
Let light bring no blindness,
Love no unkindness,
Knowledge no ruin,
Fear no undoing!
From the cradle to the grave,
    Save, oh, save !

Ghost Land.

TWENTY years,—what a mere breath in time! A turning of the sand-glass, a sweeping over the sky of a summer cloud, a sigh, a sob, a tear, such a period seems, when we look back upon it and try to apprehend the nature of time by retrospection; yet when we gauge it by the events which have crowded its onward course, what an epoch of momentous interest may not twenty years become! To traverse many lands, sound the heart-throbs, listen to the inner revealings, and learn the life mysteries of many a strange people; to trace out the panoramas of a mighty past, whose swift, silent footsteps leave no echoes in eternity, yet whose march has left imprints which strike the beholders dumb with awe and self-abasement as they contemplate the littleness of the one compared to the immensity of which that one is a part; to plunge into the fields of carnage, steel the heart to the temper of the sword, slay and stand to be slain, drown the pleadings of humanity, pity, mercy, and fraternal love in the thunder of artillery and the reverberations of deadly musketry; to lie amidst heaps of

slain, matching glory against mutilation, and hearing the
vain boasts of patriotism answered by the shrieks of
agony and the groans of torn and bleeding humanity;
to pine in the loathsome dungeon, and risk life, name,
and fame on hair-breadth escapes; to bask in the sunlight of royal favor, and hear the breath of the fickle
multitude shouting hosannas to a popular name one
day, and the next to skulk in the shadows of political
disgrace, and wander without home or land, without
where to lay a houseless head; to muster all the fires of
life upon the altar of a vain love, and see them quenched
into dust and ashes; to heap up fame and glory, knowledge and renown, love and triumph; pierce the mysteries
of space, — even to the unknowable, — and command its
legionaries, climb up to heaven and steal thence the
Promethean fire, plunge into the abyss and master its
hidden secrets, — to do all this, and then see the piled-up
treasures fade, sink, burn, consume, grow dim, cold —
nothing — or at last melt away into a vague memory!
This may be the sum of twenty years, — the twenty
years which, to recall in the aggregate, is but a breath
in time, a turning of the sand-glass, but which to
live, minute by minute, is all this and more; for all this,
and more, formed the sum of my twenty years of life
after I parted from the kindest, best of friends, John
Cavendish Dudley, on a London wharf, to sail away for
the burning land of Hindostan.

Such retrospects taken in detail are of little use to
humanity, save as sources of amusement. One, will
listen shudderingly, and, turning away from the stormy
picture, sigh for the rest which human life never grants.
Some "Desdemonas" may weave out ideal heroes from
the narrative, but still more will divide their interest in
it with a tale from the *New York Ledger* or a London

melodrama. None can know, *or ought to know*, the worth of a single life's experience to any but the actor therein, unless that life has a specialty in which all mankind can share, and in which the immediate interests of humanity are concerned. It is because I have such a specialty to offer that I now write.

I have something that has followed me, or rather infilled my soul, through every changing scene, in every wild mutation of fortune,— on the battle-field, in the dungeon, in the cabinet of princes, in the hut of the charcoal-burner, in the deep crypts of Central India, and amidst the awful rites of Oriental mysticism, in the paradises of love, and the shipwreck of every hope,— something which has never forsaken or left me alone; something which stands by me now, as I write in my sea-girt island dwelling, on the shores of the blue Mediterranean; something which has spoken peace to my soul when the storm raged the fiercest and the fever burned the highest; something that promises me, not a dwelling-place merely, but a sweet home, a long rest, and a happy awakening in eternal sunlight, amidst friends and love and blossoms that never fade, " when life's fitful fever is burnt out" and all is done with earth: and that something is the voice of an ever-faithful spirit friend, murmuring in my ear, " There is another and a better world."

LOVE and TRUTH! These are the fruits which the bruised hands of humanity can gather from the tree of spiritual life which grows in the midst of earth-life's barren wilderness. Were it not so, I never would have written these pages; never have opened the vest of the careless cosmopolitan to expose to view the scarred breast that throbs beneath it; but knowing as I do that mortal life with all its tremendous pains and penalties becomes not only endurable, but a boon and a blessing, when heaven is the goal, and rest and glory beckon us on, so I have determined to pause in the midst of my wild career, and give such scattered rays of light as I have gathered up to the world that suffers as I have done, and that perishes as I should have done amidst life's storms and tempests, had I not felt the grasp of a spirit hand upon my sinking form, and heard the precious whisper of assurance staying me in the deepest trough of the stormiest sea.

Hitherto I have been compelled to make personal adventures the vehicle in which strange spiritual experiences were to be given to the world. The mysterious processes of animal magnetism and their silent but formative effects for good and evil were, I know, more potentially illustrated in my own case than any other that I could have cited.

The "life transfer" which the fanaticism of affection, unlighted by the knowledge of immortality, induced, and the absolute, personal obsession of a human body by a foreign spirit, are items of such a rare and exceptional character, that I have ventured far out of the track which I had laid down for myself in dealing with the world when I communicate them. Even now, whilst I am writing these peculiar experiences, and tearing open unhealed wounds for the guidance of future explorers, I can see with prophetic clairvoyance the curl of many a scornful lip over my narrative; rude disbelief and reckless denial, some doubt and still less acceptance,— acceptance from those who know the writer and his unflinching fidelity to truth, acceptance from some few others who will remember passages of kindred marvel in their own history: these will make up the different phases of mind that are destined to speculate over a testimony so painful to give, so shocking to see trampled beneath the feet of coarse, unspiritual misunderstanding. Yet I did not dare grieve the Paraclete of life, who makes me and all creatures that have a truth to tell, his messengers, by withholding my strange experiences. From this point, however, I have but little more to write of myself except as an instrument for illustrating the truths my life conserves. Henceforth I shall write only of that ghost land which I shall soon enter, and to whose stern inquisition I shall have to account for every talent committed to my charge. Heaven help me to answer, " I have done thy bidding."

Looking back upon a single life, or the life of the race as revealed by ethnological science, we cannot perceive a foot of land trodden by humanity without a circle of luminous haze encompassing it. This haze is not the reflection of a dark body intercepting the rays of light, but is a light *per se*, a radiance which proceeds from some luminous body, a beam cast from some world or inhabitant of a world in which the ordinary rule of lights and shadows is reversed. History, tradition, prose and poetry, religion and even stern dogmatic science itself, all unite to record the fact of these luminous interventions pervading human history; and as we can no more have an idea without a name, or a name without some idea of which it is the signification, so we have given to the ideas which these world-wide, ages-long, luminous interventions suggest, the names of magic, religion, supernaturalism, and spiritism.

The last is the only truly comprehensive term that has ever been applied in this direction, for magic is the science by which spiritism can be reduced to an art and has been peculiar to a few epochs of time, whilst it is measurably lost in others; religion signifies only the ideas which a special people entertain on this universal realm of luminosity; supernaturalism implies something out-side of nature, which this thing is not: hence, spirit-ism alone defines what it is, because spiritism implies the science of spirit, which is what we claim for the phenomena under consideration. Spiritualism applies to a condition of mind and refers to spiritually-minded people; hence, to my apprehension, the word "spiritual-ism" though much more commonly used in this connec-tion, is a misnomer. Spiritism, or the science of spirit, can exist without spiritists being spiritual; hence when I write of the science which treats of spirits, I ask my readers to understand me in the term spiritism. Heaven speed the day when all spiritists may merit the cogno-men of spiritualists now so much abused and perverted!

Spiritism alone can explain the phenomena of life and death, as well as all the extra-mundane sounds, sights, monitions, antipathies, and attractions which are not explicable on human hypotheses, but which have accom-panied the race in all time, varying in character and proportion at different periods and also under different external influences.

The intense eagerness with which the archives of the past have been ransacked leaves this age in very wide-spread enjoyment of the most popular spiritualis-tic testimony, ancient, classical, mediæval, and modern, concerning the nature of apparitions, spiritual powers, gifts, and forces. It might with justice be asked what any fresh writer can have to say on subjects so exhaus-tively considered already, and almost the first criticism which now greets the issue of a new spiritualistic work is, "Pshaw! there is nothing new here. I have known and seen all that before." In some instances, especially in my own life experiences, there may be this variation in the popular cry: "Pshaw! that cannot be true, *because I have not seen it all before.*" But for both classes of readers there exists a necessity, which is, that we should become more exact in defining, cataloguing, and labelling the truths we have, and placing them in more appropriate niches than the memory or disjointed entries of any single generation can afford; hence my present task. Follow me who will, in my attempts to execute it.

Evidently, to me, spiritual existence is the Alpha and Omega of being. Matter is only one of the forms in which spiritual existence becomes demonstrated; perhaps I should more correctly say, it is the formative element through which spirit becomes individualized,[*] but as whole libraries of theories are now before the world on these subjects, and every theory is supported by lists of authorities, whose very names alone would fill volumes, let me confine my basic statements to the present moment, and sum up what my researches have revealed to me in the *to-day,* and that without attempting to erect my column of belief upon the foundation of other men's opinions. My facts, and the facts open to all industrious explorers, have shown me that the universe visible to man is vitalized and permeated with animated beings, which correspond in all degrees and grades of existence to the varieties of matter, from the lowest inorganic atom—if such a finality as an atom exists—to the most perfected of organisms, which are GLOBES in space, every one of which I believe to be as much *a living creature* as man himself is. The link of connection between spirit and matter is force, and the

---

[*] For a full analysis of the order of being, a definition of God, the scheme of creation, the nature of spirit forces, the fall of man or spirit, the origin, progress, and destiny of soul, etc., read the first part and earlier sections of the author's work on "Art Magic."—ED. GHOST LAND.

exhibition of force is motion in all its infinite varieties. To sum up briefly the order of existence as it has been shown to me, I commence with realms of pure spiritual life, endless in number, infinite in extent, where spiritual essences dwell, — beings without passions, vices, or virtues, the Adams and Eves of inconceivable paradises, whose genius is INNOCENCE. Incapable of growth or progress until they have become incarnated in matter and individualized by experience, these spiritual essences are attracted to material earths, where they become the germ-seed of human souls by running an embryotic race through the elements and all the different grades of matter.

Thus the seed of soul existence is planted in that diffused state of matter known as gas or air; in that condition of combustion known as fire; in the fluidic state recognized as water; in the solids called generically the earth. It also assimilates to the separate parts of earth, such as rocks, stones, crystals, gems, plants, herbs, flowers, trees, and all the grades of the animal kingdom; in short, through all tonal varieties of nature. In these successive states spirits are born through the mould of a rudimental form of matter; they grow, die, become spirits, are again attracted to earths, where they are incarnated, by virtue of a previous progress, into a higher state of being than they formerly occupied. Their bodies are composed of matter, it is true, but matter in conditions so embryotic and unparticled as to be invisible to mortal eyes, except through occasional clairvoyance; and yet they occupy space, and live in grades of being appropriate to their stage of progress.

These grades of being are realms which inhere in matter, permeating its every space and particle; in fact, the life of the ELEMENTARIES, as these embryotic spirits are called, is the life principle of matter, the cause of motion, and that FORCE which scientists affirm to be an attribute of matter. In hundreds of clairvoyant visits made by my spirit to the country of the elementaries, it was given me to perceive that their collective life principle, that which clothes their spirits, and forms their rudimental bodies, is in the aggregate the life principle of the earth and all that composes it, or that mysterious realm of FORCE, which, as above stated, is erroneously supposed to be a mere attribute of matter. Again and again it has been shown me how the germ of soul, through an infinite succession of births, lives, deaths, and incarnations in elementary existence, at last attains to that final spiritual state from whence it becomes for the last time attracted to matter, and is born into the climax of material existence, MANHOOD. The progress of spirit through the conditions of elementary being has been explained to me as correspondential to the subsequent embryotic periods of human gestation. As an elementary it progresses through the matrix of nature. As a human being it is subject to a much shorter but perfectly analogous progress through the matrix of human maternity. The one is necessary to the growth and individualization of an immortal spirit; the other to the growth and individualization of a mortal body, in which the spirit's final career through matter is effected. The two states are so perfectly analogous that when, after some years of clairvoyant practices amongst the Berlin Brotherhood, Professor von Marx subjected me to a course of study in anatomy and medicine, I was enabled to point out to him in the different stages of growth attained by the human fœtus, the most perfect analogies with similar stages of being amongst the elementaries.

The moment the pilgrim spirit has passed through the embryotic life of human maternity, its incarnations through matter are accomplished, and it is born on earth with the new function of SELF-CONSCIOUSNESS, or I should more properly say, CONSCIOUS INDIVIDUALITY. Let it ever be remembered that there is no realization known to man of the awkward and impossible word "annihilation." No particle of matter, no function of being can become the subject of annihilation. Self-consciousness is the function of the human soul, and individuality is the result of self-consciousness. Can this individuality be lost, this self-consciousness be ever quenched? Impossible! Quoting from a lecture by Emma Hardinge Britten on this subject, I re-echo her unanswerable argument for immortality,—ay, ETERNAL being, — when she says, "Could you alter, change, or impinge upon that individualism which enables each human being to say I AM, you find annihilation; for self-consciousness is individuality, and individuality is the distinguishing characteristic of human life; so when man has attained individuality he has attained immortality, for you can no more annihilate a function than you can an atom."

After the death of the mortal body the soul commences a fresh series of pilgrimages, starting from the exact grade of progress it has attained through its incarnations in matter; but its progress now is as a spirit, with the memory, individuality, and identity it has gained in its incarnations through the rudimental states of matter. Born at last as a soul, its new states or series of progressions commence in the spirit spheres, where every grade of spiritual unfoldment and future progress is amply provided for.

To my dim apprehension, and in view of my long years

of wandering through spirit spheres, where teaching spirits and blessed angels guided my soul's ardent explorations, this brief summary of our pre-existent states explains all that the reincarnationists have labored so sedulously to theorize upon. I dare not touch those theories with the pen of satire or rude denial, for those who urge them command my deep respect for their sincerity, humanity, and love of justice; but whilst the scheme thus opened up to me explained my soul's origin, the universal and reiterated assurances of myriads of spirits in every stage of a progressive beyond, convinced me there was no return to mortal birth, no retrogression in the scale of cosmic being, as a return to material incarnations would undoubtedly be, and that all the demands of progress, justice, and advancement are supplied by the opportunties afforded the soul in the spheres of spiritual existence.

In my boyhood's years I had been taught to regard spirit as the Alpha only, not the Omega; taught that it was infinite and eternal in essence, but not in individuality; that it lived forever, progressed forever, but only on the earth: hence, the miserably narrow, almost infantile theories of materialistic science, to wit, limiting life, the great glorious, and eternal boon of immortal life, to a mere speck in infinity; to the sand-grain of time of which an earthly life is made up, and to the shadowy, vague, and transitory organism of matter! With what different views of human destiny have I lived since I became a spiritist! Night after night, whilst my body was sleeping on the cold dungeon floors of my prison at P——, where I spent nearly a year; or, as I lay for many a dreary hour on the battle-field amidst the dead and dying, waiting for some trampling steed to crush me out of life, or some assassin's *miserecorde* to put an end to raging thirst and intolerable pain, spirit friends have come and waved their kind, white hands over me, liberated my struggling spirit, laid my weary form to peaceful rest, and carried me through space in every realm of spiritual existence to which a frail and sinful human soul could attain, until I have stood on the threshold of glorious lands, where my eyes could perceive the radiance of celestial spheres, the memory of whose brightness will warn and beckon me upwards forever.

CHAPTER XVIII.

FOR several years after my departure from England, I became a traveller through various countries of the East, and for the most part was engaged, as stated in a former chapter, in the busy and *exigeant* cares of active public life. Few who remember the dreamy somnambulist of the Berlin Brotherhood would have recognized in him the stern soldier, earnest statesman, and energetic worker in many directions. As I considered the numerous spheres of activity in which I seemed destined to become immersed, I could not but think that Felix von Marx had kept his word; that he had indeed died to add his noble manhood to my constitutional weakness, and that I must be indebted to the influence of his towering spirit for the capacity to achieve an amount of physical and intellectual labor under which many a more vigorous physique would have sunk. But although I never allowed myself even to pause in the career of urgent life-work I was pressed into, neither did I lose sight of the one great end and aim of my earthly pilgrimage, which ever has been to obtain positive knowledge on the mystery of the unseen universe. I had lived to be assured there were many phases of spiritual life open to the understanding of man besides those which formed the subject of study and practice amongst the Berlin Brotherhood. During my residence with my esteemed friend, John Dudley, I knew that his pure and innocent family delighted themselves in the sweet intercourse they maintained with their spirit friends. I never joined their happy séances, nor sought to impose my restless nature and troubled moods upon their harmonious gatherings; but I often hovered around them in spirit, and from thence, as well as in many less holy scenes, have learned the methods of communing with spirits, through the simple telegraphy induced by automatic passivity in what is called spirit mediumship.

I knew too, that without circles, invocations, or formulæ of any kind, my own beloved friends could reach me from the far side of that mystic river, on the shores of which they had disappeared from my straining eyes, but from whence they have all returned, one after the other, keeping watch and ward over my stormy life, with even more than the fidelity of their earthly care and tenderness.

The beautiful and gracious Constance, my brave father, my fair and gentle mother, my young brother, and many kind friends and companions who had fallen in their tracks, leaving me alone ere I knew the strength as well as the weakness of an isolated manhood, — all, all have come back to me, speaking in the tones of old, and hovering around my footsteps like beams of sunlight as they are ; making me realize the full meaning of the sublime words, " the ministry of angels." Felix von Marx, too, — he, the very pulse-beat of my heart, he has never left me, never failed me. In experiences nearer, dearer, and more sacred than any besides, he has still continued to pour out upon me that deep, unselfish love, which inspired in him the wild desire to give his life for me.

And yet who will sympathize with or understand me, when I own that the apparitions of these precious beings, with all their varied and ingenious methods of unsought, uninvoked telegraphy, could not always satisfy or convince me of my own soul's immortality, or their continued identity beyond a brief span of evanescent spiritual existence, a transitory state in which that identity might be preserved for a while, to be engulfed, swallowed up, cancelled again, by the horrible necessity of running the rounds of never-ending, material existences. I apologized to myself and to my beloved comforters for these morbid fantasies,—fantasies which fled like the shadows of night before the sunlight of their glorious presence, and yet returned again and again to haunt me when my feverish spirit was left to prey upon itself. That for which my soul hungered, was a grander, broader perception of the divine scheme than I could realize from the spheres of being absolutely known to us. I longed for a philosophy of life here and hereafter, to perceive the finger of Deity pointing to the beyond, beyond the grave, beyond the origin and ultimate of a single life, and I would far rather have been assured I should soon "sleep the sleep that knows no waking," than to be tossed thus restlessly on an ocean of speculation without compass, rudder, pilot, or anchor.

Sometimes I saw, felt, and encountered, face to face, my own "atmospheric spirit." I realized no loss of physical strength from this mysterious manifestation of duality, but it never occurred without impressing me with an unaccountable sense of awe, I might almost add, a nameless fear, which caused me to shrink away from this presence as if I were facing my worst enemy. Sometimes this hateful vision addressed me, using the language of rebuke, scorn, and irony, and commenting upon its relationship to me, like a mocking fiend, rather than the astral essence of my own spiritual body.

The spirits of those I most loved and could have trusted, conversed with me and often manifested intelligence foreign to my own consciousness, and such as proved the identity of the special individuals who rendered it; but that which they communicated failed to elucidate the mysteries by which I was surrounded.

Although they were constantly demonstrating by a thousand ingenious modes the fact that a foreign intelligence addressed me and a halo of unceasing love and watchfulness surrounded me, their revelations in other respects were slight and inconsequential, consisting for the most part of petty items of information, monitions, warnings, and prophecies, all of which I soon found to be true; yet beyond these and other small platitudes there seemed to be no common ground of ideality between us.

I longed, oh, how passionately I longed for something higher! but when I pressed home my urgent pleadings for light upon my spiritual visitants, an unaccountable weariness possessed me, and compelled me to suspend an intercourse which seemed impossible to maintain and live. Sometimes the terrible theory of the Berlin Brotherhood recurred to me, and I would be almost disposed to believe, with them, that these apparitions were in reality nothing more than "astral spirits" exhaled from the material casket in death, but that the soul was, like the body, dissipated into the elements, or else was taken up again in fresh forms with which its past existence maintained no sympathetic relations. Let me add at once that these vague and most miserable theories were sure to be refuted almost as soon as formed, for some blessed messenger from the life beyond would present itself immediately, and after proving how completely my thoughts had been scanned, give me slight but deeply significant tokens, connecting them with the continued life, individuality, and personal ministry of my angel visitant, and leaving me, for the time being, firmly fixed in the assurance of immortal life and love beyond the confines of the grave. Besides the various societies for the study of occultism to which I belonged in Europe, I became affiliated with many others during my wanderings through the East.

Like most persons interested in the occult side of nature, I had no sooner returned to India, where indeed, my earliest days of childhood had been passed, than I became fascinated with the extraordinary and preternatural powers displayed by Oriental ecstatics. Had I published these pages ten or twenty years ago I might have acceptably filled a volume with a record of the marvels I witnessed. As it is, every cheap periodical has become so redolent of East Indian magic that the *gamin* who polishes your boots in the streets of Paris or London, will tell you half-a-dozen snake-charming stories in as many minutes; the smirking damsel who hands you a light for your cigar will recite to you more tales of exhumed fakirs than she can count havannas in her show-case; and the *frizeur* who trims your beard will descant upon the facility with which dervishes can cut off heads and put them on again, how mango-trees can be grown in a given number of seconds, or thieves discovered by self-locomotive cups and balls. The public mind in Europe has been filled *ad nauseum* with such wonders; but whilst listening to details which I have myself beheld enacted with ever-deepening interest, taken part in, and spent years in searching out the producing causes of, I do not find this same glib-tongued, popular voice of rumor giving any philosophical explanation of how these phenomena occur.*   Of course we must acknowledge that their only importance is derived from the fact that their causation is occult, and transcends the power of the most enlightened scientists to explain.   Even when referred to legerdemain as the easiest way of disposing of a problem which science is too ignorant to master and too proud to study out, I do not find the marvels of Oriental spiritism reproduced on any other soil, and as I know they are in many instances, at least, indications of the occult forces in nature, it may not be wholly uninteresting to touch upon the methods which I myself adopted to master the secret of their production.

My first step was to secure the services of two of the most accomplished as well as respectable members of the fakir fraternity, and having taken all the available means at command to attach them to my interest, not forgetting to separate them from each other, so as to avoid the possibility of collusion or a systematic attempt to deceive me, I had opportunity enough to observe many of the most astounding evidences of the power these men possessed, as well as to analyze at leisure their claims for its origin.   In each case, as well as in numerous others, where incredible feats of preternatural wonder were exhibited, the fakirs assured me the *pitris*, or ancestral spirits, were the invisible wonder-workers.†

Again and again they protested they could do nothing without the aid of these spiritual allies.   Their own agency in the work, they gave me to understand, consisted in preparing themselves for the service of the

---

* See " Art Magic," sections 11, 12, and 13.— ED. GHOST LAND.
† Ibid.

pitris. They alleged that the material body was only a vehicle for the invisible soul, the spiritual or astral clothing of which was an element evidently analogous to the "spiritual body" of the apostle Paul, the "magnetic body" or "life principle" of the spiritists, the "astral spirit" of the Rosicrucians, and the "atmospheric spirit" of the Berlin Brotherhood. This element the Hindoo and Arabian ecstatics termed AGASA, or the life-fluid. They said that in proportion to the quantity and potency of agasa in the system, so was the power to work marvels by the aid of spirits. Spirits, they added, used agasa as their means of coming in contact with matter, and when it was abundant and very powerful, the invisibles could draw it from the bodies of the ecstatics and perform with it feats only possible to themselves and the gods. "Mutilate the body, lop off the limbs, if you will," said a Brahmin, whom I had also enlisted in my service as a teacher of occultism, "and with a sufficient amount of agasa, you can instantaneously heal the wound. Agasa is the element which keeps the atoms of matter together; the knife or sword severs it, the fire expels it from its lodgement in those atoms; put the agasa back to the severed or burned parts before they have had time to fester or wither, and the parts must reunite and become whole as before."

It is by virtue of agasa that the seed germinates in the ground and grows up to be a tree, with leaves, fruit, and flowers. Pour streams of agasa on the seed, and you quicken in a minute what would else, with less of the life-fluid, occupy a month to grow. Charge stones or other inanimate objects with agasa drawn from a human body, and spirits can make such objects move, fly, swim, or travel hither and thither at will; in short, it is through the power of agasa,— by which I mean

FORCE, the LIFE of things,—that all the most intelligent
Hindoos with whom I studied, insisted that preternatural
marvels could be wrought, always adding, however, that
pitris must assist in the operation, first, because their
spiritual bodies were all agasa, and next, because they
had a knowledge of this great living force and how to
apply it, which they could not communicate to mortals.

The methods of initiation into these wonder-working
powers were, I was assured, asceticism, chastity, frequent ablutions, long fasts, seasons of profound abstraction, a spirit exalted to the contemplation of deity, heaven
and heavenly things, and a mind wholly sublimated from
earth and earthly things. By these processes, it was
claimed, the body would become subdued and the quantity of agasa communicated through the elements and
by favor of the gods, would be immensely increased.
It would also be more readily liberated, and under the
control of spiritual agencies.

'"Behold me!" cried one of my instructors on a certain
occasion. "I am all agasa. This thin film of matter
wherewith I am covered, these meshes of bone that form
my framework of life, are they not fined away to the
tenuity of the elements? They hinder not my flight
through space, neither can they bind me to the earth I
am casting off."

He proved the truth of his boast by springing upwards
from the ground which he spurned with his foot, when
lo! he ascended into mid-air, and whilst his entranced
eyes were rolled upwards, and his lean, rigid arms and
thin hands were clasped in ecstasy above his head, he
continued to soar away nearly to the roof of the vast
temple in which we were. I have already alluded
in the earlier chapters of this work to the methods by
which many Eastern ecstatics promoted the "mantic

frenzy," such as leaping, dancing, whirling, spinning, the use of drugs and vapors of an intoxicating character, noise, music, and all other methods which might tend to distract the senses and stimulate the mind to temporary mania.

Another and very general mode of wonder-working amongst Eastern ecstatics is by *illusion*, a word which but ill expresses the extent of the psychological impression which a powerful adept can produce upon a number of persons at one time. It is almost impossible to describe the methods by which this haze, hallucination, or enchantment can be spread over a whole assembly, compelling them to see the chief operator in an illusory light, and imagine he is visible or invisible, or performing wholly impossible actions with wholly impossible instruments, just as he wills the spectators to believe. Those who are most successful in this species of illusion are not only "mediums" for spirits, and powerful psychologists, but they have a faculty of so enclosing themselves in agasa (spiritual atmosphere) that they can present almost any illusory appearance they please.

By way of experiment, some of the best practitioners of this singular species of enchantment have, on more than one occasion, magnetized me, — I use this modern phrase for the sake of being better understood, — that is to say, they have whirled, spun, and danced around me, pointing their lean fingers the whole time towards me, until, when they left me, giddy, speechless, and fixed, yet fully conscious of my curious situation, I have seen several persons pass without perceiving me, and when invited by the fakirs to describe my appearance, the strangers they addressed have stoutly affirmed there was no visible object on the spot of ground where I stood. Again, on some occasions, these men have not only clothed me, but other persons, with this atmosphere of invisibility. They have also caused an immense assemblage gathered together in one of the temples of Siva, at Benares, to see tigers, lions, and other terrific sights, when there was positively no such objects at the spot indicated. To perform these acts of illusion successfully, the operator must be a good psychologist, surround himself with powerful bands of spirits, prepare his body by a long fast, excite the mantic frenzy by pungent essences and anointings, and thus accumulate that powerful charge of agasa which will enable his spirit band to work through him as their human instrument. When I add that the natives of the East, with their slender, lithe forms, and natural taste for such exercises, delight to practise the arts of legerdemain, until they arrive at a degree of skill wholly unknown to the people of other lands, I believe I have presented to the curious reader the *rationale* of all the methods in which Oriental marvels are performed.

Let us not mistake or confound, however, the acts of the professed juggler with those of the religious ecstatic. The two classes are not only distinct in their modes of performance, but in their aims and the motives that possess them. The juggler is so by profession. He is wonderfully skilful in his art, skilful enough, indeed, to impress many an astute beholder with the belief that he must be aided by, or in league with supermundane powers. Still, those who, like myself, will take the trouble to follow his performances carefully and pay him sufficiently for the information, will find that he is but a juggler after all, and that his exhibitions are prompted by no higher motives than to obtain the petty remuneration which his skill commands. Despite the fact that many of the East Indian ecstatics prostitute their remarkable powers to the most abject system of mendicity, there are still a numerous class who are moved by far higher motives, the culminating point of their incredible acts of asceticism and self-inflicted torture being the realization of exalted religious aspirations. As the most accomplished adepts in Oriental marvels do not exhibit their power for alms, except in behalf of the temple, lamasery, or monastery to which they belong, they do not migrate into remunerative spheres of action, like other exhibitors, and their arts acquire a certain amount of dignity from their association with the rites of temple services.

It was under the conviction that there were spiritual forces involved in many of the wonderful phenomena I witnessed, and that, inconsequential as these were in the results obtained, they indicated an array of unexplored powers yet latent in human experience, that I determined to devote one consecutive twelve months and as much time as I could spare besides, to the study of this subject and a thorough personal experience of its methods of procedure. It was with this view that I abandoned my pleasant suburban residence at Benares and took up my abode with a company of devotees in the gloomy subterranean crypts of a vast range of ancient ruins, where the spirit of a grand, antique faith pervaded every stone and hallowed the scenes which were once consecrated to the loftiest and most exalted inspiration. I am bound in honor not to reveal the methods of initiation by which I graduated into the dignity of a "full-fledged ecstatic," under the guidance and instruction of self-devoted, self-sacrificing men, who had themselves attained to the mastery of the mightiest spiritual forces.

It is enough to say I became all asceticism; spent my time in the prescribed duties, and even exceeded in rigidity the discipline laid down for me. My capacity as a "natural magician," so my teachers informed me, shortened the term of my probation and modified the severity of the exercises enjoined, and amongst the Buddhist priests—with whom I studied, as well as the Brahmins—would have elevated me to any rank in prophetic dignity to which my ambition might have aspired.

Amongst the Brahmins, my lack of caste excluded me from priestly office, but my superiors entreated me to remain with them, tempting me with prospects of spiritual distinction held out to very few.

I need. hardly say my purpose was achieved when I mastered the secret of true occult power. I proved, tested, tried, and practised it, and I KNOW that every element in being can be made subject to the human soul; every achievement of spiritual or even deific power IS ATTAINABLE to man. All this, and much that I am pledged not to reveal, and which in our present corrupt and licentious condition of society, would prove a curse rather than a blessing, and convert the earth into pandemonium rather than heaven, I *learned, proved, tried, and practised*. These experiences were not undertaken during the occasion of my first visit to Hindostan, when the career of military life enjoined upon me by my family and connections enabled me to devote only a very limited amount of time to such studies; my principal successes in these directions were achieved during a second and more recent visit to the East, and I only anticipate that period by alluding to the results I obtained in this chapter. What I learned and the powers I attained to, however, were not cheaply or easily acquired. It is enough at present to declare I exchanged for the comforts of home and civilization, a life of discipline which would make most luxurious Europeans shrink back aghast and horror-struck.

In the inscrutable methods of Providence which seem to work all things together for good, I have sometimes thought I was permitted, if not impelled, to act out the desperate attempt at self-destruction induced by my frenzy of grief for the loss of my beloved friend, von Marx, chiefly to prepare me for the tremendous austerities demanded of me, ere I could cross the threshold of humanity and enter upon "the life of the gods," at least, in respect to the spirit's mastery over the hinderances of matter. (Although, like most persons of "mediumistic" or naturally prophetic tendencies, I inherited a very poor constitution, it was wonderful to me at the time, wonderful to me since to remember, with what extraordinary powers of endurance I sustained the enormous penalties I had to pay for spiritual light and prowess. Whilst many other neophytes associated with me failed utterly, and others withdrew with broken health, shattered minds, or even yielded up life itself on the altar of their vain endeavor, I passed through every ordeal like one upborne in the arms of mighty spirits, and sustained by a power which I can never attribute to merely human effort. All felt, though I alone knew *individually* the power that sustained me, and that I was permitted to pass through such extraordinary ordeals simply to demonstrate the triumph of spirit over matter, and the force by which the human soul can transcend all the limitations of time and space.

From the first moment of my arrival in Hindostan, — in fact, throughout my whole career, — I have spent my life in alternate devotion to spiritual experiences and the more material activities of such duties as circumstances impelled me to undertake. Notwithstanding the fact that I became immersed in public life, and that of the most stormy and *exigeant* character when I joined my father's connections in India, just so long as health and strength permitted I never relinquished my spiritualistic pursuits or researches, nor did I find them incompatible with the routine of other occupations. I was frequently obliged to reside in several of the large cities of Hindostan and the Deccan, besides spending some time with those relations to whom I have alluded in the commencement of these sketches, but my "Patmos" was a suburban residence near Benares, where I found all the incentives in surroundings and association to prosecute my favorite studies.

Throughout the length and breadth of India I ever encountered undying witnesses to the fervent faith and heartfelt devotion with which the ancient Hindoo cherished the principles of his religious belief. Every colossal monument, gigantic pagoda, or stupendous cave temple, is an offering, sanctified by the heart's best blood of adoring millions, to the fire-gods of antique worshippers.

Hindostan has of late years been the theme of such magnificent word painting and glowing literary imagery, that I forbear from the attempt to offer any addition to the innumerable accounts already extant of its sculptures and monumental glories. Like the performances of wonder-working fakirs and dervishes, the splendors of Elephanta, Ellora, Carli, and Orissa have become popular themes in the mouths of literary gossips.

From the learned archæologist to the humblest school child, the gigantic elephants, colossal sphinxes, mighty sculptures, and awful caverns of this solemn old land have been canvassed in large and small talk in every country of civilization. With throbbing heart and dazzled brain the traveller may wander beneath the shadows of the grim idols, the darksome caverns, the mighty banyan groves and memory-haunted forests, but the glories and wonders of ancient India have been so thoroughly popularized by measuring tourists and surveying explorers that any well-educated young lady from a London or Paris seminary will tell you the exact dimensions of the Kailasa better far than I could who have spent long days and lonely nights wandering amidst its superb colonnades of sphinxes and elephants.

During the hours which I devoted to meditation amidst these stupendous relics of a faith which has rendered its gods immortal by the miracle of its own immortal genius, it was not on measurements or styles that my mind brooded. I longed to pierce the mystery of the inspiration which suggested those sublime structures; to unveil the gigantic spirituality that embodied itself in the colossi around me; to know the mystery of that central spiritual sun whose Protean forms of representation, mirrored forth the lofty imaginings of the antique mind from all the grim, grotesque, sublime, and wonderfully-varied forms of sculpture around me. Sometimes I declaimed in wild and passionate accusation against the silent sky and speechless stars, that had revealed so much to the seers and prophets of old, and yet were so dumb to me. In their solemn brightness the ancient priest had been inspired to read the mystery of the Alpha and Omega; why were they now so coldly unsympathetic to my appeals for light? How still and motionless they seemed to my straining gaze! How swift, mighty, and powerful I knew them to be under the rule of the eternal hosts who commanded and marshalled them into living rank and file! Here, in the midst of those gigantic forms in which the mind of elder ages has veiled the secrets of deific being and embodied its perception of godlike power and godlike dealings with men, is there no vibrating echo of the voices which once resounded through these colossi, interpreting the mystery of being to rapt and listening disciples,—not a tone left to answer my passionate and urgent appeals for light?

During a residence of some months in the province of Arungabad and whilst lingering in the ruinous city of Dowletabad, I rode over nearly every night to the mountain region of Ellora, and frequently remained there wandering amidst its silent monuments or sheltering during the livelong night in one of the numerous grottos that had once been the abode of the anchorites or priests, whose duty it was to minister in the neighboring temples.

One night, when I had resolved to return to my residence, I lingered at the entrance of a low crypt, which I had fitted up in my own fashion with a couch of sweet-scented leaves and herbs, and where I was accustomed to pass many hours of my nightly wanderings. For some time I stood gazing abstractedly over the table-land which formed the central enclosure of a chain of mountains whose cathedral-like masses, towering up to the skies in a vast amphitheatre, were pierced in every direction with the openings to crypts and grottos, or adorned with those colossal sculptures which indicated the entrances to the temples.

The moon shone full, white, and glaring over these awful solitudes, more awful by far in the desolation which man had left, than in the pristine grandeur of nature. It was strange to observe how tremblingly the moonbeams lingered around the dark, cavernous mouths of crypts and temples, but never pierced the unlighted gloom within, as if her holy light was repelled by the mysterious secrets to which those solemn scenes were dedicated. A thousand fanciful shapes seemed to me to press back her flood of soft radiance, lest the light should fall on an arcanum veiled even from the speechless witness of the lamps of heaven.

My horse, which had become almost as accustomed to pilgrim life as his master, had strayed from the large grotto I had appropriated as his stable and was quietly cropping the scanty herbage of a moonlit plateau. Suddenly the sensitive creature raised his head and moved his ears with that peculiar action which announces an unusual presence approaching, long ere our duller senses can recognize it. At the same moment a shadow passed across the illuminated ground, and the figure of a man appeared, issuing from a cleft in the mountains, and for a few seconds lingering, like myself, in abstracted contemplation of the solitary scene. Presently he quitted the spot where I had first observed him, but instead of striking the path to the right which led off from the amphitheatre of mountains, he came towards me, evidently purposing to cross the plateau in the line of which I was standing.

As he neared me I observed that his monastic habit and cowl proved him to be one of those ascetics who so frequently sojourn amidst these desolate regions, not unfrequently spending their lives within the shelter of some lonely grotto or secluded crypt.

I was at no loss to guess the secret of his appearance at such an hour, believing that he, like myself, was intent upon communion with the spirit of the scene. Desiring to afford the stranger the same uninterrupted seclusion which I myself sought, I was retreating noiselessly into my hermitage, when he came towards me, with a swift and sudden action, and pausing opposite where I stood, so that the light of the moon might fall directly on my face yet leave his own in shadow, he said in a sweet and winning tone, speaking in my favorite dialect, the *Shen Tamil,* "Forgive me, sir, if I congratulate you on choosing so fair a night for a visit to this impressive scene." Ordinarily I would have resented this unwelcome invasion on my beloved solitude; besides, it was the well-understood custom of visitors to these deserted cities of the dead never to intrude upon the meditations of those who must have come there for any other purpose rather than that of social intercourse. I remembered however, that I had left home late in the evening, and that without finding time to assume my usual travelling dress; hence, that my military attire, plainly enough disclosed by the broad glare of the moonbeam, would prove that I was no ascetic, whilst my horse in the distance showed that I was a mere transient visitor to the scene. It struck me at once then, that it was the monk rather than the soldier, who might be expected to feel annoyance at the presence of a stranger, and besides this, there was something so sweet and refined in his pure accent and winning voice that I could not refuse an exchange of courtesy with him. Determined however to ascertain his right to become my associate, I said, abruptly enough, I suppose, "My father is free of this holy city. Is he then a dweller within its deep shadows?"

Without following my lead in the somewhat constrained style suggested by the poetical dialect in which he spoke, he replied simply, "Do you see yon black spot up there, far up on the mountain side? Nay sir, not there — be pleased to step a little farther out into the moonlight — there, just where yon dark line divides that clump of bushes."

" I perceive," I said. And I did perceive that he was critically scrutinizing my dress, whilst he was pointing off to the spot he wished me to notice.

" Well, sir," he rejoined, " there is the *Dharma Sala* in which I have found shelter for many a long year, when on my return from distant pilgrimages I have yearned to indulge that universal weakness to which our poor frail humanity is most subject, namely, the love of home."

"Home! " I involuntarily exclaimed. " Is that hole in the mountain side your home ? "

" Even so."

" You are then —." I paused, for despite the dark shroud which enveloped his whole form and face, there was something in the bearing of this stranger which would not admit of questioning.

"I am," he rejoined, in a quiet tone, "a native of a distant province, a *Vaidya* " (one who practises the art of the mediciner, the son of mixed castes), "but I am drawn hither by sympathy and some other motives. I have many deep interests in these mountain caves and temples, but the one nearest to the selfishness of human nature is the love of home, and in yon hole in the mountain, as you so graphically term my.retreat, that one personal interest finds its satisfaction. Don't you love home yourself, or are you so immersed in the excitement of your noble profession (pointing as he spoke to my sword), that you would prefer the battle-field to the rest of home? "

" I have no home but the camp," I answered, brusquely; " I seek none but the grave."

" Too young in age, too old in wisdom for such an answer as that," he replied, gravely. " Listen: Home is the soul's rest, not a locality; it is the scene where the wandering *Yogee* and the sainted *Irdhi* will find rest in the infinite soul; it is the goal of all the self-inflicted tortures that fakirs and lamas put upon their miserable bodies. Rest in Brahm is the aim which enables the *Bodhisattvas* to extinguish the perfume of the senses, the ecstacy of the emotions, the luxury of thought, and the sensibility of self-recognition. Home is soul absorption in the central source of being; in short," he added, starting, and changing the wild monotone of ecstacy into which he seemed to be soaring, back to the simple phraseology of the cosmopolite in which he at first addressed me, "in short, Chevalier, mask our aims in what abstractions we will, whether we pursue love of woman or love of God, love of gold or love of renown, the goal of our affections, whenever we attain to it, is home, and, here or hereafter, our home will be where our treasure is. Am I not right?"

"Pardon me, sir," I replied, without noticing his rhapsody, "you called me by a title I am little accustomed to hear from the lips of a stranger. Do you then know me?"

"You are accustomed to be addressed in military phraseology," he replied, at once naming my rank in the army. "Excuse my indiscretion."

"But who is it, then," I cried, somewhat piqued to be so completely mastered, "that is discreet enough to mask himself, yet unmask me?"

"The distinguished ones of earth marvel to find that the humbler classes look up to them as the ant regards the elephant," he answered, in a tone which matched the satire of his words; "nevertheless, if it be worth your while to know the dweller of yon *Math*, know me as *Chundra ud Deen*. To be more in the line of your own civilization, should you condescend to grant the request I shall presently make, call me, if you please, *Byga* (mediciner); and now for my request."

He then, in the most careless and off-hand way, invited me to visit him in his "hole," which he so pretentiously called a *Math* or circle of huts, such as is devoted to the use of a spiritual teacher and his disciples, but in the words of invitation he addressed to me, he interwove in a pointed way, impossible for me to mistake, the watchword of an association whose solemn bonds had set such a seal of secrecy even upon my very thoughts, to say nothing of my lips, that I started and shivered whilst the words fell on the listening air, as if their commonplace expression had been the deepest blasphemy. Had a peal of thunder broken the stillness of that breathless moonlit night, I could not have been more startled than to hear those forbidden words. Few there are on earth who know of the existence of such an association, fewer still who can claim fraternity with it; yet of that few, one stood before me now that was inevitably proved. Other words and signs were interchanged, yet we did not touch each other. It was enough, and without further hesitancy I agreed to renew our acquaintance at the same hour and place on the following night; and thus we parted, he disappearing in the impenetrable gloom of a neighboring temple, I signalling my horse to my side and preparing for a midnight ride home to Dowletabad.

CHAPTER XIX.

How the hours lagged! and how wearily I won my way through the duties of the day which must elapse ere I should again meet with the *Byga*, —that man who seemed so singularly able to medicine my restless spirit to peace. In his presence and listening to his wonderfully soothing voice, I had experienced a calm and tranquillity to which I had been for years a stranger. There was nothing remarkable in the words he uttered, still less could I regard the prospect of a visit to his " home," as he was pleased to call the hole in the mountain where he claimed to dwell, as an inviting one; yet I felt a strange longing to be there, and when I speculated upon the appearance of that " dark line dividing the bushes," which he had pointed out to me, I seemed to see white hands reaching from the mountain side and beckoning me up its savage and almost unattainable heights. I had intended to take some sleep before commencing my pilgrimage, but I was detained on business all day at Aurungabad, the capital city of the province, and could only partake of a late dinner with some brother officers, ere it was time to set off on my long ride in order to reach Ellora by midnight. I succeeded in gaining the ravine by a little after eleven, and having there stabled my horse, proceeded on foot to the temples, which I reached a few minutes before the appointed hour.

The moon was obscured by the driving clouds which predicated the approach of a storm. The table-land of the amphitheatre, around which towered the red granite rocks that formed "the great religious city," was destitute of all signs of life or movement as I approached it. Solitude, the most profound, desolation the most complete, cast a spell upon the entire panorama.

By an impulse I could not account for, unless it was the necessity of keeping pace in quick motion with the throbbing pulsations of my eager spirit, I moved on from point to point, scrutinizing every cleft in the rocks, every opening and sculpture, looking for I know not what, and striving to find out the meaning of my own feverish research. At length I paused before one of the most ancient of the cave temples, whose deep recesses were, as I well knew, to be reached only by passing through long rows of gigantic elephants, whose effigies I had often before gazed at by the gloomy light admitted through the vast portico or the fitful glare of torches. I knew the interior of that cavernous hall thoroughly, and had traversed its colossal colonnades again and again, yet now something seemed to repel my advance, and make me hesitate ere I took the first step onward. In this moment of indecision I suddenly recollected that my appointment with the *Byga* was at a spot from which I had strayed away nearly a mile.

Provoked at my own unaccountable restlessness, and fearing lest I might fail in my tryst, I turned hastily to retrace my steps, when I was violently seized from behind, my arms drawn back and tightly pinioned, a scarf tied across my eyes and another over my mouth; and all this was done with such an amount of force and incredible rapidity that before I had a moment's time to offer the least resistance I was gagged, pinioned, and

blindfolded, and in this helpless position, with hands of
iron grasping me on either side, I felt myself dragged
on in the direction of the temple and through its long
colonnades until I reached a point where there was a
slight pause, and the aroma of a damp, subterranean
atmosphere became distinctly palpable. After this
interruption my course was always descending, sometimes by rough steps, sometimes by very narrow, winding tracks. Occasionally the passages we traversed
were so confined that my conductors were obliged to
advance before and behind me, and again the chill air
assured me we were traversing vaults or large halls.
Strange to say, my usual clairvoyance, in this unexpected captivity, utterly forsook me. There seemed to
be a will stronger than my own operating to crush down
or subdue my spiritual perceptions, and for some time I
was too stunned to attempt resistance. In all this long
descent into the very bowels of the earth I heard no
other sound than that of my own footsteps. No voice
spoke, no footfall broke the portentous silence. The
strong grip of my captors was the only evidence that I
had companions. Just as we reached a certain point and
when I realized that I was being forced to descend an
almost interminable stairway, the idea occurred to me
that by planting myself firmly on my feet I might at least
manifest my determination of going no farther. This
poor show of resistance, however, was instantly met by
a push so violent that had I not been held by hands of
iron I should have been precipitated to whatever depths
awaited me below; then, as if to convince me of my utter
helplessness, I was lifted up from the ground, and despite
the fact that my conductor carried a burden of six feet
in height with a proportionate amount of diameter, I
was borne along for some time in the grasp of this Titan

as if I had been an infant. Happily, as I deemed it, the
next passage was too low and narrow to admit of such
a mode of locomotion, and I was, again set on my
feet, whilst the iron grasp of one giant before and another
behind me, sufficiently advised me of the uselessness of
further demonstrations on my part.

At length I experienced a marked change both in the
atmosphere around me and the ground on which I trod.
The air became soft, balmy, and perfumed with the
odor of aromatic essences, and the floor was smooth
and hard as if formed of polished stones. Presently I
felt busy hands about me removing the gag, bandage,
and thongs, and then it was that a sight burst upon my
eyes such as no language of mine can do justice to.
I stood in a subterranean temple of immense extent,
fashioned in the shape of a horse-shoe, the large oval
of which was arranged as an auditorium, with luxuri-
ously cushioned seats in ascending circles, on the plan of
an amphitheatre. The lofty roof was surrounded with
highly-wrought cornices, sculptured with emblems of
Egyptian and Chaldaic worship, interspersed with sentences emblazoned in gold, in Arabic, Sanskrit, and
other Oriental languages. In the midst of the roof
which sloped upwards, was a magnificent golden planisphere, formed on an azure plane, and so skilfully
designed that the interior of the temple was illuminated
from the representations of the heavenly host that
gleamed and sparkled above my head. The walls were
hewn out of the same red granite which composed the
mountains of the district, but they were thickly adorned
with gigantic images of the Hindoo and Egyptian gods,
surmounted by a border of gorgeous *bas relievos*, some
of which represented ancient Chaldaic tablets; others
were engraved with planispheres, astrological charts,

and scenes in Babylonish, Assyrian, and Chaldaic history. At the small opening of the horse-shoe was a second cavern, hewn out of the solid rock, and so designed as to form an immense raised platform or stage, on the floor of which was spread a carpet of grassy turf, or an imitation so finely executed that the difference could not be detected. A pair of gigantic sphinxes supported either side of this noble rostrum, and an immense image of the winged bull of Nineveh was suspended, in all probability by magnetic force, in mid-air, between the high vaulted roof and the grassy carpet beneath. The walls and ceiling of this huge, cavernous stage, were otherwise destitute of adornment. A golden hand held a scroll suspended over the auditorium, inscribed with a word in Arabic which corresponds to NEOPHYTES, whilst a similar hand and scroll appeared over the cornice which served as proscenium to the stage, with the Arabic inscription signifying HIEROPHANTS. Ranged in a semicircle midway on the platform were seven tripods supporting braziers, from which ascended colored flames and wreaths of deliciously perfumed vapors, whose intoxicating odors filled the temple. Behind each tripod, seated on thrones fashioned of burnished silver, so as to represent a glittering star, were seven dark-robed figures, whose masked faces and shrouded forms left no opportunity of judging of their sex or semblance. Around me, some reclining, some sitting in Oriental fashion, but all seemingly engrossed in deep abstraction, were multitudes of men attired mostly in European, but with some Hindoo costumes. Their faces were concealed, however, for they all wore masks. I observed that those who had removed the bandage from my face had invested me also with a mask, leaving my eyes entirely free, and thus enabling me to make an uninterrupted survey of the remarkable scene around me.

In all I gazed upon, there was no minutiæ of detail; all was colossal, distinct, magnificent, whilst every design, however vast its size, was executed in a style of the most perfect workmanship. The light diffused from the gorgeous planisphere of the roof was soft yet brilliant, and by an arrangement since explained to me, large shafts were so constructed as to communicate with the upper air and thus introduce a perfect supply of fresh atmosphere even into the deep abysses of this subterranean chamber.

For the first few moments of my liberation, astonishment, delight, and awe kept me motionless. It was whilst I was thus gazing around me that I beheld the entire assemblage directing their masked faces towards me, but from every quarter giving me the signs of brotherhood in one or more of the different fraternities to which I belonged. I have since learned, and believe I then understood, that there was not a person present who had not been initiated into one or more of the occult societies with which I was myself connected. The recognition of this fact placed me at once upon a footing of understanding with my companions and indicated the line of conduct that was expected from me. There was, and still is, an unspoken *cipher of signals* existing amongst certain brotherhoods, far more terse and significant than speech, and this I found in practice with my new associates. By this method I learned the special ideas upon which I was expected to rely that night. The first was the sentiment of brotherhood extended from one particular order to as many as would represent humanity at large. The next was an understanding that the aim of our gathering was the discovery of occultism and our methods of research were to be occult likewise. Another piece of instruction was, never in the most distant way to allude to the Society or its existence, to any of its members whom I should chance to meet in the world, the object in this prohibition being to avoid discussion on the nature of the intelligence communicated. I was required to reflect upon it within myself, or, if I chose to adopt its revelations as my own opinions, to communicate them to others, not members of the Society; also I might allude to the existence of such an association and describe its aims, but never reveal the names of its members or guide strangers to the many scenes where its sessions were held. The final charge impressed upon me was to be strictly attentive to the proceedings, in virtue of which I fixed my eyes upon the seven masked and robed figures on the platform, who I at first thought were simply effigies, but as soon as the whole assembly were seated and in order, I observed they arose, one after the other, each one making his sign of intelligence and then resuming his seat and moveless attitude. The first command issued in this way was for Pythagorean silence during each session. The next required from all, Platonic submission to the order during our connection with it. The third assured us of divine protection. The fourth apprised me in especial, that my most secret wishes were penetrated. The fifth (still addressed to me) promised me complete gratification of those wishes. The sixth was an universal charge for discretion in the use of the knowledge I was to receive, virtue in its application, and fraternal love in its distribution. The seventh sign I am not at liberty to explain, but I was advised by one of the masked figures near me that propositions for complete initiation would be given me hereafter.

During the time that these ciphers were being enacted, the entire auditorium was becoming enveloped in gloom, so that when this part of the proceedings ended, I found the light greatly subdued and the radiance of the noble planisphere modified to a soft twilight, such as would be dispensed by the moon and stars. And now, my most imperfect sketch of the fine temple and the opening scenes of the grand drama ended, let me essay to describe those which followed.

A deep hush reigned on every side of me, a silence that could be felt pervaded the assembly, when I perceived that the entire of the vast cavern that formed the stage at the small opening of the horse-shoe, was melting away. Walls, ceiling, hierophants, silver thrones, and braziers, all vanished, and in their place I beheld illimitable wastes of what seemed at first to be impenetrable darkness. Presently I observed there was motion,* an ever-increasing, wave-like motion, and a gradually diminishing hue in this thick blackness, which became refined into a gray, silvery vapor, and at last melted entirely away. Then I saw a boundless *univercœlum*, in which were represented myriads of hemispheres. Above, below, around, stretching away into endless horizons, and ascending from thence beyond every imaginable limitation, were piled up hemisphere upon hemisphere, densely massed yet all separate from one another, and all blazing with systems, every system sparkling with suns, planets, comets, meteors, moons, rings, belts, and nebulæ. Millions and millions of these systems swarmed through the spaces of the universe, yet all differed the one from the other, whilst all moved in the same resplendent order, swinging around some mighty and inconceivable pivotal centre. And in this stupendous scheme of harmony, every newly created cluster of fire-mist seemed as admirably adjusted to its relative point of space in the universe as the huge astral systems with their galaxies of suns, stars, and revolving satellites. I saw the spaces of the universe divided up into hemispheres,—hemispheres into sidereal heavens,—heavens studded with suns, forming systems of created worlds in every stage of progression, from unparticled fire-mist to the central sun of a perfected system.

I merely *thought* of the order in which the movements of the universe transpired, when I instantly discovered that the motions of bodies in space were not, as I had deemed them, a mere automatic revolution around a central orb. It is true that each one moved in an axial orbit of its own, having direct relation to its solar centre; that its path was circular, and bent or deflected only at its points of aphelion and perihelion; but as the observant gaze became able to master the details of planetary motion, unappreciable at first by reason of its inconceivable rapidity, it detected subordinate motions, which impressed upon every flying orb the character of an individualized life, and showed it to be endowed with an animation of its own. These sparkling worlds swam, danced, sported, floated upwards and darted downwards, with all the erratic mobility of zigzag lightning. Could they be really living, sentient beings,—glorious organisms not moved upon, but breathing, burning, rejoicing lives, acting in the inimitable procedures of fixed law? but no more so than the child who wins its way from point to point, yet is ever turning to gather flowers and butterflies in erratic divergence from the line of its path; no more so than the man whose fixed destiny between the cradle and the grave is checkered by all the turnings and windings which **a** mobile fancy and wandering imagination can prompt. Could they be all living organisms, and the immensity of the universe be filled, not with billions of manufactured autometa, but with legions of living creatures, rushing through the orbits of illimitable space in the joy and glory of life everlasting? Could our own burning sun and its shining family of planetary orbs be all creatures of parts and passions, organs and susceptibilities, with a framework of rocky ribs and mountain bones and sinews; veins and arteries coursed by the fluid-life of oceans and rivers; heaving lungs aerated by the breath of winds and atmospheres; electric life evolved from the galvanic action of metallic lodes, threading their way like a gigantic nervous system through every globe; vast reservoirs of polar force generated in the Arctic North and Antarctic South; the brain and feet of the living creature, realms of supply for the waste of physical life, in the relation which every satellite sustains to its solar centre, and one vast collective soul in the aggregated mass of soul atoms that maintain a parasitical life upon the surface of every planet? In the Apocalyptic vision now presented to my dazzled sight, every sun, star, planet, comet, moon, every fully-formed body in space, in short, was *a living being*, a body and soul, — a physical form destined to sustain a transitory material existence, composed of infinitesimal physical beings of its own grade and order, — an immortal spirit moulded and grown through the formative element of matter, destined to survive its dissolution, and live eternally as a perfected soul, carrying with it all the freight of soul atoms which it has sustained and unfolded, like the leaves and blossoms of its own parental germ seed.

I know this thought will seem like the rhapsody of a delirious fancy to those who have not read the universe

23

in its occult page of unfoldment as I have, but the time will come when the Cabala of existence shall be read as an open page. This "madness" will then be accepted as true philosophy; until then, the revelating angel bids me write — and I obey.

And next I pondered on the unknown, perhaps the unknowable, central source from which and to which, I perceived, every body in space tended, around which infinity itself becomes a revolution. I saw that millions and millions of hemispheres were swept on in paths as strictly orbital as the smallest planet of a single system. The whole vast arcanum of the universe, then, must move around some definite pivotal point.

As I reflected, the answer came. The universe of matter became translucent, and throughout its illimitable spaces I saw that creation was filled with piercing beams from the central sun of being. In a space less in magnitude than a degree marked on a child's school-map, I might have counted millions upon millions of such beams, yet the wondrous constituents of their nature were plainly revealed to me. The external or visible shaft of every ray was formed of physical light, or matter in its most sublimed condition. This shaft was lined by a ray of astral light or force, and this again by spiritual light, or the element from which is formed the imperishable soul. Conceive of the whole universe filled with these rays so thickly planted that space becomes annihilated; trace them to their source; and you will resolve them all back to one illimitable realm, into which no worlds, suns, systems, bodies in space, spirits, souls, nor men have ever penetrated; where thought becomes madness, ideality is lost; from which light, life, force, motion, matter, government, order, power go forth, but to which nothing that is returns again, and know then the source from which those rays of living light emanate; know then the central sun the body and soul of the universe, THE GOD, of whom man cannot even think and live.

One of my favorite studies at college was the chemistry of the sunbeam, and I have spent many an hour in delighted observation of such experiments as discovered the constitution, direction, and effect of this marvellous agent, in the economy of life, light, and growth; but how tame, dull, and insignificant, what mere child's play with shells and husks, became the memories of all that physical science could reveal, compared with the broader, grander vistas of causation, opened up to my view, as I penetrated into the arcanum of spiritual science. Could the dreams of the fire-worshipper, then, have a better foundation in divine truth than the asseverations of the theologian? asked my questioning soul.

The revelating angel answered by a fresh series of visions. I beheld a single planet, my own perhaps, with the light of the parent sun removed, and lo! as by an instantaneous blight, all color, beauty, shape, and form ceases. Now I behold a world from which the heat of the sun is withdrawn, and instantly life is suspended. A dull, leaden, crystalline death sets in, the wheels of being stop short, and being itself is at an end.

I behold the centripetal force of the sun withdrawn · from our solar system, and planets, moons, asteroids, comets, meteors, and all the array of embryonic elements held in solar paths fly off in ungoverned space, and become lost in endless ruin.

I see the centrifugal force withdrawn, and the solar system rushing to a point, is absorbed, swallowed up in the parent mass, and the parent mass itself becomes a mere wreck of worlds. If such are the life-giving, life-sustaining potencies of the physical sun, what must be the correlative action of the spiritual sun on the realm of immortal being?

If such is the actual physical relation of the sun of our system to the world, and to the forms which it has sown in the garden of the skies, what may we not dream of, and aspire to know, when in future ages of progression we may ascend to the heaven of heavens, and comprehend the mystery of God! Again I saw the universe outrolled and upon its shining surface worlds, with all their freight of material life, vitalized by force and inspired by spirit; and this trinity of being ranged from the gelatinous masses that floated in ancient seas to the sparkling suns that. blazed and burned in the depths of sidereal heavens.

With each fresh phase of the vision, fresh questions rose like waves in the surging sea of my storm-tossed mind.

To the next craving appeal for "light, more light," came stealing on my senses the tones of this mild rebuke: "Seek not, child, to compass eternity in a single hour of time. Be patient, and all shall be revealed, which is good for thee to know." For many and many a night, during many succeeding weeks of almost ecstatic life, these precious promises were kept to me by revelations of a similar character to that which I have noted down, and that, not in language worthy of the sublime and stupendous light that poured in on my soul, but in the simplest, plainest phrases, I could summon to my aid. As all language is unworthy when matched against thoughts which speech fails to interpret, so do I employ a form of expression so rude, that my utter powerlessness will be shown in· every line I write. Enough that the themes which an Apocalyptic angel alone could demonstrate, were shown to me in those magnificent visions, until a complete cosmic scheme was revealed, of which the following may be named as some of the subjects treated of. World building and builders, constitution of the solar universe. Of gods, men, spirits, angels, the fall, growth, and reconstruction of the spirit. The realm and destiny of souls. Light, heat, physical, astral, and spiritual light. The human soul, its powers, possibilities, forces, and destiny. Will; occult and magical powers, forces, and objects. The relation and influence of planetary bodies upon each other; the human mind, the necessity of theological myths. The permanance of being, cycles of time, cyclones of storm and sunshine in human life, etc. etc. etc.

Of these stupendous themes the treatment was ever grand, original, bold, and conclusive.

A scheme was presented, upon which, as I now solemnly believe and hope, the foundations of a new, true, and religious science and scientific religion will yet be upreared. The thoughts which shone in resplendent imagery before the eyes of my associates and myself a quarter of a century ago, have gradually been leavening the lump of civilized society during that whole period of time. They have been seen in vision, felt in soul, and taught in isolated fragments by many a solitary pioneer of the new church that shall be; but chiefly has their influence been realized as the radiation of an unknown force, whose subtile potencies are making for themselves a lever of public opinion, a giant whose will is sufficient to raise up every stone in the new temple and put them all in place, a concrete and glorious whole, when the stones of thought shall have been hewn each in its separate quarry, when every stone shall be *fair*

and square and true, and ready in its separate perfection to form a part of the sublime erection. That the
midnight assemblies gathered together in the subterranean vaults of one of the most ancient of ancient India's
cave temples has had its share in leavening the mass of
public opinion in the nineteenth century, I know, by the
experience of better soldiers in the army of metaphysical progress than myself; but as no mortal tongue or
pen can do justice to the gorgeous imagery with which
it was our great privilege to be favored, as these mere
magazine sketches, moreover, are not the fit channels
for the publication of the glowing ideality which these
visionary representations inspired, I shall presently disclose to my readers the singular *modus operandi* by
which the visions of our fraternity were impressed on
the recipients, and write of them no more.

At the close of the first grand drama enacted before
my eyes, I suddenly felt the encompassing arms of
strangers tying my hands and fastening thick bandages
over my face. This time I had no desire to resist the
movements of my captors; on the contrary, I rose at
their touch and suffered them to reconduct me through
another series of passages, for such I had instinctive
reasons for knowing was my mode of exit, until we
reached a very distant point of the amphitheatre of
mountains from that at which we had entered. The
bandages were removed as rapidly and noiselessly as
they had been adjusted; but my conductors were gone
before I had fairly recovered my sense of liberty. They
left me with the mask I had worn in my hands and a
strip of paper attached to it, on which were inscribed
in fine Sanskrit characters these words: "The night
after to-morrow at 12 midnight. *Chundra ud Deen.*"

Who can doubt that I was faithful to my appointment?

and I deemed myself sufficiently rewarded when I gained the plateau to see the tall form and monastic robes of my mysterious acquaintance there before me. He greeted me with warmth and the peculiarly sweet c. artesy which had distinguished his manner at our first interview. Before I could make any inquiry concerning his agency in my late adventure, he spoke of it, with apologies for the rough mode of my first initiation. He gave me ample reasons for the mystery in which it was deemed necessary to veil the entrances to those vast crypts and subterranean retreats, which I well knew undermined so many of the ancient temples and not unfrequently exceeded in size and grandeur the superstructures themselves. He informed me that my true initiation was to take place that night, provided I was sufficiently interested in what I had seen to desire association with the fraternity I had visited.

My name, standing, character, and spiritualistic proclivities were all known to this brotherhood; indeed, none ever had been or could be introduced amongst them who were not already known and selected for the qualities which were in harmony with the association. My mysterious friends had the advantage of me at every point, but I was entirely willing to trust them, and that night saw me a sworn brother of their order.

Amongst the many items of occult lore I learned in that wonderful convention of true spiritual scientists, was the singular and original method by which their gorgeous dramatic representations were made.

The whole temple was furnished with fine metallic lines, every one of which converged to six powerful galvanic batteries attached to the silver thrones occupied by six of the adepts. These persons, ADEPTS in the loftiest and most significant sense of the term, received their inspiration from the occupant of the seventh throne, a being who, though always present, was not always visible, although as on the first night of my attendance a presence from the realms of supernal being was always there.

The office of the adepts was to centralize and focalize the inspiration received. The thoughts of each were first focalized into one idea on the rostrum, and from thence distributed to every neophyte in the auditorium. This universal impression was produced, first, by the harmonious spirit of accordance which pervaded the assembly; next, by the influence of strong and concentrated psychology; and finally by the distributive power and force of the galvanic lines extending, as before stated, from the rostrum to every member in the auditorium.

The negative pole of this complete battery was formed by the neophytes, the positive pole by the hierophants; and I solemnly swear, as a man pledged only to record the truths of that higher realm of being into which I have been permitted most reverently to look, that the whole of the gorgeous representations enacted before my eyes during several consecutive weeks of three sessions each week were psychological images impressed upon the adepts by the presiding angel of our holy gathering, and from thence distributed and transmitted mentally to the seat of consciousness by psychology, and physically by connecting links of electric force to every member of our vast assemblage. Let no sneering sceptic doubt the possibility of transmitting thought even through the physical methods here roughly indicated.

Well-practised biologists will never question the possibility of the mental action described, except as regards

the vast number operated upon at once; but on this
point permit me to assure my readers that no inconsid-
erable part of East Indian magic depends upon psychological impressions produced by single adepts upon vast
multitudes. The science of *illusion* — a term which in
translation but ill represents the original idea — is one
in which every adept, ancient and modern, must become
au fait if he would succeed as an " enchanter " or a good
" magician." The *rationale* of magic is WILL or psychology; the success of psychology or the operation of
WILL depends upon the entire absence of intervening
obstacles. Thus, if you *will* a thought to reach another
at any distance, long or short, your thought will surely
reach its object, provided it encounters no psychological
obstacle more potent than itself. Man possesses inher-
ently the power to effect any phenomenon in or upon
matter that spirits can do, provided his spiritual forces
encounter no cross currents of magnetism, no opposing
lines of force. The potencies of will have been exalted,
known, felt, and practised by the mystics, magians,
seers, and prophets of all ages. Why WILL ever fails
to accomplish its ends arises from the fact that thousands, perhaps millions, of other wills are traversing
space in opposing lines and contrary currents, and so
the force of one will, which might else prove irresistible
if directed under carefully arranged conditions and suffered to operate unhindered upon its object, becomes
thwarted, and a single failure of this kind will be immediately quoted as an illustration of the hollow pretensions which psychologists make for the sovereign potency
of WILL. The association of which I have been speaking originated centuries ago, in a keen perception, on the
part of one mighty metaphysician, that the powers and
forces of the human soul might be so concentred as to

imitate the creative action, and give an actual sensuous embodiment to ideas. I shall not here enter into the results of experiments persevered in, as I have hinted, during centuries of time with varying success, — success proportioned to the excellence or indifference of the subjects by whom they were conducted.

The discovery and application of electric force as a means of stimulating mental power, created a complete new era in this remarkable fraternity, and urged forward its adepts to a class of fresh experiments, some of which have been of the most stupendous character. The privilege of explaining and enlarging upon them is not at present accorded to me, otherwise I could more than justify the immense claims I advance for the potency of the human will, especially when strengthened by scientific appliances.

In reference to the transmission of thought by aid of electro-magnetism, I have repeatedly proved its possibility, nay, demonstrated its infallibility, by experiments conducted with my friend, Mrs. Emma Hardinge Britten. We had already become experts in the processes of mental telegraphy, which we were enabled to practise with invariable success; but with the potential, although still more material agency of electricity evolved from mineral substances, we arrived at a means of energizing the subtile though variable powers of vital magnetism, which tended to render its operation more than ever reliable and uniform.

In fine, I feel authorized to say that none are qualified to pronounce a verdict of "unreliability" against my statements, unless they have themselves experimented in the same direction, and that with all the advantage of well-prepared conditions. The fraternity of which I have given so very brief a description surrounded their practices with a perfect bulwark of psychological defences, against which the intrusion of unfavorable conditions was impossible. Every member of that venerable association was selected for the peculiar endowments which its interests demanded. No disqualified person could, by the remotest possibility, have access to its sessions. The psychic rulers were not only adepts in the mental force necessary for their office, but practical " magicians," whose knowledge and experience of the occult in Nature placed her mysterious elements of power at their command. The teachings given in that society were derived, not only from the cumulative wisdom of the ages, but also from the inspiration of higher realms than those of mortality, and by researches into those realms through all the aids which man's spiritual endowments could supply him with.

Spiritual as well as material science was ransacked in search of truth. Practice and theory were deemed equally essential for the formation of just opinions, and from the profoundest depths of the earth's centre to the sublimest heights of astral systems, from the force which crystallizes the diamond to that which is supposed to rarefy the finest realms of ether, these philosophers continued to explore the universe in search of absolute truth. They were all Spiritualists in the best sense of the term, and their sessions were invariably composed of spiritual as well as earthly searchers. They were not ashamed of aspirational worship, never felt their manhood lowered by the act of prayer, nor did they disdain to acknowledge their dependence on higher beings than themselves, nor abstain from soliciting their protection and inspiration. They believed in sacred places and consecrated things, and whilst they esteemed and cultivated scientific knowledge as the highest aim of the human mind, they ever subordinated the *mind* to the *soul*, and deemed that spiritual science must be the complement to material science, and without the union of the two, the body and soul of true knowledge could not subsist. Neophytes on first entrance, indeed so long as it was deemed desirable, were appointed teachers, who in private sessions rendered them all the instruction and assistance they required. Such a teacher was assigned to me, and if I had gained no other advantage in this admirable fraternity, I should forever feel indebted to its leaders for procuring me the life-long friendship of Nanak Rai, the noble Brahmin to whose learning, piety, and manhood the charge of my initiatory studies was assigned.

During the many subsequent years of steady friendship that have subsisted between Nanak and myself, I have never known him to utter a word or perform an act unworthy of the most exalted saint in the Christian calendar. What model religionist can transcend such a spotless record? Soon after my admission to the fraternity of which I write, I became selected as one of their adepts, an office I endeavored to excuse myself from accepting, on the ground of inevitable absorption in other duties and too frequent absence from the places of assemblage. The latter objection was overruled in a mode which impels me to record the fact of my election to the position of adept. I was induced to accept the nomination, after having occupied the seventh throne spiritually, on three occasions when my body lay sleeping at a distance of several hundreds of miles from the scene of assemblage. If my readers shrink from this acknowledgment in utter or even partial disbelief of its veracity, I can only say they have not as yet crossed the threshold of that temple which initiates them into a knowledge of their own souls' powers and forces.

They, like me, are immortal spirits, infinite in capacity, boundless in power. The only horizon which limits the executive functions of their spirits is not so much the clog and fetter of a material body, as the lack of knowledge how to control and subdue that body. So long as that body is entirely subjected to the will by abstinence, asceticism, chastity, and discipline, it is a mere fleshly vehicle, enabling the soul to come into contact with matter. The moment the sway of the passions or even the mental emotions, compels the spirit to yield to the impulses of the body, the spiritual reign is ended, and henceforth the spirit exercises only a temporary, broken, and spasmodic rule over its own transcendent faculties, just as "material conditions" are favorable or otherwise for that exercise. I candidly present my own case in evidence of both positions.

When I was first elected to the supreme power of an adept in the nameless fraternity alluded to in this chapter, I was a spirit rather than a man, in the world, but not of it. Every function of humanity was subordinated to the power of my soul and its spirit allies, and I scarcely realized, in the midst of all life's active duties and pressing cares, that my mortal body was more to me than the garments I put on and off at pleasure. I do not contend for the naturalness or reasonableness of such a condition; I only claim it is possible and attainable, and I dwell upon it the more forcibly to illustrate the complete subversion of those exalted powers when, a few short years later, the wear and tear of human passion and passionate emotion had enveloped my spirit and its exalted transcendentalism in robes of mortality more dense and clinging than the garments which now shelter me. Be it so!

Perhaps the highest perfection of the soul hereafter can only be attained through a complete realization of the pathetic words, "He was a man of sorrows." Perhaps the Magdalene shall win her way to the kingdom more readily than the dainty lady who never sinned because she was never tempted. In the touching legend of the Christian God's crucifixion, the penitent thief will surely gain that Paradise which the Pharisee seeks in vain. And yet I would have gladly lived and died a spiritual ecstatic, but the Lord of life had willed it otherwise.

CHAPTER XX.

THE progress of my narrative brings me to a period during which the unhappy land of Hindostan seemed to have had a moment's breathing-time granted her in the midst of ever-accumulating intestine and foreign calamity. It was during one of those seasons of false peace and hollow truce that have occasionally lifted the war demon's hand from the bleeding breast of hapless India that I found leisure to cultivate systematically the teachings which exalted my soul to the gods of antiquity and brought me into communion with the holy beings that would fill our world with the tracks of angels, did we not drive them back with the work of devils.

Almost the happiest hours of my life were those devoted to the sessions of the glorious Brotherhood, of whose teachings I have given a slight and most imperfect sketch in the preceding chapter. So long as the influence of those séances was upon me I felt as if I had been living with gods, angels, and spirits, and as I grew more and more familiar with the sublime ideas they opened up to me, I became reconciled to the chaotic present and hopeful for the inevitable future. Still, I realized then, as I do now, when I recall those ecstatic communings derived from the heaven of heavens, that they measurably unfitted me for earth, and rendered a return to its spoliation and licentiousness weary and distasteful to me. Yet I knew it was my lot to return, ay, and to take an earnest and active part in the terrible era that impended, — a *dance of death* more gaunt and grim than any that had of late desolated the doomed land of the Orient. I knew too, by the force of that prophetic nature which is the ban as well as blessing of its possessor, that there was an episode in my life to be passed through of a totally different character to any that had preceded or could follow it, and though these monitions could neither be banished nor modified, they did not enable me to avoid the breakers, or steer my life's barque out of the stormy sea that threatened to wreck it. Our holy séances had closed for the time being. The mystic Bygas, the noble Brahmins, and the associated brothers, many of them strangers from distant lands, must all separate, and depart each on their several ways. The bright angels who ministered amongst us would wing their way hence to fairer though none the less worshipful scenes. The attendant spirits would rise, by virtue of their labors in our behalf, another round higher on the ladder of progression, whilst the solemn crypts of the ancient temples would become silent, deserted, given up to the desolation which falls upon every thing and every creature where life has been and life is not.

Of the throng that had assembled in our subterranean temple to partake of the sublime teachings there imparted, all were scattered like the snows of a past winter, save my Brahminical friend, Nanak Rai, and myself. In our departure from the neighborhood of Ellora we were accompanied by Capt. Graham, a young Scotchman whose acquaintance I had made some years before while travelling with Professor von Marx, and whom I had subsequently encountered wandering, like myself, amidst the stupendous cave temples. Some years had elapsed since we first met, and time had worked great changes in us both, yet we immediately recognized each other, and gladly renewed an acquaintance which had already ripened into friendship.

In his own country Capt. Graham was an *habitué* of the best society, not only on account of his birth and connections, but also for the sake of his amiable manners, genial disposition, and cultivated intellect. With a remarkably handsome person, the clear blue eye and ruddy complexion of his Highland progenitors, this young officer united qualities of mind and physique which endeared him to all who knew him. The specialty which first attracted him to me was his strong sympathy with my spiritualistic pursuits, and the fact that he was gifted with the peculiar faculty of what the Scotch call "second-sight." Having obtained a short furlough, he had left his regiment at Allahabad in order to make a visit to the 'famous cave temples at Ellora, where I was fortunate enough to meet him and become useful in guiding him through the intricacies of the wonderful ruins with which I was myself familiar.

I perceived that he was no subject for our association, the existence of which he, like thousands of others who trod over the very ground which our halls of meeting undermined, was profoundly ignorant of. Still I found him eager and yearning for metaphysical knowledge, and an apt student in that school of philosophy wherein Nanak Rai was an especial proficient. I presented him, therefore, to that learned Brahmin, happy in realizing the treasures of wisdom which the young neophyte would receive from such an admirable instructor. And these were the two esteemed companions who journeyed with me to Benares, where the Brahmin resided and

24

near which I had made for myself a temporary abiding-
place. Although there was nothing in our external circumstances to create a bond of association between the
young Scotch officer and myself, I have said it was the
season of rest and treacherous lull in the political life
of hapless Hindostan; there was therefore nothing to
disturb the interchange of the most kindly relations
between us, or mar the interest with which we entered
upon the discussion of abstruse points in occultism and
metaphysics whilst he remained my guest. It was during a conversation of this character, as we lay beneath
the luxuriant shadows of a clustering palm-grove smoking fragrant cheroots, that my friend with some hesitation began to question me concerning the occult powers
of certain fakirs whom I entertained in my establishment.

It was only after a considerable amount of circumlo-
cution that I ascertained the drift of his questioning,
and found that he wished to learn how far the magical
acquirements attributed to these ecstatics could be made
available in procuring the love of the opposite sex. At
first, I treated the subject with the contempt and indifference which I felt it merited; but when I found Capt.
Graham was not only in deep earnest, but actually proposed to avail himself of the power which he was so
curiously seeking to understand, I became considerably
startled, and asked him, bluntly enough, I suppose, how
it was possible that a man of his fine mind could propose to avail himself of arts so unworthy and for purposes so base. Fixing his clear blue eyes upon me, and
without any show of resentment for the unintentional
severity of my rebuke, he said, "My dear Chevalier, do
you believe that the exercise of any powers with which
nature endows us is wrong?"

"That all depends upon the purpose for which we employ our powers," I replied.

"Granted," he answered; "but suppose nature has endowed me with strong psychological powers, would you deem it a base and unworthy act if I exerted them to induce a return of affection from the woman I love?"

"I can see nothing unnatural or objectionable in that, Graham."

"Again you grant the only position I contend for," said my friend. "Then, wherein can the wrong exist of adding to the powers with which nature has endowed me, occult powers of a still stronger kind? that is, provided the purpose be the same, and that I only seek to secure the affection of the woman I love."

"Does she whom you love fail to return your affection?"

"Just so."

"And you would compel her to do so, even against her will?"

"I would bend that will to my own, Chevalier; and if I could succeed, do you deem me capable of misusing my advantage? I desire to marry a woman whom I cannot as yet succeed in inspiring with my own devotion. Could I do so, how should I wrong her by spending my life in ministering to her happiness?"

"Graham," I answered, "if you yourself were an ascended spirit, freed from all the gross desires and selfishness of earth; in a sphere of higher and holier aspirations than earth ever engendered; would you devote your exalted powers to satisfy the promptings of a merely sensual human passion?"

"By heavens, Chevalier!" replied my friend, starting up and pacing the ground in great agitation, "I never thought of the matter in such a light. Why, the very idea of asking blessed spirits to engage in such a work, as you present it, is blasphemy."

"I am answered, Graham; but where does your confession lead you to? Do you not perceive that you rule out the intervention of *good* spirits in the acts under consideration? and if this be so, what class of beings do you suppose would be attracted to your service or willing to aid in your enchantments?"

"Wicked spirits, of course, or if not actually wicked, still beings of a less exalted grade than I could desire companionship with; but, my friend, you know there are powers inherent in ourselves, occult forces, too, in nature, which could achieve the end desired without the aid of spirits. You yourself, Chevalier, have often proved your resistless power of will and ability to bend the will of others to your desire. Why cannot I use a similar influence to impress the object of my affections with sentiments of reciprocity?"

"You have constantly tried to do this?"

"I have."

"And without success?"

"Entirely so."

"Then you have simply proved what I have so often told you concerning the conditions which may interpose to hinder the effect of psychological impressions."

"Will you not repeat the substance of your theory?"

"I believe my will, clothed with the force of my magnetism, which is LIFE, powerful enough to remove mountains, provided there be no intervening obstacle between the current of my magnetism and the mountain I would act on. You can compel whom you will to love, hate, or obey you, irrespective of distance or material obstacles, provided there be no cross magnetism intervening between you and your object, no more powerful will than your own operating against you; in that case, your will must be thwarted and the currents of your magnetism will be dissipated in space."

" But how can I be aware of this, or, knowing its probability, how prevent it? "

" You can but take your chance. We are not yet clairvoyant enough to be masters of every situation we would experiment with. Be assured these baffling cross magnetisms, projected from a thousand sources unknown to us, are the causes of the many failures which occur in just such cases as yours. Successes are most frequent when the operator is potential or electrically positive, and the subject is passive and negative. Such is the relation sustained by that worst and meanest of all criminals, the licentious seducer, towards his victim. He projects his foul psychology upon a negative and wholly unguarded subject. Those around her, probably unsuspicious of her danger, exert no counteracting influence, no cross magnetism to thwart his: the result is the subjection of the weak to the strong, the passive to the negative, an angel perhaps, to a devil assuredly."

" I must accept your positions," replied Graham. " I know you have often claimed sovereign potency for the will, and yet urged the reasons just assigned why it is so successful in some instances, and so inoperative in others. Be it so. I must abandon two contingent resources then, — the aid of good spirits and the exercise of psychological power; but is there nothing left for me, — no medicaments in the realm of Nature, no spells, enchantments, or talismans whereby her occult power may be exerted for my benefit? I know I shock you, my friend; you will despise if not hate me for these questionings, to me so importunate, to you so lowering

and contemptible.   But, Chevalier, remember you do
not love, you never did love, nor can you know what
that name means.   Oh! believe me, love is stronger
than death, more cruel than the grave.   All else,—wit,
wisdom, piety, learning, hope of heaven or fear of per-
dition, pale before the strength of this giant passion;
but I see I speak to empty air: you can not understand
me."

"You are mistaken," I replied, kindly pressing my
poor friend's hand, and addressing him in the most
sympathizing tone I could command.   "I can and do
understand you, although no mortal has ever yet moved
me to the master passion; but the day will come, Graham, when I shall be thus moved; nay, more, when I
shall love, as you do now, in despair and hopelessness,
in life-long endurance and silent misery; and yet I would
despise myself and renounce my art, did I deem it possible I could be induced to use it for the unholy purpose
of captivating the woman I prophetically know I shall
be doomed to love in vain."

"You love in vain! you, Chevalier!" exclaimed my
friend with equal *naïveté* and amazement.   "Nay, that is
impossible."

"Your partiality makes you egotistical for your friend,
Graham, neither do you justly estimate the character
of woman in her noblest, highest phases.   What I tell
you is the truth, and though I have never yet seen her
of whom I prophesy, except in spirit, I know she is not
of the class who give men occasion to boast of their
too easy conquests.   The women who are marketable
commodities are only worthy of the men who buy them.
For every true man in creation there is a woman who
should be, nay, who must be and is, his angel side.
One such I shall fail to win on earth, but gain in

heaven; but let us return to your last proposition, consulting together as students of occultism, rather than
as men striving to win the affections of women by
aid of impure arts. Charms, spells, and enchantments
depend for their success on the aid of spirits and psychological impression. I have already endeavored to
show you that the spirits who could or would assist in
such rites are unholy, and in obtaining their aid you
would league yourself to them in such relations that
when you become like themselves a spirit, you would
find yourself bound to them in the chains of a magnetic
rapport which would be horrible to endure and difficult
to break. We have already considered the chance of
success or failure in psychological impression: what
other art would you inquire about?"

"You have not answered me concerning the effect
of charms and talismans, Chevalier. Is their alleged
potency only an idle fiction?"

"See this handkerchief, Graham; it was but yesterday
taken from the bazaar: what virtue inhered in its fabric
as it lay exposed for sale?"

"Surely, none that I know of."

"As you say, none. But supposing you were to
place it now in the hands of a sensitive or psychometrist,
you would find my character and physique, nay, my
very motives and the most secret intentions of my mind
impressed upon its every fibre, is it not so?"

"We have proved the possibility of such soul read-
ings. Go on."

"Supposing, then, I should add to the magnetism
which already adheres to this fabric, some strongly
concentrated idea, wish, or purpose: do you not suppose that idea, wish, or purpose would also be detected
there? and would not that voluntary impression of my

mind upon this inanimate substance constitute it a
. talisman?"

"Talismanic virtue is no fiction, then," cried Graham,
triumphantly.

"Be patient," I replied. "Before we speculate further
upon the possibility of effecting your purpose through
any occult means, let me lay before you the general
effect of such procedures; you may then be better enabled to determine the worth of what you propose.
You think I do not understand the nature of human
love. Philosophically speaking, I comprehend it better
than you do. Love, or the motive so called, is generally one of three impulses: The first is 'magnetic affinity,' or a movement of the material atoms which compose the human body, and these being brought into the
presence of another set of atoms for which they have a
strong affinity, impress upon their subject that powerful
sense of attraction which is commonly called love. I
insist that the emotion I describe is magnetic affinity
only, and corresponds to the chemical affinity which
exists between inanimate atoms of nature. The difference between the two modes of attraction is this, however. Chemical affinities in atoms are permanent and
changeless. If you separate the atoms, they still maintain their affinities, and when placed in the same relations again will manifest the same attractions; but
magnetic affinities are not permanent. Their special
attribute is change, and their attractions are merely temporary, soon wearing out, and when once exhausted,
never renewed. The chemical affinity which subsists
between sulphur and gold will ever be the same. It
existed ten thousand years ago, and will be as manifest
ten thousand years hence as now; but the magnetic
attractions which draw the libertine to the fair face of

his victim almost invariably end in depolarization; then ensues coldness, neglect, indifference, followed by dislike and even loathing; hence it is that many intrigues based upon mere passional attraction, have ended, ay, and will again, in the intense repulsion which impels the seducer even to the murder of his victim. Believe me, it is not in idle fantasy that the phrenologist associates the cranial organs which impel to licentiousness and destructiveness in close proximity to each other. The demons of lust and murder are twin brothers, and follow on each other's track, from the law of which I speak. The swing of the mental pendulum which prompts the one carries the mind to the other extreme, and thus accounts for the aversion which so often succeeds the excess of violent and unbridled passion."

"Admirable, my dear philosopher!" cried poor Graham, almost excited to mirth by my grave analysis of a passion which he still insisted could only be known experimentally. " You have given me case No. 1; now for your secondly. What sort of a phase is that, may I ask?"

"Oh! secondly, is not love at all," I replied. "It is simply friendship, and as such it may be an excellent basis of union between man and woman, far more likely also to remain a permanent sentiment than any evanescent passion; still, it is not love, and those who unite upon such a foundation, although restrained from infidelity to each other by principle, may yet experience emotions of love for others."

" Very good! I am with you there. Friendship between husband and wife! Pshaw! just the same as between man and man. I may and do feel the warmest sentiments of friendship for you, Chevalier, yet I do not wish to marry you, however I might feel if you were a

woman. No, no, my Mentor! friendship is not love, of
that I am quite certain; but now for your No. 3. Ah,
you sigh! I almost begin to imagine you are more
committed than you choose to acknowledge. No?
Well, that emphatic shake of the head is your confession, and I must wait until I see you stricken down
as I am; but come, I long to hear about your No. 3.
What is it, I pray?"

"It is *soul affinity*, Graham,—the realization that man
and woman have no actual existence apart from each
other; that they are, in fact, counterparts, without which
their separate lives are imperfect and unformed. Life
is dual, Graham, and love, true soul-love, is the bond
of union which reunites the severed parts. It exists
independent of personal charms or mental acquirements.
It annihilates self and selfishness; prefers the beloved
object beyond all adventitious acquirements; subsists
through sickness or in health, through good or evil
report, lives for the one beloved, dies and realizes
heaven only in the union which death may interrupt
but cannot sever. Divine spiritual affinity survives
death and the grave, unites the two halves of the one
soul, and in eternity perfects the dual nature of man
and woman into the one angel."

"Chevalier," replied my friend, "if you have not yet
loved, you deserve to; and thrice blessed will she be who
can secure to herself the affection you thus describe.
That heavy sigh again! Why, you will compel me presently to believe you are the rejected one, and I the
happy lover. But come, my Socratic and Platonic
friend, you have not yet informed me what effect I
might expect from the love potions, philters, or other
approved methods of magical art, of which your famous
fakirs are the expert professors."

"My fakirs are occultists, Graham, not Vaudoo charmers, nor would they be mine much longer if Vaudooism were amongst their practices; but to recur to your question: I answer; though the use of certain drugs, vapors, or other physical means might produce a temporary excitement in the person upon whom they were exercised, nevertheless, like psychology or other arts of enchantment, the effect is but temporary. They can impress, but not create the will; arouse passional attraction, but not permanent sentiment. They excite illusions, cast spells, induce impulses, but their transitory effects are always followed by depolarization and revulsive reaction, in which antipathy sets in as proportionably strong as the attraction was violent."

"I see it all," cried my poor friend. "You are a severe teacher, but I believe a truthful one; besides, our mutual experiences assure me you are correct. I would have risked my life and, Heaven forgive me! perilled my very soul to secure the love of her I adore, but the bare possibility that she who now tolerates me might one day learn to loathe me is too terrible to risk. It is enough. There is no hope for me. And now, Chevalier, the very lowest depths of my weakness having been laid open before you, let us return to our occultism. You say it is the magnetism and psychology impressed on an object which impart to it talismanic virtue: are there, then, no natural talismans in nature?"

"Thousands and millions, Graham, had we but the clear sight to discern them. There are myriads of herbs and stones full of virtue to heal, gladden, or sadden us; objects which can and do affect the senses and impress the spirit; links of connection between the visible and invisible worlds; and those who, with sapient self-sufficiency, scoff at these occult forces in nature and think to extinguish faith in them by the bugbear word, 'super-stition,' are themselves the dunces, rather than those who unwittingly believe without being able to prove their belief."

"O my friend!" cried the enthusiastic young Scotch-man, "why will you not lead me into those realms of occult power?"

"Because I am not there myself, Graham," I replied. "I have as yet only stood upon the threshold and glanced down the endless corridors of the invisible universe. I know such things are. Some of their powers and dangers I have tested, but only enough to warn and encourage me in yet deeper researches."

"You know enough," replied Graham, "to explain to me what talismanic influence is impressed upon this object."

As he spoke he drew from his vest a small package which he put into my hand, but even as he did so he started with astonishment and dismay at the effect his talisman produced upon me. Had the deadly cobra stung me, I could scarcely have experienced a pang more poignant. Something unconquerably antagonistic to my nature was contained in that package. The face and form of a very beautiful woman rose up before me, but the most loathsome dwellers on the threshold of humanity that ever drove the neophyte back from the country of the elementaries would have been more sympathetic to me than this terrible visionary woman. Almost breathless with emotion, I poured out to my friend a hurried description of the portrait — for such I knew it to be — that I held in my hand, and the effect that it produced upon me, and then the feeling of antipathy gave place to an irrepressible passion of grief as humiliating to myself as inexplicable to my friend.

Meantime doleful shapes flitted before my eyes, wailing sounds were in the air, and a sorrow as profound as unaccountable weighed me down and impelled me to push away my sympathizing companion and bury my face in the sheltering grass ere I could regain composure. Rebuked, indignant, and amazed to find myself the sport of such incomprehensible emotions, I at length succeeded in freeing my clenched hand from the odious package, which I returned to Graham, entreating him to keep from me all such influences in future. He listened to and watched me with evident pain as well as interest. He said that I was correct in my description of the beautiful female whose portrait was enclosed in that package, but why her image should be associated with such presages of sorrow and excite sentiments of antipathy in his best friend he was at a loss to conceive.

"Graham," I exclaimed, as we arose to separate, "if that portrait represents the woman you love, thank your guardian angel that your enchantments have failed. Better wind around your neck the slime of the boa-constrictor than the arms of that fatal woman."

"Chevalier de B——," cried the young Scotchman, in high wrath, "you shall answer for this!" Then returning, and grasping my hand which he had just flung from him, he murmured in his usually affectionate manner, "Forgive me, Louis, I am a half-dazed fool, I know, and as to you—why, you are only a mystic."

CHAPTER XXI.

THE sun of Hindostan compels a reversal of many of the social customs which obtain in Europe, prominent amongst which is that of turning night into day, an arrangement which the higher classes of European society establish on the basis of inclination, but which in India becomes the law of necessity, provided we would maintain the activities of life without the contingency of melting out before the duties of the day are fully achieved.

Graham and myself had parted after an 11-o'clock-P. M. dinner, and high-noon coffee at twelve. Towards the sweet hour of dawning, when both of us had retired to the spacious halls which in Europe we are accustomed to call "bedrooms," but which in this tropical land simply signify the place of sleep, or the scene of the day's long siesta, after the conversation recorded in the last chapter, I sat speculating on the singular influence which my friend's talismanic package had exerted over me; on the wonderful calm of the holy moonlight, lighting up the sacred Ganges, which washed the descending flight of steps that led from the terrace outside my chamber to the river's brink; on the silver-tipped minarets, domes, towers, and metallic ornaments of temples, pagodas, palaces, and fanes that everywhere sparkled with mild and softened lustre in the pale moonlight; on the mystery of the beyond; the life, the death, the everlasting progress, perhaps the everlasting sleep, of the very power by which I speculated! Everything. assumed a new idea beneath the transfiguring light of the soft and holy queen of heaven; every idea took a personal shape beneath the influence of the same tranquillizing power. Suddenly I felt that a new presence was near me. In the vast and spacious apartment which I occupied, the moonlight, the only lamp I permitted that night, failed to penetrate the farthest point or deepest recesses; it only cast its radiant halo on a circle of which I was myself the centre as I lay on a divan placed between the open glass doors which led out on the terrace overhanging the river. I knew a fresh presence was in my apartment, though no sound of footfall broke the stillness and no shadow as yet streamed over the polished floor, yet it came on, threaded its way amongst the groups of statuary scattered through the place, lingered near the tubs of orange-trees and other tropical shrubs and plants that formed arcades on every side, and now approached me, penetrated the circle of moonlight in which I lay, passed noiselessly around the divan, and standing between me and the pillars which supported the veranda without, disclosed to me the shrouded form and cowled head of the Byga of Ellora, Chundra ud Deen.

"My father comes at last," I said, rising to receive him. "He is indeed welcome."

The Byga, for the first time during the many occasions that we had met, extended his hand to me. He had never before touched me; nay, he had evidently avoided such contact, nor did I wonder at it, for now I took his hand in mine it was as cold as death, and sent a chill through every fibre of my frame.

"My son has become my brother!" said the Byga, in his sweet, low voice and Tamul accent. "He is now an adept like Chundra. What can Ud Deen tell him more than he knows?"

"Much, much!" I exclaimed passionately, and forgetting, in my desire to become a pupil again, all the self-possession and immobile reserve which belonged to my character as a fellow-adept. Let it be understood that I did not marvel at this man's unexpected presence, nor venture to comment on it.

During my attendance at the sessions of the Ellora Brotherhood, I knew Chundra ud Deen was one of the adepts. I believe he was an occupant of the *seventh* throne only. I knew he came and went like a spirit. I had visited him in his mountain home, but never could realize with external sense how I reached or left that giddy height. I had never seen his face or touched him until that night; never understood who or what he was, save as one who came between me and the light, when, where, and how he would, — no more.

"What would you ask, Louis?" he said; and O Heaven! how the sound of that name, grown unfamiliar in my ears, thrilled on my heart, pronounced by that stranger!

It was forbidden to the neophytes, though not to the adepts of the Ellora Brotherhood, to converse with each other on the teachings they received. From this prohibition both Chundra and myself were exempt; hence, I knew I was at liberty to press upon him many of the spiritualistic problems that now disturbed me. Had I not understood how perfectly the power of transmitting thought could be practised amongst us, I should have been startled to find every question I designed to put anticipated and dealt with, even where it was not fully met by my associate, ere I had framed it into speech. In the mental contest between us I placed myself in the negative relation to my respondent, hence for the time being he read and mastered me. We could have reversed this position, but we could not both maintain the same attitude towards each other. As my questionings on this occasion refer to what I have since learned to be common problems amongst spiritists, and he who answered me did so upon sufficient authority, I will here transcribe such portions of the dialogue that ensued as may be of general interest to the reader. (I inquired why the spirits who appeared to me, or at times manifested proofs of their identity with my deceased friends, could not give me more philosophy, higher intelligence, and above all, a more perfect description of their lives in spiritual existence.)

Chundra replied as follows: "You are constantly impressed with a morbid anxiety to relieve that class of mendicants whom you imagine to be suffering from hunger, you are often warned that the objects of your solicitude are unworthy; but the thought that any human being may be suffering from hunger, transports you into fanatical acts of alms-giving. Is it not so?"

My readers must pardon me for recording the above remarks, which referred to a specialty of mine, induced, as I well know, by my vivid recollection of the agony which hunger inflicted upon me in early life, rendering me painfully sensitive on the subject, and ready to commit any act of extravagance rather than endure the sight of any human being wanting food.

He continued, "Now, what would you say if on earth, as in spirit life, you found that every time you had bestowed alms on a necessitous fellow-creature, a flower had spontaneously blossomed in your garden?"

"I should require to understand the connection between my act and the flower," I replied.

"You are a successful soldier," he continued, "and the men under your command have been efficient on the battle-field. Suppose I were to tell you that for every drop of blood you have shed, or caused to be shed, one of those blossoms engendered by your charity would fade and wither away?" I started. "Three days ago," he resumed, "you entertained a party of friends at your dinner-table. Supposing your real thoughts at the time had been known, how much would your guests have enjoyed your hospitality?"

Again I felt committed. At the time of which he spoke, I had the most intense desire to be at another place, and wished my visitors anywhere rather than at my own table.

"Last night," he went on to say, "you were present at an entertainment. How would you have felt had you seen, as you would have done in spirit land, the beautiful lady who smiled on you so graciously, assuming to all who approached her the appearance of a deadly snake, and your royal host wearing the semblance of a ferocious tiger? Look around you! Yon forms of stone which your imagination connects with the gods of antiquity and the inspiration of prophets, magicians, and hierophants,—how would you endure to gaze upon them and repose in their midst, should they suddenly present to you all the crimes, obscenities, follies, and errors committed by countless generations, in the atmosphere which has swept over those images, impressing them with every shape, thought, motive, or act with which that atmosphere was charged? These walls now adorned with works of art,—how would you like to see them displaying, as they would in spirit land, every

act of your life, your most secret thoughts, hidden motives, and concealed wishes? All grimly hideous or
gracefully beautiful, no matter which? Could you
endure this? You were thinking a while ago of a
return to Europe. Could you comprehend how you
could be there by the simple impulse of your will, and
that without steamboats, cars, horses, chariots, or other
known means of transit? Could you understand how
you might stand beneath arcades of waving trees, fragrant blossoms, and sunlit skies, yet another stand by
your side and converse with you, immersed in a pelt-
ing storm, blown about by fierce winds, or surrounded
by desolation, barren wastes, and darkness that could
be felt?"

" You speak to me in enigmas, Chundra," I exclaimed.

"And yet I speak of the actualities in which your
spirit friends live, Louis. All of which I have spoken,
transpires each moment in the spirit world and form
the experiences of the spirits that visit you. Their
gardens are planted by good deeds and destroyed by
bad; their banquets are spread and dissipated by conditions of mental growth and moral excellence; their
images, pictures, houses, cities, trees, flowers, roads,
mountains, rivers, scenery,—ay! all that they have or
gaze upon, are not only written over and inscribed with
their acts, thoughts, words, and characters, but are
absolutely formed, shaped, and colored by their soul
emanations. They go and come by mental power and
intellectual activity only. They build and destroy under
conditions of mental and moral achievement, of which
no human speech can convey an idea. You have visited their spheres, seen, heard, and felt the truth of
much that I now touch upon, and yet you are confused,
bewildered, and incredulous at what I say. You would

ask, too, Is there, then, nothing real in spiritual existence?
Are all things seeming only,—spirit life but shadows?
Louis, if I confuse and bewilder you in attempting to
image forth some of the conditions of spirit life, and
you begin to doubt the reality of anything in a state
of being far more real than your own, how do you
expect your spirit friends could converse intelligibly
with you, or find topics of common interest with which
to converse about, except such as belong to the earth
they have left? Do you not see there is no common
ground for the interchange of thought between spirits
and mortals? Nothing would be comprehensible to
you of their existence, whilst, except for your sake, the
life they have left behind has lost all interest for them.
Man *knows* nothing but what he has absolutely experienced, although he may believe much more than he
knows through reading and hearsay, yet even then
he can not appreciate anything that he has not at some
time or other had connection with, or realized through
similitude or kindred knowledge. Mortals impatiently
demand information concerning spiritual existence. You
might as well talk to the African savage of telegraphy
and electricity, or declare what the microscope and telescope reveal to the aborigines of Australasia, as to ask
your spirit friends to explain to you the conditions,
employments, and aspirations of the state of being to
which they have attained."

"Why this new spiritual movement which is now pal-
pitating through the world then, Chundra? this evidently systematic attempt of the spirit world to commune
with mortals, which is now so spontaneously planting
its standards through every land of civilization?"

"Humanity MUST MOVE ON," he answered. "It is
ordained that the world must at length attain to a true

understanding of spiritual existence, and that the fictions of vain theological beliefs shall disappear.

"Physical science has conducted the race up to the threshold where spiritual science commences. Louis, you know that in this generation is the opening of the sixth seal. There is yet another to be broken. Be in no haste. God can wait: shall not his creatures do so likewise?"

"The trance mediums of whom John Dudley writes such glowing accounts from America and England,— they profess to be inspired by earth's great ones and to give accurate accounts of that spirit land, to describe which you and I find human speech so inadequate."

"They are sensitives, magnetized by spirits, and give such teachings as the world is able to receive. Fancy the most abstruse problems of Euclid reduced to the comprehension of the child who has just begun to study his multiplication table, and you have by analogy a description of the spirit land, as it comes filtered through the lips of magnetized somnambules, in phrases adapted to the comprehension of children studying earth's multiplication tables. As to the great names, so long as the world depends upon the authority of great names, great names will be in the mouths of those who are as much magnetized by their auditors as by the spirits who labor only to give such meat as their audiences require."

"But all this is deception, Chundra, and unworthy of a great religious movement."

"The world must grow, Louis, and Spiritualism is one of its means of growth. Do you inquire how your bread is made? Perhaps you would never consume another morsel if you were fully answered. Yet you grow and are sustained by the result, let the details be what they may. This modern movement is but the chaotic reflec-

tion of the ignorance, bigotry, credulity, and materialism of the age. Still it is the first step towards breaking
the seals of that apocalyptic age that is even now upon
us. This step, too, is the most necessary of all that are
to follow. Man will advance nearer and nearer to the
spiritual realms, the elementaries will advance nearer to
man; and all creation, moving upwards, hinges on the
first step; this inauguration of the new and breaking up
of the old order. Be patient!"

"Chundra," I said, anxious to share my thoughts
with some one who could understand me, "last month
I visited a village community who were tormented with
a *Bhuta.** The honest people deemed the disturbances
they suffered from were all caused by the spirit of an
evil woman, a reputed sorceress, who had lived amongst
them, but who had been set upon and murdered by
Bheels under the charge of having bewitched their children. Directly after this wretched woman's death, their
own children were waylaid, beaten, and spit upon by
invisible powers. Their cattle, property, and houses
were injured, and their clothes torn and destroyed.
Shrieks, cries, groans, and knockings filled their dwell-
ings and drove them nearly frantic. The poor villagers
had performed faithfully all the ceremonies of exorcism
and propitiation which they deemed necessary, but without effect; and when I visited them, the 'Headman' of
the village was in despair, and the Brahmins they had
hired to perform the rites of exorcism were despatched
for a still larger and more powerful band to help them.
I saw the *Bhuta* clairvoyantly, and by suffering myself
to enter the somnambulic condition I could return with
her to her spiritual captivity.

* The *Polter Gheist* or ghost that throws; the haunting spirit of an evil
or ill-disposed mortal. — ED. GHOST LAND.

"I found her in the country of the worst and most evil-minded of the elementaries who belong to the lower conditions of earth, but she did not know any difference between them and multitudes of wicked and degraded human spirits who had been attracted there likewise. The habitations of these wretched beings were in a dark, desolate land. Their cities were formed of piles of cinders, ashes, and the wrecks of worlds. Their occupation was to fashion machinery and implements of war as models for mortals whom they were compelled to inspire with constructive or inventive ideas in this particular department of mechanical skill; but the elementaries of this sphere were all too rudimental in conception to succeed in their work. They never made anything complete; they could not achieve a single form right, and yet they felt the influence and inspiration of higher orders, who did succeed in modelling ideas into complete shape; and these poor embryos would therefore keep on trying and trying until they died, and progressed to a sphere of greater completeness and higher power. But many amongst them, in frantic haste and passion, destroyed, broke, and burned up their abortive models.

"I learned it had only been in a recent period of time that they had tried to make anything, and that in future they were, the best of them, destined to succeed inimitably. I wandered over their blighted, doleful land in many districts; found they delighted to attract human spirits, however evil, to them, because it enabled them to come into closer *rapport* with humanity; and though they worked mischief and rejoiced in helping human spirits to annoy and haunt mortals, they learned much in their contact with earth, and would ultimately improve. It seemed strange to me to see that the human spirits who gravitated there did not understand the difference between themselves and the elementaries, so nearly did they resemble each other. All, alas! were stamped with the characteristics of fierce and destructive animals, and some, although strictly human, resembled the loathsome reptiles with whose passions they had sympathy. I was told that the demands of earth inspire these lower worlds with inventive ideas. The rude and half-fashioned instruments they construct are man's thoughts in embryo; hence, when I saw these poor antitypes of humanity clumsily trying to draw swords through ungovernable fires, and found cannon amidst mountains of cinders piled up to the black skies, I lamented that I, amongst others, had ever used or required for use weapons of offence and missiles of war. If the demands of our bad passions stimulate these lower worlds to answer us, what a mighty responsibility rests upon us, who are to the elementaries what the realms of angelic inspiration are to us!"

"Did these wretched beings see your spirit, Louis, and how did they receive you?"

" They could not see me, but they felt my presence, and they were impelled to acts of worship although in rags and ruin, and knelt amidst their wrecked world and addressed my spirit as a god. They could not aspire to any existence higher than the soul of a pitying mortal, and my presence amongst them was both felt and signified by spirit lights. They wept as they prayed, and as I prayed myself, the *Bhuta* became inspired and preached to them. She uttered my thoughts, though not my words,—perhaps like the world's trance mediums. I left them so, for I was recalled to the earth, but I have heard since, that the disturbances in the haunted village have ceased, and all is peace there again. Chundra, if mortals were better informed concerning the condition of these 'hells,' could they not elevate the miserable dwellers there, and thus save the race of men from their evil influence, their promptings to wrong and mischief breathed through the atmosphere, and the failures which humanity makes through abortive effort?"

The Byga silently pointed to a pair of pistols lying on a table near me, and my sword laid across a divan.

"So long as you demand those instruments of destruction," he said, in a low but impressive tone, "poorer, more necessitous, and less responsible beings will make capital out of the demands of their superiors. Louis de B——, assure yourself the universe moves *en masse*. One redeemed soul in any department of being pushes creation forward everywhere, whilst one who sinks, sinks a host with him. Let those who preach, point the way by practice. Creation's road.is onward, not downward. Man must sooner or later learn to recognize and acknowledge the existence of other worlds above, beneath, and around him besides his own; when he does, his knowledge will warn him that there are legions of beings who rise or fall with him. Meantime, the purification even of one human soul is triumph enough for a lifetime, for, as you say, it is in the realms of evil and mischievous elementaries that the hells of humanity are found. Elevate the one class of being, and your work will create a heart-throb throughout the whole dark realms of being."

"Chundra, you who know, tell me who is Metron?"

"A chief amongst the elementaries who correspond to the electric and magnetic forces generated in the Arctic and Antarctic circles. These regions form the brain and feet of the living earth, and sustain vast

realms of elementary beings who correspond to the
prevailing influence and quality of their *locale.* They
derive their peculiarly magnetic temperaments from
the regions they inhabit, and react upon those regions
by filling them with the immense activity of their own
magnetic natures.　Metron is a prince amongst these
radiant elementaries.

"Is he himself an elementary?"

"Not so; he is a spirit, a tutelary spirit, even as the
Eloihim of the ancient cabalists were princes or rulers
in different departments of creation.　You, as a caba-
list, should understand that regions, countries, nations,
planets, and even the individuals who reside upon their
surfaces, are under the guardianship of special tutelary
spirits, of whom Metron, himself a planetary angel, is
a type."

"I do understand this, and should be as poor a caba-
list as my Christian brothers, did I fail to recognize the
doctrine of tutelary spirits and guardian angels.　The
Christians might find this doctrine fully and even elab-
orately taught in their own Scriptures, especially in the
books of Ezekiel, Daniel, and the Apocalypse.　I find
it in the Oriental as well as the Jewish cabalas, believe,
and fully realize it; but that which perplexes me is the
strange fantasy that possesses me of a similarity between the radiant Metron and that most beloved friend
of my soul, Felix von Marx.　Sometimes I have half
imagined Metron might be his transfigured spirit, but
again I have endeavored to banish this idea, lest it
should lead me into the realms of fanaticism and hallucination."

"Resemblances in the spiritual kingdom are not those
of the physical form, but mental similitudes.　Every
tutelary angel rules over realms of being imbued with

special mental or moral qualities, as well as certain regions of space, and all great leading minds in the spirit
spheres form the nucleus of circles whose harmony of
thought or purpose creates a similitude of appearance.
On earth the wheat and the tares are grown together,
and all classes of mind, morals, and estate, are hetero-
geneously gathered into that vortex of life called "society," or grouped together into nationalities.

"In the spiritual kingdom, Death the harvest-angel,
separates the wheat from the tares, and ranges the
specialties which mark human character on earth or
conditions of progress in eternity, each in their special
department of life; each is garnered up in the place and
association to which he belongs. Felix von Marx, a
profound student and adept in the mysteries of vital
magnetism, gravitates as a spirit to those spheres of
thought which are devoted to the occult in creation, but
especially does he belong to the realms of force, the magnetism or life of the universe, the all-pervading element
whose grand reservoir and generating centre upon this
planet is governed by the tutelary angel, Metron.

"Speaking to you in the imperfect verbiage of human
speech, Felix von Marx is one of the legionaries in those
realms of elementary life of which Metron is the prince,
hence, he partakes of the similitude which pervades his
sphere of being. Artists, poets, sculptors, musicians,
inventors, all classes of mind whose aggregate makes
up the order and harmony of creation, gravitate to
special spheres on their first entrance to the realms of
spiritual existence; and until they have ranged through
all departments of the universe and mastered all its
separate elements, you see them grouped into circles,
presided over by tutelary spirits of their own order, and
attracted to realms of thought where their peculiar char-

acteristics find the grander fields of culture and expression which spirit life affords to the graduates from earth."

"But Metron is the tutelary angel of the elementaries, not of human spirits."

Of all minds, human, elementary, mortal or immortal, who are attracted to the kingdom in which he rules. "Look to the north when the pencilled glory of the Boreal lights are flaming through the evening skies! Look to the silent finger of the magnetic compass pointing out the mariner's path through the boundless wastes of ocean, yet ever faithful to the invisible polar brain of the earth, fixed in the Arctic regions! Look to the growing tree, the springing grass, the shooting flower, throbbing with the silent influence of the all-pervading spirit of life. Watch mankind's thronging millions, whirled through space with a force which would suffice to throw off from the earth's surface every particle of matter into unmeasured space, yet gravitation suffices to attach all living forms to that surface, enabling them to move upon it without the slightest sense of insecurity. The glorious lights of the flaming Aurora, the invisible power of the magnet, and the potential fires of life and gravitation, are all but so many phases of that one mighty realm of force, generated in the brain regions of the polar North and distributed in endless lines of radiation through the system of earth and its freight of animate and inanimate kingdoms.

"Looking upon the order of being throughout which this stupendous realm of force is the life principle, you behold the kingdom of Metron and his legions of magnetic elementaries, whose station is in the North, whose sphere is the realm of force, and whose legionaries correspond to the magnetic and electric life which courses through every fibre of this planet.

"Although this class of the elementaries are still embryotic and unvitalized by an immortal spirit, in which all elementaries are lacking, they form a bright and radiant grade of existence, with high aspirations for knowledge, goodness, and immortality.

"It is a realm of elementary existence of this character which is ministered to by Metron, himself a tutelary angel whose nature is in harmony with those he rules over, whose deepest sympathies are engaged in preparing them for their ultimate destiny as immortal beings, and who leaves the celestial regions to which he belongs to preach to and teach these subordinate races, and help them to attain to his own purified condition."

"Why does the presence of spirits and my efforts to converse with them always weaken me physically," I asked, "when in intention I would spend my life in that communion?"

"Because spirits can not renew intercourse with earth without borrowing from you the life element by which they approach you and make themselves palpable to your senses. They must rob you of physical strength ere they can reclothe their sublimated forms in material pabulum."

"Will it ever be so?"

"No. As men grow into spiritual light and knowledge, they will better understand the methods of communion. This earth is full of occult forces; trees, plants, herbs, stones, minerals, vapors, gases, and fluids are all teeming with magnetism. To comprehend these forces, draw them forth and apply them, was the art of the ancient magian, and will be the next phase of science which humanity will achieve. The living forces of the body will then be reserved, and the occult powers of nature be substituted as a means of communing with

spirits. Man will take part in that communion, instead
of being the mere passive instrument of beings whom
he does not know or understand, and this will be the
period when spiritual and physical sciences will supplement each other, instead of being, as now, arrayed against
each other by the ignorance and prejudice of man.
The communion between mortals and those spheres of
human spiritual existence that have as yet been able to
manifest to mortals, is but a faint indication of the
approaches which the earth is making towards the
inauguration of a new era; a time fulfilled, a judgment
passed; a dawning day of new life, new light, new
heavens, and a new earth. Occult science, words which
at present have but little meaning in the ears of men,
must be understood, studied, and mastered ere humanity
can enter the temple of spiritism, or worship in spirit
and in truth that God who is a spirit."

The Byga here made a movement to go, but as he
did so, he stretched out his hand to me as before. I
attempted to take it, but felt nothing, and shrank from
him in confusion, exclaiming, " Have I lost my sense of
touch, or what is this I would clasp? "

"As an adept in occult science you should know the
difference between mortal substance and the still more
potential touch of force." So saying he grasped my hand
with a power that would have imprisoned me had I been
a Titan, then releasing me as suddenly, I saw the
shrouded form and cowled head gradually becoming
transfigured. A dimness was on my eyes; the walls, gardens, terraces, moon-lit river, and the distant city, with
its glittering domes and minarets, all seemed to be
whirling around me with frightful rapidity; the vast
crystal vault of the heavens, with its sparkling lamps
and spangled immensity, looked so close to me that it

might be about to descend and crush me. In the midst of this awful chaos I experienced a sensation as if I were being lifted up in the arms of some being who was all force, and then laid tenderly on the couch from which I had risen on the Byga's entrance.

I became environed in an atmosphere of fire-mist; corruscations of radiant lights flashed around me, a mingled sentiment of oppression and ecstacy overpowered me, and yet I was able to perceive a glorious form bending over me. For an instant only I beheld the divine face of Metron gazing upon me with such love as only an angel can feel for its mortal charge; then, as the blinding rays of light which enveloped him vanished or faded out, I know not which, the form of my guardian spirit, still stationary by my side, still fixing its eyes of tenderest affection upon me, seemed to become transfigured, and I beheld plainly, distinctly, and with emotions of the most profound calmness, trust, and rest, the noble form and face of Felix von Marx. Many words passed between us, words that dispelled the mists of doubt and error from my mind, soothing my troubled spirit with a foretaste of heavenly peace ere I sank into a deep and refreshing slumber.

If my readers would know what relation this vision bore to the strange visitor whom I have named "the Byga," I am wholly unable to answer them. I never knew who or what this mystic was. I never fully understood why, in his atmosphere, spirits could come and go like images on the sensitive plate of the photographer. He himself, his nature and relation to the world of the unseen around me, have formed a part of those mysteries which the researches of a single life or a single generation cannot master. I have often listened with regret to statements purporting to emanate from the inspiration of "very high spirits," which assumed to explain all the mysteries of spiritual manifestations, and that upon the ground of material science and secularized analogies, simply ridiculous.

I have read essays of a similar character, claiming to emanate from the most exalted dwellers of the spheres, and their perusal has filled me with pain and humiliation.

In the light of such revealings, the universe of spiritual existence becomes a mere reflex of this human world, with all its human conditions, grovelling ideas, and limited if not atheistical views of Deity and the scheme of causation.

To my apprehension, the spiritual life beyond the grave bears the same relation to earth that the life of the embryo during its period of gestation bears to that of the infant immediately after its mortal birth, — no more. Looking back upon the scenes of my own past life, with its various acts of spiritual intervention, I confess I can only perceive through the enclosing mists, the white hands of angels weaving the woof of human life, and feel the supporting arms of spirit guardians but half revealed. The longer I live and search, and strive to gauge the infinite and eternal with finite senses and temporal capacity, the less I find I really know, and the more stupendous appears to become the ocean of immensity over which I must sail before I can venture to offer any chart of the path I have followed to those who shall come after me.

I have written TRULY, FAITHFULLY of the "Ghost-Land" through which I have been searching. The "Cassandras" of life are never believed in, and still they must vaticinate. Perhaps it will be so with me. Many more will scoff and sneer and disbelieve than strive as I have done to find the clue that might explain my strange experiences. Flippant egotism may either deny them altogether, or offer such silly and secular attempts at explanation as deprive spiritual life and science of all dignity, religious grace, or holiness; but to me it becomes more and more apparent every day that a bridge of occult science must span the gulf between the visible and invisible worlds ere man can venture to say he knows as he is known.

26

CHAPTER XXII.

THE ENCHANTRESS.

THE time was fast approaching when I had resolved
I would make a complete change in my mode of life
and the sphere of its action. Eight years had passed
away since I left England, and I had grown so weary
of military life beneath the burning sun of Hindostan,
that I seriously contemplated a change of service which
would enable me to return to my own country and
scenes more congenial to my early education. I did
not venture to suggest these proposed changes to my
Hindoo connections, who built largely upon my continuance amongst them, as a means of aggrandizing their
own power and improving my fortunes.

My relatives exalted my slight successes beyond their
true worth, and the mere hint of my wish to return to
Europe was met with strenuous opposition. I had
another object in view too, and one that was far more
congenial to me than any earthly chances of achieving
fame or fortune, and this was the prospect of soon com-
pleting my term of initiatory probation in a society of
extremely antique origin, with which it had been my
passionate yearning to become affiliated. It little matters to my readers where the *locale* of this society is to
be found, or of what its rites and exercises consist.

The nineteenth century is perhaps the very coldest
possible culmination of the materialistic philosophy,

which has been growing up like a fungus upon the civilization of the last five hundred years; so the nineteenth century is the last which could appreciate the objects of an association contemplating amongst other ideas, the reversal and obliteration of all theological myths, and the inauguration of a true spiritual king-. dom, in which truth itself will be the Bible, God the high-priest, ministering spirits the acolytes, and occult science the connecting link between the past and the present, the spiritual and the natural world. The very few that in this generation are fitted for affiliation with this society will be called, as I was, without any previous knowledge of its existence; the rest of the world may and will seek it in vain.

I *had* been called, I repeat, and was *obliged* to join its ranks, but I had to undergo a long and painful series of probations ere I could hope to arrive at all that that society could confer upon me. I had labored and suffered for it, abnegated self, and given up for its sake much that renders life beautiful, cheerful, and happy. I had given up my very body and soul to gain what I sought, and soon, very soon I was to be rewarded.

As the time for complete realization approached, my intense devotion to the idea before me deepened, and it was only by a great effort that I could bring myself to fulfil the daily cares that pressed upon me, and combine together the meshes of the various activities I had undertaken, so as to be ready when the time should come to devote myself wholly to the work before me, and quit the land of Hindostan without one feeling of compunction for duties unfulfilled or actions which I could look back upon with regret.

All was progressing under my silent and secret purpose, when a day arrived, — a day ever memorable to

me, as that which was to usher in an episode of my life's
history, the shadow of which I darkly felt, but the form
whereof I could not discern.

"My dear friend, I must start for Calcutta immediately, — this packet of letters compels my departure
at once; yet how I grieve to leave you and the delightful quarters you have afforded me, I can never fully
express."

"Wait till to-night, Graham, and I shall be your travelling companion to Calcutta, for thither I too must go
as soon as possible."

This was the conversation that passed between myself
and my friend Graham at our breakfast-table, as we sat
reading our letters on the day which succeeded the visit
recorded in the last chapter. Besides the business matters which summoned me to Calcutta, I found a strong
impelling motive in a letter just received from my
esteemed friend, John Dudley, but one which for some
unexplained reason I ought to have had many months
before. By a perusal of its contents I learned that
Mr. Dudley had succeeded to the earldom of D——,
in consequence of the demise of the intervening heirs.
His elevation to the peerage was entirely unexpected,
and seemed to have had no effect in changing the
hearty and affectionate cordiality of my friend's character, nor had it, as he emphatically assured me,
wrought any alteration in the feelings of his "dear
girls, except some little astonishment at their awakening
one fine morning to hear themselves called the *Ladies*
Sophia Edith, and Blanche." He frequently alluded to
his experiences amongst the Spiritualists of America;
his unquenched enthusiasm for "the cause," and his
abiding faith that I should keep my promise and revisit
his family at the expiration of ten years from the time

of my departure. IIe reminded me that the ten years would soon elapse now, adding that I should have a good excuse for returning to England, were it only to escort back his best-beloved child, the Lady Blanche Dudley, who, as he informed me, had been induced to accompany her aunt, Lady Emily R——, to India for a visit of two years. Lady Emily, the sister of the new Countess of D——, had, in my absence, espoused her cousin, the Viscount R——, whom I should remember, said the writer, "as a sour, unspiritual relative" of his family, one between whom and the Dudleys no great intimacy had ever been maintained. My friend continued thus: "Now, Emily was just one of the best and most genial of human beings, besides being a capital medium, which is better than all, you know. What under the sun could induce this dear sister-in-law of mine to wed a prig of a Scotch viscount, and a Presbyterian to boot, none can say except those who are more versed in the mysteries of womankind than I am.

"The fact is, I suppose, poor Emily grew tired of lone widowhood, and as my lord was appointed to a high position in India, and offered my dear relative a handsome establishment and all the privileges of *Begumship*, etc. etc., the thing was too much for the aforesaid womankind, and dear Emmy consented to become the Viscountess R—— and depart with her yellow-visaged spouse to India forthwith. But that is n't the whole or the worst of it, Louis. Would you believe it? They have actually carried my little Blanche, the very 'light of my harem' and the apple of my eye, along with them. Of course you will wonder how such a miracle could have come about, and to tell you the truth, I have not got over my own astonishment in the matter, even now that she has been gone — my precious

darling! more than two months. All I can do is to tell
you the way the thing came round.

"Emily received a splendid settlement in her marriage,
and as she is not very likely to bring her noble spouse
any heirs, she, with his full consent, offered to adopt my
Blanche as her heiress, provided she were permitted to
accompany her aunt on her two years' mission to Calcutta. You know that Blanche was always her aunt's
favorite, as she was mine and everybody else's. Well,
I don't know how they arranged it all, but they made
out that as my two boys would have the bulk of the
estate, and the girls had but little prospect beyond
slim settlements, or rich marriages, of course this offer
of my lady the viscountess was far too magnificent to
be slighted. Thus they got it all settled to their satisfaction, and I verily believe had fitted my little fairy
out with all the gauzes and finery proper on such occasions, when suddenly they bethought them of coming
to ask my consent to my darling's abstraction. Now,
Louis, you know me well enough to be aware how hard
it would be for me to oppose one woman at a time; but
when I tell you that they came in a band, and asked me
en masse to consent to what they had already fully made
up their minds to do, you may 'guess,' as our American cousins have it, what sort of a chance I stood
amongst them. However, I thought I would just try
it on a little; so, summoning up my most potential air
of authority, I stated my decided objection to any child
of mine taking up her residence amongst lions and
tigers, snake charmers and charmeresses; but before I
could get out another word—rap, rap, rap! comes 'the
spirits,' and instantly my whole band of feminines set
to work spelling out communications from what I was
informed was the spirit of 'a fakir' who had lived six

thousand years ago, and who peremptorily commanded that the Lady Blanche Dudley should proceed forthwith to India, ' to meet her fat.'

"'Meet her fat!' I exclaimed. 'In heaven's name, why should she go so far to meet fat? That fakir does n't know much about my family arrangements, I take it.'

"'May it not be to make her fat?' suggested my wife.

"But no, the spirits would n't have it that way either; then, after a considerable amount of bungling, the fakir corrected his spelling, and the sentence read thus: ' To meet her fate.'

"Well, when a body of women, backed up by a man six thousand years old, undertake to have their own way Louis, rely upon it, the best thing one can do is to make a virtue of necessity and give the consent they 'd just as soon do without; and so, to make a long story short, she sailed away last March Louis, and the sunlight of my life sailed with her. That 's all.

"Now, my dear fellow," continued my friend, " don't think I want to tax your good-nature or impose any burdens upon you in the philandering line, but what I would say is this: See my little Sunshine, and just find out, as you can do if you choose, if she is happy; whether she does n't want to return to her old father, or whether she would rather stay till my lord's term expires. Which ever it is Louis, I give you *carte blanche* to act as if she were your own child, or, for the matter of that, your grandchild. If she prefers her native moon, that is, the moon of her native land, to that blazing old luminary you keep for warming purposes in Hindostan, take her away in her father's name. Pack her up, with a legion of Ayahs to wait on her, and a regiment of Sepoys to escort her, and I'll pawn my earldom but I'll recompense you, if her transit home costs a king's ransom."

Such was the substance of my old friend's letter, and though I was vexed enough to find it ought to have been delivered to me so many months ago, I still hoped to be in time to ascertain how far the fair Lady Blanche had become reconciled to meeting " her fate " in India, or whether she might not wish to return to her native land. Devoting the next hour to writing explanatory letters to my old friend, and the rest of the day to my preparations for departure, I was ready to set out that night with Graham for Calcutta, which "City of Palaces " we reached in due time, and after taking a cordial leave of each other, we departed to our separate destinations.

I took an early opportunity after my arrival to call at the Viscount R——'s residence, to inquire for his wife and niece. ●The ladies were away at their country seat, I was informed, but would return to-morrow. I left cards for them, but none for the Scotch dignitary. The next morning however, brought the viscount's servant to my residence with his master's card, and a singularly cordial invitation to dine *en famille* at his house the next day, when his wife and niece would have returned to the city. At the appointed time, and whilst I was preparing for my visit, Capt. Graham entered my room with his usual unceremonious frankness, and tendering me a highly perfumed and extravagantly embossed billet, accompanied it by the urgent request that I would oblige him by accepting the invitation it contained, which was nothing less than to attend a fashionable entertainment at the residence of Madame Hélène Laval, the widow of an eminent East Indian

nabob, and the reigning queen of a certain class of
fashionable society, for that season, at Calcutta. When
Graham first tendered me the scented piece of frivolity
that conveyed this invitation, I was half angry with
him, and despite the sincere regard we entertained for
each other, I was somewhat hurt that he should have
so far mistaken me as to imagine that I should be willing to spend my time in assemblies of mere fops
and flirts. He knew that I was often compelled to
take part in stately ceremonial or official gatherings,
but he also knew that in my most charitable moods, I
could not regard what is popularly called "society"
with toleration; how then, could he expect me I asked
coldly, to make one of the gilded butterflies whom
a vain and ambitious woman gathered around her for
the sake of exhibiting the homage offered up at her
shrine?

Poor Graham bore my reproaches very patiently, but
would not yield his point nevertheless. He said *la
belle Hélène* was like myself a "mystic" and devoted
"occultist"; she had long known me by reputation as a
student of her favorite sciences, and was eager to meet
me; that it was no gilded butterflies, but profound
thinkers, grave reformers, and speculative metaphysi-
cians who were in the habit of attending her *soirées.*
Some rank and fashion of course, was permitted to
exhibit there, but for the most part it was to be an
assembly of those whom I should acknowledge to be
"the best people in the city." Graham added, with an
earnestness peculiarly irresistible to me, his attached
friend, "But it is not for the society's sake I urge you
Chevalier, it is for my own that I plead; there will be
one person there to-night, whom I entreat you to
meet, to look upon and speak to, if for no other pur-

pose, at least to oblige the friend who would nevei refuse anything you could ask."

"Enough!" I replied, "you wish me to see your enchantress, Graham. As soon as I can extricate myself from the dinner engagement I am about to fulfil, I will meet you at Madame Laval's."

On arriving at Viscount R——'s, I was received by him with much more cordiality than he had deigned to bestow on the German mystic of olden times, but his fair wife, now in the full blush of her Hindoo dignities expanded into a portly, magnificent "Begum," greeted me with all the affectionate interest of our former acquaintance. By her side, and almost overshadowed in the amplitude of her gorgeous robes, stood her beautiful niece, not the little Blanche of old; no more the merry, light-hearted "little Sunshine" of her doting father's home, but the graceful and *distingué* Lady Blanche Dudley, somewhat grown it is true, but still *petite,* slight, fragile, — ethereal perhaps, would be the better word, — and beautiful; heavens! what a wondrously beautiful creature she was! All the poet's ideals of sylphs, undines, or fairy beings, "too fair for earth, too frail for heaven," would have paled and grown cold, plain, and insignificant before the beauty of this wondrous, unearthly-looking girl. I gazed at her as I would have done at the cunning workmanship of an Apelles, a Phidias, or an Angelo. At that time, at least, I regarded her more as a marble goddess than a very lovely mortal. Her beauty had a touch of sadness quite unlike the Blanche of old, and there was so much dignity in the turn of her graceful form, veiled by masses of golden ringlets, that I stood like a worshipper of the beautiful in art, as I have ever been, and I suppose stared at her in equal surprise and admiration ere I had the sense or good-breeding to greet her. She was as much changed in manner as appearance, I found, for though she met me with kindness and *empressment*, there was a womanly reserve and a far-off, dreamy air of abstraction about her which completely removed her from my memory as the merry, laughing girl I had parted with eight years before.

Ever a dreamer, a vision arose in my mind of the many hearts that would ache, and the many gallants that would sigh in vain for this creature of light and ether, this peerless Undine, and that too in a city where the tropic skies and burning sun kindle up warmer emotions than in any other fashionable capitol of the known world. And this was all, absolutely all, that I thought about the Lady Blanche Dudley during the many succeeding months that I became her constant attendant, escorting her in her rides and drives, waiting upon her in her uncle's stately official entertainments, listening to her thrilling voice, sweeter than the fabled syren's, as she accompanied herself with masterly skill on the harp; watching crowds of adorers hovering around her, and the richest and noblest in the land emulating each other for the honor of winning one glance from her wonderful violet eyes. And all this I watched, and looked upon her meanwhile as I would upon a beautiful and ingenious piece of mechanism, or as those of my comrades who knew me best affirmed, "like an Arctic iceberg, reflecting back the rays of a Southern sun, but never melting beneath them." And this fair Lady Blanche never changed the soft, white, fleecy gauzes in which she veiled her exquisite form for any other dress, and never substituted the fresh flowers and leaves which constituted her only ornaments for the radiant jewels and burnished gold that flashed on every side around her. Who can wonder that she moved in the midst of India's highest magnates like a descended star of light and purity?

Who can wonder that she became the cynosure of all admiring eyes, save mine? For her good father's sake, and because I remembered how tenderly in times gone by, the kind-hearted little one, had wept in sympathy with my strange afflictions, I devoted to her now all the spare time I had to give, and delighted to escort her and her good-natured aunt to those scenes of ancient art and antique splendor with which Hindostan abounds, but in which so few of the fashionable crowds around them took the deep interest they appeared to do.

Sometimes I wondered at this fair creature's beauty; sometimes lifted one of her golden curls to kiss, or placed choice flowers amongst them. She never raised her eyes to mine, scarcely ever looked at or spoke to me, and yet I knew this was not unkindness.

On the evening of my first visit to the viscount's I informed my friends that I must leave them soon after dinner, as I had resolved to keep tryst with poor Graham. We did not dine until 10 p. m., so that it was midnight before I was free. I then stated the nature of my engagement, and prepared to take my leave. Great was my surprise however, when the viscount asked me if I would take his place as an escort to his wife and niece who were also engaged to attend Madame Laval's entertainment, from which he should still be detained for an hour or so.

"Are you then acquainted with this lady?" I asked of the viscountess, as we drove to Madame Laval's residence."

"Oh, yes," replied Lady Emily, "of course we are. Hélène is our Blanche's dearest friend; in fact, they are almost inseparable; besides," she added, lowering her tone mysteriously, "she is one of our sort, you know, Chevalier; a mystic and a medium, and all that sort of thing, and of course, we are delighted to cultivate her, with our present terribly materialistic surroundings. She reads the stars, too, distils potions, and—"

"Dearest aunt," interposed Blanche, "do not suffer yourself to speak so wildly of Hélène. She is a woman far beyond her surroundings, Chevalier," she added, turning to me, and blushing in the warmth of her friend's defence.

"Why don't you call me Louis, as you used to do?" I asked. "Is it because I am now expected to address you as *Lady* Blanche Dudley?"

"Louis!" she said in an accent so pathetic that it rings in my ears to this day. "Louis, then, now and forever!"

Of Madame Laval's entertainment, her royal and distinguished guests, and the splendor which flashed through her *salons* at every turn, it would require a writer more skilled and interested in such scenes than myself to dilate on. It is enough to say that as we entered the principal *salon*, Lady Blanche, in defiance of all etiquette, left me, and hastened forward to greet her beloved friend with a sister's kiss, and then returned leading that friend, with something like her old look of girlish impulse, through the gay crowds, to present to me. As she approached, I saw that she led in triumph and obvious delight, a tall, graceful, splendid brunette, with large, searching, oriental eyes, heavy masses of raven hair, glittering with diamonds, a majestic presence, fascinating smile, and—the impersonation of the horrible vision I had beheld when psychometrizing Graham's "talismanic" package!

This lady, whom I subsequently found had been named in the fashionable circles that thronged around her, "the enchantress," received me with marked *prestige*. She held my hand in hers some time longer than was necessary for the formalities of presentation; informed me I was no stranger to her, though she, of course, she said, was unknown to me; told me she had seen me at ——, and here she named several scenes of my public life when I might have been in presence of many persons of whom I knew nothing; that she had followed my career with the deepest interest, sympathized with certain of those pursuits which vulgar rumor attributed to me, and was especially delighted to meet me on account of her darling friend,—here she glanced patronizingly down upon Blanche,—and finally she released my hand, but not before she had given me the peculiar grip accompanied by the sign of a certain society, to which I belonged, but to which I never knew that any ladies had been admitted. Before I had time to breathe or recover from the shock her identification with my vision occasioned me, still less to follow the drift of her many complimentary remarks and the extraordinary signs of understanding she gave me, she again claimed my attention for the purpose of presenting her brother, Monsieur Paul Perrault, a tall, handsome Frenchman, who strongly resembled his sister, but the touch of whose ungloved hand sent a thrill through mine which reminded me of nothing so much as plunging my hand into a nest of crawling adders.

Oh, fatal gift of occult sight! Oh, ban of mortal life,— that power which pierces the veil, wisely, providentially, hung before the holy of holies in each one's secret nature! That fatal occult sight was mine from the moment that woman fixed her talismanic eyes upon me.

That veil was lifted instantly as I beheld her standing side by side with her obsequious brother. Near them gleamed the snow-white, misty robes of the golden-haired Blanche, and above their heads grinned and chattered a triad of hideous elementaries, invisible to all but me, yet graphically revealing the characteristics of the couple to whom they were attracted as attendant spirits, and glowering at the unconscious Blanche like the demons of some hideous rite, to whom she, the pure victim, was to be offered up as a sacrifice.

Near this group stood my friend Graham, and I was fairly shocked by the look of pain and anxiety with which he was scrutinizing me as I endured this intro-duction. I have often marvelled why the exercise of spiritual insight is so seldom accompanied by the power to use it. (The seer is compelled to behold the innermost of natures all masked to others, yet the cramp-ing bonds of society interpose to neutralize the value of what he discovers.)

Had I obeyed the monitions which my spiritual per-ceptions suggested at that moment, I should have spurned, ay, spat upon that brother and sister instead of bowing before them and suffering them to touch my shivering hand; I should have shut them out from all that was good and fair and beautiful; above all, I should have laid that golden-headed Blanche low in the quiet grave ere I had suffered their baleful presence to come like a blight between her and the sunlight of her young life. As it was, the shadow of the future clung around me like a cold, damp shroud, and as I caught the eye of poor Graham, I felt giddy, lost, wretched, and he *knew* I understood that the original of *the vision* stood before me. When the host and hostess left me to pay their compliments to others, Graham approached and said

earnestly, "You have my secret, Chevalier, and see my
enchantress. You cannot wonder at my fascination, nor
do I marvel at yours." He glanced as he spoke at the
fair Blanche. "Oh!" I said as if waking from a dream,
" I have no fascination here, Graham. These scenes are
hateful to me, and the atmosphere is so unendurable I
can stay no longer." As I spoke, the Viscount R——
and a party of his friends entered the *salon*. Pleading
the indisposition I really felt, I hastened to resign my
charge to him, and left the place.

It was towards the close of the same night, just as the
first faint streaks of dawning light had begun to dispel
the darkness, that I awoke with an indescribable sense of
mental oppression. I felt as if all that was good and true
had abandoned me and I was left in the toils of some foul
and hateful captivity. As I started up from my pillow,
determined to shake off this terrible nightmare by exercise, I saw distinctly, standing between me and the
faintly illumined sky as it gleamed through the open
glass doors of my chamber, the figure of Madame
Hélène Laval, — graceful, beautiful, and commanding
as a Pythoness, a veritable Medea, though but little of
a woman. In one hand she held a short curl of black
hair, in the other a square case, the nature of which I
could not at first discern. Her voice, which though
deep was singularly sweet and sympathetic, sounded a
long way off as she said, "Do not seek to fly me! I love
you, have long loved and followed you. Give me your
affection or — yourself, and I will worship you. Reject me, and I will destroy all you love best."

She then raised the square case she held in her hand,
and I saw it was an ivory miniature, a likeness of myself, that Mr. Dudley had caused to be taken before I
left England. I was not informed how this portrait was

to be disposed of, but I was under the impression that it belonged to the family generally.

Without any definite idea of what I was going to do, I sprang from my bed and grasped the figure I beheld by the arm, endeavoring at the same time to seize the portrait she held. What I touched gave me the impression of being a substance like stiff gauze, or lace inflated by air; but instantly, beneath my hand, this substance began to recede, the figure collapsed, shrank together, and melted down to the floor. The last portion I saw of it was a pair of black, long, almond-shaped eyes, gleaming at me with an expression I would fain blot out from my memory forever.

I have often touched the "atmospheric spirit" or *Döppel Ganger* of others, *my own included*, and felt a sense of resistance like the application of my hand to a body of compressed air, but I never before experienced such a concrete mass of *materialized life essence* as this terrible wraith displayed. It vanished, however, though from that time forth it haunted me day and night for many a long month.

When my phantom visitor disappeared, I mechanically raised my hand to my head, and discovered where a lock of hair had been cut away from the back; but how or when was as much a mystery as how it had come into the visionary hand where it had just been displayed.

It was about a week after this occurrence, and when I was engaged to dine at Viscount R——'s, that on entering his drawing-room, I saw Lady Emily standing looking out of the window with her back towards me. She was alone. I knew her impressibility, and had but to exert my will for one instant to place her under its psychological influence. I then caused her to turn

round, sit down on an ottoman before me, and answer
the following questions: —

"Lady Emily, tell me truly, to whom was my portrait
given after I left England?"

"To Blanche, my niece."

"For what reason?"

"She asked permission of her mother to copy it, as a
work of art."

"For whom?"

"For herself. She confided to me her wish to possess a copy, and I agreed that it should be asked for in
my name."

"Where is that copy now?"

Lady Emily began to tremble violently as she
answered, though with great apparent reluctance, "In
the possession of Hélène de Laval."

"How came it there?"

"Hélène asked Blanche for it, with the expressed
wish of copying it, and Blanche, who can refuse Hélène
nothing, was obliged to comply."

"How did Madame Laval know Blanche possessed
such a picture?"

"O heavens! that woman knows everything. She
has a complete mastery over Blanche, and can read the
inmost secrets of her heart."

"And yours also, Lady Emily."

"Not so well. She has never magnetized me, but she
has Blanche."

"Can you not interpose your authority to prevent the
continuance of this intimacy?"

"I will try, but I am afraid of Hélène. She can come
and go as a spirit, whenever and wherever she pleases."

"Have you ever seen her as a spirit?"

"Many times; coming out of Blanche's apartments."

" Have others seen her? "

" Certainly. Blanche's maid, also the viscount and my housekeeper."

" Why did she desire to have my picture? "

I felt condemned as I asked this question, and the self-reproach that arose in my mind, occasioning a feeling of irresolution, evidently shook my *rapport* with the somnambulist. I saw that she too was irresolute and doubtful. I immediately closed the séance, therefore, and, demagnetizing my kind subject, presented myself before her as if I had just entered the drawing-room. Lady Emily started, and holding out her hand, exclaimed, " Why, Louis! is it possible you have found me napping? I believe I am hardly awake yet, for I am strangely sleepy."

For many months I was detained by the duties of my position in the vicinity of Calcutta, and during the constant intimacy I maintained with my English friends, I discovered three well-marked features of our relative situations. The first was that Blanche Dudley was completely infatuated by, and in the power of, Madame Hélène Laval. Next, that the lady's brother, M. Perrault, was equally infatuated with the beautiful English lady; and despite the fact that his rivals were, some of them, native princes and nobles of the highest rank and official distinction in Hindostan, he had conceived the audacious design of appropriating this precious prize, despite all odds against him. That he was weaving a spell around this beautiful creature by aid of other arts than those of his own personal attractions was a fact of which I became more and more distressingly conscious every day; whilst the third and most repulsive idea which ranged itself before me in the category of certainties, was that his magnificent sister was directing a battery of the same magical character against myself; furthermore, that it required all the knowledge of occultism that I possessed, to baffle and thwart the arts she employed to fascinate me.

Not an hour of the day or night passed, during which I disposed myself to slumber, that I did not awaken to find her "atmospheric spirit" hovering over me. Exorcism, concentrated will, all were in vain to banish this dreadful haunting. The terrible wraith could neither touch nor magnetize me, but she was herself so powerful an adept and so reckless in her alliance with the most potential of elementaries, that the best I could do was to guard myself during my waking hours against the mighty spells she used to subdue me. There were means by which I could have utterly broken those spells, and cast them back upon herself; but in this case I must have left the unfortunate Lady Blanche an unprotected prey to the arts of this vile woman and her bad brother; and for the sake of the innocent girl herself, no less than in my steady friendship for her excellent father, I silently, secretly vowed myself to her defence against her unprincipled assailants. The problematical part of this network of evil lay in the fact that Blanche had become completely spell-bound before my arrival in Calcutta. When I attempted to modify her unlimited confidence in Hélène, she expressed the utmost regret and astonishment at my aversion for so charming a person, and asked mournfully why I wished to take' from her, her only friend.

"Has she told you she was your only friend, Blanche," I asked,—"you, who are surrounded, not with friends alone, but with positive worshippers?"

"What are they all to me?" replied the poor girl, in a pleading, bewildered tone. "One true friend is worth a legion of interested acquaintances. Hélène is *true*. She alone understands me. Whom else can I trust?"

"Can you not trust me, Blanche?" I inquired, though with much hesitation.

Flushing instantly to the hue of the crimson roses which adorned her white dress, she answered evasively, "Hélène told me before you came hither, you would cruelly misunderstand her, and warn me against her. She knew this by aid of those powerful spirits who surround her. She told me, too, the hour would come when I should have no one to rely upon but her. Is it not come now?"

There was an air of utter desolation in the accents of this young and beautiful creature, which formed a strange contrast between the splendor of her surroundings, the attractions which brought half a kingdom to her feet, and the forlorn expression with which she clasped her little hands and gazed into the far-off distance, like a hunted deer seeking for shelter.

The piteous though unspoken appeal made its way into the depths of my heart, and would certainly have enchained me in the bonds I so much dreaded, had not a happy alternative suggested itself. I suddenly remembered her good father's letter, and knew how much he would at that moment have felt indebted to me if I assumed his office, and urged upon the poor, bewildered girl an immediate return to his paternal care and protection.

I knew the fearful peril in which she stood, and though I could never make her pure and innocent nature comprehend the force of evil spells or the actual potency of psychological arts, I succeeded in impressing her with the dangers she incurred by sub-

jecting herself any longer to the possibility of a controlling influence from her friend, Hélène, in favor of
her audacious brother, Paul Perrault.

I found here that I had touched a chord, to which
every fibre in the refined and high-toned lady's being
instantly responded. She truly loved Hélène, but detested
her brother. She perfectly understood his pretensions,
but never for one moment believed that even Hélène's
influence could convert her loathing for Perrault into
toleration. From this source, she said, she expected no
other result than the pain she felt in inflicting pain on
her friend. My arguments, however, proved resistless.
I brought such an array of reasons before her to show
why she should return, for her father's sake, her own,
and — alas! more potential than all — for mine, that,
putting both her hands into mine, and fixing her wonderfully lovely eyes upon me with the devotion of a
saint for a deity, she murmured, " Order my destiny as
you will: I obey." Hating myself for my resolution to
send her away, yet more resolved than ever to remove
her from scenes and places where there was not one
human being worthy of her, least of all myself, I left
her, having undertaken the very difficult, very ungra-
cious, and certainly untruthful task of persuading her
aunt and uncle that she was pining to return to her
home, wearying for the society of her own family, and
must be sent back by the very next ship that sailed.

CHAPTER XXIII.

BLACK MAGIC OR VAUDOOISM.

It was with considerable hesitation that I presented my plea to the Viscount R—— for his fair niece's return to England.

I had nothing to excuse my interference in such a matter but her father's letter *and her own wish;* for this was the ground on which Blanche herself had desired me to found my proposition. The viscount received my request very coldly, but said he would refer the matter to his wife and niece, with whom he promised to consult before arriving at any conclusion on his own account; meantime, he added, as I had thought proper to open up the subject of his niece's welfare, he deemed it a favorable opportunity to present another view of her interests, and one in which he thought I was more immediately concerned. He then, in stately phraseology, and with considerable show of patronage, made me a formal offer of the lady's hand. He acknowledged that I had given him no reason to suppose I sought such an alliance, but he could hardly imagine that the honor for which princes contended would be unappreciated by me. He confessed that he was impelled to " this extraodinary breach of etiquette," first, by what he knew to have long been the sincere wish of the Lady Blanche's excellent parents; next, because his "own dear wife " had set her heart upon the match. In addition to this, he said, it was evident that there was some powerful obstacle to the young lady's settlement in life, when she so pertinaciously refused all the splendid opportunities that were open to her; and finally, he trusted to my chivalry and sense of honor not to misunderstand him when he hinted his opinion, that I was the particular obstacle in the way; in a word, that it was for my sake that she had rejected the many desirable offers of brilliant settlement that had been made to her.

My principal sentiment towards Lord R—— for this very flattering address was one of gratitude, as it gave me an opportunity to explain to him my position with perfect candor. I told him, with all the deep and affectionate interest I cherished for Earl D—— and his family, to say nothing of my fraternal regard for sweet Blanche herself, it was yet impossible that I could marry. I was a man devoted to a special idea, consecrated to aims wholly foreign to the marriage relation, the duties of which I could not undertake consistently with the religious engagements to which I referred. I assured him that it was chiefly because I was unable to contribute to Blanche's happiness or peace of mind, that I had pleaded with him to permit her return to her native land and her father's protection.

"To her father's protection most surely," replied the viscount bitterly. "Handsome men that *can't* marry ought decidedly to devote themselves to a *religious* life; and beautiful young ladies that *won't* marry should never be absent from the paternal roof."

Without resenting the tone of sarcastic disappointment in which the poor viscount spoke, I again took advantage of our awkward game of fence to urge my plea for Blanche's departure. I knew that Lord R—— had no valid excuse for finding fault with me in this rejection of an engagement I had never given him the least reason to suppose I desired, yet I pitied his mortification, and felt neither surprised nor angry to observe that he could scarcely master his sense of humiliation, or address me with common civility.

He at length assumed an air of submission, which ill-concealed his anger and disappointment; and as I was about to take my leave, he suggested that as perhaps the ladies might suspect *what a blockhead he had been making of himself* if I departed thus suddenly, he should feel obliged if I would *deign* to bestow a few moments more of my valuable time upon them in the drawing-room. I followed him in silence to Lady Emily's boudoir, where we found Blanche extended on a couch, suffering from a severe headache. I uttered a few of the commonplace pieces of advice usual under such circumstances, and was about to make this indisposition a plea for my immediate departure, when Blanche rose suddenly, and shaking back her glorious veil of golden curls from her flushed face, she exclaimed, "Hélène will cure me; she calls me even now. I know her soothing influence."

For a few moments she stood, evidently magnetized by some unseen power, in the attitude of a Pythia waiting for the inspiration of the divine efflatus; then as the force of somnambulism deepened upon her, her beautiful face became almost transfigured. Every one present continued to gaze upon her with breathless admiration, when suddenly she commenced to sing a song so full of sympathetic tenderness and exquisite melody that it was almost impossible to listen to her without tears. This wonderful piece of musical improvisation was addressed to me, and breathed the language of hopeless love combined with a warning of impending evil. It might have

applied to the songstress herself, but seemed more
designed to express the passion of the sibylline Hélène,
whose "atmospheric spirit" I could discern, standing
beside, and inspiring the beautiful somnambulist. Even
the viscount, cold and passionless as he was, had sufficient artistic culture to be amazed and enchanted at the
irresistible beauty of the song. Most fortunately, too,
he had seen enough of the magnetic trance to understand it. He was none the less displeased, however, and
declared that since his niece was given to "such fits of
vaticination as that," the only safe and proper place for
her was beneath her father's roof, and the sooner she was
there the more relieved he should feel.

Meantime poor Lady Emily wept and smiled and
clapped her hands with delight, and when at last the
fair somnambulist returned to consciousness, and hid
her face in her aunt's arms, the latter expressed her
unbounded satisfaction that her Blanche had not lost
that wonderful gift of "trance improvisation" which had
made her the star of those happy home séances which
had proceeded under her father's roof, and in which
Blanche had been the principal medium and Lady
Emily one of the admiring witnesses.

When Blanche was entirely restored to herself, I
asked her gently, whether Madame Laval had been in
the habit of magnetizing her. "Oh, yes," she answered,
"frequently. She can not only relieve my headaches
when I have one, but she can call me to her at any
distance. We have frequently tried this experiment,
and I know she could make me come to her, should she
will me to do so, from the end of the world."

I looked significantly at the viscount, and then rose
to take my leave. He followed me from the room, saying with much cordiality, as we shook hands at parting,

" Chevalier, you are right. This poor girl's place is with her father and mother. I have been wrong to allow her to engage in these dangerous magnetic practices; and since they cannot be broken through if she stays here, go the must, and that with the least possible . delay."

" Has not the error been in allowing one so pure, innocent, and impressible as Blanche," I replied, " to become subjugated by the baleful influence of Madame Laval? "

The viscount colored highly, and in the elaborate defence which he attempted of Madame Laval, simply confirmed my suspicions that he, like his niece and many another unsuspecting victim, had succumbed to the spell which this enchantress delighted to cast on all around her, especially when, as in the present instance, she had something to gain by the exercise of her fascinations. It was agreed between the viscount and myself, that Blanche should sail for England in about ten days, that in the mean time she should be taken by Lady Emily to their country-seat, some seven miles from Calcutta, under pretence of allowing her full leisure to complete her preparations for departure, whilst the viscount and myself further arranged that I should ride out to see her as often as was necessary, to consult about the most perfect conditions for her comfort and welfare during her passage homeward.

My mind set at rest on that subject, I felt free to devote myself a little more to my friend Graham, who had at last induced me to promise that I would that very night, conduct him to a Vaudoo woman, from whom he hoped to obtain some gift or information which would aid him in the prosecution of his almost hopeless suit. I had in vain attempted to dissuade him from this step. Graham either would not or could not open his eyes to the real character of the woman he so frantically loved. Some of the arts she had put upon him in common with others whom she desired to fascinate, had led him to believe that it only required a certain amount of influence on his part to turn the scale of her vacillating mind in his favor. He had heard much, he said, of a certain Vaudoo woman of Calcutta, named Anine, who to his certain knowledge had brought together many couples whom he named.

All the philosophy I had formerly urged against these practices were reiterated in vain. He was resolved to try the effect of Vaudooism, and, with or without me, he would visit Anine.

Now, it so happened that I had in my service a fakir named Nazir Sahib, who was remarkably skilful in all feats of occultism, especially in such as were produced through the ecstacy of motion, an art he had learned in Egypt from the famous "whirling dervishes." This fakir was a Malay, and brother to that very Anine who had obtained a high reputation for her success in those arts of sorcery, which more properly come under the cognomen of "Vaudooism." I had never seen Nazir's sister, nor had I any desire to do so; but as my little fakir was much attached to me, and delighted to recount for my edification his sister's remarkable experiences with her distinguished patrons and patronesses, I became unwittingly, the repository of many singular and un-sought-for confidences, amongst which was one that I deemed might be peculiarly serviceable to my friend Graham at this juncture.

It was by a private arrangement then with Nazir, that I selected a certain night for our visit to Anine, and this was the result. Directing our steps towards the lowest and most obscure part of the "black city," we arrived about midnight at the door of a low dwelling, when I paused to advise Graham that he was to walk unswervingly and as nearly as he could in my footsteps, keep close to me, and neither turn aside or speak. He need not marvel, I added, that no one who might chance to meet us would observe or address us, for we should be invisible and unheard.

If my readers should question whether I was serious in this last assertion, I answer YES, *in every iota.* If they still further desire to know how I could command such a power, I reply, By such means as enables the Hindoo fakir to saturate his body with living force, and subdue all its physical elements to the power of his spirit. This power is gained by long-protracted fasts and other ascetic practices, continued for years, when the actual changes wrought in the system, render the *rapport* between the votary and the spirit world very close and intimate. The subject, almost a spirit himself, can easily be enveloped in the agasa (life essence) of the spirit's astral body, and in this envelope he walks in spiritual invisibility, commanding the physical elements of earth at will. The processes by which a determined Eastern ecstatic can attain to these spiritual states would be as useless to describe to self-indulgent European sybarites as to expect an English life-guardsman to fly through the air like an East Indian *Irdha-pada*, who has spent his life in probationary exercises, besides inheriting an organism fitted for the part he plays.

It is enough to say that I had earned the power I possessed, and was aided by spirits to exercise it and dispense it to my companion.

After passing through the outer dwelling and a succession of mean, deserted courts, we came to a ruinous old temple, in one angle of which I advanced to the door of a crypt, which opened from within at my signal, and admitted us, by a descent of a few steps, into a large stone chamber partly hewn out of the rock. Here we found a tank and other preparations for the performance of ancient priestly rites. Three veiled females were sitting huddled together on a stone bench at the side of the hall, and their attire proved that they were attendants on some lady of consequence.

"Do not mind them," I said to Graham aloud. "Step as I have desired you, and they will not see us." In proof of what I said, I led my companion close to the group, speaking aloud as we advanced, but they neither looked up or noticed us. We then moved on to a second door at the farther end of the hall, which, like the first, swung open for our passage through. Beyond this door we found the scene of operations, which was a stone chamber similar to the first, though somewhat larger. I placed myself and my companion at the foot of a broken peristyle, around the base of which we found a heap of stones, on which we leaned whilst the following scene was enacted.

A party of half nude fakirs, amongst whom I recognized my lively little follower Nazir, danced, spun, and whirled in a circle round a female, who, attired simply in a loose white robe, with bare arms and feet, and a profusion of raven-black tresses falling almost to the ground, stood, with arms folded across her breast, in the centre of the dancers. These ecstatics whirled round, each on his own pivot as it were, with such inconceivable rapidity that they looked like spinning columns rather than human beings, and the immense charge of agasa or magnetism they liberated, so completely filled the apartment that it could be almost seen as a vapor, as well as felt as a force; certain it is, that it nearly over-· powered Graham, who would have fallen to the ground under its tremendous influence, had I not held his hand firmly and willed him to be calm. At the upper end of the hall was an altar covered with cabalistic characters, on which were placed three braziers dispensing fumigations. Before the altar was a red charcoal fire, whilst moving around the fire and feeding the brazier with strong, pungent odors, was the sister of Nazir, a Malay woman with handsome features, bright, sparkling eyes, and wearing a short, white tunic edged with cabalistic signs, and a sort of glittering coronet, similarly adorned.

At a certain portion of the dance the whirling fakirs all paused instantaneously, stood for a moment motionless, as if they had been turned to stone by the touch of an enchanter's wand. They then each raised their lean arms and pointed their forefingers at the female in the centre. By this change of posture Graham was enabled to see plainly what I already knew, namely, that the female was Madame Hélène Laval. His horror and dismay at this discovery had nearly destroyed the *rapport* in which I held him. He soon recovered himself, however, and with a muttered exclamation resumed his place by my side.

As the fakirs continued to point their fingers at the lady, her features assumed an expression so rapt and superb, that my admiration for the beautiful overcame my disgust for her character, and I regarded her for the time being with breathless interest. It is no exaggera-
,tion to say that at this juncture, the luminous fluid which streamed from the outstretched fingers of the fakirs, shone like tongues of flame, and so transported their deeply-

entranced subject that she tossed her arms aloft, with wild cries and convulsive shudderings. At length she seemed to make one bound high up in air, when she was held suspended three feet above the ground for several minutes. At this sight the circle of ecstatics around her uttered fresh cries, and imitating her action by tossing their arms in the air, prostrated themselves, with their faces on the ground, where they remained motionless during the rest of what ensued. The Malay woman now approached the floating figure, and extending her arms towards her with an imperative gesture, whilst she chanted a monotonous invocation to the spirits of the air, gradually drew her subject down to the earth, when, taking her by the hand, she led her to a seat placed opposite the fire and within a circle traced on the ground. From this point she commenced a series of invocations to the spirits of the elements, during which she kept incessantly pacing round and round, including the altar, the fire, and the lady in her gyrating path, feeding the fire and braziers meanwhile with essences, which continued to dispense their aromatic and pungent odors through the chamber.

To those Spiritualists who may have been accustomed to behold mediums floating in air in the midst of the commonplaces that ordinarily prevail at modern spirit circles, such phenomena may occasion no surprise, nor will the above recital convey the slightest idea of the weird and ghastly effect which this scene produced. The gloom and antique solemnity of the rock-hewn cavern; the strange aspect of the fetish objects which surrounded us; the wild, almost demoniac appearance of the crouching fakirs, and the half-frenzied mistress of the rites; but above all, the preternatural appearance of the white-robed ecstatic, whose suspension in air, baffling all the known laws of nature, must have been the effect of powers unknown and incomprehensible, or else the action of invisible beings no less terrible than the sorceress whom they aided.

All this was so new and startling to Graham that I could not feel surprised when he—as brave a soldier as ever drew sword—stood grasping my hand, whilst his own was as cold as death, and trembling like an aspen leaf, as he leaned for support on my shoulder.

The following words form a rough translation of the first verse, which the sibyl chanted, as she paced round and round in her magic circle: —

" O beauteous creature of Fire,
   Endow this mortal with thy ardor!
   Let the flame of her life draw all creatures to her feet in worship !
   Let her power consume them
   And burn into dust and ashes all who bend not the knee before her !
   O Spirit of Fire ! Spirit of Heat ! Spirit of Flame ! Spirit of the
      blazing elements ! Hear and be obedient ! "

Three verses addressed to the spirits of the other elements followed, but the ardor of the language and the reckless wickedness which was implied in them, although masked in the synthetical flow of the sweet *Shen Tamil* language, will not endure translation.

When these abominable invocations were ended, a sensation of rocking and quivering followed, which not only pervaded our systems, but seemed to thrill through the whole mass of rock from which the ancient fane was hewn. An indescribable disturbance, too, agitated the air around us. The perception of a sound rather than a sound itself, wailed in our ears, something between a long-drawn sigh and the moaning of the wind. Faint indications of grotesque forms and glittering eyes flitted through the gloomy cavern, lighted as it was only by the dull glare of the fire

28

and braziers, and tongues of flame glinted through the atmosphere everywhere. Those who, like myself, have ever taken part in or witnessed an act of combined Vaudooism and ecstacy like the one I am attempting to describe, will have experienced what both Graham and I felt at the time, namely, an oppression of spirits almost amounting to despair, terrible to realize, but almost impossible to express in words. I have known many travellers in Oriental lands, who, from motives of curiosity or special interest, have attended such scenes, and no matter how unimpressible they may have been by nature, I have never conversed with or heard of one who did not realize something of the same kind of desolation and abandonment of God and the good which possessed us on this occasion.

When the invocations of the Malay woman were ended, she made a profound Oriental salutation to Madame Laval; then crossing her arms upon her breast, she stood like an ebony statue or an impersonation of the spirit of darkness and thus addressed her employer: —

"What more would the daughter of Indra require of her slave? Lo, she is now fairer than Parvati in the eyes of mortals, more powerful than he of the sacred Bull! What more does she demand?"

"Anine!" said the lady in a tone of deeper dejection than I had ever heard her clear tones sinking to before, "Anine, I have already proved your power upon all men but one. He whom alone I love, alone has resisted me; nay more, I know now — oh, too well, too well! — that he actually abhors me."

"He loves another," said the Malay, coldly. "Is not that enough?"

"Hush, hush!" cried the lady, fiercely, "you shall not tell me that, nor do I yet believe it. Listen to me, woman! You have a woman's heart in your breast: that I know, despite your reckless indifference to the woes of others. Is there nothing you can do to help me, — nothing yet left to be tried, Anine?"

Here she poured out a tale of passion so wild and fierce that again my pen halts before the attempt to transcribe her words. Reckless and pitiful, wicked, yet touching, as they were, they afforded terrible evidence of the woe and wreck which human passion can make when once its stormy power is suffered to usurp the throne of reason.

Anine replied, "Have I not confessed to thee, lady, that this master of spirits is stronger than I? I can bring all other men to my feet, but not him. Even now, it seems to me that his influence is upon us; this place is full of him, and he beats down my power as if I thrashed the wind.

"Lady, I have told you there is but one way left by which you can subdue him: *you must hurt him,*—nearly kill his body before you can touch his spirit!"

As she spoke, she advanced to the space behind the altar and withdrew a dark curtain, when we at once discovered the background of the scene. I must confess I was less surprised than my friend, to perceive that this veil had concealed a large, coarse, but well-executed portrait of myself, beneath which was a waxen image, which I had no difficulty in recognizing as also intended to represent me.

Graham started wildly as this exhibition met his eyes. For the first time, as it would seem, the real truth flashed upon his mind; and when the lady, with a mixture of passionate sobs, adjurations, and execrations, began apostrophizing these effigies in language that admitted of but one interpretation, my poor friend's agitation exceeded all bounds, and would certainly have destroyed my power to shield him from discovery, had I not retained a strong grasp upon him.

"Let us go, Chevalier!" he murmured. "For God's sake, let us leave this scene of shame and horror! Is this Vaudooism? Is this what I was about to enter upon with unhallowed purpose and reckless intent? O Heaven, forgive me for my involuntary crime!"

It was useless to try and soothe him, or attempt to detain him longer in a scene of which I well knew he had beheld enough already to effect his perfect restoration to a sense of honor, manliness, and piety. For myself, I knew well enough the nature of the performance that was to ensue. I knew also that whatever it was would fall harmless upon my well-guarded spirit. I have already intimated to my readers, that the success or strength and potency of all magical rites lies in their psychological effect, or the power of mind projected from one individual upon another. Permit me also to recur to the theory so often alluded to in these pages, namely, that all the effect of will or psychological impress depends upon its uninterrupted action. So long as it can reach its subject without the intervention of cross-magnetism or opposing currents it will surely succeed; but when, as in my case, the subject is aware of the work in hand, guarded against it by a stronger will and more potential spiritual power than that of the operator, the spell fails, the potency is overpowered, and the whole attempt is baffled.

According to the conventional ideas upon which tales of fiction are founded, the writers—being in general well-meaning persons, who conceive themselves bound to uphold what they term "the interests of morality" —depict their scenic effects with a view to the "triumph of virtue over vice," hence the Vaudoo workers' power to harm the pure and good should utterly fail. Unhappily the physical and psychological laws of being do not suspend their action in favor of the moral. The pure and pious share the fate of the wicked and blasphemous in the sinking ship or burning house, and the good and sinless parent is just as apt, if not more so, to love the bad and sinful child as the good and pure one.

Blind force is inexorable, whether it be directed in the interests of vice or virtue. Let us not mistake laws for principles. The law of psychological effect is the law of strength, of magnetic potency, of positive and negative reciprocity.

The principles of good and evil operate in circles of an entirely different character; hence the arts of Vaudooism would and could affect the pure and innocent Blanche Dudley, wholly unguarded as she was by any influence strong enough to repel the magnetism to which having once yielded she had become subject. On me this power failed because I was positive to the projector, and was enclosed, moreover, in a circle of influence which she could not penetrate.

As to the intrinsic power of Vaudooism, let me endeavor to define it in the following comments. That wicked spirits both of mortals and elementaries attend such scenes and aid in the effects produced, no well-experienced spiritist can deny; that the strong passion infused into the rites must aid their phenomenal power is equally certain. The rites themselves, the chants, invocations, fumigations, and mock tortures inflicted on pictures, images, and other inanimate objects, are absolutely worthless either for good or harm, save and except as they are instrumental in stimulating the mind of the operators to psychological fury and ecstatic frenzy.

The true potency of all such scenes lies in the motive,
the amount of mental power infused into the work, the
strength of the will with which it is enacted, and the
attraction which it has for evil and mischievous spirits,
who delight to aid mortals in such acts as they themselves are in sympathy with. ·

It may be asked, Where, then, are our good angels,
and why do they not interpose to save us from these dark
and malignant powers? I answer, They are ever near;
potential to aid and prompt to inspire us either to fly from,
or resist the evil; but that they are always successful
the facts of human history emphatically deny. Perhaps
coarse, gross, and material spirits are nearer to earth than
the pure and refined. Whatever be the cause, it is as idle
as injurious to disregard facts for the sake of upholding
a theory of morals which is only valuable when it is
proved to be practical. (Our best safeguard against
evil powers and evil machinations in general, is to
cultivate a pure and innocent nature, which in itself is
a repelling force against evil.)But when that pure and
innocent nature has become the subject of *magnetic influence*, it is imperative for us to deal no longer with moral
but with magnetic laws, and these, as I have frequently
alleged before, act upon principles of their own which
do not regard morals at all. We must adopt the principles of nature as we find them, not as we deem they
ought to be nor as we in our egotism suppose they
will become in deference to our peculiar excellence,
neither must we delude ourselves with the idea that our
ignorance will shield us from dangers we know nothing
about. I have heard many well-meaning people affirm
they were quite safe from all evil influences, etc. etc.,
because they knew nothing about such subjects, deeming their security lay in their ignorance.

In former chapters on the subject of obsession, I have referred to the vast multitude of obsessed persons whose example proves that innocence and ignorance form no protection against the assaults of evil powers. All were attacked indiscriminately without any reference to their knowledge or ignorance of their state. Sweet young children, innocent and ignorant enough to illustrate this position, frequently become the subjects of obsession, and I could cite innumerable cases wherein good and pure women have fallen victims to the arts of base-minded psychologists, whilst far less worthy persons, aware of their danger, have escaped.

(The true safeguard against all occult influence of an adverse or malignant character, is an understanding of its nature and existence, the laws that govern it and the means of thwarting and overruling its effects.) It may be very satisfactory to remain in ignorance of the fact that the midnight marauder is prowling around our doors, provided he takes no advantage of our fancied security to break in upon us, but when we are aware of his presence and our liability to danger from his incursions, we shall be able to guard against him without any proviso.

KNOWLEDGE IS POWER, IGNORANCE IS IMBECILITY. It is for this reason that I would induce all truly philosophical thinkers to investigate the occult, and study out in the grand lyceum of nature's laws, the various sources of good and evil influences by which we are constantly surrounded and constantly affected. Were mankind once aware of its danger in this, as in every other direction, it would be proof against it.

The limitations of time and space forbid my enlarging upon this subject further. It is enough to know what all mankind will sooner or later realize, namely, that WILL is the sovereign potency ruling creation for good or evil; and until we educate the race in the knowledge, use, and abuse of psychology, we shall continue to sin and suffer, become the victims of blind forces which are continually operating upon us whether we know it or not, filling the lunatic asylums with subjects obsessed by evil spirits, the prisons with imbeciles impressed with the contagion of criminal propensities, and the home, with immoral men and women, laboring under the epidemic of evil passions, infused into their natures by the very atmosphere they breathe.

Knowledge and science to the rescue! The knowledge of occultism and the science of soul!

CHAPTER XXIV.

THE day at length arrived preceding that fixed for the departure of Lady Blanche Dudley from Calcutta.

Early in the morning I rode over to the viscount's country house to communicate my final arrangements to Blanche, and inquire how I could still further contribute to her comfort. The poor girl perfectly well understood that I was the cause of her banishment, in fact she had so informed me; but she only thanked me for my frater-nal care, and assured me in her own gentle way that she was confident I had studied her best interest and happi-ness, and that she was quite willing to go.

Throughout this interview there was a dreamy, ab-stracted manner about her which strangely troubled me. It was not coldness nor absence, but a sort of duality, if I may use the term, which made me feel as if it were not Blanche who addressed me, but her spirit or the spirit of another speaking through her. When I addressed her she listened, but apparently to some one else, not me; and in her answers there was a halting, incompre-hensible air of distance which perplexed and pained me inexpressibly.

With a view of arousing her from this lost condition, I separated some of the flowers I had brought her and attempted to arrange them, as I had frequently done before, with the simple fondness I should have mani-

fested for a cherished sister, amongst her beautiful
ringlets; but for the first time in our lives I believe,
she repelled me, and shrinking from me like a startled
fawn, she waved her hand in farewell, and darted out
of the apartment, nor did she again return whilst I remained at the villa. Like all individuals susceptible of
spirit influence or psychological impressions, I am compelled to acknowledge myself to be a creature of moods,
for which I am not always prepared to render, even to
myself, any sufficient explanation. That night I knew
the impress of a strange and occult power was upon
me. An unconquerable restlessness possessed me, peo-
pling every lonely place with unendurable visions, yet
compelling me to withdraw from all human companionship. Towards midnight I became weary of wandering through the gardens and over the terraces of my
own residence, and wayworn and wretched as I felt, but
without any clew to analyze or control my miserable
sensations, I retired to my own chamber, determined to
try if by fastening my attention on a mass of accounts
and other details of a business character, I could conquer the occult influences that beset me. All would not
do, however. I could neither write, read, or even sit
still. Again I re-entered the gardens of the once splendid, though now ruinous old villa I inhabited, and
walked about, without aim, purpose, or relief, until I
was foot-sore and weary. At length I returned to my
dozing attendants, who were waiting up for me. Almost as much aggravated by the presence of these poor,
patient drudges, as I was angry with myself for impos-
ing upon them, I hastily dismissed them and prepared
to retire for the night, determined to compel the sleep I
longed for, yet dreaded. When I was but half undressed, the same restless fit returned upon me, and the

same sense of a nameless, formless presence haunted
me. Then, as ever in my experience, I found that when
the mind is most disturbed, the lucidity of the spirit is
most obscured. One of the earliest lessons of initiation
I had to learn for the attainment of high spiritual exaltation, was self-control and the entire subjugation of all
exciting impulses, passions, or emotions. I had been
taught, and now believe, that the highest grades of
spiritual power, require for their achievement, a life of
complete abstinence, chastity, and, as before stated, the
subjugation not only of the passions, but even of the
social affections, tastes, and appetites. To be the perfect master of one's self, is the first necessary preparation
for mastery over others, or the attainment of that complete condition of mental equilibrium in which Nature,
with all her realms of occult unfoldment, becomes subject to the power of the adept. Naturally impulsive,
passionate, and emotional, I know I should never have
succeeded in attaining to the conditions of spiritual exaltation I aimed at, had I not inherited by nature those
gifts of the spirit, which I had not passivity enough to
earn by culture. Still, I had labored faithfully through
the probationary exercises enjoined upon me. Already
I had succeeded in a thousand self-conquests that few
young men of my age could have accomplished, and it
was only at very rare intervals now, that poor fallible
human nature triumphed over the acquired stoicism of
the adept. The present occasion however, witnessed
one of those mental defeats for which I had before paid
many penalties. At length I determined that my wisest
course was not to exhaust myself any further by maintaining the spiritual warfare that was distracting me.
" Let the powers of evil do their worst," I mentally
exclaimed, " I will heed them no more."

Throwing myself on my bed, half undressed as I was, I fell asleep almost as soon as my head touched the pillow, nor did I awake again until the moon was low in the heavens, and the stars were beginning to pale; then, and not till then, I awoke suddenly, disturbed by a noise I could not at first distinguish the nature of. With heavy, half-closed eyes I lay still, waiting for a repetition of the disturbance. It came in the sound of a low sob, — a sob of woe, a sound so plaintive and heart-rending that I shuddered as I listened. Again and yet again, this piteous moan resounded in my ears. It was no dream; I soon became convinced it was a reality; that it came from the terrace outside my room, was approaching nearer and nearer, and was now mingled with another sound, namely, that of a very light, but slow footstep on the veranda. The next moment a white, fleecy form passed through the open glass doors of my chamber, and bare-headed, except for the profusion of golden curls that fell around her neck and shoulders, in a floating white evening dress, soiled, torn, and trailing as if dragged through brambles and stony places, appeared the bending, wayworn form of the hapless Blanche Dudley. One glance sufficed to show me there was no speculation in those fixed but lustrous eyes which looked straight forward, staring, yet heart-broken, into vacancy. Her beautiful face was deathly pale, she walked like one in a deep sleep, with a stately onward motion; yet her little feet halted, and were evidently cut and bruised, for her white shoes were torn and stained with blood. Her hands hung drooping by her side. In her bosom were placed the flowers I had that day brought her; but except for the white gauze evening dress she wore, she had no shelter from the chill night air, more chill at that season of the year and hour of the night, than is often experienced even in northern latitudes.

As she passed through the open doors of my room, she walked forward with the automatic air of a magnetized subject, until she reached the foot of my bed, when she paused, uttered a low cry, as if she had been suddenly struck, and sank to the ground, where she lay on the lace that shaded the couch, like a mass of newly-fallen snow.

To extricate myself from the enclosing curtains, so arranged as to protect the sleeper from the insects of that tropical land, and raise the white and seemingly lifeless form from the ground, was but the work of a few moments; but even as I held her in my arms, almost paralyzed for the instant with astonishment and dismay, the flash of lights from without streamed into my chamber, and seven or eight Brahmins, who were associated with me in one of the most important occult societies to which I belonged, appeared upon the veranda, some of them deliberately entering the room, others standing without and gazing upon me sternly through the open doors.

" In the name of Heaven," I cried, choking with rage and indignation, "what do you want here, gentlemen? "

" We have come here to convince ourselves that an evil tale we have heard of your unworthiness, Louis de B——, is no slander," said one of the oldest of my visitors, a noble Guroo, to whom, as one of my teachers, I had pledged myself in the most solemn vows to observe for a given time the strictest asceticism in thought, word, and deed.

"What, sir!" I answered indignantly, "have you then the right to enter my private apartments, intrude upon my most sacred hours of retirement, and invade every custom of honor and good-breeding in this fashion?" I had laid the unfortunate lady on a divan as I saw the strangers at my window, and now stood between her and the invaders.

"Louis," said the first speaker, advancing towards me mildly but firmly, "we have been this night informed, that by your arts you have lured away an unfortunate lady from her home, and beguiled her here for her destruction. You know the awful penalties you incur for breaking your vows during the time you have pledged to fulfil them; but even the honor due to our order is as nothing compared to the duty we, as your spiritual fathers, are called upon to perform, when we attempt to save you from the base act with which you are charged."

"Who charges me?" I asked.

"One who is himself a neophyte of our order," answered the Guroo.

"Ferdinand Perrault," said a low voice at my side, and turning hastily round, I saw the shrouded form and cowled head of the Byga, Chundra ud Deen.

Before I could appeal to him, as I knew I could successfully, for aid in my dreadful emergency, he glided quietly up to a group of statues placed in a distant part of the chamber, interspersed with rose-trees and tropical plants, and adding in his low but thrilling voice, "and here is the enchantress," he dragged forward, seemingly by his own volition rather than any force he used, a masked and veiled female, who had up to that moment been concealed amongst the trees and statues. This person the Byga' led forward, obviously with no effort on his part, but with a terrible show of reluctance and terror on hers, until he placed her in the centre of the group that clustered around me. In an instant I had dragged the veil from her head and the mask from her face, discovering, as I was confident I should, the deathly pale yet defiant features of Madame Hélène Laval.

"See how you have wronged me, gentlemen!" I exclaimed passionately. "Here is the demon that has wrought this destruction. Here is the enchantress by whose remorseless arts this unhappy lady, her trusting friend, her warm-hearted defender, her most miserable magnetic subject, has been drawn hither, whilst you have simply been invited to bear witness to the shame and ruin this fiend has planned." Who could doubt or misunderstand further the character of this foul plot? Long before she had any such vile purposes to gain by her arts, Madame Laval had openly boasted of her magnetic control over the hapless Lady Blanche Dudley, and by way of what she called "interesting psychological experiments," she had on several occasions exhibited her power by biologizing the unconscious and innocent victim to her side, when she was at some distance from her. Who could have conceived those powers, which appeared to have been exercised merely in pastime on the one side by an interested student of spiritual science, and on the other by a pure, unsuspecting, and loving-hearted friend, could thus have been turned to the base design of destroying that friend's peace of mind and honorable name, to say nothing of the shame and disgrace intended to fall upon me.

Had I been sufficiently composed to have noted the details of the sad scene in which I was engaged, I could not have failed to remark the extraordinary palsy of fear or mental subjugation that had fallen on the once commanding Hélène. She stood with eyes glaring fury and defiance, yet vainly striving to protest her innocence. A spell stronger than her own over-powered her, and so long as the clasp of the shrouded Byga was on her arm she could only glance fiercely from one to the other of those who surrounded her without being able to utter an intelligible sentence. As to the Brahmins, they knew and really trusted me. My kind friend, Nanak Rai, was one of their party, and my little fakir, Nazir, flitted from one to another, explaining to them who this new intruder on the scene really was, and the arts she had practised with his sister Anine, for the express purpose of subduing me and injuring the poor innocent lady.

" This is all my sister's work," cried the little fakir impetuously. " Alas, alas! that ever the blood of Nazir Sahib should flow in the veins of so base a *Chandala!* But O my fathers! " he cried, suddenly starting into a new passion and gesticulating towards the gardens with frantic energy, " there is still worse woe in store for the innocent ones. Hide the poor lady, Chevalier! Hide her, if you value her life! Yonder comes her proud uncle, led on by that base-born son of a Sudra, Perrault. See where they come with torches in search of the absent lady, whom Perrault well knows is to be found in this fatal place. We are too late! " he added, dropping into the background. " The enemy is upon us." He was right, for before any of us could recover from the shock his disclosures occasioned, the Viscount R——, accompanied by Perrault, and a nephew of his, who happened to be visiting at the house when the absence of the unfortunate Lady Blanche was discovered, entered the apartment from the gardens without. Lady Blanche had, as I afterwards learned, been missing since ten o'clock that evening.

Knowing how fond she was of rambling through the

gardens by moonlight, the domestics had been despatched in every direction to seek and recall her. Hour after hour passed away in fruitless search, and it was about an hour after midnight, and just as the infamous Perrault knew that his sister's horrible scheme must be on the eve of accomplishment, that he appeared before the viscount, simulating haste and an eager desire to serve an afflicted family, with the terrible tidings that he had beeen informed by the famous Vaudoo woman, Anine, that I, "the Chevalier de B——," had been working charms to entice the hapless girl to my residence, and that she was in all probability there even at that very moment. When this piece of intelligence was first communicated to the proud nobleman, the tale-bearer had nearly lost his life for his pains, so infuriated did the viscount become at what he deemed a shameful slander; but when Perrault had succeeded in evading his first explosion of wrath, and reiterated again and again the truth of his assertions, the viscount called upon his nephew, who was then on a visit at his house, for advice and aid. It was agreed between them that Perrault should be their prisoner, and either make good his words or pay the penalty of their utterance. They compelled him, therefore, to enter the carriage with them, in which they drove off, with a speed inadequate to satisfy their frantic impatience, to my residence.

Such were the circumstances that complicated the scene of misery which surrounded me on that fatal night. I believe it was to the preternatural power of the Byga, and the steady, calm friendship of Nanak Rai, that I owed the preservation of my senses throughout those trying hours; certainly it was due to the latter's humanity and firm control over me that Madame Hélène Laval and her infamous brother escaped from my hands

with their lives. It was also to the Brahmin's force of
character, commanding presence, and clear, straightforward explanation that I owed my own life, which the
viscount was determined to sacrifice the moment he
found that the unfortunate Lady Blanche was in my
chamber.

"Be still, all of you," said the good man, "and listen
to the story I have to tell." He then, in simple, earnest
language, gave the sum of my fakir's narrative; a con-
cise but scathing description of the arts practised by
Madame Laval, and a glowing account of myself,
and my incapacity, as he steadily affirmed, for the base
part attributed to me. He dared Madame Laval or her
brother to controvert his statements; and when both
these wretched and baffled plotters were silent, he
pointed as the climax of his evidence, to the unfortunate girl, who, still under the spell of the somnambulic
trance, lay extended on the divan where I had placed
her. Putting me gently aside as I stood by to guard
her, — the only poor act of reparation I could now
make, — this kind and true gentleman, who was also a
well-skilled magnetizer, took her tenderly by the hand,
and set her on her feet, still unconscious as she was, in
our midst.

Her forlorn and wayworn appearance, her torn dress,
blood-stained shoes, dishevelled curls, and the indescribable aspect of woe and innocence that marked those set
and rigid features, the soiled and fluttering rags of her
fleecy evening dress, and the fact that the hapless girl
had been dragged for more than seven long miles
through a rough country during a chill night, and
amidst dangers that froze the blood to reflect upon, —
all these circumstances combined, had the effect which
the wise pleader expected they would. The viscount

turned aside his head, and buried his face in his hand-kerchief; the good Brahmins murmured words of pity; and even the ruthless enchantress was moved, and hid her face from the sight of her much-wronged victim in the folds of her veil. At that moment a strange phenomenon appeared amongst us.

Above that young, sunny head, so beautiful, yet so touching in its innocence and desolation, appeared what seemed to be at first, a little glimmering light, a spark no larger than a fire-fly, which might have been imprisoned in her golden curls; but presently it increased in size, expanded and diffused into a luminous, misty halo, which increased in extent and brilliancy until it formed a complete coronet of glory above and around the beautiful somnambulist's head.

I know not what may have been the experience of others. I have frequently heard the spiritists since then describe the beauty of the spirit lights they have seen and the variety of the modes in which these luminous appearances were made visible. I only know that never before or since have I beheld any phenomenon of this kind, so directly in contact with a mortal, never any sign of angelic presence and guardianship that produced upon the witnesses so deep, reverent, and hallowing an influence. In the midst of the hush which ensued as this phenomenon became perfected, the good Brahmin said in his gentlest accents, "Blanche, my child, what brings you here? Answer as if you were in the presence of your God."

"*She is* in the presence of her God, Brahmin," replied the entranced lips of Blanche, though the voice and accent was that of another. "Her spirit is with the angels, and a stronger than her shall answer you. There is the cause of her coming," and as she spoke, she advanced with a stately step towards the veiled figure of Hélène, who was still held firmly by one of the Brahmins, — *for the Byga was gone.* With an authoritative gesture she threw back Madame Laval's veil, and then said in a deep and searching tone, "Answer, Hélène de Laval. Why have you brought hither Blanche Dudley? By what power and for what purpose? Answer! for you are in the presence of your God!" There was not an individual there who did not experience a thrill of awe as that slight creature, now seemingly a tall and stately presence, stood like an accusing angel, encircled by a halo of divine light, confronting her evil genius.

"What have I done?" murmured the dark-browed sibyl, the psychological spell evidently becoming reversed, and the frail subject commanding the operator.

"Speak the truth, Hélène, and answer!" repeated the beautiful ecstatic in a voice that made her enemy shudder.

"I lured her hither by my power of will," muttered the sibyl, as if each word were wrung from her by tortures.

"For what purpose?" thundered the viscount. "Answer that, foul enchantress!"

But Hélène heard him not; she was wholly in the power of one magnetizer, and under that spell she had no senses for any other. The hand of the somnambulist was laid on her arm and she was enthralled.

"For what purpose?" repeated Blanche, turning with mild dignity upon the viscount. "Can you ask? Know you not she purposed to destroy the name and fame of her victim?"

"Let her confess it, then," said one of the Brahmins, fiercely.

"Enough has been said to right the wrong and clear

the innocent," answered the sleeper, with inexpressible sweetness and command. "Vengeance is mine, saith the Lord, I will requite;" then releasing the arm of Madame Laval, she clasped her own fair hands together, and raising her eyes to heaven with an ecstatic expression impossible to describe, she murmured, "Forgive us our trespasses as we forgive them that trespass against us!"

The halo then gradually faded from her head. Nanak stretched out his arms to receive her, as a father would have sheltered his child; then raising her as if she had been an infant, at a sign from me he carried her through the glass doors, and down to where the viscount's carriage waited below. It was then that, as if moved by a burst of honest indignation which would no longer endure repression, the fakir Nazir exclaimed, "She is a hard and cruel woman that!" pointing to Hélène, who stood confronting us all with an expression of the fiercest rage and hardihood.

"She deserves the reprobation of men as well as the judgments of Bramah. I know not how far she may have come with her poor victim, but I saw her riding in her carriage over the rough roads and stony paths, whilst the sweet young lady, in her unsheltered garments and her little feet torn and bleeding, toiled on behind her. She went on like one in her sleep, ever straight forward, over rough ways and smooth, whilst yon woman leaned from her carriage-window, and beckoned to her with her hand, and mocked her with her mouth, and laughed and jeered at her. I heard her cry, 'Faster, my gay bird! Come on faster, faster yet! I am guiding you to your bridegroom, my pretty piece of purity, and we'll have a fine wedding before the stars are set; and many a one shall hear how the fine Lady

Blanche Dudley offered herself to an unwilling lover before another sun has set upon her dishonored head.'"

I dashed my hand over the fakir's mouth and bade him be silent or I would call him to account for not rescuing her. Some of the Brahmins then took a kind leave of me, whilst others remained to offer me service. Leaving the detested brother and sister in their charge, and the fakir engaged in telling his story to the viscount, I went out to seek Nanak, whom I found standing at the carriage-window, speaking in his own kind, fatherly way, words of cheer and consolation to the now awakened lady, who was weeping bitterly. Gently pushing him aside I sprang into the carriage, and taking a seat by her side, with my arms closely folded round her, I whispered, "The day has dawned, my Blanche; the day that is to see you leave not for your father's, but for your husband's home.

"Let your maids attire you in your simplest, whitest robe, my Blanche. Let them smooth these poor, disordered tresses, and place in them the sweet white flowers I will send you, and at eight o'clock to-night I will be with you, and in the face of friends and enemies you shall give me a husband's right to shield you henceforth from every harm that may befall so long as you and I do stay in life on earth." A few more whispered words of cheer and promise, and then I left her.

"Your carriage waits you, madame," I said to the now closely-veiled form of the woman who encountered me on the threshold of my door. "No words! There is your place."

I saw my servants hand her in, and then bid the coachman drive her away.

"Not so fast, sir!" I said, as I saw her brother hastening after the carriage, which he tried to detain.

"Let me go!" he screamed, as I seized and dragged him back. "You wouldn't murder me, would you? Help!" he shouted. "I am being strangled, murdered!"

"What would you do, Louis?" exclaimed Nanak, vainly trying to extricate the struggling wretch from my grasp. "Let him go, I say! You shall not steep your soul in sin for such a worm as that. Nay, I command you by a word you *must* obey!" ·

The word was spoken and I was disarmed.

"I'll have a reckoning with him yet," I muttered, all the Hindoo in my veins rising against the wretch upon whom I had resolved to avenge his own no less than his sister's villany. At this moment the viscount and his nephew joined the Brahmin in pleading for the poltroon's escape.

, Contenting myself for the present with hurling him amongst the bushes and rank weeds of the garden, I bid him remember, my hour of full requital was yet to come.

That night, at eight o'clock, saw me the husband of sweet, pure, innocent Blanche Dudley. Her haughty uncle was well satisfied, and her own loving, guileless heart leaped with the purest joy she had ever known on earth. As to me, I bid farewell to my hopes of life amongst the stars, to the mysteries of the occult, my dreams of spiritual exaltation, and all my wanderings in the realms of supernal glory.

Hopes and aspirations,—all were dashed to the earth, and I set myself lovingly, tenderly to fulfil the life of new duties that honor and compassion had thrust upon me.

CHAPTER XXV.

IT was just nine years from the time when I parted with the excellent friend whom I still delight to call by the familiar name of John Cavendish Dudley, that I became the husband of his most beloved and cherished youngest daughter. I knew that this event would fulfil the dearest wishes of himself and his amiable wife, but when I parted from him and listened to his pathetic lamentation that he might never hope to call me his son, little did I think that I should return to him in the very character he so earnestly desired me to fill.

I had resolved to spend the year which succeeded my marriage in closing up every engagement that could bind me to the land of my birth. For eight months I spent my time partly in these arrangements and partly in the effort to embellish the life of the sweet and loving creature I had taken to my arms, if not entirely to my heart. Heaven knows how completely she deserved the devotion of heart, life, and all that life could give, in return for the sinless nature and undivided affection she laid upon the altar of her young heart's idolatry!

I had planned our departure for the close of our marriage year. It was all one to Blanche, — anywhere with me. To follow the movement of my finger, or anticipate the glance of my eye, made up the sum of her life's occupation; yet she was no mere automatic companion. Her bright intellect and vivid imagination might have far eclipsed her wayward husband's, had not her passionate admiration for him and her modest diffidence of herself, kept her own brilliant powers of mind in abeyance.

Eight months had passed away, when duties of an urgent and personal nature demanded my presence in a distant province. My fair bride had scarcely quitted my sight since our marriage, yet now it was impossible for me to escape this journey, equally impossible that she should accompany me. The hated enemies to whom, if I owed them anything but abhorrence, I owed the precious boon of my little girl's companionship, had never appeared on the panorama of our lives since the momentous night described in the last chapter; indeed, I had not even heard of them, save a report that Madame Hélène had become a devotee to a new sect of religionists just arisen in the land, and that her scoundrel brother had succeeded in worming himself into a good official position. The very names of these people were tabooed in my household and amongst all who visited us; indeed, we saw but few persons who could remind us of them, for the circle in which my own and my Blanche's relatives moved were closed against them. No cloud dimmed the lustre of those sweet blue eyes, ever fixed on me with an expression of mute adoration.

No sorrow had ever stained that blooming face with one tear, since the night when I called Blanche my own. Her aunt and uncle were very proud of her, and constantly urged us to spend our time with them, but she loved her husband's home better than any place on earth; and to care for the flowers I admired, arrange my books, statues, paintings, or make the old ruinous villa I rented, ring with the music of her delightful voice or the thrilling chords of her plaintive harp, was happiness enough for Blanche.

My fakirs often entertained her with their wondrous feats of incomprehensible art, and even those apathetic ascetics would raise their dull heads and smile, or their veiled eyes would light up with gleams of pleasure, as they heard the ringing laugh of the bright fairy, or the merry sound of her little hands as she clapped them in wondering admiration at their *tours de force.*

She had many living pets also amongst odd birds and stray animals whom she coaxed into companionship with her. She tooked great delight in "educating" them, as she called it, and talked to them as if they understood her. I think they did, and listened to her childish wisdom and womanly play with as much solemn admiration as did any or all the dependents who approached her.

But what did all this lead to? Let me turn again the pages of the only record that remains to tell how the last act was played out. That record is her own journal, written evidently with a prophetic view of how it would some day be needed, and how it would become a silent witness of the tale no human lips have ever spoken. I found it in the loneliness of a cold and empty room from which the life had fled and the sunshine died out; when the ringing laugh was hushed, the wonderful voice silent, and the harpstrings run down or snapped forever. The extracts that relate to the crisis of which I am now writing ran thus: —

"*Jan. 10, 18*—. O mother, mother, how I wish you could see me now! Dearest sisters, would you not almost envy me? I do believe you would, just a little, — though all the time you would rejoice for me, for I am sure you used to admire that 'magnificent Chevalier,'

as we were accustomed to call him, almost as much as I
did when he was amongst us at N——. But O my
mother and sisters! what is the admiration which you
and I and every one else must feel for my Louis, compared to the love which moves my heart, not because
he is so handsome, but because he is *himself,* and O
Heaven! because he is so good and kind and dear to
me! How could I fail to love him? And yet I think you
would laugh to see what a little creature I am, when I
take his arm and try to look dignified and keep pace
with him as we enter Uncle Frederick's *salon,* or go to
the numerous receptions we have to attend. Louis is
so tall and stately and splendid, whilst as to me, I am—
no matter what. *He* says I am a "little sprig of summer
and winter; a snow-flake and a rose-bud in one," and
only just fit to stick in his button-hole. But ah, my
mother! I wish you were near me just now. Shall I
ever see you more, — ever, ever tell you how much better I have understood what mother's love is within the
last few months? I know not. Aunt Emily tells me
all young creatures, when they hover on the wonderful
verge of the *new path,* the path that reaches heaven
through the life of a new-born being, all tremble and
shrink, and fear to enter upon that awful responsibility,
and think they cannot live to go through with the
mighty change. I have no fear; on the contrary, I
have sometimes a hope, a strange, unnatural hope perhaps; it is that my good and noble Louis, my generous
husband, who never was my lover, only my friend and
protector, — that he will be released again, and become
free to follow the lead of his towering mind and lofty
inspirations. I know not! I have written these words
before, and feel now as if they were not true, for I do
know; I know that in the midst of all my great joy,

there is ever a strange dimness upon me. Even when
my Louis hides me away in his heart, — there where I
am safest and strongest, or when I am looking up into
his splendid eyes, so kind, so true, that everything false
or unholy quails beneath them, even then the dimness
comes, comes between me and the light that sparkles in
the dark eyes of my Louis."

"*Jan. 20.* There is a great secret constantly pressing
upon my mind and ever urging me to confide in him;
yet just as I am on the point of doing so, I see upon
his face that sad, appealing look I have before referred
to, that look which pierces my heart like the eye of Fate,
and seems to plead with me to spare him further sorrow.

" No, I have not the heart to tell him, and don't know
that I shall ever be able to do so, though I think I ought.
Would I could banish the remembrance of it! Perhaps,
if I write about it, it will fade away like the ghost of a
haunting air, which only needs singing to chase it
away. Yes, I will write it down; perhaps it may some
day explain away what is mysterious when — when — I
know not what. — That doubt of the future again!
God's future. Why then should I fear it? But to my
secret.

Just before I met my Louis for the first time in India,
Hélène, she whom I so loved once, and alas! so
tenderly think of still, that Hélène who was then so
very dear to me, so kind, so wise, so strong, — she asked
me for a long curl of my hair. She said it would serve
to bring us together at any time, and I knew it would,
for she proved it and taught me how. When I gave
her leave to cut off that curl, how I shivered, and felt as
if a part of my life had gone out from me; but I did not
mind it then. She asked me afterwards to give her
a locket or something I had worn, to enclose a piece

of the hair in. She was quite particular in asking for something that I had worn, so I gave her a small gold locket that my dearest sister Edith had given me for a keepsake when we were both children. Edith and I have exchanged many presents since then, so I didn't mind parting with this trifle to Hélène, especially as she preferred it to all the other rich jewels I offered her. She had her name engraved upon it, and when she had enclosed a piece of my hair in it, she said my curl outshone the gold it was enclosed in.

That was a compliment worthy of my Chevalier, it was so like the sweet things he says to me; but what he says is always true and like his own noble self, whilst as to Hélène — ah me! I wish she were as true and pure and good as he is. But that unfortunate lock of hair! Oh, how I wish it were back on my head again or in my Louis's keeping! What would he say if he knew that lady still possessed it, besides having another piece in the locket I gave her? But then again she may have lost all interest in me, and forgot that she has such things in her possession, or, having them, the desire to use them may, — nay, *must* have passed away. I am nothing to her now, only a memory; perhaps not even that. Poor Hélène! she had no female friend except me. I do think she loved me once, and sometimes I believe she must miss me. Oh, why could she not continue to love me even though she did love Louis? That is nothing strange, — every one must love him; and as to her, she was so fascinating and in everything so far superior to me, that I should never have been surprised if he had preferred her to me."

"*Feb. 12.* Alas, alas! I know too well now that Hélène remembers that dreadful lock of hair. I fear me, too, she has been tempted to use it for — O Heaven!

how I shudder when I think of it — last night I was gone, I know not where. I am confident I was not sleeping, for I distinctly remember seeing the palm-trees waving in the breeze, and listening to the midnight songs of the boatmen as they floated down the river; and yet I was away somewhere, — away where my Louis could not reach me, away in some terrible imprisonment, in some place where I saw the form of Hélène. I saw, too, that she wore a beautiful India muslin dress embroidered with gold, and that she stood somewhere near me, like a priestess of Valhalla, with her long, waving tresses of raven hair falling around her, crowned with a wreath of bay leaves. I know this scene was not a mere dream. I think it took place in some old temple where I have never been; but O Heaven! this may not be the end of it! Would I had told Louis, but I could not, I could not! Perhaps I shall have courage to do so to-morrow."

"*Feb. 15.* Louis has gone away for three weeks. Louis is gone, and the sunlight has all gone with him. He has explained to me the urgency of the affairs that called him hence, and I knew he ought to go, so I never opposed him or tried to detain him. I knew I ought not to do so. He wished me to go and stay with my aunt, who was very urgent that I should do so; but I pleaded to be allowed to remain here in my happy, happy home, with all my pets round me, and the tracery of my dearest love's presence on every side of me. Oh, I could not go away! I could not leave such a scene, for my aunt's gay home, with so many visitors coming and going all day, and nothing there of Louis except that splendid portrait of him my uncle has had painted, just for every one that comes in to admire, as of course every one does. I know my kind Louis feared to hurt me by opposing my wishes, so he consented to let me stay, but I heard him charging

my aunt so earnestly to come and see me every day, and
besides that he has filled the house with so many attendants, and left so many persons in charge of me, that I am
never alone. This would trouble me a little if I did not
perceive in it fresh evidences of his tender care. I dare
not trust myself to write anything about his absence, but
it is a· wonderful joy to me to know that he will be home
again in three weeks. Three weeks! Ah me! the sun
will shine upon me then, though all is so dark and desolate now."

"*Feb. 19.* Heaven have mercy on me! The worst
has come at last. O misery unutterable! Where shall
I go, what shall I do to escape this awful fate? O
Louis, Louis! where are you and why can you not
realize the shipwreck and woe that has befallen your
unhappy 'fairy'?

"Last night Hélène called me away, dragged my
spirit forth, though she mercifully left my helpless, woeful body sleeping in my bed. Alas, alas! what an
afflicted, captive soul was mine as I stood in her presence, with her dark and dreadful brother by her side,
and all around them a crowd of awful shapes, demons,
or elementaries, I know not which or what! O cruel,
remorseless woman! What have I ever done to deserve
such a dreadful doom? She mocked and taunted me,
told me she could control me, body and soul, and I felt
too well she could.

"I saw my fatal lock of hair, half consumed and
crisped by fire, laying. on an altar that might have been
dedicated to the dark god, Juggernaut. I knew when
I was called; I knew that I must go, for I felt the sharp
sting of the burning lock upon my forehead, and ere I
had time to pray, or call upon thee, my Louis, lo! I was
there. O Heaven, pity me! Angels of mercy, help me!

There is still so much left of that fatal lock of hair that I know not how many more times she may summon me, nor when, nor how, those fiendish rites may be exercised again. I have prayed all night and day since then, and believe I am at last a little stronger. To-day a fresh calamity has befallen me. My uncle, who has been so very kind to me, my poor uncle, who seems to have become so fond of me, went up the country some forty miles on official business, and has been seized with malarious fever. My dear, good aunt has been obliged to join him, and I have lent her my best ayah to help her nurse him. I fear Louis would not be pleased if he knew my nurse was gone, because she is so good, so much better a physician than poor, stupid Dr. S——. Why could he not see this morning how worn and sad I was? Alas, no one knows me but Louis, and he is so far away! How lonely and deserted this place appears to be, and oh, the dimness! it has now become quite a thick cloud.

"I believe I could summon Louis if I were to try, and send out this trembling soul of mine to fetch him home, but I know how fearfully sensitive he is, and what terrible pangs he would suffer before he could reach me. No, no! I cannot brave the consequences.

"He has been gone ten days now. A little more than another week, and he will return. I will tell him all then, and I know he will and can save me, at least before my time of trial comes."

"*Feb. 22.* Again, again! Another fearful ordeal! Last night they called me again, and there was none to save me. Surely, surely, God has forgotten me, and good angels have deserted me!"

"*Feb. 25.* Oh, joy, joy! The lock of hair has been restored to me, and now it is burned, consumed in

the fire my Louis calls so sacred, and I am saved, at
least till Louis, returns, and then what power can harm
me? Still, he shall know it all, and I will write it down
just as it happened, so that he may know everything
correctly. Early yesterday morning whilst I was
absorbed in lamentation, wringing my hands, and pray-
ing that Heaven would send me help, who should I see
crossing the veranda and stopping opposite my couch,
with low obeisances, but that dear, good, droll little
fakir, Nazir, the little sprite whom my Louis likes so
well and who made such pleasant entertainment for us
when we were first married.

"I had not seen him for a long time because he has
been away on a pilgrimage, he said; but he had now
returned, and brought with him a pair of those sweet
birds we call in England 'love birds.' He brought
them as a present to me, the precious little ones! He
said they were not half good enough for me. Poor little
Nazir! but I answered him that I thought it was just
like his fatherly care to bring me such a present. Then
the good little fakir asked if he could do nothing else
for me; was I quite sure? no commission that he could
execute, — nothing that madame could think of which
Sahib could do to beguile her loneliness? It seemed
strange that he should linger so; stranger still that
just then I could think of nothing for him to do, though
I knew it would please him so much to be of use to
me, — the kind heart!

"At last I remembered that fatal lock of hair. The
memory of it came upon me like a thunder-cloud just
as I was making friends with my little birds. Then as
it all came back to me, I told Nazir the whole story, and
asked him what I could do until my husband returned
to help me. Good Nazir! he is a man after all, though

30

he is a fakir, and has a heart though he has studied how to encase it in a crust of seeming apathy. He frowned darkly when I mentioned Hélène's name, but when I told him how they had treated me I thought the sparks of fire emitted by his glittering black eyes would have consumed Hélène had she beheld their lurid glare.

"When all was told, he said, literally hissing between his clenched teeth, 'Madame shall have her golden lock again; the sun of my lord's existence shall have the shorn beam restored to her.'

"Oh, how glad I was when I heard these words! I knew that Nazir had done more wonderful things than spiriting away a little lock of hair. At one of my husband's dinner parties, three fakirs caused a whole set of china to walk across the floor, and wait on each member of the company separately; they brought jewels through the air from my aunt's dressing-room, seven miles away, and caused my uncle's cane to leave our house, fly through the air, I suppose, and drop down before the family, as they sat at dinner two miles distant. Oh, I felt sure Nazir could restore my lock of hair. Why did I not think of that before?

"Just one hour ago I went into my dressing-room, and there I saw Granger, my English maid, standing like a statue of fright, bending over something that lay upon the ground just inside the French window. 'Look there, my lady,' she cried, 'what can that be on the ground?'

"I looked and saw what it was in a moment, and requested her quite calmly to pick it up and hand it to me. It was indeed my poor lock of hair, tumbled, soiled, and half-burned; still it was mine, and that was all I cared for; but that was not the only thing there; by the side of the hair lay Hélène's locket! O Nazir!

that was quite wrong, and far exceeded your commission. I never meant that he should have taken that locket away. Why, that is stealing, and a very ugly way of stealing, too! I must have the hair taken out, and Nazir must just spirit the locket back again in the same manner that he abstracted it. I shall be perfectly miserable until it is returned. What an error to commit! I hope he will come to-morrow and enable me to return it before she discovers her loss. If she still perseveres in her wicked designs against me, and finds the hair gone, as hair I know is a very essential part of the dreadful invocation, of course she will resort to the little piece in the locket, and if that is missing too, I don't know what she may think."

"*Feb. 24.* The whole day has passed, and that tiresome Nazir has not made his appearance. I feel so safe and composed now that I have my lock of hair again, that I can afford to be a little troubled about the locket. Still I wish my good, kind little fakir would come. I cannot rest till that fatal jewel is out of my possession. It seems to cast such an evil spell upon me that I cannot shake off its effects. No! not though I am holding in my hand another precious letter from the star of my existence. Sweet, fragrant leaves are between the pages, but oh, how much more fragrant is the aroma of goodness and protective care and kindest sympathy that breathes through these precious lines! He is coming home soon, and says, home is where I am. Oh, thank Heaven he is coming! Would he were here now! How coldly the stars gleam upon me to-night; and I have a strange fancy, as I look at them, that they seem to be calling me away. This old house is full of sounds, but I never feared them till to-night. Hark! there's another string of my poor harp gone. No, surely it is a hand wandering amidst the strings! Can it be a hand? Perhaps it is only the night breezes. How they sigh and moan amongst the tall palms!˙ They sound like the rushing winds of our own Scottish moors rather than the balmy breathings of a tropic land. If there are spirits of the air abroad this night, they are calling me hence, for surely I hear my name sounding amongst the tree-tops. There it is again! *Blanche, Blanche! come home!* Who is it that calls? Home is where my Louis is. Oh, will they take me from him? . . . Granger has just been here to inquire whose voices were singing in my chamber. Poor girl! how terrified she was when I could not answer her. My people creep about the house and look so strangely upon me. There is a mortal fear upon them all to-night, and I can not now sustain and cheer them as I used to do when I was a gay girl at home. How calm I was when my Louis slept so long, that all around thought him dead but me, and I crept to his side and gazed upon him, and thought how beautiful he looked. I wish I could recall the courage of those days now. Hark! some one is pacing my chamber. Who can it be? Now the footsteps die away, and — now some hand is on my harp again. That is not the wind; those chords resound beneath a master's touch. O Heaven! what a sad and mournful˙ strain that was. Who could the player be? O spirits of the solemn stars; bright planetary angels! You who know so well, and love my Louis, — oh, protect and guard him! And if it is thy will, Father of spirits, return him to this sad and lonely heart of mine ere I go hence! Louis, my Louis, star-beam of my soul! would thou wert with me now! Good-night, dear love, good-night."

CHAPTER XXVI.

"Good-night, dear love, good-night!" This was the last entry in that journal wherein a pure and innocent heart had poured out in every line the treasures of an unrequited love; in which such mines of unwrought gold were opened up to the gaze of the shipwrecked man, who only realized their true value at the moment when he was to behold them all sinking in the ocean of a vanished past.

Her diary ends with those words of tender farewell, and to me has fallen the task of finishing up the history. I have set myself this work to do for a special purpose, and painful as it is I must fulfil it.

Since the night when I determined to devote myself to the care and protection of John Dudley's child, I had silently but resolutely abandoned my pursuit of the occult, my association with the various societies with which I had been connected, and all that formerly fascinated me and filled my soul with spiritual light and knowledge. I felt that the new duties I had voluntarily incurred, must not be divided with the old pursuits, and whilst I could not overcome the bitter disappointment I felt at being thus shut out from the realms of the unseen, in communion with which I had lived from boyhood, I never faltered in my purpose. I knew then and still believe, that the devotion so absolutely required to attain to the highest good in any condition of life admits of no compromise or divided interests. To stifle my heart's yearnings for the spiritual in which my whole being had been bound up, I plunged into the cares of public life, the duties of home, and the entertainment of my sweet bride, as if I had never known any other aims or employments. I devoted myself, moreover, to all those materialistic occupations with a restless and untiring energy which left me no time to think.

I accompanied my young wife and her friends to all the various scenes which I thought would interest them, and although I permitted my fakirs to amuse them with feats of occult art, I never took part in them, or suffered myself for one moment to brood over my altered career. This abandonment of my past life's dearest aspirations cost me many a pang, but I never thought my fairy understood this until I read her precious confidences to herself, and that at a time when all chance of changing the tide of her regrets was at an end.

During my enforced absence from her, I began to realize the monitions of my true nature crowding in upon me again. Visions haunted my pillow, voices sounded in my ears, and the fluttering wings of other worlds of being stirred the air around me. I steadily resisted these phenomena up to one dreadful night, when a vision of such intense horror flitted before me, that I was compelled to spring from my bed, dress hastily, and spend the rest of the night pacing the streets ere I could regain peace of mind and composure. The next night and the next, witnessed a recurrence of the same horrible representations, and on each occasion they forced upon my mind the conviction that what I beheld was the reflex of an actuality, not the mere distorted images of an unquiet vision. I saw, or seemed to see, my fair young bride dragged before an altar, where a scene of "black magic" was being enacted, and the forms of Hélène Laval and her infamous brother were the presiding demons of the foul rites. I could almost hear the voices of these remorseless fiends mocking, insulting, and taunting my gentle wife, whilst I, a bound and helpless captive, stood looking on in vacant imbecility.

At first I regarded these representations as the result of an overstrained condition of mind, but at length their resistless force made their recurrence unendurable, and I was compelled to accept their spectral imagery as visions of prophetic if not of present reality. Spirit voices, too, — the spirits of those I had known and loved, but whom I had abandoned, whilst I sullenly complained that in thickening the mists of my destiny upon me they had abandoned me — now sounded in my ears, and in tones like muttering thunder, tones that could not be mistaken, insisted on being heard. They assured me of their constant love and untiring affection; pointed out to me the impossibility of their interference to alter my fate or change the purposes of the Infinite; they reminded me that whilst they could neither make nor mar the scheme in which the Creator had spun the woof of every living creature's destiny on an immutable plan, they were still commissioned to dispense in angelic ministry the strength which would enable me to bear the shafts of affliction and the wisdom which must overrule all things for good. They would be heard; they would enclose me in their arms of love; and in the names of those I had known and trusted on earth I was bidden to arise from my attitude of rebellion·against the power of the spirits, and when I

bent my stubborn soul and once more leaned in submission upon them, I was warned to depart for my
home, to ride for life and death, by day and night, not
to pause or linger, but hasten to her to whom I had
been given as her earthly protector; to her whom I
could not save from an inevitable fate, though I might
share it with her and help her to endure it.

The constant echo of my present life, is a hymn of
thankfulness that I did at last listen to these spirit
voices and obey them.

Summoning my servants around me I distributed to
each his task. Like the pilgrims of the ancient pass-
over, we each fulfilled the duties I marked out with a
speed which admitted of no let or hinderance. When
all my arrangements were completed, I set out on my
journey alone, and partly by train, partly on horseback,
travelled two hundred miles to Calcutta, with an urgent
haste that increased every instant as I neared the city.
The last twenty miles I rode, in the heat of a scorching
day, on horseback. The train which I might have
taken, had I waited, would not leave till night, but the
impetuous eagerness to which I had worked myself up,
would have urged me to go on foot, had I been unable
to hire horses to carry me. As it was, I had to change
them every hour, for I loved and pitied the noble animals
and would not for worlds have subjected them to the
heat and toil of a journey, the hardships of which
seemed to have lost all effect upon me. As I rode on,
the voices deepened to the roar of a torrent in my ears,
and the shadows of impending fate closed down so
thickly upon me that I could see nothing but my little
girl, forlorn, wayworn, and broken-hearted, just as I
had beheld her on the dreadful night when the spell of
the foul enchantress lured her to my home.

Five miles from the city, a little, dusty, wayworn figure threw itself before my horse and with much difficulty succeeded in stopping my headlong career. It was the fakir Nazir; he would speak, he *must*, he said, speak with me, and as he leaned breathless against my panting horse, he poured out a horrible, an almost incredible story. My wife, my fair and gentle wife, that delicately nurtured lady who had never known any ruder shelter than the luxurious homes of her father and husband, was in a common prison, thrown there under charge of stealing a gold locket from Madame Hélène Laval. The shocking tale, poured out amidst tears — ay! actually tears from those unused eyes that had never wept before — was this. He told me how at the lady's supplication he had spirited away her fatal lock of hair, but finding that another portion of this precious talismanic curl was enclosed in a gold locket, and fearing that if this remained, the base enchantress would still torment her victim, he had rashly added that paltry jewel to the abstracted lock.

It would seem that the loss of these means to work injury, was realized almost immediately. Madame Laval, who no doubt suspected the nature of the arts as well as the source by which she was thus baffled, sent for a *Chulah*, and by means of one of these singular and expert conjurers, a "magic ball" was set in motion, which she was assured would travel on, and, followed by the conjurer, never stop until it reached the place where the lost jewel was to be found. Nazir rightly conjectured this explanation of the mode in which it was ascertained that the lost locket was in my house. He had met the operator, he said, who confessed to him there was some power which prevented his crossing my threshold, at which point the magic ball became suddenly arrested. The fact that it was traced thus far, however, must have been sufficient for the plotters, who availed themselves of this clew to follow out the rest of their hellish plan.

What I afterwards learned let me here state in brief. The vile brother and sister knew I was far away from my hapless wife. They doubtless suspected the power by which the unfortunate lady had obtained possession of the missing locket, and convinced by their magician's art that it was still in my house, they secretly and swiftly executed their direful plan of vengeance.

By aid of an immense bribe and the civic influence possessed by Perrault, the remorseless wretches first obtained a warrant to search my house, where the missing locket was immediately discovered; they then proceeded to arrest my hapless girl, my little sinless fairy, the high-born Lady Blanche, and actually removed her to a common felon's prison, before, as I have since had reason to believe, the city magistrates or any officials, save a set of hired, bribed, and remorseless myrmidons, knew aught of the shameful transaction.

It was not until night of that same fatal day, the fakir added, that he, who had been out of the city, returned to find the woe and wreck his indiscretion had occasioned. Graham, the viscount, all my friends were absent or not to be found till night. My servants scattered themselves in every direction to seek for help, but none of them really understood the facts of what had happened until Nazir returned and in frantic self-accusation ran from place to place, rousing my friends and telling his shocking story. Still the night had to elapse before aid and rescue could be procured, and then — it came too late, too late!

What the miserable and insane persecutors expected

to effect by their daring act, none can say. They must have known that the entire community would rise against them, and their horrible act of vengeance recoil on themselves with crushing force. As it was, they were so swift in their work, and kept it so silent and secret for many hours, that it was not until the fakir's return, that the tidings became noised abroad, and rescue could be obtained. The viscount and his lady were at length reached, the magistrates apprised of the horrible plot, and my entire circle of friends aroused by the indomitable energy and remorse of the unhappy Nazir. Friends and officials alike had hastened to the prison to release the unfortunate girl. Why she was still there and could not be removed, alas, alas! I too well knew. I could hear no more; indeed, I knew nothing more until I reached the city, and my servants crowded round me with assistance, for the horse I rode, fell at the gate of my own house, — my house all void and empty now! How I reached the prison I know not, or how, or whether, the darkness that fell around my way was in the air or in my own dim eyes.

Every gate was opened, and many hands were outstretched to me as I made my way from point to point and passed gloomy cells and through damp, dark passages. Fit resting-place for my fairy bride! Meet shelter for a crushed and broken flower like her!

Presently the Viscount R——, very pale and very kind, and several of my brother officers encountered me. I never paused to greet them, though they surrounded me and would have kept me back. I heard many voices speaking in tones of deep sympathy, indignation, and regret.

I never answered them. I did not speak, I had no thought but of her, — knew nothing but her.

As I passed on I was met at the threshold of 'an open door by the viscountess and a group of women, one of whom, my wife's favorite ayah, held a small bundle in her arms. As I advanced she removed the folds of a dainty shawl and showed me the face of a dead child. I stopped and kissed it and then passed on, — on till I reached a wretched pallet gorgeously covered with splendid shawls and strewed with fragrant flowers. I heard a wild cry, — my name pronounced in those soft, tender accents so like the tones of her own broken harp, — white arms wound round me, soft hands clasping my neck, a fair golden head nestling in my bosom, and — so she died.

Back in the old ruinous house, ruins covered up with gorgeous art until it had once shone like a fairy palace; back in the house she had so loved and where her presence had made the place a paradise, amidst the flowers and bloom, the pale statues, and deep, unbroken silence; back with my fairy bride and my dead child, — alone and still and quiet, I spent that long, long night, whilst the storm of fierce passion, prompting men to riot and ruin, filled the streets without. The real truths that surround great tragedies are never known to the world, but there is an element of generosity in public sentiment, a depth of honest manliness in the human heart which, however crowded down by the artifices and sordid cares of civilization, can always be aroused to indignant protest by the action of injustice or wanton cruelty. Such a sentiment seemed to have been awakened by the impassioned utterances of my poor little fakir, who, in his frantic anxiety to right the great wrong done to his hapless lady had again exceeded the bounds of prudence in declaiming against the authors of the cruel deed.

The viscount had made strenuous efforts to keep the

matter secret, fearing lest its publication in some gar-
bled form should attach disgrace to his noble family;
in fact he had caused the report to be industriously
circulated, that the lady so shamefully wronged was
a domestic attached to his wife's household, not one
of his own immediate connections, — an interpretation
of the tale which I believe prevails to this day in the
city where this great tragedy of my life really occurred.

A portion of the populace, who had learned something
of the fakir's story, and with it understood that the
lady's imprisonment and death were connected with the
enchantments practised by the well-known adventuress,
Madame Laval, had surrounded her house, and without further inquiry into the right or wrong of what
they did, had burned it to the ground. All this caused
a restless wave of riot and destruction to surge through
the streets that night which might have disturbed any
sleep but *hers*, or aroused any mourning but such as
mine; but the storm raged on, — *we were all still and
quiet within.*

It was about nine o'clock the next night that I left
my house, — a home no longer, — accompanied by Capt.
Graham and Col. M——, a noble-hearted gentleman,
between whom and myself a warm friendship subsisted.

We threaded our way through the lowest and most
obscure part of the city, until we gained the miserable
hut which Graham and I had before visited, the dwelling of Anine, the sister of Nazir. The door was barred
and bolted within, but at my signal Nazir himself
opened it, and after carefully fastening it again, led me
on from the dwelling through several courts and ruinous
buildings, when we gained the door which I knew led
into the halls where we had witnessed the scenes of
"black magic" described in a previous chapter. We

crossed the outer hall, and paused before the entrance which led to the interior chamber. Here I stopped to gain breath and strength enough to proceed, but whilst I leaned against the door, I heard the voices of those I came to seek, the accursed brother and sister who had wrought my great ruin, in angry altercation within. The sound of those hateful tones supplied the stimulus I needed and impelled me at once to push open the door and enter. Crouching on the threshold inside was Anine, awaiting our coming, according to Nazir's directions.

Perrault and his sister had, it seemed, sought temporary shelter there, fearing to trust themselves to the rage of an excited populace in the streets. They were both seated at a table on which refreshments were spread, but the altar, braziers, and all the abominable paraphernalia of fetish rites, were strewed around in disorder and neglect. The guilty pair started to their feet as we entered, and the woman uttered a faint cry of alarm. Our plans were already laid, however, and no time was lost in idle parley. Graham and the fakir seized Perrault, and Col. M——, laying his hand firmly on Madame Laval's arm, told her sternly that the least cry or attempt at resistance would cost them both their lives. I then proceeded to cut to pieces the fatal pictures of myself and their victim,— which last they had recently hung up beside my own,— throw down and stamp upon the waxen images, and break up or rend apart all the instruments and machinery of their vile art.

Anine, under my directions, then gathered up the fragments in a heap, cast them into a large, dry, stone tank, and set fire to them. All this I did without haste, rage, or passion. I was very calm, and conducted my work with the utmost deliberation. When this was accomplished, I directed Anine and the fakir to take charge of Madame Laval, towards whom I never once trusted myself to look, nor did I speak to or notice her, although she often addressed me in terms of supplication. I then motioned my friends to retire to one of the large, desolate courts which we had before crossed, leading the brother and sister prisoners with us.

Arrived at our destination, Col. M—— addressed Perrault, and without enlarging upon the misery he and his accomplices had wrought, he simply told him the hour of reckoning so long ago promised had arrived. He reminded them both that they were utterly at our mercy; that a dreadful fate awaited them should we, as we might, give them up to justice, but instead, I had resolved, little as he deserved such grace, to deal with him as *if he were a gentleman*, rather than what he was; in short, that I was now prepared to give him the only chance for his life which mortal combat afforded.

Without suffering him to answer, the colonel directed him to assume a position opposite me, and briefly, yet still with the military courtesy which never for one moment forsook him, introduced him to Graham, who had, with the utmost reluctance and disgust, consented for my sake to act as Perrault's second.

Baffled and hopeless, the trembling coward took the place assigned him, exchanged a few words of formality with Graham, received from him one of my pistols, and instantly, without waiting for the dropping of the handkerchief, which was the signal agreed upon for firing, discharged the weapon at me. Whether the treacherous villain's hand shook or he was but an indifferent marksman I know not, but the shot was ill sped and only took effect upon my left arm.

Furious at this murderous act, my gallant friends seized him on either side, and shouting to me to kill him, bravely held him between them, awaiting the result of my fire. My aim was deliberate and my purpose fixed. I determined not to charge my soul with an act of murder for so worthless a being, I would only maim him for life. I said as much before I drew the trigger, and then fired, and *I know* succeeded in my design. He fell, but not to die. Better for him if he had. After this deed of retribution, my friends and myself quitted the accursed spot forever.

It had been my intention to proceed to England immediately, taking with me all that I now had to return to the bereaved father of his precious child, contained in a splendid sarcophagus; but I had drawn too largely on the forces of Nature and she demanded immunity for the heavy draught. For many weeks I hovered between life and death, consumed by a raging fever.

The viscount and his kind wife, to both of whom I had become very dear, desired to have me removed to their own country seat, but though by their provident care my once bright home had been despoiled, shut up, and all my household dispersed, it was not to their house that I was carried. My kind and loving friend, Nanak Rai, claimed the charge of me, and attended only by my well-tried and faithful Arab servant Ali, I was conveyed to his residence, where he watched and ministered to me with the skill of a physician and the care of a tender father.

For many a long day and succeeding week, this excellent friend's untiring efforts were exerted to snatch me from the confines of the grave. With his remarkable skill, and under his benign and holy influence, I became at length restored to health alike of body and mind.

In the peaceful retirement of his home, I became also

reconciled to myself, my fate, and the ministry of the angels whom I had once so sullenly rejected. All my spiritual powers and aspirations returned to me, but returned with a nearer and dearer sense of the sweet companionship which the spirits of beloved earthly friends alone can bring. How many times during my long nights of weariness and pain, have I heard the light step of my fairy, running through the hall, and stopping just as she used to do when she meant to surprise me, and then stealing close, very close to me! Her ringing laugh sounded softly, though still very subdued in my ears, her golden tresses swept over my burning face, and her tender tones once more whispered words of love and consolation, ever ending by a promise of "the rest in heaven," to which she had herself attained.

Good and gracious Father of spirits, with what deep ingratitude and pitiful self-denial do poor mortals reject thy best blessing, when they refuse to accept or scoff at, the precious truths of spiritual communion!

The thirty years of life experience, the summary of which I have sketched out in these pages, have pointed candidly and dispassionately to the abuse as well as the use of the vast and wondrous powers that lay occultly hidden away in man, and the unseen universe by which he is surrounded. But whatever may be the dangers, terrors, and mysteries of occultism, let suffering humanity assure itself there is ever an angel side to this realm of being, one on which the soul may lean as the anchor let down for its support from the hand of the Creator.

Had it not been for the power which bridged over the Lethean river that separated me from all that I had loved on earth, health might have resumed her sway,

31

but reason would have fled from its shattered throne within my mind forever. One by one I had seen the fondest, the truest, the best, all upon whom I had anchored my warmest affections, fall by my side, vanish from my sight, and leave me alone. With a heart full of passionate impulses veiled by the cold exterior of disciplined asceticism, I had been compelled to see every tie of affection snapped, every earthly hope shipwrecked.

I had borne so much and strained at the cords of mental effort with such fearful energy, that I know I must have become a raving lunatic if I had turned despairing glances to the land of the hereafter, and sought in vain there for my vanished loves and my own goal of rest.

Looking through the eyes of my beloved ones, as they all returned to me, one by one, each assuming his or her place in the bright procession, with all the well-remembered tokens that could bring me the assurance there was no death, only change, I could see bright angels, higher still than the spirits of earth, and a Deity over all, upon whom I could lean my trembling soul and be at rest. Once more the tides of spiritual life and force rolled in upon the storm-beaten shores of my destiny; once more the grand scheme of the universe and the philosophy of existence was unrolled before me. I began again to recognize myself as the link between the lower and higher worlds, at the same time that I learned the necessity of hedging in the aspiring intellect by the safe boundary lines of matter and mystery, lest the soul, penetrating too far into the arcanum of the illimitable beyond, should become lost, wrecked, overwhelmed in immensities of being, too vast for finite humanity to comprehend.

I know I have not always remembered or applied these salutary lessons. Removed from the wise and philosophic teachings of my excellent Brahminical friend, restored to health and reconciled to myself, my angels, and my destiny, the spring of my wild aspirations has impelled me into the profoundest realms of occultism, into the depths yawning beneath my feet, and the heights stretching away above my head; piercing the path of the stars and plunging into regions of mystery beyond the safe limitations of human spiritual guidance.

In scaling these tremendous ladders of knowledge, I have experienced many a fearful fall, paid many a heavy penalty. Again and again I have returned from these awful pilgrimages with a wounded, bruised, and way-worn spirit; but ever, as I came, I have found rest, peace, and consolation in the loving ministration of earth's enfranchised spirit friends. I have learned to believe that communion between the denizens of this planet and her spirit spheres, should constitute the highest, purest, most normal and healthful exercise of our soul's religious faculties. Mortals have but an imperfect realization of this sublime truth, amidst the folly, fanaticism, wrong, and imposture that have disgraced the movement miscalled Spiritualism, — a movement which has served to externalize much of the darkest features of human nature, but as yet has been permitted to do little more than point to the mines of unwrought treasure that lay hidden beneath the possibilities of that communion. As yet it is all too human and too redolent of human short-comings.

I dare not pause now even to hint at what we may hope for in the better day of spiritual communion, when its *modus operandi* shall be understood by science, and its sublime revelations be received in the spirit of religious reverence. Time and space, however, I now find have become limited in this volume to a closing sentence.

When strength of mind and body returned to me, I left my noble friend's peaceful dwelling with the benison of a thankful heart upon its hospitable roof-tree. Then I stood once more on shipboard, waving farewell to groups of the dear and warm-hearted friends who had trod with me life's rough and rugged paths in India; and with many a "God-speed" sounding in my ears, and many a moistened eye following the track of the ship out into the pathless wastes of ocean, sailed away to commence a new career of research into the realms of spiritual existence.

EDITOR'S NOTE IN CONCLUSION.

THE reader will observe that the foregoing sketches only account for ten years of the author's career after his departure from England, and constitute simply one portion of the "Ghost Land" papers, the remainder of which include an equally interesting and thrilling record extending over nearly twenty years more of the author's eventful and varied experiences in occult spiritism, many of which I have shared with him. As the ample dimensions of this volume forbid further additions, I take advantage of the epoch recorded in the last chapter to close these sketches, at least for the present.

By the favor of the author, I am in possession of another series of papers from his pen, of even more importance to the thinking part of the community than either of his previous works. This valuable MSS. I hope to present to the world on some future occasion.

Time and experience invariably regulate the demands of public opinion for the quality of the literature it can assimilate. Guided by that standard, no less than the means open to me, I shall determine how far I may be enabled to publish the rest of the fascinating sketches commenced in this volume, as well as the MSS. above referred to, the merits of which will be sufficiently well understood by the readers of "Art Magic," when I add that it treats of and enlarges upon the same subjects as those contained in that extraordinary work.

Life is short, but its responsibilities are to my mind continued throughout eternity; were it not so, the harassing cares, duties, and burdens which belong to the editorship of works so startling and revolutionary as those put forth by the Chevalier de B—— would never be assumed or endured by his friend and the world's faithful worker,

EMMA HARDINGE BRITTEN,
Ed. Ghost Land.

ANOTHER WORK ON OCCULT SPIRITISM,

BY THE AUTHOR OF

"ART MAGIC."

GHOST LAND;

OR,

RESEARCHES INTO THE MYSTERIES OF OCCULT SPIRITISM.

Being a series of autobiographical papers, with extracts
from the records of

MAGICAL SÉANCES, Etc. Etc.

Translated and edited by EMMA HARDINGE BRITTEN.

This magnificent and thrilling record of spiritual experiences was prepared for and commenced in the " WESTERN STAR " some four years ago. Since the suspension of that periodical — necessitated by the Boston fires — Mrs. Hardinge Britten has been repeatedly solicited to publish the admired and fascinating " GHOST LAND " papers in a connected series. The great demand for another book from the author of " ART MAGIC," the earnest desire of the subscribers to that CELEBRATED WORK to know more about its author, and the interest which exists at the present hour in philosophical and progressive views of Spiritualism, combine to induce the editor to put forth the present highly instructive and wonderful volume, with the special view of meeting the above requirements.

Orders addressed to Mrs. Emma Hardinge Britten at her residence, 118 West Chester Park, Boston, Mass., will be promptly filled.

Price, $3.00. Postage, 33 cents. Express charges at the purchaser's cost. Remittances to be made by P. O. Order or Registered Letter.

OR,

MUNDANE, SUB-MUNDANE, AND SUPER-MUNDANE

SPIRITISM.

———◆◆◆———

A TREATISE IN THREE PARTS

· ON

Art magic, natural magic, modern spiritualism, the different orders
of spirits in the universe known to be related to or in communication with man, together with directions for
invoking, controlling, and discharging spirits, and
the uses and abuses, dangers and
possibilities, of magical art.

————————